African Words, African Voices

AFRICAN SYSTEMS OF THOUGHT

General Editors
Charles S. Bird
Ivan Karp

Contributing Editors
James W. Fernandez
Luc de Heusch
John Middleton
Roy Willis

African Words, African Voices

Critical Practices in Oral History

EDITED BY

Luise White, Stephan F. Miescher,

AND

David William Cohen

Indiana University Press

BLOOMINGTON AND INDIANAPOLIS

This book is a publication of

Indiana University Press
601 North Morton Street
Bloomington, IN 47404-3797 USA

http://iupress.indiana.edu

Telephone orders   800-842-6796
Fax orders   812-855-7931
Orders by e-mail   iuporder@indiana.edu

© 2001 by Indiana University Press

The paper used in this publication meets the minimum requirements of American National Standard for Information Sciences—Permanence of Paper for Printed Library Materials, ANSI Z39.48-1984.

Manufactured in the United States of America

Library of Congress Cataloging-in-Publication Data

African words, African voices : critical practices in oral history / edited by Luise White, Stephan F. Miescher, and David William Cohen.
    p. cm. — (African systems of thought)
Includes bibliographical references (p.) and index.
    ISBN 0-253-33948-0 (cloth : alk. paper)—ISBN 0-253-21468-8 (paper : alk. paper)
    1. Africa—Historiography. 2. Oral tradition—Africa. I. White, Luise. II. Miescher, Stephan. III. Cohen, David William. IV. Series.
    DT19 .A344 2001
    960—dc21

                            2001001889

1 2 3 4 5 06 05 04 03 02 01

Contents

Acknowledgments

The Rockefeller Foundation, the Wenner-Gren Foundation, and the University of Michigan provided generous support, making possible the two "Words and Voices" conferences at Bellagio and Ann Arbor in February and March 1997. At the University of Michigan the International Institute, the Dean's office of the College of Literature, Science, and the Arts, and the Office of Academic and Multicultural Affairs contributed support to the project at several stages, including making possible the sustained collaboration of the editors and the participation in the follow-up conference of an extraordinary group of young scholars from graduate programs around North America. We are especially grateful to Dr. Sydel Silverman (Wenner-Gren), Alberta Arthurs (Rockefeller), Susan Garfield (Rockefeller), Dean Edie Goldenberg (Michigan), and Associate Provost Lester Monts (Michigan) for their interest in and support of this project. They, along with Bryn Mawr College, Swarthmore College, Northwestern University, Rice University, and the University of Pennsylvania, helped assure the full participation of colleagues in Africa-based institutions in the Bellagio and Ann Arbor conferences.

Staff of the International Institute at the University of Michigan and the Bellagio Study and Conference Center contributed to and facilitated the meetings. We are grateful to John Godfrey, Violet Elder, and Christy Yenkel of Michigan and Pasquale Pesce and Gianna Celli of the Bellagio Center for the high quality of arrangements that graced and supported the work of the conferees at Bellagio and Ann Arbor.

From her office at the University of Michigan, Christy Yenkel provided an exceptional anchorage for this collaboration, from its first beginnings through the conferences and the first revisions of the conference papers. After a long struggle with cancer, she passed away on 5 October 2000, before this project, in which she played such an important role, was completed. We hope that readers who knew Christy will recognize in this volume the grace, energy, and sense of community she brought to every aspect of her life.

We are grateful to the participants in the two conferences, including those who have contributed their papers to this volume. In many instances, their home institutions provided support for their participation in the conferences. Many other colleagues in our field provided good counsel in the development of the project from the original position paper to the completion of the this work: Boubacar Barry, Timothy Burke, Susan Geiger, Carolyn Hamilton, Ivan Karp, David Newbury, and E. S. Atieno Odhiambo. Apollo Amoko provided valuable assistance in the editing of the conference papers. Finally, Janet Rabinowitch, Dee Mortensen, and the staff of Indiana University Press have with grace and wisdom moved this "Words and Voices" project to print.

African Words, African Voices

Introduction

VOICES, WORDS, AND AFRICAN HISTORY

David William Cohen, Stephan F. Miescher,
and Luise White

The essays brought together here offer an extraordinary range of engagement with the production of African history. They reflect a shift from an era when oral histories and oral traditions were reckoned fragile, critical, problematic sources for the past of the continent. Far from melting in the face of the historical profession's codes of *objectivity*, African oral history has been opening important inquiries into the very nature of African *subjectivity*. The collection comprises papers first presented at the Rockefeller Foundation's Bellagio Conference Center in February 1997 and subsequently discussed at a follow-up conference at Ann Arbor, Michigan, in March 1997. The papers were developed by the contributors in response to a position paper circulated in 1995.

The relevance and significance of the history of Africa is today acknowledged in universities in Africa and across Europe and North America. Two major compilations of historical studies—the multi-volume *Cambridge History of Africa* and the *UNESCO History of Africa*—have assumed prominent positions in libraries across the globe, while dozens of journals have emerged that focus on the study of the African past. Specialized textbooks and course programs have brought Africa's history into the secondary school curriculum. Debates over how African history should be taught to younger students have displaced older debates as to whether Africa's past can be or should be taught amid the broad pedagogical challenges facing educators across the globe. There are today departments of history—with appropriately Africanist signatures and emphases—in virtually every university on the African continent. Notably, the *discipline* of history has gained preeminence among all the disciplines that have taken up Africa as a subject of interest, with deep influence upon the adjacent fields of politics, anthropology, archaeology, conservation, museology, art and architecture, economics, urban studies, journalism, literature, musicology, performance studies, and the applied fields of law, health, human rights, development, women's rights, and tourism. From status as a veritable oxymoron in the world of learning, the field of African history has moved to the vital center of learning, understanding, and interpretation of African culture, economy, society, law, and politics. Two scholars of African oral history, Philip D. Curtin and Joseph C. Miller, have served as presidents of the American Historical Association.

In less than five decades, the field of African history has emerged from a relatively obscure and marginal position among the varieties of scholarship in and on Africa. The youngest field in the broad domain of world historical scholarship, African history has established itself as the most dynamic of the academic disciplines addressing Africa, albeit one of as-yet-unrealized influence on the fates of the continent. The field has developed at a faster pace than has any other field of professional history at any time. Within this extraordinary development—one might say "fast professionalization"—no element has served as a clearer signature of and for African historiography than the development of a central position for *the oral source* and *oral history* within the programs of recovering the African past.

The Bellagio conference and ensuing book project unfolded in the 1990s, yet both sought to draw attention to several transformations that marked, made, unmade, and made again the programs of African historiography. In the 1960s, historians of Africa were caught between the potential force of local evidence and the power of universal vocabularies that fixed scholarship easily within nationalist projects. By the 1990s, the African nation-state was seen to accord poorly with classical ideas of progress and national integration; historians had begun to recognize that universal vocabularies had obscured the power and meanings of local evidence. In the 1960s, African history was an academic discipline that could legitimate the postcolonial nation by historicizing precolonial sovereignty; dissertations and monographs on precolonial states, traditions, and dynastic history, two by an author of this introduction, were commonplace in historical scholarship. In the 1990s, precolonial African history was exceptional, rarely done and difficult to fund. In the 1960s, historians of Africa recognized the possibility of giving the continent a past and, at the same time, valorizing Africa and its cultures before a world audience by constructing, unveiling, the record of that past. By the 1990s, historians of Africa had come to doubt the possibility of a *unified* treatment of Africa's past. Knowledge of Africa's cultures and past was a site of new conflicts among diverse scholarly communities, fixed on such notions as "inside" and "outside," or such ambits as Afrocentric approaches, postmodernism, and feminism. In the 1960s, African history was hardly concerned at all with African lives, African individuals not being considered a fit subject matter for historical studies. In the 1990s, life history had become an unproblematic and much practiced mode of historical scholarship.[1] In the 1960s, historians of Africa recognized the demand that oral sources be read and tested critically in the light of diverse bodies of evidence from documents, and against evidence from anthropology, archaeology, climatology, ethno-botany, geography, and linguistics. By the 1990s, oral testimonies had achieved a transcendent status by which they could stand by themselves as authoritative accounts of lived experience, unmediated and uncorrected by the domains of knowledge that professional historians of Africa were trained to bring to the evaluation of texts. In the 1960s, the historian of Africa was expected to play a critical and professional role in the collection, transcription, translation, and interpretation of African oral sources, and in the broad dissemination of African primary materials to wider audiences. By the 1990s, critical mediations, including the deployment of elaborate research methodologies, could be read as evidence of "silencing the African voice."[2]

WORDS AND VOICES

The essays collected here bring critical regard, as well as historical illumination, to these transformations, and to the certainties and uncertainties that have marked the work of African oral history over the more than four decades since professional historians announced the objective of "giving Africa a past." From the inception of this present project we have chosen two interrelated motifs—"words" and "voices"—to frame our discussions of the story of African oral historiography.

"Words" stands for the fraught struggles for historical evidence through the generation of an authoritative and scientific program of African history. Here, we are concerned with the hermeneutics of transfiguring text into historical knowledge and meaning. And we have been interested in the connections between these hermeneutics and the social and intellectual histories of a professional field of African history. After all, this professional field developed out of the search for historical substance and meaning within the speaking practices of a people held to be without literacy and without written documents until quite recently.

"Voices" stands for the equally fraught quest for *authentic* African voices amidst tumultuous changes in the lives of Africans and in Africa's relations with the world. Struggles over the control of the crafting of the history of Africa and Africans have positioned "voice" not only as a means to knowledge but also as a frame of authority. While in other fields of history truth and authority may at times be rife with tension, one with the other, perhaps no field of historical research and writing has been more shaped, essentially wrought, by the tensions *between* the quest for truth and the search for authority.

The very absence of a larger sensibility regarding African history's own recent history has implanted within Africanist scholarship a quixotic relationship to values and programs of authenticity and objectivity. In postcolonial Africa, specific issues of representation, leadership, and authority have continually resituated "voices" as authentic or appropriated, representative or distinctive, intrinsic or democratic, reinforcing the identity of a "voice" heard or surveilled and the voice's associated moral and ideological properties.

Transnational organizations such as Amnesty International have compounded the appropriation of "voices" through "speaking for" as opposed to just "speaking of," and such organizations have claimed—some would say earned—authority to speak for Africans within global and international forums. The elaboration of international conferences, with the constitution of national and regional delegations from the African continent, with delegates and delegations speaking "to the world" *from* and *for* Africa, has even given African "voices" representational authority in global settings with precedence over the diplomatic representation of sovereign states. The African "voice"—cradled, massaged, liberated, and authenticated within the expert approaches of the African historian—comes to represent (or at least presents the opportunity to reach for) truth while it bolsters scholarly claims to objectivity.

The valorization of African "voices" and their association with notions of authenticity and truth may also be understood in relation to the locations of "Africa" within writings on African-American history and culture, as Africa has come to represent, on its own, a truth within African-American letters. Similarly, an African women's oral historiography developed in the 1980s around the idea that voices captured in interviews could most closely report or represent women's experience. The emphasis on capturing the voice through an interview focused the attention of scholars on the interview itself. Paradoxically, this attention to the interview—which came in the same period as calls for reflexivity and self-critical work in anthropology, cultural studies, and feminist scholarship—reconstituted this research encounter as one between a powerful and reflexive scholar and an unreflective, powerless, and colonized woman. If the informant could not be made to speak for herself, the interviewer or scholar was to be responsible for nothing less than the colonization or recolonization of the subject-informant (Smith and Watson 1992; Hoppe 1993). The politics of the collection of oral testimony, focused on the scholar-informant relationship, were assuming precedence over the critical practices of analysis and interpretation of texts.

THE STRANGE CAREER OF AFRICAN VOICES

"Voice" has had a marvelous and yet tortured history within writings on Africa over the past two hundred years. At the end of the eighteenth century and through the first decades of the nineteenth century, antislavery literature offered a central place to the first-person narrative, enabling the reception of a critique of slavery and the slave trade from within the consciousness of those who most fully experienced their brutality (Curtin 1968b). But from the second half of the nineteenth century, and through much of the twentieth century, the rising power and authority of scientific writing on Africa divorced itself from African informants, narrators, and writers. Africa could, in this new age, be studied, known, understood, and represented without reference to the narrative and interpretive practices of Africans themselves. Indeed, the act of coming to know the continent of Africa became a heroic experience for Europeans, paralleling and eventually supplanting other forms of adventurous heroism. Although from the late nineteenth century Africans were authoring major accounts of their histories, their cultures, and their polities, experts from Europe, trained outside the continent, would shape and control knowledge of Africa. Their methods and epistemologies were largely divorced from any notion that Africans could themselves comprehend, interpret, and narrate their worlds in a usable manner. Indeed, the "science" of such studies was substantially constructed around the notion of the absence of indigenous intellectual and scientific authority. Ironically, some of the better-known studies produced by Europeans within the new science—for example, John Roscoe (1911, 1915)—were developed upon or out of works authored by African intellectuals and informants.

This displacement of African "voices," developing from an intersection of the rise of science and the organization of European power "on the ground" in Africa, could not long be sustained. Already in the early twentieth century, commissions of inquiry sought out Africans to provide expert testimony on issues relating to land tenure, marriage, and labor. Whatever the constraints of these commissions and the dubious circumstances in which they were conceived, many Africans were encouraged to speak unfettered. Irrelevant testimony, wrote the authors of the report into the 1935 "disturbances" on the Copperbelt of Northern Rhodesia, was necessary if Africans were to feel they could speak freely.[3] Moreover, whatever Africans were encouraged to do, some would use these venues as sites of personal performance, speaking outside the framework of colonial surveillance before the commissioners. Before such commissions in southern Africa, African miners not only spoke about the hardships underground, but revealed their own modes of evaluation of the conditions of work, including savings and consumption strategies, the relative values—in their terms—of different specie, and the informal arrangements relating to the recruitment and control of labor.[4] But these documents, and the words within them, were subject to a kind of amnesia not uncommon in colonial circles: in the 1930s and 1940s scholars and experts on Africans came to imagine that they were the first to allow Africans to testify.

African testimony was alive and of growing import in other settings organized within the European colonial order. Works by Marcel Griaule in the 1930s and 1940s and by his student Jean Rouch in the 1950s were breaches in long-standing protocols of research and representation, especially in francophone circuits of scholarship. Such work centered African testimony and life history as means to explore the realms of African culture that seemed to stand outside of, or to resist, the great imperial projects of civilization and modernization, if not also to unmake the naturalized protocols of descriptive ethnography. Griaule's recension of Ogotemmêli's knowledge of the world

(Griaule 1948) and Rouch's cinematic explorations of ecstatic states were not only opening views of the richness and complexity of African thought and belief to broader audiences, they were also attaching, albeit with European editing, an authority to African "voices" that had previously—so these works suggested—"lived" outside the scientific observation of Africa. More, the developments associated with *Présence Africaine* thickened and orchestrated this extraordinary shift in the orientation of writings about Africa (Mudimbe 1992). In 1938, Jomo Kenyatta published his ethnography of the Kikuyu—"anthropology begins at home," wrote Bronislaw Malinowski, Kenyatta's professor at the London School of Economics, in the introduction to the first edition.

By the 1950s, as colonial powers saw their empires fragment and then unravel, ethnographers and a few officials wrote outside surveillance, and writings about Africans once again came to be legitimated by the voices of Africans. It is no surprise that African "voices" would gain a new authority in writings on Africa at the very time, just after the Second World War, when Europeans and Africans were awakening to nationalist rhetoric from many arenas across the continent and around the world. Seen another way, the reevaluation of the costs of empire in the postwar era occasioned a rising recognition of African "voices," in both the mass actions that characterized postwar nationalism and in the halls of negotiation of the termination of empire. The unity of the "voice" distilled from domestic servants' religious practices or copper miners' dances was simultaneously claimed by nationalists and investigated by social scientists. Colonial social surveys, including studies of urban social change, not only relied heavily on the words of the ethnographic subject but quoted them at great length. In Ghana, these social surveys were conducted by a new generation of university-trained African social scientists. K. A. Busia, the first West African appointed to the Colonial Administrative Service, published the social survey of Sekondi-Takoradi in 1950. Combining the "methods of the Survey with those of the Social Anthropologist," Busia and his "two field-assistants" engaged in "'free' interview, questionnaire, and interview by schedule" (1950: 120).[5] Laura Longmore's study of single African women in Johannesburg (1959), using testimony in juvenile courts to read family relations, was a key contribution to urban sociology. A. L. Epstein's work on gossip and slang on the Northern Rhodesian Copperbelt (1958) placed language and culture firmly in the crucible of industrialization and political economy. Epstein had heard in courtroom testimony the fissures of marriage and domesticity in mine laborers' families (1953). Also on the Copperbelt, Clyde Mitchell (1956) had listened to dance society songs to understand mine workers' ideas about ethnicity, work, and status. Aidan Southall and Peter Gutkind's study of Kampala's slums (1957) allowed informants to do a great deal of the work of ethnographic analysis. This trend did not disappear in the onslaught of independence, either. Hortense Powdermaker's *Copper Town* was published in 1962; in it, Africans spoke about what reading the newspaper meant to them, what they liked about going to the movies, and what striking miners would sell in order to prolong a strike. In 1969 Lloyd Fallers published his study of law in colonial Busoga, in which chiefs and magistrates made clear the difficulties in distilling political processes from the overlapping histories of kingdom, colony, and empire (Fallers 1969; see Cohen 1991). Also in the 1960s, J. A. K. Leslie's *A Survey of Dar es Salaam* (1963) included accounts of prostitutes, transvestites, and the young men who dressed as cowboys in the colonial city. If such examples of inclusion suggested profound change in the relations between Africans and Europeans, some Africans could see these shifts quite critically. As Abdullahi Ibrahim points out in his paper in this volume, Africans outside European schools of training would make linear and barbed connections between the interrogations of sympathetic researchers and those of colonial officials.

An Africa that "spoke" found further elaboration in the publication and celebration of négritude poetry, in the appearances of novels and autobiographies, in testimonies before public tribunals and treason trials of the anticolonial struggles, and in the employment of African voices in late-imperial short-wave broadcasts. There was an *economy* in this production of African voices in the late colonial period, as authority was attached to the narration of African subjects, which merits close scrutiny and close historicization. One might argue that, just as early colonial authorities found it possible, and even necessary, to create an illusion of "silent subjects" as a means of establishing colonial administrations and governance (Africans as audiences, spoken about and dictated to), they found it equally appropriate, if not also enabling, to create an illusion of "speaking subjects" to make possible a most interested and highly negotiated exit from colonial responsibility.[6] A new African historiography arose in this postwar period, one increasingly attentive to "voices," to African sources and African actors, within the course of the imperial epoch. These fresh approaches would comfortably accommodate the emergent frames of nationalist historiography. In their papers written for this volume, Joe Alagoa, Bethwell Allan Ogot, and Megan Vaughan address some of the ways the writing of African history was linked to the process of building African nations. Their papers remind us of the unsettled nature of the question: whose history was this African history to be, with which actors, to be found and interviewed where? In his paper, Alagoa narrates the fidgety negotiations between community and historian as to how history is to be properly constituted. He asks, rhetorically, who controls the historical narrative: the professional historian or the actors in the community? Ibrahim, Laura Fair, and Kwesi Yankah join this discussion, considering the work and force of audiences in the construction of the past. Yankah tells how the singer Nana Ampadu achieved a popularity so strong, so exceptional, that his sung-tale titles, like "Ebi Te Yie" ("Some are favorably positioned"), have been accorded proverbial status, no small achievement in Akan daily life. Fair's account of the singer Siti binti Saadi shows how her lyrics came to live in, virtually as, a public domain. Siti became an authority; Fair's informants validated and proved their opinions by quoting a Siti lyric about whatever they were discussing. This program of authorization was virtually restaged in the Ouko saga in Kenya, as David William Cohen narrates it, with the New Scotland Yard experts instantiating the authority of a housemaid's observation, testing other evidence, statements, and witnesses against it. Ibrahim takes such concerns further, focusing critical attention on the conditions of power within the interview itself, pointing out that the informant may have far more experience managing and suffering interrogations by policemen and district officers than participating in the field projects of anthropologists and historians. Here, the ethical issues of interviewing come to the fore. Some have reflected more closely on the complex and dynamic relationships constituted (or sometimes not constituted) between narrator and researcher (Strobel 1977; Mbilinyi 1989; van Onselen 1993, 1996; Tonkin 1992). Corinne Kratz and Stephan Miescher go still further, narrating critically and self-critically the methodological, political, and ethical presumptions associated with the life history mode regarding whose story is being constructed or told. Within the genre of life history, several scholars have emphasized the bonding experience between the researcher and his and her subject (Shostak 1981, 1987; Geiger 1986; Davison 1989; Mirza and Strobel 1989).

In his elaborated methodology, Jan Vansina was rather dismissive of personal recollections (1965: 160; 1980: 265–72 and 1985: 8–10), since they were considered unreliable, hence most removed from his quest for a historical truth in oral sources. Over the last ten years, social historians of twentieth-century Africa, interested in historical actors at the margins—rural dwellers, migrant workers, and especially women—have increasingly focused on individual "life histories" in order to give "voice" to people subjected to the colonial project. Life histories, it has been said, complement silences in the archives. Materials in archives, particularly missionary archives, could be transformed and translated into life histories (Wright 1993).

Historians, animated by distinguished and accessible work of this kind, have asked African women and men to talk about their personal lives, to share tales and memories of repression and resistance experienced within the colonial and postcolonial context. Listening to and transcribing these accounts, a group of researchers—most influentially those with a feminist agenda focusing on women and women's struggle—created something of a genre, presenting African history through the collection and publication of life histories (e.g., Mirza and Strobel 1989; Davison 1989; Staunton 1990). While it has evidently been important to some scholars to present "unmediated voices"—first-person accounts kept separated from any interpretation and contextualization—such work tended to ignore the literature that was arguing that women's life histories required subtle interrogations (Geiger 1986, 1990, 1997; White 1994). Others have very successfully explored the oral reconstruction of lives by supplementing them with archival records and careful interpretation (White 1990; van Onselen 1996; Geiger 1997; Miescher 1997 and this volume).

In a shift that is part and parcel of the development of oral history methodology within African history, the genre of women's life histories was all but divorced from earlier written life histories, such as Donald Barnett's "Life Histories from the Revolution" pamphlets and *Mau Mau from Within* (1966), written with Karari Njama. In these earlier works there is clear evidence of struggle, of battle over whose project each was to be. In Barnett and Njama's antagonistic collaboration, Barnett sought to make Mau Mau coherent to the 1960s, calling it "the Movement," and Njama used the text to rehabilitate Dedan Kimathi for whatever Kenyan audience would read the book. The idea of life history as contest, in which researcher and informant would have antagonistic goals, revealing different worlds of thought and history, was submerged by the feminist project (e.g., Menchú 1984; Mbilinyi 1989; Bozzoli 1991). It was likewise a genre that could not recognize how life history methodology was borrowed and adapted from anthropologists, who had written and published life histories since the 1920s (Radin 1926; Smith 1954; Mintz 1974, 1979; Shostak 1981). In this volume, Kratz traces the history of this anthropological genre as it came to be taken up in African studies.

The earliest feminist work on African life history did contain an implicit critique of the use of oral sources by African historians, but one different from that raised here by Kratz and Tamara Giles-Vernick. Claire Robertson (1983) and Susan Geiger (1986) addressed the question of subjectivity not in terms of subject position, but in terms of what to do with sources that were not objective. Within this volume, Babacar Fall turns to life history as an accessible and refreshed means of understanding state-society relations in Senegal, as a means of gaining a sense of difference in experience and in the representation of experience. Miescher thickens the values of life history by using multiple sources, both oral and written, to bring into a central position the subject's own sense of self and history. Giles-Vernick and Kratz demonstrate the multiple genres that underlie the notion of "life history." Subtly deconstructing the naturalized mode of "life history," Kratz and Giles-Vernick in their contributions here enlarge on Elizabeth Tonkin (1992) in arguing that the use of life history as a method has tended to force African ideas about life and self into a universal, Western model. Readers seeking a more unified and universal address to Africa's past may paradoxically find it in the familiar genre of individual life narratives while lamenting the loss of the unified historical treatment of the African continent. Largely due to Geiger's work (1986, 1990, 1997), the life history method found additional authority because it had application cross-culturally. Here was a way for women in Africa, Latin America, and North America to speak—to others and to one another—in ways that had never been included in more conventional histories with conventional sources.

Looking across the two centuries briefly sketched here, we observe that popular and academic engagements with Africa have fluctuated—sometimes moderately, sometimes wildly—between two extremes. Either African accounts of African experience had no authority in and of themselves—African experience would have to be mediated by, represented through, documents, archives, and the practices of Western scientific thought—or African "voices" held an essential authority and power to represent Africa and its past across all the complexities of racism, colonialism, and suppression, and could best do so, or could only do so, without mediation and interpretation. Perhaps there is no stronger indication of the shift to "voice" than the *naturalization* of "life history" within recent African historiography. This was very striking at the Ann Arbor follow-up meeting to the Bellagio conference, as the younger participants (in different stages of dissertation research and writing) used "life history" as a synonym for oral history research.

DECODING WORDS

A half-century ago few professional historians labored in the fields of African history, and still fewer reached beyond attention to the story of Europeans and European power on the African continent. In the arenas of colonial governance and development and of decolonization, Africa had a present full of challenge and a future only faintly perceived. Significantly, Africa had a past hardly at all beyond its invocation as alibi for the trials and failures of governance and development. Europeans with interest in and knowledge of Africa saw Africa's deeper history as irrelevant, uninteresting, or unknowable. But the protocols of decolonization and the movements of nationalism would challenge earlier European suppositions and prejudices at almost every juncture, and not least on this question of the utilities and possibilities of an African history, or histories, that would be a central program in the liberation of the continent. The "usable past" (Ranger 1976; Jewsiewicki and Newbury 1986; Jewsiewicki 1989) was to give a foundation, as well as pride, to the project of nation-building.

Caught in complex webs between a growing demand in the 1950s and 1960s for a historiography that would recenter Africans within the stream of colonial and national history and a growing call for a historiographical practice imbued with the methods and values of science, it was not long until historians of Africa attempted to join science to the study of African "voices." Published in its English translation in 1965, but rehearsed in the 1960 inaugural number of the *Journal of African History,* Jan Vansina's *Oral Tradition* opened a three-decade-long exploration of how Africa's past could be recovered from the "voices" of Africa. Vansina's treatise and his subsequent writings attempted to codify a methodology for the handling of oral sources, the testimonies of Africans, oral narrative, verbal art, and gossip (but see Yankah 1989, 1995; Barber 1991; White 1994).

The essential challenge for Vansina, and for others who joined these discussions of methodology and epistemology, was to construct methods that would allow the trained historian to transcend the very facts of colonialism and its descendant postcolonial contexts. The training for oral history—revised by Vansina and others in concert with two generations of his students' and colleagues' research—gave confidence that the components of an oral narrative could be disembedded from the present and from the performance (Curtin 1968a). Between the 1960s and the 1980s, Vansina honed his definition of oral tradition into a form of "verbal messages which are reported statements from the past beyond the present generation" (Vansina 1985: 27). It was assumed that this evidence could be disembedded from stories taken from films or the Bible, from ways of talking about colonial governors or postcolonial despots. For the historian, "the truly distinctive characteristic of oral tradition is its transmission by word of mouth over a period longer than the contemporary generation. This means that a tradition should be seen as a series of successive historical documents all lost except for the last one and usually interpreted by every link in the chain of transmissions" (1985: 29). In short, oral traditions contained much that was true; what was false had simply been added over the course of a generation or two. All that was needed was a method to remove these later additions.

For Vansina, and for those who followed his call, trained historians could gain the capacity to "un-read" this context from the sources themselves, to engage the precolonial past through the spoken text. That Africans had given oral testimonies in a wide variety of colonial and postcolonial venues was worthy of neither consideration nor interrogation. What partially underwrote the claim to science was the very claim to the "discovery" of new and original sources. Like the pre-"discovery" Nile River, which had been long explored, known, and navigated by Africans, the new oral sources drawn into the purview of scientific method had long been examined, evaluated, debated, and reworked within Africa itself.

Nevertheless, Vansina's early writings on the methodology of oral history announced themselves and were broadly received as opening a new age of possibility of historiography on the continent.[7] The heady sense of discovery, of new beginnings, in the 1960s bundled the academic field of African history with the project of African independence, while it paradoxically restaged the heroic modes of the Victorian era's scientific and discovery literature. Not least did this "new field" mythologize and anathematize the discipline and practitioners (in Africa) of anthropology as antithetical to history, furnishing additional armature to the heroic mode.[8] This new African history was an African history uncoupled from the written history of Africa begun in the nineteenth century by Africans who based their research on oral accounts of the past (Reindorf 1895; Johnson, writing in the 1890s but published in 1921; cf. Alagoa 1990, Jenkins 1998). Significantly, the heady sense of new beginnings in the 1960s obscured—most particularly within the new African historiography—the trend from the 1940s that recognized that African "voices" could and would speak outside the framework of colonial institutions and colonial surveillance.

Following Vansina's early publications, questions and debates developed around whether the breakthrough to a new historical practice and a new African history was achievable, whether the methods worked or not (see, for example, Henige 1974), rather than how the science itself came to be constituted as a program. Like other late-twentieth-century scientific projects, African oral historiography has distanced itself from a regard of its own history in which the search for and representation of African voices was part of a larger search for authenticity in addressing an African continent in its transition from colonialism. It is in this context, between an African oral historiography searching for an objective accounting of the continent's past and an African oral historiography searching for an authentic rendering of past, event, and meaning from within African textualities, that this *African Words, African Voices* project and the two 1997 conferences at its core were framed.

The foundational status of Vansina's *Oral Tradition* in the development of a new African historiography was not everywhere as pronounced as it was in the North American academy and especially among Vansina's own students. The papers by Alagoa, Vaughan, and Ogot remind observers of the field that the stories of its foundation are elsewhere inscribed differently. If Vansina and his students succeeded in codifying a methodology for the handling of oral sources, and of legitimating oral sources in advanced-degree programs at prestigious research institutions, they did so at least in part by distinguishing their work from the field methodologies engaged in by scholars and research students who were not part of the founding myths of the field: Ogot; J. Bertin Webster, instrumental in oral history projects in Nigeria, Uganda, and Malawi; and a number of other dissertation advisors, many of whom did not work with oral materials but allowed and sometimes required their students to use them. At Bellagio, Alagoa mentioned that he thought Ogot, not Vansina, was the acclaimed founder of the field.

Back in North America, Vansina's books and those of his students established a method for the historical use of oral materials. However archivally based Vansina's first students' first books were (Isaacman 1972; Miller 1976), all did fieldwork, interviewed, and argued the importance of oral tradition. There were challenges, of course. Thoughtful scholars argued with one another about the usefulness of oral tradition for historical reconstruction.[9] Some have debated within the terms set by Vansina's programmatic writings,[10] while others have challenged the very terms set by him,[11] but virtually all insisted that oral tradition and oral testimony were useful for something. But in terms of a discipline, the force of the foundational narrative of African oral historiography stirred many pots. On the African continent, in the United States, and in Europe, courses of study, seminars, workshops, curricula, conferences, guidebooks, further treatises, methodological essays, and dissertations elaborated upon the discussions of method, working within the idea that scientific address to the study of spoken history and oral history was

possible, and that through these media one could move toward an authoritative, and scientifically educed, reconstruction of the precolonial African past.

The authors of this introduction are all professional African historians.
All were trained as such—at different times—in four institutions with long-
standing programs in African history. These institutions were themselves
marked by the developments of the 1960s in Africa, Europe, and North
America, in which graduate programs in African history—with all the extra-
curricular forms of knowledge, conferences and workshops and the like—
were founded, funded, and expanded. All of these programs stressed the
possibility of the scientific study of oral history as a way to recapture Africa's
past. The historical methods for analyzing oral traditions implied that Africans carried traditions from the past that could be recorded from living persons whose memories were not wholly transformed by the lived experiences
of colonialism. Even if these elders, informants, local historians, or griots (as
they have variously been called) were influenced by colonialism, by written
texts, by the Bible, by presentism, excellent historical practice could educe
usable tradition for the reconstruction of Africa's precolonial past (Ewald
1985, 1987; Tonkin 1982, 1986; Hamilton 1987; Barber and Farias 1989).

The challenge for the founders of the field and for those who joined
these discussions of methodology and epistemology was to construct guidelines by which trained historians could transcend the very facts of colonialism
and independence: to ask questions and receive answers free of what an
informant had read, or heard, or seen in a movie. Participants in debates
over the possibilities of African history held a range of positions in regard to
the weight of colonialism on historical consciousness and African historical
practice. Some, such as David Henige (1973, 1982b), argued that literacy
and written texts had profound—and virtually unrecoverable—effects on
oral tradition. But others saw the experience of African contact with Europe
differently. One of the founding figures of African history, Jacob Ajayi, remarked in the mid-1960s that

> in any long-term historical view of African history, European rule becomes
> just another episode. In relation to wars and conflicts of people, the rise and
> fall of empires, linguistic, cultural and religious change and the cultivation
> of new ideas and new ways of life, new economic orientations and so on, in
> relation to all these, colonialism must be seen not as a complete departure
> from the African past, but as one episode in the continuous flow of African
> history. (Ajayi 1968: 194)

Others viewed the problem differently. Carolyn Hamilton (1987) and Karin
Barber (1991) saw the shifting nature and meaning of oral tradition not so
much as a barrier to understanding the past but rather as a means to get at
shifting ideological ground not only in the colonial era but also during precolonial times. Cohen (1986, 1989) likewise expressed concern about the

reifications of "oral tradition" in the methodological writings of Vansina (esp. 1971, 1974, 1978a, 1978b, 1981, 1983, 1989) and Henige (esp. 1973, 1982a, 1982b, 1986). He sought to recognize the active work of Africans in producing and transforming histories in the colonial period not as an obstacle to historians but as a fit and important subject for the historian and the historical anthropologist. Nevertheless, African historians were trained to see through the colonial and postcolonial context not because anyone had told them it was transparent, but because they were trained to believe in the power and solidity of oral traditions that would remain intact in colonial and postcolonial times. Leroy Vail and Landeg White (1991) made this argument more generally as they looked at the historiography of praise poetry in Southern Africa. Studies of orality (e.g., Ong 1982, Tedlock 1983) had shifted scholars' focus away from the poets and performers of Albert Lord (1960) and Milman Parry (1971), away from their storehouse of allusions and historical references, and toward an "oral man," unimaginative and uninventive, and too unmodern to be thought to use the past as a way to criticize the present.

Vail and White's discussion of African oral literature in the context of the history and historiography of orality was an exception, however. Broader approaches to the study of history, and to the history of historical method, were hardly addressed within the schools of training that attended to Vansina's mission. Oral history became a narrow and thickly programmed frame of reference. "Oral" and "written" became reified as concrete things (Goody 1968, 1986, 2000; Miller 1980; Ewald 1987; Hofmeyr 1992, 1994), further apart in scholarship than they could ever be in practice. Indeed, although Vansina's first Kuba informants had originally told him about oral tradition by saying "We too we know the past, because we carry our newspapers in our heads" (1994: 17), this became, in the development of a field of inquiry, a statement about equivalencies, not an example of a Kuba way of talking. In this volume Isabel Hofmeyr, Miescher, and Luise White argue that oral and written genres are both media and reservoirs: no form of knowledge is intrinsic to one or the other; rather, individuals use both of them to communicate with specific audiences and to tell better stories (cf. Irwin 1981; Ewald 1987; Hofmeyr 1992, Barber 1995). The logic and utilities of the overworked distinction between orality and literacy, especially in the work of Jack Goody (1968, 1986, 2000) and Walter Ong (1982), fall away as one sees the workings of the Bunyan text under the scrutiny of Hofmeyr, the multiple competencies of Boakye Yiadom under the eyes of Miescher, and the itineraries of a remark about a white car observed in Cohen's essay. Hofmeyr goes further, arguing against the histories of worlds circumscribed and overdefined by area histories, showing how Bunyan's *Pilgrim's Progress* worked in different settings, speaking to senses of locality and outside the restrictive rhetorics of nations and empires.

The bastard in the first years of the new academic African history was colonial history. Colonialism was too dubious a field to merit serious methodological consideration. After all, should historians of the colonial era seek to do interviews—and many of the Wisconsin generation, as well as most colonial historians trained by the University of London's School of Oriental and African Studies, did not (see, for example, Fetter 1976)—they would be interviewing people about things that were within living memory; oral testimonies could be checked against published and archival materials. Such a presumption privileged written accounts over the spoken (White 1990) and implied that mythical heroes and social imaginaries were things that vanished in the modern era. Historians who sought to establish differences between written and oral sources never fully developed them: in colonial history, oral and written were supposed to be different (White 1990, 1995). After all, the best colonial histories revealed the different realities experienced by colonialists and the colonized (Vaughan 1991).

But if African oral history—as opposed to oral tradition research—meant adding an "African voice" or another perspective to archival histories, it was also, by the late 1980s and early 1990s, a way to access a more true, more accurate, and more authentic colonial experience than that which could be teased out of the writings of white male administrators and their official reports.[12] Oral history—often in the service of women's history—gained legitimacy not because of any methodological claims, but because it was argued to be more authentic, and thus more objective, than any colonial text could be. At the same time historians in Europe and North America began to do a different kind of oral history: they were less concerned with adding specific perspectives or voices to a national master narrative than with recording everyday experiences within history (Johnson 1980; Passerini 1987, 1992) and with seeing oral interviewing as a way to get at another kind of history, a genre that recorded the private, the personal, and the political in dialogue with the present day (Portelli 1991, 1997). Again, these works entered conversations about African history largely through women's history (Personal Narratives Group 1989), but they nevertheless revealed a realm of possible uses for oral accounts that went far beyond what social historians usually meant by "experience" (e.g., Mugambi 1994; White 1994). Within African history, the work of one of us began to query whether oral history should be about "what really happened" at all (White 1993, 2000). Peoples' accounts of the fantastic and the formulaic were not off the mark of historical practices, but could problematize the entire project of oral historiography. Rather than defend oral materials as being as good as, as reliable as, as accurate as a document, could historians discover in them something different, a way to access ideas from the past, embedded in descriptions of the extraordinary? In their papers here, White, Fair, and Cohen all argue that what has been called historical memory is valuable precisely because it is not necessarily an accurate memory—that is, it is not the historical veracity of a statement or memory that gives that statement or memory constitutive power. The thing that happened, and the ideas transmitted by its distorted reporting, silencing, or even and most especially invention, reveal a space of colonial and postcolonial conflict.

Arguing such a position actually made African historians backtrack to some of the paths not taken in oral history. In 1987, Hamilton pointed out in an article that oral tradition research and oral history were not different domains: people used ways of talking about the precolonial past to talk about more recent events, and vice versa. Ben Blount's 1975 description of Luo elders negotiating a lineage history had not been taken up by African historians, despite the best efforts of two of the conference organizers. Yet Blount insisted that scholars cannot talk about methodology without talking about the institutional and intimate structures within which methods were developed and practiced. More than anyone else—with the possible exception of Beidelman in his 1970 critiques of oral tradition—Blount understood that these structures existed not only in graduate schools but on the ground, among Africans.

Most of the authors presented here—including the editors—insist that the various and varied oral and written forms found "on the ground" in Africa are what give the field its history; there was no one founding moment and no one founding methodology. While Vansina's writings introduced or pressed discussions and debates that have been fertile, the essays presented here propose a far more complex matrix of issues, concerns, and contingencies than the early programmatic writings suggested (but see Rosaldo 1980, Price 1983). In these papers, the teleologies inherent in foundation myths of disciplines are transcended, if not also identified and deconstructed (Alagoa, Ogot, Vaughan, White). More importantly, the papers reveal an open sensibility toward source genres (Hofmeyr, Miescher, Vaughan, Yankah) and a critical regard to fixed genres (Kratz, White); an attendance to intertextuality (Hofmeyr, Miescher, Ogot, White, Yankah); a complex regard for relations between source or audience and scholar (Alagoa, Fair, Giles-Vernick, Ibrahim, Miescher); an understanding of different modes or regimes of truth and the force of different "truths" on the composition and work of knowledge (Alagoa, Cohen, Ibrahim, Vaughan, White); and a readiness to comprehend diversity in the modes of historical narrative (Alagoa, Miescher, Ogot).

THE CONFERENCES

The collection here arises out of a broadly circulated position paper and two conferences, one at the Rockefeller Foundation Research and Conference Center at Bellagio, Italy, and the other at Ann Arbor at the University of Michigan some three weeks later. It was the three organizers' intention that the Bellagio meeting would be a site for the presentation and discussion of a diverse group of papers by both senior and junior scholars. These papers would define the historical trajectories of African oral historiography: locating problems whether epistemological or methodological, identifying important areas of debate, and suggesting certain new paths for scholars of history. The Ann Arbor conference would be a follow-up, with a small number of Bellagio participants present. Young scholars enrolled in doctoral programs in North American universities would discuss the Bellagio papers. These young scholars, who were involved with organizing dissertation research or drafting sections of their dissertations, were identified and selected through an application process. The motif of the Bellagio-to-Ann-Arbor itinerary was one of early dissemination of the original scholarly papers presented at Bellagio, the first international conference in the field of African oral history in some twenty years.

Just three weeks apart, the two conferences unexpectedly juxtaposed a remarkable set of polarities, which themselves enriched and now frame our agenda, an agenda unlikely to have been realized had the two conferences and their different protocols and constituencies not been organized within a single plan. The papers at Bellagio, and their discussions there, ably defined the itineraries of the field of African oral historiography from its beginnings. These itineraries mattered, as they left critical marks on the practices of African history as a discipline and a profession. The individual papers, and the papers taken as a whole, largely avoided the teleologies so readily available for the definition of routes from here to there. The papers at Bellagio demonstrated a diverse, at times inchoate, field, practiced here and there, then and now, in different ways, with different suppositions about the values and challenges of oral material. Not least was the distinction between a North American (and to some extent European) notion that a history had to be found and given to Africa (in the manner of overseas assistance) and a recognition that Africa had always had, and had always been producing, histories. But even this distinction was recognized as a rather unsteady one; North American and European practitioners sought to animate oral historical research at different sites on the African continent, as Vaughan narrates, while Africans received some of their formative historical education in European settings, as Ogot recounts. Still more important was the distinction between a North American understanding that only methodological breakthroughs would make possible the incorporation of the practice of African history within the Western history profession and the claim, neatly framed by Bellagio conference participant Ogot of Kenya, that "Africans know their history and get on with their lives." The "insider-outsider" point actually traveled rather poorly through both the Bellagio and Ann Arbor discussions, and has gained attention in the papers largely as a topic for intellectual history rather than as a fundamental problem for the field. The movements of scholars across different institutional and geographical terrains, and the recognized banality of such an issue in many settings—as Alagoa, Hofmeyr, and

Vaughan suggest in their papers—have sucked value away from this cliché, though it has from time to time gained prominence in scholarly and public conferences, and nearly everywhere in public history and museum work.

But among the younger Africanist scholars at the Ann Arbor meeting, such issues hardly mattered. African history was reasonably part of the historical profession and part of the lived worlds of Africans. Regardless of their sometimes heroic aspect, the complicated itineraries from methodological programs to common-sense values and then to important universal understandings of history and the human condition seemed irrelevant, if not spurious. Doing African history was no more or less challenging than doing history in other societies. The heated debates around the programs of oral tradition research and the calls for training in ancillary disciplines needed in order to understand and verify oral tradition were no longer crucial for the young African historians being formed in the late 1990s, many of whom were exceptionally sophisticated in their use of archives alongside oral testimony. In short, there were fewer war stories at Bellagio and Ann Arbor than at conferences twenty or more years ago. Indeed, the discussions at Bellagio and Ann Arbor differed in manner from the autobiographical writings of senior figures in the field, especially Vansina (1994) and Roland Oliver (1997), which offer heroic scripts of the foundation of a modern field of African history. Vansina sees the passing of an era, as the unified purpose of the field of African history falls into disarray in the West, while Oliver laments the decline of African institutions dedicated to the recovery of the African past.

At Bellagio, questions regarding the struggles for objectivity—to give African historiography authority within the historical profession, to meet the evident, prevailing standards of the discipline—lay within and around many of the papers. Historical research from oral testimonies and oral traditions did involve the generation of methods of collection, evaluation, and interpretation that would yield equivalence to the written document. Orality and literacy were qualities, conditions, which did matter. Whether or not they labored on these questions of the essentialities of *the oral,* most of the authors of papers presented at Bellagio did recognize the special conditions and limitations of oral testimonies and traditions. But in discussions—even where they had been set up explicitly in the conference schedule—most of the Bellagio attendants seemed wholly uninterested in reconvening the debates on methodology and objectivity that had been the subject of so many discussions of such uneven quality in so many sites and venues of African historiography in North America through the 1960s and 1970s. Indeed, such debates inspired the foundation of *History in Africa: A Journal of Method,* which itself became a site for debates about oral tradition long after most journals ceased to publish such material.

For the organizers of the two conferences, the question of how oral sources gained important footholds within a professional African historiography overlay self-critical concerns that historians may have moved to credit the oral with greater objective substantiality than might have been reasonably warranted in the context of the "higher goal" of "giving Africa a history." The organizers explicitly wished to regain and reopen the seemingly formative debates of the 1950s through the 1970s on the usability of oral materials, if only to provide more senior scholars space and time for reflection amidst the developing work of the younger scholars.

At the Ann Arbor meeting, few of these younger scholars had even taken a methods course specifically geared to African historical research or oral historical research. As noted, they hardly remarked on "objectivity" as a special burden of the Africa field. More significantly and unapologetically, they saw their work developing quite far from an engagement with the objectivity debates and protocols of the historical profession. Rather, most saw their applications of oral historical research as the means of documenting and historicizing African subjectivities, and they took their respective studies to be in direct conversation with scholarship on fields other than African.

Whereas more senior participants at Bellagio could regain, heuristically, a sense of the problematic aspects of the subjective in the sources they drew on for their own research, most of the graduate students at the Ann Arbor meeting, as well as some of the younger presenters at Bellagio (Fair, Giles-Vernick, and Miescher), readily and undefensively saw that oral testimony was subjective. The challenge they had chosen to take on was not to affirm the truth or falsity of such testimony, as if in a judicial process, nor to cleverly identify and extract overlying falsities to get at underlying truth, but rather to work through the gathering and interpretation of oral testimony as a means of comprehending how Africans saw their lives, their worlds, their histories. The younger participants were less interested in how Africans recalled the past than how they *felt* about—or understood and represented—the experience of being African, or being male, or female, or poor, or sick, in the heady conditions of the twentieth century. Far from seeing their sources' subjectivity as a problem or hazard, the younger scholars took subjectivity to be their core interest. "Life history" is a way of getting at this subjectivity.

Among the students presenting their projects at Ann Arbor, life history was the historical modality, and oral history was the means to—so to speak—gain a "life," gain understanding. At Bellagio, life history was a method of history, one route of recovery of the African past among many that had moved the field to a central, dominating position across several decades. More than others, the papers here by Fall, Giles-Vernick, Kratz, and Miescher take up life history as a research modality and as a means to understanding. They leave the discussion far richer, remarking the inchoate and variant textualities comprising the genre, while alerting readers to the problems and limitations of life history as a contribution to historical knowledge.

*   *   *

The differences in the orientations of the two meetings—and the complete set of Bellagio papers were distributed in advance to and discussed by all the participants in both meetings—unmade and redefined the present editors' original program. The juxtaposition of the two meetings and of their substantive discussions brought into dramatic relief the complex lineages of thought and work on the project of writing Africa's history . . . and of writing that history through broad and generous inclusion of the so-called oral record. On the last day of the Ann Arbor conference, Professor Ogot, one of the founding figures of African oral historiography and a man fully aware of the instrumental role he played in the research of many scholars, including two of the conference organizers, related to the conference participants a previous night's dream. In Ann Arbor, Ogot dreamt that Jomo Kenyatta, the first president of Kenya, had come to see him. For the next two hours the two men debated the future of Kenya. While we leave it to Professor Ogot to write about the content of his debate with Kenyatta, we do suspect that Kenyatta's nocturnal visit has still further complicated the notions of orality and literacy in the constitution of Africa's past, present, and future, as historians' and anthropologists' explorations of dream-worlds have complicated and enriched our ideas of what lived experience means in other places, other times.

The papers here address the complexities of storytelling and history in Africa, and we believe they leave the field much enriched, if also far more complicated. These papers contradict some of the prevailing concerns of African historical scholarship—a scholarship based once on voices speaking from their pasts and more recently on them speaking on their own. In this scholarship, specially trained experts were first to rescue, recuperate, and recapture the glories of the African past for Africans and then to stand aside and let Africans speak for themselves. How did the field of African history, and within it African oral history, move across different working contexts—institutional, spatial, temporal—from a program holding "the oral" to be the means of unlocking the histories of peoples without writing to one in which "the oral" would move scholarship toward objectives seemingly unrealizable in the documentary record?

NOTES

1. The topics that have serially captured the attention of South African historian Charles van Onselen (1976, 1982, 1996) across more than two decades, and produced distinguished work of very different kinds, are revealing. Another example: an early exploration in African women's history, Mary Smith's *Baba of Karo* (1954), went out of print almost at once. As a feminist critique of historical research in general became widespread, *Baba of Karo* was reprinted in 1981 as a woman's life history and has remained in print for most of the last twenty years.

2. See especially the debates developing around the work of Belinda Bozzoli and Mmantho Nkotsoe (1991).

3. Commission Appointed to Enquire into the April 1935 Disturbances on the Copperbelt of Northern Rhodesia, *Report* (Lusaka: Government Printer, 1936), 5.

4. The practices of speaking freely and using commissions of enquiry for one's

own purposes are not limited to Africans, of course. White mine managers testifying before this commission often used the occasion to decry the inexperience and lack of discipline of skilled white miners.

5. For a similar endeavor in Accra, see Acquah 1958.

6. One might observe, whimsically, that if Europeans needed chiefs at the outset of the colonial period, they very badly needed "voices" at its close.

7. Jan Vansina's (1994) account of his medievalist professors rejecting his Kuba oral history is meant to describe the prejudices against oral history, but it is often taken as a foundation moment in African history. Similarly, Trevor-Roper's pronouncement that without writing there was no history, only "unrewarding gyrations of barbarous tribes in picturesque but irrelevant corners of the globe" (1963: 871), became a rallying cry for African historians: the struggles of the new field were not about content, method, or audience, but against European historians who could not imagine a world beyond their documents.

8. Not only did this view of anthropology as ahistorical find presence in the new "schools" of training of African historians, but it also constituted an epistemological break that some rising scholars would seek to overcome in yet another, and different, heroic mode. Remarkably, Jan Vansina, in his memoir (1994), kept alive this myth. Among others, Richard Werbner has readily identified and deconstructed it (1996).

9. Beidelman 1970; Pender-Cudlip 1972; Feierman 1974; Miller 1978; MacGaffey 1978; Miller 1980; Spear 1981; Irwin 1981; Cohen 1986; Ewald 1985, 1987, 1990.

10. Henige 1973, 1982a, 1982b, 1986; Vansina 1974; Miller 1980.

11. Cohen 1986, 1989, 1994; Hamilton 1987; Barber 1991; Comaroff and Comaroff 1992; Tonkin 1992. Also see White, chapter 13, this volume.

12. Strobel 1979; Robertson 1983, 1997; Geiger 1986, 1997; Romero 1988; White 1990.

BIBLIOGRAPHY

Acquah, Ioné. 1958. *Accra Survey: A Social Survey of the Capital of Ghana, Formerly Called the Gold Coast, Undertaken for the West African Institute of Social and Economic Research, 1953–1956.* London: University of London Press.

Ajayi, J. F. Ade. 1968. "The Continuity of African Institutions under Colonialism." In *Emerging Themes of African History,* ed. T. O. Ranger, 189–200. Dar es Salaam: East African Publishing House.

Alagoa, Ebiegberi J., ed. 1990. *Oral Tradition and Oral History in Africa and the Diaspora: Theory and Practice.* Lagos: Centre for Black and African Arts and Civilization.

Barber, Karin. 1991. *I Could Speak until Tomorrow: Oriki, Women, and the Past in a Yoruba Town.* Washington, D.C.: Smithsonian Institution Press.

———. 1995. "Literacy, Improvisation, and the Public in Yoruba Popular Theatre." In *The Pressures of the Text: Orality, Texts, and the Telling of Tales,* ed. Stewart Brown, 6–27. Birmingham: Centre of West African Studies, University of Birmingham.

Barber, Karin, and P. F. de Moraes Farias, eds. 1989. *Discourse and Its Disguises: The Interpretation of African Oral Texts.* Birmingham: Centre of West African Studies, University of Birmingham.

Barnett, Donald, and Karari Njama. 1966. *Mau Mau from Within: Autobiography and Analysis of Kenya's Peasant Revolt.* New York: Monthly Press.

Beidelman, Thomas O. 1970. "Myth, Legend, and Oral History: A Kaguru Traditional Text." *Anthropos* 65, nos. 5–6: 74–97.

Blount, Ben G. 1975. "Agreeing to Agree on Genealogy: A Luo Sociology of Knowledge." In *Sociocultural Dimensions of Language Use,* ed. Mary Sanches and Ben G. Blount, 117–35. New York: Academic Press.

Bozzoli, Belinda, with the assistance of Mmantho Nkotsoe. 1991. *Women of Phokeng: Consciousness, Life Strategy, and Migrancy in South Africa, 1900–1983.* Portsmouth, N.H.: Heinemann.

Busia, K. A. 1950. *Report on the Social Survey of Sekondi-Takoradi.* London: Crown Agents.

Cohen, David William. 1977. *Womunafu's Bunafu: A Study of Authority in a Nineteenth-Century African Community.* Princeton: Princeton University Press.

———. 1980. "Reconstructing a Conflict in Bunafu: Seeking Evidence outside the Narrative Tradition." In *The African Past Speaks: Essays on Oral Tradition and History,* ed. Joseph C. Miller, 201–20. Hamden, Conn.: Archon.

———. 1989. "The Undefining of Oral Tradition." *Ethnohistory* 36, no. 1: 9–18.

———. 1991. "'A Case for the Basoga': Lloyd Fallers and the Construction of an African Legal System." In *Law in Colonial Africa,* ed. Kristin Mann and Richard Roberts, 239–54. Portsmouth, N.H.: Heinemann; London: James Currey.

———. 1994. *The Combing of History.* Chicago: University of Chicago Press.

———, ed. and trans. 1986. *Towards a Reconstructed Past: Historical Texts from Busoga, Uganda.* London: The British Academy and Oxford University Press.

Comaroff, Jean, and John L. Comaroff. 1992. *Ethnography and the Historical Imagination.* Boulder: Westview.

Curtin, Philip D. 1968a. "Field Techniques for Collecting and Processing Oral Data." *Journal of African History* 9, no. 3: 367–85.

———, ed. 1968b. *Africa Remembered: Narratives by West Africans from the Era of the Slave Trade.* Madison: University of Wisconsin Press.

Davison, Jean, with the women of Mutira. 1989. *Voices from Mutira: Lives of Rural Gikuyu Women.* Boulder: L. Rienner.

Epstein, A. L. 1953. *The Administration of Justice and the Urban African: A Study of Urban Native Courts in Northern Rhodesia.* London: H. M. Stationery Office.

———. 1958. *Politics in an Urban African Community.* Manchester: Manchester University Press for the Rhodes-Livingstone Institute.

Ewald, Janet. 1985. "History and Speculation: History and Founding Stories in the Kingdom of Taqali, 1780–1935." *International Journal of African Historical Studies* 18, no. 2: 265–87.

———. 1987. "Speaking, Writing, and Authority: Explorations in and from the Kingdom of Taqali." *Comparative Studies in Society and History* 30, no. 2: 199–224.

———. 1990. *Soldiers, Traders, and Slaves: State Formation and Economic Transformation in the Greater Nile Valley, 1700–1885.* Madison: University of Wisconsin Press.

Fallers, Lloyd A. 1969. *Law without Precedent: Legal Ideas in Action in the Courts of Busoga.* Chicago: University of Chicago Press.

Feierman, Steven. 1974. *The Shambaa Kingdom: A History.* Madison: University of Wisconsin Press.

Fetter, Bruce S. 1976. *The Creation of Elisabethville, 1910–1940.* Stanford: Stanford University Press.

Geiger, Susan. 1986. "Women's Life Histories: Method and Content." *Signs* 11, no. 2: 334–51.

———. 1990. "What's So Feminist about Women's Oral History?" *Journal of Women's History* 2, no. 1: 169–82.

———. 1997. *TANU Women: Gender and Culture in the Making of Tanganyikan Nationalism, 1955–1965.* Portsmouth, N.H.: Heinemann.

Goody, Jack. 1986. *The Interface between the Written and the Oral.* Cambridge: Cambridge University Press.

———. 2000. *The Power of the Written Tradition.* Washington, D.C.: Smithsonian Institution Press.

———, ed. 1968. *Literacy in Traditional Societies.* Cambridge: Cambridge University Press.

Goody, Jack, and Ian Watt. 1963. "The Consequences of Literacy." *Comparative Studies in Society and History* 5, no. 3: 304–45.

Griaule, Marcel. 1948. *Dieu d'eau. Entretiens avec Ogotemmêli.* Paris: Chêne.

Hamilton, C. A. 1987. "Ideology and Oral Traditions: Listening to the Voices 'from Below.'" *History in Africa* 14: 67–86.

Henige, David. 1973. "The Problem of Feedback in Oral Tradition." *Journal of African History* 14, no. 2: 223–35.

———. 1974. *The Chronology of Oral Tradition: Quest for a Chimera.* Oxford: Clarendon.

———. 1982a. *Oral Historiography.* New York: Longman.

———. 1982b. "Truths Yet Unborn? Oral Tradition as a Casualty of Culture Contact." *Journal of African History* 23, no. 2: 395–412.

———. 1986. "Where Seldom Is Heard a Discouraging Word: Method in Oral History." *Oral History Review* 14: 35–42.

Hofmeyr, Isabel. 1992. "'Nterata'/'The Wire': Fences, Boundaries, Orality, Literacy." In *International Annual of Oral History, 1990: Subjectivity and Multiculturalism in Oral History,* ed. Ron J. Grele, 69–91. New York: Greenwood Press.

———. 1994. *"We Spend Our Years as a Tale That Is Told": Oral Historical Narrative in a South African Chiefdom.* Portsmouth, N.H.: Heinemann.

Hoppe, Kirk. 1993. "Whose Life Is It Anyway? Issues of Representation in Life Narrative Texts of African Women." *International Journal of African Historical Studies* 26, no. 3: 623–36.

Irwin, Paul. 1981. *Liptako Speaks: History from Oral Tradition in Africa.* Princeton: Princeton University Press.

Isaacman, Allen. 1972. *Mozambique: The Africanization of a European Institution; The Zambezi Prazos, 1750–1902.* Madison: University of Wisconsin Press.

Jenkins, Paul, ed. 1998. *The Recovery of the West African Past: African Pastors and African History in the Nineteenth Century, C. C. Reindorf & Samuel Johnson.* Basel: Basler Afrika Bibliographien.

Jewsiewicki, Bogumil. 1989. "African Historical Studies: Academic Knowledge as Usable Past." *African Studies Review* 32, no. 3: 32–76.

Jewsiewicki, Bogumil, and David Newbury, eds. 1986. *African Historiographies: What History for Which Africa?* Beverly Hills: Sage.

Johnson, Richard, ed. 1980. *Making Histories: Studies in History-Writing and Politics.* London: Hutchinson in association with the Centre for Contemporary Cultural Studies, University of Birmingham.

Johnson, Samuel. 1921. *The History of the Yorubas from the Earliest Times to the Beginnings of the British Protectorate.* Ed. O. Johnson. Lagos: C. M. S. Bookshops.

Kenyatta, Jomo. 1938. *Facing Mount Kenya: The Tribal Life of the Gikuyu.* London: Secker and Warburg.

Leslie, J. A. K. 1963. *A Survey of Dar es Salaam.* London: Oxford University Press for the East African Institute for Social Research.

Longmore, Laura. 1959. *The Dispossessed: A Study of the Sex-Life of Bantu Women in Urban Areas in and around Johannesburg.* London: J. Cape.

Lord, Albert B. 1960. *The Singer of Tales.* Cambridge, Mass.: Harvard University Press.

MacGaffey, Wyatt. 1974. "Oral Tradition in Central Africa." *International Journal of African Historical Studies* 7: 417–26.

———. 1978. "African History, Anthropology, and the Rationality of Natives." *History in Africa* 5: 101–20.

Mbilinyi, Marjorie. 1989. "'I'd Have Been a Man': Politics and the Labor Process in Producing Personal Narratives." In *Interpreting Women's Lives: Feminist Theory and Personal Narratives,* ed. Personal Narratives Group, 204–207. Bloomington: Indiana University Press.

Menchú, Rigoberta. 1984. *I, Rigoberta Menchú: An Indian Woman in Guatemala.* Ed. Elisabeth Burgos-Debray, trans. Ann Wright. London: Verso.

Miescher, Stephan F. 1997. "Becoming a Man in Kwawu: Gender, Law, Personhood, and the Construction of Masculinities in Colonial Ghana, 1875–1957." Ph.D. dissertation, Northwestern University.

Miller, Joseph C. 1976. *Kings and Kingsmen: Early Mbundu States in Angola.* Oxford: Clarendon.

———. 1978. "The Dynamics of Oral Tradition in Africa." In *Fonti Orali: Antropologia e Storia,* ed. Bernardo Bernardi, 75–101. Milan: F. Angeli.

———, ed. 1980. *The African Past Speaks: Essays on Oral Tradition and History.* Hamden, Conn.: Archon.

Mintz, Sidney. 1974. *Worker in the Cane: A Puerto Rican Life History.* 1960. Reprint, New York: Norton.

———. 1979. "The Anthropological Interview and the Life History." *Oral History Review* 7: 18–26.

Mirza, Sara, and Margaret Strobel. 1989. *Three Swahili Women: Life Histories from Mombasa, Kenya.* Bloomington: Indiana University Press.

Mitchell, James Clyde. 1956. *The Kalela Dance: Aspects of Social Relationships among Urban Africans in Northern Rhodesia.* Manchester: Manchester University Press.

Mudimbe, Valentin Y. 1992. *The Surreptitious Speech: Présence Africaine and the Politics of Otherness, 1947–1987.* Chicago: University of Chicago Press.

Mugambi, Helen. 1994. "Intersections: Gender, Orality, Text, and Female Space in Contemporary Kiganda Radio Songs." *Research in African Literatures* 25, no. 1: 47–70.

Oliver, Roland. 1997. *In the Realms of Gold: Pioneering in African History.* Madison: University of Wisconsin Press.

Ong, Walter J. 1982. *Orality and Literacy: The Technologizing of the World.* London: Methuen.

Parry, Milman. 1971. *The Making of Homeric Verse.* Oxford: Clarendon.

Passerini, Luisa. 1987. *Fascism in Popular Memory: The Cultural Experience of the Turin Working Class.* Cambridge: Cambridge University Press.

———, ed. 1992. *Memory and Totalitarianism.* International Yearbook of Oral History and Life Stories, vol. 1. London: Oxford University Press.

Pender-Cudlip, P. 1972. "Oral Traditions and Anthropological Analysis: Some Contemporary Myths." *Azania* 7: 3–24.

Personal Narratives Group, ed. 1989. *Interpreting Women's Lives: Feminist Theory and Personal Narratives.* Bloomington: Indiana University Press.

Portelli, Alessandro. 1991. *The Death of Luigi Trastulli and Other Stories: Form and Meaning in Oral History.* Albany: State University of New York Press.

———. 1997. *The Battle of Valle Giulia: Oral History and the Art of Dialogue.* Madison: University of Wisconsin Press.

Powdermaker, Hortense. 1962. *Copper Town: The Human Situation on the Rhodesian Copperbelt.* New York: Harper and Row.

Price, Richard. 1983. *First-Time: The Historical View of an Afro-American People.* Baltimore: Johns Hopkins University Press.

Radin, Paul, ed. 1926. *Crashing Thunder: The Autobiography of an American Indian.* New York: Appleton.

Ranger, T. O. 1976. "Towards a Usable African Past." In *African Studies since 1945: A Tribute to Basil Davidson,* ed. Christopher Fyfe, 17–30. London: Longman.

Reindorf, Carl Christian. 1895. *History of the Gold Coast and Asante.* Basel: Missionsbuchhandlung.

Robertson, Claire C. 1983. "Post-emancipation Slavery in Accra: A Female Affair?" In *Women and Slavery in Africa,* ed. Claire C. Robertson and Martin A. Klein, 220–45. Madison: University of Wisconsin Press.

———. 1997. *"Trouble Showed the Way": Women, Men, and Trade in the Nairobi Area, 1890–1990.* Bloomington: Indiana University Press.

Romero, Patricia W. ed. 1988. *Life Histories of African Women.* London and Atlantic Heights, N.J.: Ashfield.

Rosaldo, Renato. 1980. "Doing Oral History." *Social Analysis* 4: 89–99.

Roscoe, John. 1911. *The Baganda.* Cambridge: Cambridge University Press.

———. 1915. *The Northern Bantu.* Cambridge: Cambridge University Press.

Shostak, Marjorie. 1981. *Nisa: The Life and Words of a !Kung Woman.* Cambridge, Mass.: Harvard University Press.

———. 1987. "What the Wind Won't Take Away: The Oral History of an African Foraging Woman." *International Journal for Oral History* 8, no. 3: 171–81.

Smith, M. F. 1954. *Baba of Karo: A Woman of the Muslim Hausa.* London: Faber and Faber.

Smith, Sidonie, and Julia Watson, eds. 1992. *Decolonizing the Subject: The Politics of Gender in Women's Autobiography.* Minneapolis: University of Minnesota Press.

Southall, Aidan, and Peter Gutkind. 1957. *Townsmen in the Making: Kampala and Its Suburbs.* Kampala: East African Institute of Social Research.

Spear, Thomas. 1981. "Oral Traditions: Whose History?" *History in Africa* 8: 165–81.

Staunton, Irene. 1990. *Mothers of the Revolution: The War Experience of Thirty Zimbabwean Women.* Bloomington: Indiana University Press.

Strobel, Margaret. 1977. "Doing Oral History as an Outsider." *Frontiers: A Journal of Women's Studies* 2, no. 2: 68–72.

————. 1979. *Muslim Women in Mombasa, 1890–1975.* New Haven: Yale University Press.

Strobel, Margaret, and Sarah Mirza. 1989. *Three Swahili Women: Life Histories from Mombasa, Kenya.* Bloomington: Indiana University Press.

Tedlock, Dennis. 1983. *The Spoken Word and the Work of Interpretation.* Philadelphia: University of Pennsylvania Press.

Tonkin, Elizabeth. 1982. "The Boundaries of History in Oral Performance." *History in Africa* 9: 273–84.

————. 1986. "Investigating Oral Tradition." *Journal of African History* 27: 203–13.

————. 1992. *Narrating Our Pasts: The Social Construction of Oral History.* Cambridge: Cambridge University Press.

Trevor-Roper, Hugh. 1963. "The Rise of Christian Europe." *The Listener,* 28 November 1963, 871.

Vail, Leroy, and Landeg White. 1991. *Power and the Praise Poem: Southern African Voices in History.* Charlottesville: University Press of Virginia.

van Onselen, Charles. 1976. *Chibaro: African Mine Labour in Southern Rhodesia, 1900–1933.* London: Pluto Press.

————. 1982. *Studies in the Social and Economic History of the Witwatersrand, 1886–1914.* 2 vols. New York: Longman.

————. 1993. "Peasants Speak: The Reconstruction of a Rural Life from Oral Testimony: Critical Notes on the Methodology Employed in the Study of a Black South African Sharecropper." *Journal of Peasant Studies* 20, no. 3: 494–514.

————. 1996. *The Seed Is Mine: The Life of Kas Maine, a South African Sharecropper, 1894–1985.* New York: Hill and Wang.

Vansina, Jan. 1960. "Recording the Oral History of the Bakuba." Parts 1 and 2. *Journal of African History* 1, no. 1: 43–51; no. 2: 257–70.

————. 1965. *Oral Tradition: A Study in Historical Methodology.* Trans. H. M. Wright. London: Routledge and Kegan Paul.

————. 1971. "Once upon a Time: Oral Traditions as History in Africa." *Daedalus* 100: 442–68.

————. 1974. "Comment: Tradition of Genesis." *Journal of African History* 15: 317–22.

————. 1978a. *The Children of Woot: A History of the Kuba Peoples.* Madison: University of Wisconsin Press.

————. 1978b. "For Oral Tradition (But Not against Braudel)." *History in Africa* 5: 351–56.

————. 1980. "Memory and Oral Tradition." In *The African Past Speaks: Essays on Oral Tradition and History,* ed. Joseph C. Miller, 262–79. Hamden, Conn.: Archon.

————. 1981. "Oral Tradition and Its Methodology." In *General History of Africa,* Vol. 1, *Methodology and African Prehistory,* ed. Joseph Ki-Zerbo, 142–65. Paris: UNESCO.

————. 1983. "Is Elegance Proof? Structuralism and African History." *History in Africa* 10: 317–48.

————. 1985. *Oral Tradition as History.* Madison: University of Wisconsin Press.

————. 1989. "Western Bantu Tradition and the Notion of Tradition." *Paideuma* 35: 289–300.

―――. 1994. *Living with Africa.* Madison: University of Wisconsin Press.

Vaughan, Megan. 1991. *Curing Their Ills: Colonial Power and African Illness.* Stanford: Stanford University Press.

Werbner, Richard. 1996. "African Past, American Present: An Anglicised American Reads an Americanised Belgian." Review of *Living with Africa,* by Jan Vansina. *Cultural Dynamics* 8, no. 1: 101–10.

White, Luise. 1990. *The Comforts of Home: Prostitution in Colonial Nairobi.* Chicago: University of Chicago Press.

―――. 1993. "Cars out of Place: Vampires, Technology, and Labor in East and Central Africa." *Representations* 43: 27–50.

―――. 1994. "Between Gluckman and Foucault: Historicizing Rumor and Gossip." *Social Dynamics* 20: 75–92.

―――. 1995. "'They Could Make Their Victims Dull': Genders and Genres, Fantasies and Cures in Colonial Southern Uganda." *American Historical Review* 100, no. 5: 1379–1402.

―――. 2000. *Speaking with Vampires: Rumor and History in Colonial Africa.* Berkeley: University of California Press.

Wright, Marcia. 1993. *Strategies of Slaves and Women: Life-Stories from East/Central Africa.* New York: L. Barber.

Yankah, Kwesi. 1989. *The Proverb in the Context of Akan Rhetoric: A Theory of Proverb Praxis.* Bern: Peter Lang.

―――. 1995. *Speaking for the Chief: Ökyeame and the Politics of Akan Royal Oratory.* Bloomington: Indiana University Press.

PART I

Giving Africa a History

1

The Construction of Luo Identity and History

Bethwell A. Ogot

For the last four decades, heated debates have been conducted in learned journals and books about the use and importance of oral traditions in African studies. Are they reliable? Are they valid? Can we use them for dating? Are they relevant to the contemporary situations in Africa or are they merely of antiquarian interest? Such questions, I wish to argue in this paper, do not deal with the real issues we should seriously debate. We need studies which seek to achieve an understanding of a people through a study of their treasure chest, the profounder aspects of their culture, knowledge of their history, literature, and world-view, their philosophy, language and art; not for curiosity, or out of antiquarian interest, but as fit explanation for contemporary situations.

In my own field of history, the use of oral traditions as sources of African history has continued to win great recognition from modern African historians. Efforts have been made to produce general works which seek to offer guidelines on the nature of oral traditions, the problems involved in their use and interpretation, how they become historical texts, and their integrity as historical evidence.

But a much more fundamental question we should be discussing in this context is the nature of historical reality and its relation to historical method. This, in turn, determines the fundamental orientation of perception and thought as components of a given approach to reality. For example, one of the major concerns of anthropologists and historians dealing with oral traditions is whether or not they are "true." What we normally mean by this question is whether oral tradition conforms to *our* concept of truth. But we should also be concerned about how other people view the past and how they define historical truth. For one of the aims of collecting oral traditions must be to get the people's view of history—call it folk history—as opposed to *our* view of *their* history. If that is the case, then veracity in their terms is more important than veracity in our terms. This is because primary sources do not directly determine the mode of reconstructing the past; they only offer a narrative space for several explanatory accounts.

Furthermore, in our attempt to understand the nature of historical reality, we should address ourselves to such questions as the forms and criteria by which history is understood. How did historical consciousness evolve in a particular tradition, and in what specific forms? What things are worth remembering and why? What is the historical foundation of self-understanding, and how is it formed? What is the role of individual experiences in the common memory? What are the nature and form of communication between different traditions and experiences of history?

The answers to all these questions should emphasize the point that an evaluation of oral tradition as historical evidence must depend upon detailed ethnographic knowledge of the social functions of folk history, its manner of transmission, its variability within any one society, the criteria of historical truth, and other features of history as a system within the culture under study. We have to study the way in which whole societies and segments of society have thought about themselves in relation to what they understood as their past and their knowledge of it. We will discover that such a concept of history is logically related to other fundamental concepts in a particular society, and that such a concept of history itself has a historiography.

Roots of Luo Historiography

The Luo, like all other people, have always thought about the past as reflected in the present and as a basis for predicting the future. Lessons from experience were worked out collectively and preserved through the participation of many people in their construction, recitation, and performance. Individuals had to know the history of their communities, because their own identity and status derived from connections to a community. Oral traditions were developed to record such histories, and they changed in response to new challenges and situations. Within their broadly collective narratives, individuals also reflected on their personal experiences and on those of other communities, and constructed their own visions of the past. In other words, for many centuries the Luo have been producing popular historical literature in their language. These histories had authority, significance, and meaning for individuals, as well as for collectivities.

The construction of Luo identity and history is therefore a process in which many people, both African and non-African, have taken part. This has produced different discourses of knowledge through which different experts have constructed the Luo past in order to gain credibility for their versions of it. This, inevitably, has led to a struggle for control of voices and texts, initially among the popular historians and later between them and academic guild historians.

By the eighteenth century, the *chir,* a kind of informal school, had evolved among the Luo. Leaders from neighboring settlements met and agreed on where they could establish their chir. It was usually situated under a big tree at the junction of a number of paths. On any normal day, it lasted from ten until two o'clock. Young males between ten and thirty years old attended chir for instruction, while male adults discussed current affairs and played the game of *ajwa* (bao).

The traditional historians taught the young men the stories of their *gwenge*, or settlements (singular *gweng'*), and how these had combined to form the larger *pinje* (singular *piny*), autonomous territorial units into which, by the nineteenth century, the Luo people were divided. Each piny (Asembo, Uyoma, Sakwa, Gem, Alego, Nyakach, Kano, Ugenya, Kisumo, Seme, Karachuonyo, Karungu, Kadem, etc.) taught its youth about its history before its arrival in Siaya, its settlement in Luoland, its evolution in Central Nyanza or later in South Nyanza. In practice, all these pinje were multi-clan and multi-ethnic political groupings. Hence their histories had to deal with the histories of the different non-Luo groups, their identities, their statuses—for example, people who were conquered and remained on the land and hence continued to sacrifice on behalf of the land, and *jomotur* (refugees) or *jodak* (clients) who worked for the landowners. The youth were also taught about leadership and the evolution of the different types of leaders in the pinje—those who had a traditional claim to positions of authority and those who earned positions of influence because of their talents: *jobilo* (priest-diviners or prophets), *ogaye* (peacemakers), *osumba mirwayi* (generals), *jodong' lweny* (war leaders), *okebe* (wealthy people).

Instruction at the chir also included *sigana* (history or oral literature), covering the history of the interactions among the Luo and the Bantu and other Nilotic groups in southern Uganda and western Kenya. There was, for example, considerable exchange of knowledge and ideas—economic, religious, cultural, and linguistic—between the Luo and the Bantu-speaking groups. Besides sigana, instruction was also given in agriculture, wealth creation, war, and customary law.

The *duol* gathering ("duol" means a hut in the middle of a *gunda bur*, a multi-clan or multi-lineage village) took place from about seven in the evening until bedtime. It was a much smaller group, a kind of tutorial group, where similar subjects were covered, except there was time for the young to raise questions about any obscure points (Ogot 1950).

Young girls' education was carried out in *siwidhe* (the house of a *pim*, or respectable old lady). Cookery, good behavior, storytelling, and singing were the most important subjects (Cohen 1985).

Thus, in the chir, duol, and siwidhe individual and collective identities were constructed as history by the various experts. In the words of the Bellagio Conference organizers, Luise White, Stephan F. Miescher, and David William Cohen, in their conference proposal (1996), Africa in general and the Luo in particular could during this time "be studied, known, understood and represented" with "reference to the narrative and interpretive practices of Africans themselves." In short, Africans "could themselves comprehend, interpret and narrate in a useable manner their worlds." Their voices were dominant. The constructed identities and histories may not have been true, but they were acceptable because they did not conflict with their audience's conception of identity. And as they forged identities at the village, local, and regional levels, the Luo were simultaneously forging an identity for themselves as a nation.

FROM ORALITY TO LITERACY, OR THE CONTAINMENT OF AFRICAN VOICES

With the onset of colonialism in Kenya in 1895, the written word gradually replaced orality. A people without writing, it was alleged, could not have history, or culture, or religion. The Africans suddenly became voiceless and memories could no longer be reconstructed. The chir, duol, and siwidhe were soon replaced by mission schools where emphasis was on the word of God, the white God. In the rest of Luoland, silence prevailed, which the visitors construed to mean ignorance and helplessness.

European eyewitnesses now replaced the African experts on Luo culture and history. Their accounts usually took the form of lists of numerous details of material culture, social divisions, customs, and beliefs. Sir Harry H. Johnson, Special Commissioner for East Africa, wrote about Luo villages, clothes, agriculture, cooking, hunting, smoking, religion, health, and games (Johnston 1902). Missionaries such as Reverend N. Stam (1910) and Reverend H. Hartman (1928) published articles describing Luo religious beliefs and practices, marriage and burial customs, physical ornamentation, diet, rites, sexual habits, taboos, and life cycles; these articles revealed their idea that most customs of the "poor slaves of ignorance" were unchristian and bad. A colonial administrator, G. A. S. Northcote, wrote an article (1907) on the relationship of the Luo to other Nilotic peoples and their physical characteristics, dress, weapons, politics, system of land ownership, settlement patterns, rules of inheritance, marriage ceremonies, funerals, religion, and witchcraft (cf. Hobley 1898, 1902, 1903). Obviously, the treatment of all these topics in one article would not be comprehensive.

Such studies by amateur anthropologists did not show how the society was integrated. No serious efforts were made to relate the society's traditions to its environment, or to investigate the circumstances of transmission or testimony. The interest of the pioneer administrators and missionaries in writing on the history and culture of the Luo people derived more from a wish to record the quaint and strange than from a desire to achieve what Evans-Pritchard called a "constructive integration of events" (1962: 24).

But unlike in other places, such as West Africa, South Africa, Buganda, and Kikuyuland, these European writers produced no "historical model" that could influence local and international readers and students. Indeed, no serious or standard work on Luo culture or history was produced at this time.

The Luo also did not have the Leakeys, who could claim authority based on having grown among them. Nor did they have colonial administrators or missionaries claiming to know their traditions from the insider's point of view, merely by having spent many years amongst them. C. W. Hobley and W. E. Owen were the nearest one could find to foreign experts on the Luo. But neither produced any substantial work on the Luo. Hobley published a few descriptive articles in journals (1896, 1902, 1903), while Owen, who had a long, relatively uninterrupted residence in western Kenya (1918–1945), is less known for the article (1932) he wrote on food production amongst the Luo than for his archaeological and paleontological study of western Kenya. He also acted as an informant to Evans-Pritchard during the latter's brief survey of Luo "tribes" and clans in 1936. The Luo were thus able to retain autonomy over their past and traditions, albeit in silence, until after the Second World War.

In 1946, when the Colonial Social Science Research Council decided to post four social anthropologists to Kenya, the colonial government admitted that the ethnic groups which it was most anxious to have studied, because they were the groups about which the ethnographical literature on Kenya was most deficient, were the Luo, the Gusii, the Abaluhya, and the Bantu of the Coastal Province (Mijikenda, Taita, Taveta). The Abaluhya had been studied fairly thoroughly by Dr. G. Wagner shortly before the war, and the results of his research were later published under the title *The Bantu of North Kavirondo* in two volumes in 1949. Dr. P. Mayer was assigned to study the Gusii, while Dr. A. H. J. Prins carried out extensive research on the Coastal Bantu. Dr. Andrzej Waligorski, a Polish scholar, seems to have carried out extensive research among the Luo. When Isaac Schapera, who had been appointed by the Kenyan government on the advice of the Colonial Social Science Research Council as consultant for the research project, visited Waligorski in the field in 1946, he was impressed by his thoroughness and his command of the Luo language, which enabled him to converse with elders (Schapera 1947).

Aidan Southall later appreciated the generous way in which Waligorski shared his own knowledge of the Luo with him. He, however, regretted that circumstances had "prevented [Waligorski] from publishing his own much more extensive material" (Southall 1952: 4). Whoever prevented the publication and whatever the circumstances, it is unfortunate that the only results of Waligorski's extensive research seem to have been two articles published in Polish and an unpublished paper on "Soil Selection among the Luo" (n.d.).

By 1936, when the first Luo voices were heard after three decades of silence, the process of "knowing the other" in colonial Kenya had not produced European experts on the Luo. Hence, the first Luo writers (who wrote in Dholuo) did not write in response to colonial works or to correct biased versions of the past, as no serious colonial historiography had developed with regard to the Luo. This contrasts sharply with the situation in Kikuyuland at this time. By the time Jomo Kenyatta was giving the African point of view on Kikuyu customs and traditions in *Facing Mount Kenya* (1938), W. Scoresby and Katherine Routledge, who were settlers with academic training, had produced *With a Prehistoric People: The Akikuyu of British East Africa* (1910) and Father Cagnolo of the Catholic Mission of the Consolata Fathers had published *The Akikuyu: Their Customs, Traditions, and Folklore* (1933). Kenyatta himself had studied anthropology under Bronislaw Malinowski in London, where he was exposed to foreign methodologies and epistemologies. His book should therefore be placed within the colonial setting where Africans were now beginning to use the new academic sites to engage in colonial debate. In his book, the African voice is heard clearly on such important and controversial matters as land tenure, female circumcision, the Gikuyu system of education as distinguished from the European, European civilization, and Christianity.

ENCYCLOPEDIC INFORMANTS

How were historical traditions preserved and transmitted amongst the Luo? This is a question which has received inadequate attention. The Luo had no court historians, no griots or professional tellers of accounts. But they had recognized specialists who instructed the youth in chir and duol. They also had ritual experts, such as keepers of *tong liswa* (sacred spears), *jojimb koth* (rainmakers), and jobilo. Such specialists were experts in the traditions that were historically relevant to their functions and they acted as guardians of those traditions.

But, in addition to specialists, there were also a few individuals who were recognized as experts on all aspects of local history. They learned many different versions of tradition and then used these to reconstruct their own histories of communities. These are the people P. Pender-Cudlip (1973) called "encyclopedic informants." But how reliable is the testimony of such encyclopedic informants? And are they informants or historians? Whatever answer we give to these questions, one thing is clear: the practice of history consists of a discussion of the relations between the texts of historians and the real past. Do these specialists engage in such a discussion?

The first works by Luo encyclopedic informants were published before the Second World War. Their primary objective was to preserve for posterity the traditions and customs of the Luo: how the ancestors lived. They represented the first major writings by the first generation of mission-educated Luo. Written in Dholuo and intended for Luo audiences, they constituted powerful African voices on the traditions, customs, history, and identity of the Luo people. They did not merely record traditions: they carried out serious investigations from which they produced authoritative reference works. True, they did not give the names of their informants or discuss methodology; nevertheless, they represent serious attempts to construct Luo history and identity.

Weche Moko Mag Luo (Luo traditions, customs, and folklore) was written by Zablon Okola and Michael Were (1936). The former came from Gem in Siaya and was a teacher, a pastor, and later a president of the African Tribunal. In his foreword to the book, W. E. Owen recommended it on three grounds: it was the first book to be written by Luo people from Central Nyanza; the traditions and customs recorded would enable Europeans to understand the way of life of the Luo; and it might inspire other Luo people to write books. In other words, Owen, who had already lived in Nyanza for about eighteen years and who regarded himself as an expert on Luo culture, was conceding that this was an authentic African voice which deserved respect. Another missionary, A. W. Mayor, headmaster of the Maseno School, wrote the preface to the book. He stated that the book would promote development in two ways. First, it would provide new literates with serious reading material, and this was likely to encourage the culture of reading, particularly since the authors were Luo. Second, he was concerned that the children of Luo Christians were already ignorant of the customs and traditions of their people, and the book would, in his view, provide a corrective. The book covered migration and settlement, how the Luo preserved traditions and how they aided memory, war and peace, leadership, long-distance journeys, rainmaking, birth rituals, the meaning of Luo names, religion, witchcraft, taboos, "wife inheritance," proverbs, customary law, and wealth.

The second book by an encyclopedic informant was *Luo Kitgi gi Timbegi* (Luo customs and traditions). The author, Paul Mboya, who hailed from Karachuonyo in South Nyanza, was a Seventh Day Adventist pastor before he became chief of Karachuonyo and, later, secretary of the African District Council, South Nyanza. This book (1938) covered Luo leaders, the council of elders, religion, war and warriors, food and eating habits, fishing, oath taking, establishing a new home and house construction, landowners and their clients, marriage customs, mothers and children, deaths of elders, tragic deaths, animal husbandry, leisure activities and sports, farming and rainmaking, trade and cooperative work, witchcraft, hunting, boat making and boat-making ritual, going on a journey, diseases, and folktales and proverbs.

Mboya explained that he wrote this book with the intention of preserving Luo customs and traditions, for he believed that a country's development cannot be based on foreign ideas and practices. The indigenous culture must therefore provide the firm foundation on which new structures and institutions can be erected. God provided all communities with the wisdom to devise their own customs and institutions. We would be acting contrary to God's wishes if we borrowed other people's cultures and institutions wholesale. In any case, history has shown that people who live by borrowed ideas are never respected even by the people from whom they borrow. Hence the necessity to be one's self. But one cannot do this unless one knows the culture of one's people. Paul Mboya was thus preaching authenticity with a very clear and powerful voice in 1938.

Both of these works were, in effect, distillations of the corpus of knowledge that had for many years been imparted at chir and duol. They represented the first major movement from orality to literacy in the process of constructing Luo history and identity. They soon became classics, read in primary and intermediate schools. They formed part of the cultural baggage Luo carried along with them from childhood to adulthood and they provided a firm ethnic base as well as an armor against the corrosive impact of foreign cultures. Their value, in fact, increased with the passing of the years, so that, today, they have become sanctified as the final authorities on Luo culture and traditions.

But that is the problem. Once written, these traditions became codified and frozen. Today, they do not reflect the many cultural changes which have taken place since that time. They convey the impression that Luo culture has remained static despite the momentous changes which have taken place. To the youth, and even to the present generation of adults, many of these revered customs appear irrelevant and do not help them to understand their history, their identity, or the complexities of the human predicament.

CONTRIBUTIONS OF PROFESSIONAL SOCIAL ANTHROPOLOGISTS

As we have seen above, the results of the research by Waligorski, the first professional social anthropologist to work in Luoland, were never published in English. Hence the two papers published by Evans-Pritchard in 1949 and 1950, based on research carried out in Central Nyanza in 1936, marked the first significant contribution to Luo studies by a professional anthropologist. The two essays were, on the whole, excellent in their detail, given the short period he spent in Central Nyanza, and are a remembrance of one of the greatest field research anthropologists of the twentieth century.

Professor Edward Evans-Pritchard (1902–1973) took his M.A. in modern history at Oxford in 1924 and his Ph.D. in social anthropology at the London School of Economics, with C. G. Seligman and Bronislaw Malinowski as his teachers. His thesis was based on field work among the Azande of the southern Sudan, and in 1931 and 1932 he carried out field work among the Nuer (Naath) of the southern Sudan. He gave invaluable help to his teacher Seligman in his compilation of the *Pagan Tribes of the Nilotic Sudan.* Between 1932 and 1939, he worked among the Anuak (another Jii-speaking group) and the Luo of Kenya. In 1937, he published one of his most influential works, *Witchcraft, Oracles, and Magic among the Azande,* and 1940 saw the publication of *The Nuer,* the first of the Nuer trilogy which was to end with *Nuer Religion* in 1956.

During a six-week visit to Luoland in 1936, Evans-Pritchard was assisted by Archdeacon W. E. Owen, Mrs. Owen, and, especially, by a Luo pastor, Rev. Ezekial Apindi from Alego. In his introduction to his first paper on the Luo, "Luo Tribes and Clans" (1965b), he states, "This paper is sketchy and the survey on which it is based was superficial. . . . All [it] claims to do is to show that the Luo have the same type of [social] structure as the Nuer" (205).

The claim is not proved anywhere in the paper—it is simply assumed. And the concepts of tribe, subtribe, clan, and lineage are not properly defined. He identifies each Luo *oganda*, or subtribe, and gives its approximate population and density. According to him, each oganda was an autonomous unit and had a dominant clan or lineage, with maximal, minimal, and stranger lineages attached to it. He wrongly assumes that no political offices existed, just influential men. He asserts that among the Luo, political values were expressed in kinship terms and "the politico-territorial system is reflected in the lineage system" (1965b: 214).

Evans-Pritchard introduced the incorrect, but influential, theory that the "Luo tribes" (pinje), like other "tribes," are segmentary societies made up of a series of agnatic lineages, all of which trace real or mythical descent from a common ancestor, usually the eponym. He produced genealogies to show that all the twelve "tribes" of Central Nyanza—Kano, Alego, Gem, Nyakach, Kisumo, Kajulu, Seme, Asembo, Uyoma, Sakwa, Yimbo, and Ugenya—trace descent from their eponyms.

But his theoretical model did not apply to many of the pinje he studied. His concepts were derived from Western thought and were often not adequate to analyze some aspects of African life. For the most important factor in tribal identification was not kinship; ideology and leadership roles (ritual, spiritual, military, political, and economic) were important factors in the determination of collective identities in the pinje, which, incidentally, were not simply kin groups. They were territorially defined multi-ethnic polities composed of several semi-autonomous settlements and settlement clusters. And they varied greatly in both their political diversity and their degree of political centralization.

Another area in which Evans-Pritchard's article was influential, in a negative sense, was the study of Luo expansion into formerly Bantu areas. He provided a simplistic and somewhat mechanical formula, saying that "Luo expansion at the expense of the Bantu was like a line of shunting trucks, each Tribe driving out the one in front of it to seek compensation from one yet further in front, generally a Bantu Tribe" (209). What actually happened is that in most areas where Luo immigrants encountered Bantu groups, they formed multi-ethnic "plural" communities. In Bunyala, Yimbo, Rusinga Island, Mfang'ano Island, Kano, Seme, Kisumu, Gem, and Ugenya, Bantu groups considerably influenced the nature of the societies they eventually united with the Luo to form. Hence it is the histories and identities of these plural societies that we should be constructing from the fifteenth century onward. And it was these collectivities that evolved to form the Luo nation by the early 1950s.

On the other hand, it is worth noting that the detailed traditions of each piny that Evans-Pritchard collected are extremely valuable, and the collections compare favorably with those that S. Malo made in the late 1940s and early 1950s. Nevertheless, though a trained historian, Evans-Pritchard paid little attention to the historical dimensions of these traditions, even though, in the seminal articles he wrote on the Zande culture, he emphasized internal changes in an African society in an African setting (Evans-Pritchard 1960, 1963, 1965a).

Evans-Pritchard's second paper on the Luo, "Marriage Customs of the Luo of Kenya" (1950), was also based on the information provided by Ezekial Apindi. It represented an attempt to provide a parallel account, a scholarly analysis, of Luo marriage customs. However, it did not go beyond the accounts that had already been provided by the encyclopedic informants, especially as it was confined to information obtained from one piny, Alego.

Aidan Southall was the third anthropologist to work in Luoland. He paid two visits to South Nyanza in 1950, accompanied by two former Makerere students, B. F. F. Oluande from Gem and N. C. Otieno from Ugenya, as his research assistants and interpreters. Most of the information seems to have been provided by Paul Mboya. Southall was greatly influenced by Evans-Pritchard's ideas on lineage formation among the Luo. Furthermore, he based his theoretical model on the piny of Karachuonyo, which was atypical in that many of the settlements in Karachuonyo were based on kinship relations. No wonder he concluded that the Luo see segmentation and the establishment of a gweng' by the segments as a natural extension of family relationships (Southall 1952).

The works of Evans-Pritchard and Southall were to influence considerably the researches of Dr. Gordon Mc. L. Wilson, an American who was appointed to work among the Luo as a government sociologist in the 1950s. He produced two reports. The first one, on "Luo Customary Law," published in 1954, adopts the models of indigenous political structure and lineage formation prescribed by Evans-Pritchard and Southall, respectively. It is based on court records and information supplied by Central Nyanza elders and discussed with South Nyanza elders for corroboration. It restricts itself to Luo customary law pertaining to land.

His second report, on marriage laws and customs, was published in 1955. It owes much to Evans-Pritchard's paper on the same subject. His other sources were Shadrack Malo, then president of the African Appeal Court, Central Nyanza, "who wrote a paper in Dholuo which I translated and checked with groups of elders of all locations and with the three research assistants, representing three different Luo tribes, who wrote brief essays from information supplied to them by their own LIBAMBA elders on headings supplied to them by myself; from Mr. Paul Mboya's unpublished manuscript; and, finally from my own field research" (Wilson 1955). The two reports were later combined into one volume and published under the title of *Luo Customary Law and Marriage Laws and Customs* in 1961.

The thing to note about these anthropological studies is that none of them covered the entire Luo national system. The authors had done narrowly focused research, relying on one or two informants, usually the same people, through interpreters. Their training tended to foster the use of Western analytical models to interpret their findings. And, writing in English, they directed their works, *ipso facto*, largely to their foreign professional colleagues. But more importantly, their research contributed to freezing and reifying fluid African cultures into "tribes" that became the exclusive identities of the Luo. Their texts were socially constituted as authorities in competition with the encyclopedic informants. On the other hand, their works marked the beginning of a process in which social scientists tried to listen to the voices of those who had apparently been silent. But were they capable of describing "the other"? And apart from foreign methodology, were they saying anything that the encyclopedic informants, on whom they relied anyway, had not said?

FROM ANTHROPOLOGY TO HISTORY

The collection and publication of the historical traditions of Central Nyanza by Shadrack Malo (1953) inaugurated the "age of history." He collected these materials between 1948 and 1951 and published them initially as pamphlets, one for each clan, as they were collected. The texts deal mainly with the movements of the Central Nyanza clans after they arrived in Kenya.

Malo himself was not a trained historian. He was a teacher of Kiswahili at Maseno School who through personal effort gradually became one of the recognized encyclopedic informants on Luo culture and history. He belonged to one of the submerged Gusii clans—Sidho—in the piny of Kano. He wrote *Luo without Tears,* a Luo language textbook that included grammar and conversation, and *Sigend Luo ma duogo Chuny* (Luo merry stories), a collection of stories, tongue twisters, and riddles. He later became president of the African Tribunal Court, and, in that capacity, made a substantial contribution to Wilson's book on Luo customary law, as discussed above.

Informants were assembled for him at chiefs' *barazas* (assemblies), where the different versions of traditions were hammered out into authorized versions, one for each piny. These were soon accepted by the public as standard texts, representing the true stories of "what actually happened." Oral traditions were thus transformed into historical texts to which the historian was supposed to apply his tools. Malo later edited these texts, omitting some sections or versions which appeared to contradict the authorized version, and published them in a book entitled *Dhoudi Mag Central Nyanza* (Clans of Central Nyanza, 1953). The book represents an elaboration of the traditions collected by Evans-Pritchard in 1936. The only difference is that Malo's book had the stamp of authority of the Luo elders in the different Central Nyanza pinje and hence did for historical traditions what the Okola and Were and Mboya books had done for cultural traditions—froze and sancti-fied them. Malo himself does not show any awareness of the problems in-volved in collecting oral traditions and in treating them as history.

Samuel G. Ayany's book *Kar Chakruok Mar Luo* (The beginnings of the Luo, 1952) was based on material he collected in 1947. He also read the works of the Luo encyclopedic informants—Okola, Were, Mboya, and Malo. Above all, he was greatly influenced by the articles written by Father Crazzo-lara which were published in the *Uganda Journal*. These he read when he was a student at Makerere College, where he studied history. In his book, he talks vaguely about information he derived from talking to his friends among the Acholi, Lango, and Padhola, but without identifying them. He therefore emphasizes the common heritage of the Jii-speaking people as an important factor in the construction of Luo history and identity. Indeed, for Ayany, Luo history encompasses the histories of the Northern, Central, and Southern Luo, which he regards as constituting the *national* history of the Luo. At the same time he is acutely aware of the extensive interactions and intermarriage that have occurred between the Luo and their neighbors. He therefore stresses the physical, cultural, and economic impact of these non-Luo peoples on Luo history and identity.

Unlike the earlier works, *Kar Chakruok Mar Luo* was written as a work of history in Dholuo and therefore addressed to a Luo audience, to whom he passionately stressed the importance of knowing their history and of working diligently and honestly to develop their nation in close collaboration with their neighbors.

Though a trained historian, Ayany provided no theoretical framework within which his reconstruction of the past could be examined. Nor did he discuss his methodology or how a tradition becomes a text and how a text is transformed into history. Furthermore, he did not critically analyze Luo traditions or Crazzolara's evidence, but merely reproduced them to support his populist history of the Luo nation. His book should, therefore, be re-garded as a continuation of the popular processing of the Luo past outside the work of the academic guild.

THE MAKERERE ARTS RESEARCH PRIZE AND ALL THAT

The Makerere Arts Research Prize was founded by the Makerere College Council in 1946 and was awarded for research in an approved subject in the faculty of arts. The first recipient of this prize was Simeon H. Ominde, a Luo from Kisumu, Nyahera, for his essay "The Luo Girl from Infancy to Mar-riage." His fieldwork was done during successive vacations under the supervision of Aidan Southall. The essay discusses in great detail the education of a Luo girl and can be taken to document the kind of education that took place in siwidhe under the supervision and guidance of pim. It was first published in 1952 and has been reprinted several times. Its impact on the definition of the place and role of a Luo woman in society and history has been enormous.

In presenting an analytical interpretation of *The Luo Girl from Infancy to Marriage,* Atieno Odhiambo (1992) has written,

> The text was a witness to a process of recovery: the recovery of what was embedded in Luo tradition. In this process Ominde acts as a communicator for his oral informants. The print culture through which the author ushered the Luo Girl had its own hallowed history: it empowered them through content: they knew the bible and the prescribed syllabi. The Luo girl empowered Luo tradition. It was a message, but at the same time it was a new message . . . that amplified and reinforced ideological statement about continuity between the past and the present. (10)

The book appeared at the time of what Odhiambo termed "the Luo Renaissance." The Luo "articulate citizens" were engaged in constructing the Luo nation and forging the Luo identity, and Ominde's *Luo girl* made a contribution to this process.

For the next two years no prize was awarded. But in 1950, I won the prize for my essay "Social and Economic History of the Luo of Kenya, 1870–1910" (1950). My chief informant was Michael Were. Although he had coauthored a book with Okola on Luo customs and traditions, I discovered that his knowledge of Luo national history, which included the histories of the Jii-speaking peoples, was wide and deep. He was particularly knowledgeable about the Luo religion and system of education, and how these had changed during the period under discussion. The information he gave me on these two topics was new, original, and detailed, but up to now I have seen no reference to it in any other publication. When I embarked on my professional research on Luo history in 1959, Were again played a major role in assisting me to construct Luo history and identity.

In the following year, 1951, another Arts Research Prize was awarded to Henry Owuor Anyumba for his essay "The Place of Folk Tales in the Education of Luo Children." For Anyumba, this was the beginning of a distinguished career during which he made enormous contributions to the study of Luo oral literature. He published papers on *ogio* (love) songs, *nyatiti* (harp) music, spirit possession among the Luo, and Luo folk tales. Later, at the University of Nairobi, Anyumba together with Taban lo Liyong and Okot p'Bitek provided a major center for the study of Luo oral literature. Okot p'Bitek wrote his *Song of Lawino* and *Song of Ocol* and Taban lo Liyong wrote his *Eating Chiefs.* The spirit of the time is reflected in Liyong's introduction to his book. He explains that from Malakal in the north, on the banks of the greatest African river, which the Luo call Kir (the White Nile), to the bottom of Lolwe (Lake Victoria) live a people who call themselves Luo. He asserts that he was not interested in collecting traditions, mythologies, folktales; anthropologists had done that. His job was to create literary works from what anthropologists only collect and record, and he proceeded to create forty-three literary pieces. He is, of course, aware that among the Luo each subgroup has its own slant to each story. He is also aware that the retelling of these stories is likely to touch on some nationalistic feelings. This, he says, is as it should be. He concludes, "To live, our traditions have to be topical; to be topical they must be used as part and parcel of our contemporary contentions and controversies" (Liyong 1970: ix–x).

Okot p'Bitek's *The Religion of the Central Luo,* Anyumba's work on spirit possession among the Luo, Maura Gary's on Jok Lagoro of Pajule, Aidan Southall's on the concept of *jok* in Aluruland: all these raised a host of fascinating questions about the relationship between religion and politics among the Jii-speakers.

When oral literature was introduced in the Department of Literature at the University of Nairobi, Anyumba became its head, and until his death he carried out major researches on Luo oral literature, defined to include music and dance. The Luo now felt they were a people with a rich culture, including literature, music, and dance. In short, they were a people with a distinct identity and a rich heritage.

Traditions, History, Identity, and Pragmatism

From the 1950s on, the Luo increasingly used history and traditions in a pragmatic manner in order to create identity. For example, in an attempt to provide a solution to African (especially Luo) social and economic disabilities, Oginga Odinga founded the Luo Thrift and Trading Corporation (LUTATCO). The founding of this corporation also represented a determination to get rid of the colonial notion of the "lazy Luo" who could be only a clerk and not a businessman. LUTATCO built Ramogi House, established Ramogi Press, and bought Ramogi Farm. Odinga baptized himself "Jaramogi," and Richard Achieng' Oneko became Ramogi Achieng' Oneko. Business had to be organized on ethnic lines to create a new image of the Luo as entrepreneurs. It was also at this time that the Luo Union, whose first branch had been founded in Nairobi in 1922, developed into a major political and social organization in both urban and rural areas. Wherever two or three Luo were gathered together in East Africa, the occasion called for the formation of a Luo Union branch. Soon branches were formed in all the major towns of East Africa and in all the Luo pinje in Nyanza. In 1953, the branches came together to form Luo Union (East Africa), with Odinga as the first elected *Ker,* or president.

The choice of the title was significant. "Ker" is the term for political power in Alur, Acholi, Padhola, Joluo, Luo, and Shilluk. Whoever possesses ker is the ruler. These peoples had similar royal regalia (*jamiker* or *masana miker*), such as *kom ker* (a royal stool), *bul ker* (a royal sacred drum), *tong ker* (a royal spear), and *la ker* (a royal garment). Thus the Luo deliberately chose an ancient title of great symbolic significance for the leader of their Union.

The merger of the two movements, economic and cultural, in Odinga led to the emergence of a strong cultural identity, and history was invoked to sustain it. At all public rallies and meetings, the Luo now referred to themselves as *Joka-Nyanam* (the river-lake people) or *Nyikwa Ramogi* (the descendants of Ramogi), thereby implying or asserting that all Luo groups descended from one person—Ramogi. The works of Paul Mboya, Zablon Okola, and Michael Were became their cultural bibles.

As part of decolonization, more and more Western-educated elite began to develop an interest in their cultural and historical background, especially in the late 1950s and early 1960s. This cultural nationalism eventually resulted in the formation of a nationalist movement. It sustained Oginga Odinga between 1966 and 1969, when he formed an opposition political party, the Kenya People's Union, and it enabled him to form another opposition political party in 1991, Ford-Kenya. In short, this cultural nationalism, responding to various political and economic challenges of modern Kenya, has produced a powerful Luo subnationalism.

PROFESSIONAL HISTORIANS TAKE OVER

In the late 1950s and early 1960s, academic historians were beginning to hear the voices of those who had been voiceless. At the same time, doubt was mounting that historians and other social scientists were at all capable of describing the Other. How do you accommodate the new voices and at the same time understand "otherness"? Ultimately the crucial question being raised in the 1950s was, were non-Western histories legitimate subjects of historical research? As Steven Feierman has written,

> The specialist work of historical reconstruction served to take the people about whom anthropologists had always written and to insist that they be placed within the larger historical narrative. The change in context required a change in how historians understood agency. Previously mute people had now to be seen as authors and actors. Exotic cultures were not new to the academic imagination, but the style of description was new. The new knowledge broke with a long intellectual tradition that treated exotic cultures as though they existed at a different time from the rest of humanity, stone age, or bronze age, or iron age peoples, remnants of the past, not living in the

same world where historians live, not subject to the same political and economic forces. (1995: 52)

In the 1960s and 1970s, African academic historians began to play an active part in the description and analysis of African history. From being mere observers, African historians became both observers and actors. But the problem was how to translate oral traditions, the vehicles of historical information, into a form of history that befitted modern times.

There was also the epistemological problem. An African past, with its own social forms, mythologies, and values, was not to be fitted into an alien Western model. Finding a more appropriate model was the task some of us had to undertake. This meant going beyond Malo, Ayany, and Crazzolara, who did not have to bother with theoretical reflections on the nature of oral traditions and their significance as a historical source. In their production of popular texts they followed their sources closely without too much comment on their historicity, thereby reifying oral tradition.

But I was working toward a Ph.D. at the University of London, and my work did have conform to certain Western historical canons. The methodological problems were enormous, and, like my fellow students, I was aware of the difficulties.

In my research, I collected traditions from as many informants and across as wide a geographical spread as possible. In this task, I had to confront the problem of feedback. Most of my informants had participated in the Malo meetings where standard versions were worked out. The question I had to ask myself, therefore, was, are these new oral traditions or the regurgitations of formalized texts? The contents and also the textures of oral and written sources had been interacting since 1936. I was therefore confronted in the 1960s with a mixture of oral and written discourses.

I was also convinced that oral sources were primary sources analogous to written documents. I therefore tried to put forward a convincing case that a verifiable past could be reconstructed from these primary sources. That argument ignored what this paper has already demonstrated, that oral traditions are synthetic products of communal and individual historical composition which change constantly over time. They could not therefore be compared to documentary evidence.

The work of constructing Luo history and identity was to be greatly extended in two directions. First, David William Cohen in Busoga and J. B. Webster and his team at Makerere University showed that the assumption that the early Southern Luo migrants shared a common culture ignored their contacts with various non-Luo groups, such as Madi, Bantu, and Ateker-speakers, and their experiences in diverse environmental zones (Cohen 1983 [much of which had appeared in the 1970s]; Webster and Odongo 1976; Webster and Denoon n.d.) These diverse influences led to the development of many differences, not only between the Southern Luo and their Sudanese

and northern Ugandan relatives, but also among the Southern Luo communities themselves (Ogot 1996). These differences and mergers had to be ac-
commodated in any construction of Luo history and identity. Luo attempts to
frame a collective identity by distinguishing themselves from their neighbors
were critiqued and rejected.

Second, within Nyanza itself, the complexity of Luo history and identity
was confirmed through the painstaking researches of many scholars: P. A.
Abuso, H. O. Ayot, J. Butterman, M. J. Hay, W. R. Ochieng, A. Odira, P. C.
Oloo, L. D. Schiller, O. J. Opinya, and E. Onyango Odiyo. But the main objective of these works was still to demonstrate that a verifiable past for Africa
could be reconstructed by using oral traditions as primary sources.

From the 1970s, however, oral traditions increasingly came under heavy
criticism as sources for African history. It was argued that reliable chronicles
would never emerge from these sources, which, in my case, were constantly
changing through time. Such critiques were summarized in David Henige's
Oral Historiography (1982). Heated debates continued to be conducted in
an annual journal of historical methods, *History in Africa*, edited by Henige
since 1974. Basically, oral traditions were being rejected as "objective sources"
for the reconstruction of the African past.

As African historians, we failed to articulate any new definition of autonomy. In fact, we felt helpless as we realized that African historical scholarship, which in many regions had existed for over four hundred years,
was being assimilated into Western epistemology. Indeed, the "idea of Africa"
was being reinvented by Western scholarship, and, consequently, African historiography was being westernized and hence alienated. We abandoned researches on, and studies of, the precolonial history of Africa.

But for how long can we continue to isolate Africa from the rest of the
world? Is it enough to continue to affirm differences? I think the time has
come when we should reintegrate and reintroduce Africa into world history by adding African experience to global historical patterns. This implies
understanding Africans on their own terms, using their perspective. It also
means recognizing oral traditions as key sources for the writing of intellectual and cultural histories of Africa.

In recent works in the various disciplines, such as anthropology, linguistics, and archaeology, this point is being appreciated. For a long time, this
"idea of Africa" for many outsiders was anthropological; it helped to define
the Other in Africa: barbarian, uncivilized, pagan, animist, primitive, colonized. Currently, great efforts are being made to reintegrate anthropology
with African history, and hence to assimilate the Other in Africa into world
history. In the case of the Luo, David William Cohen and E. S. Atieno Odhiambo's book *Siaya: The Historical Anthropology of an African Landscape*
(1989) is a gallant move in this direction.

But for the other outsiders, the "idea of Africa" was archaeological. An
evolutionary model that introduced significant distortions into African his-

tory was adopted by archaeologists in the nineteenth century. It demonstrated the progressive course of human society from a primitive stage of savagery to an advanced stage of civilization. By the mid–twentieth century, the typological stages of savagery, barbarism, and civilization were replaced by hunter-gatherer bands, tribal chiefdoms, and states. But recent research in archaeology has increasingly questioned the suitability of applying to Africa evolutionist models that produced universal histories tying together the world's parts in a coherent narrative of a rise to civilization from savagery and barbarism. Similarly, historical linguists are replacing linguistic classifications based on dubious racial theories and, like archaeologists, are adding a major chronological depth to African history.

We learn from the Jewish tradition that in the beginning was the word. In other words, language is regarded as the origin of formed reality. If this is the case, then it is imperative that we understand the origin of formed reality. What is the character of this reality? What are the fundamental words and how does truth arise in sound? What is the language of revelation in Africa? Is there any special language of mystical experience? We need to know how language in Africa has been used to symbolize things, the worldview, essential beings, ideals, and reality as a whole. A bold attempt toward this goal has been made by Jan Vansina in another pioneering book, *Paths in the Rainforests* (1990), in which he has applied the "words and things" approach to produce a brilliant synthesis of three thousand years of equatorial African history. He defines traditions as "self-regulating processes" which "consist of a changing, inherited, collective body of cognitive and physical representations shared by their members. They inform the understanding of the physical realm, and do so in terms of the guiding principles of the tradition. Such innovations in turn offer the substance of the cognitive world itself" (Vansina 1990: 259–60).

We thus see that in the search for the universality of human experience in Africa, emphasis has shifted from the institutional to the social, from facts to processes. Anthropologists have turned to history; archaeologists are increasingly emphasizing process. Cultural sociologists, in their recent studies, and linguists are closely collaborating with historians. The interdisciplinary character of African history has been revived and it has become possible to synthesize a coherent, continuous, convincing, and reasonably comprehensive narrative of Africa's pasts, stretching back several millennia. In this endeavor, oral traditions are again being accepted as valuable expressions of African perspectives. They have to be interrogated afresh and new questions raised. And the current broad intellectual concerns with memory, history, meaning, and experience are already yielding insights into the historical consciousness of those whose experiences have rested mostly in the hands of others.

Several problems, however, remain to be tackled. First, there is the urgent need to define the relationship between popular productions of knowledge, which are going on all the time, and those of the academic guild. What status do we give to historical knowledge produced outside the work of the guild? Vansina, for example, has recently designated 1948 as the birth date, not of African history, but of African history in academia. But he is aware that African history existed before 1948, complete with its historians, both official and communal. Vansina noted that this trend never died. As they became literate, local historians all over tropical Africa began to write histories in vernacular languages for the benefit of their communities (Vansina 1994: 42). But is this part of African historiography? Vansina does not think so, because much of it is written by nonacademic historians. But why should the historiographical field be restricted to the academic guild alone? He gives no answer to this question.

Second, there is the fundamental problem of the relationship between the scholar and his or her audience. Historians do not reconstruct the past *in vacuo,* but with particular audiences in mind. Despite Vansina's attempt to assimilate African historiography into universal categories, he realizes the dilemma into which such an assimilation would lead us. He is concerned by the fact that Africa is the only continent whose history is dominated on a large scale by outsiders even today. He writes,

> This is a continuing anomaly. In all other major parts of the world, and that includes the major so-called Third World areas, the writing of history, academic history included, has primarily been conducted in the area itself, by authors of the area, in the languages of the area, and for audiences in the area. But in tropical Africa the writing of academic history was organized by 'outsiders,' and ever since, the epicenters of this activity have remained outside Africa, despite all effort to alter the situation. It is a crucial anomaly. . . . Outsiders initiated academic history here. They created the university departments, and they wrote the first substantive histories. They set up the framework within which African historians later worked, and they 'trained' them how to write academic history. The pioneers wrote for an outside audience which shared their world views and social practice, not for an audience in Africa itself, except for African historians of Africa and a few others who had absorbed Euro-American academic culture. When African scholars began to take their destinies into their own hands they unwittingly continued to write their major works to a large extent for the same academic audience rather then for their own natural populations. . . . While these authors attacked imperial history and promoted national history, they continued to write in English or in French, thus limiting access of their local audiences. (Vansina 1994: 239–40)

Vansina strongly believes that this anomaly goes to the heart of historiography because it affects the fundamental relationship between author and audience. He would like us to address two questions: Whose history are we writing? And is it for ourselves or for the African audience? He then concludes that, "[h]owever difficult to achieve, authors, insiders and outsiders alike, must strive to reach 'natural' audiences and thus end this anomaly of African historiography" (Vansina 1994: 242). I agree.

Africa needs to reclaim its history. We have done it in the past, we can do it in the future. And the future began a long time ago.

BIBLIOGRAPHY

Adefuye, A. T. 1973. "Political History of the Paluo, 1840–1911." Ph.D. dissertation, University of Ibadan.

Atkinson, Ronald R. 1978. "A History of the Western Acholi of Uganda, c. 1695–1900." Ph.D. dissertation, Northwestern University.

Ayany, S. G. 1952. *Kar Chakruok Mar Luo* (The beginnings of the Luo). Kisumu: Equatorial Publishers.

Ayot, Henry O. 1979. *A History of the Luo-Abasuba of Western Kenya from A.D. 1760–1940.* Nairobi: Kenya Literature Bureau.

Butterman, Judith M. 1979. "Luo Social Formations in Change: Karachuonyo and Kanyamkago, c. 1800–1945." Ph.D. dissertation, Syracuse University.

Cagnolo, Father. 1933. *The Akikuyu: Their Customs, Traditions, and Folklore.* Nyeri, Kenya.

Cohen, David William. 1983. "Luo Camps in Seventeenth-Century Eastern Uganda: The Use of Migration Tradition in the Reconstruction of Culture." *Sprache und Geschichte in Africa (SUGIA)* 5: 145–75.

———. 1985. "Doing Social History from Pim's Doorway." In *Reliving the Past: The Worlds of Social History,* ed. Oliver Zunz, 191–235. Chapel Hill: University of North Carolina Press.

———. 1994. *The Combing of History.* Chicago: University of Chicago Press.

Cohen, David William, and E. S. Atieno Odhiambo. 1989. *Siaya: The Historical Anthropology of an African Landscape.* Nairobi: Heinemann.

Evans-Pritchard, E. E. 1950. "Marriage Customs of the Luo of Kenya." *Africa* 20, no. 2: 132–42.

———. 1960. "A Contribution to the Study of Zande Culture." *Africa* 30, no. 4: 309–23.

———. 1962. *Social Anthropology and Other Essays.* New York: Macmillan.

———. 1963. "A Further Contribution to the Study of Zande Culture." *Africa* 33, no. 3: 183–97.

———. 1965a. "A Final Contribution to the Study of Zande Culture." *Africa* 35, no. 1: 1–7.

———. 1965b. "Luo Tribes and Clans." In *The Position of Women in Primitive Societies and Other Essays in Social Anthropology,* 205–27. London: Farber and Farber. First published in *Rhodes-Livingstone Journal* 7 (1949): 24–40.

Feierman, S. 1995. "Africa in History: The End of Universal Narratives." In *After Colonialism: Imperial Histories and Postcolonial Placements,* ed. Gyan Prakash, 40–65. Princeton: Princeton University Press.

Hartman, Rev. H. 1928. "Some Customs of the Luo (or Nilotic Kavirondo) Living in South Kavirondo." *Anthropos* 23, nos. 1–2: 263–75.

Hay, Margaret. J. 1972. "Economic Change in Luoland: Kowe, 1890–1945." Ph.D. dissertation, University of Wisconsin.

Henige, David P. 1974. *The Chronology of Oral Tradition: Quest for a Chimera.* Oxford: Clarendon.

———, 1982. *Oral Historiography.* New York: Longman.

Herring, Ralph S. 1974. "A History of the Labwor Hills." Ph.D. dissertation, University of California, Santa Barbara.

Hobley, C. W. 1896. "Kavirondo." *The Geographical Journal* 12: 361–72.

———. 1902. "Nilotic Tribes of Kavirondo." In *Eastern Uganda: An Ethnological Survey,* 26–35. Occasional Papers, No. 1. London: Royal Anthropological Institute of Great Britain and Ireland.

———. 1903. "Anthropological Studies in Kavirondo and Nandi." *Journal of the Royal Anthropological Institute of Great Britain and Ireland* 33 (July–December): 325–59.

Johnston, Sir Harry H. 1902. *The Uganda Protectorate.* Volume 2. London: Hutchinson.

Kenny, Michael. 1977. "The Relation of Oral History to Social Structure in South Nyanza, Kenya." *Africa* 47, no. 3: 276–88.

Kenyatta, Jomo. 1938. *Facing Mount Kenya: The Tribal Life of the Gikuyu.* London: Secker and Warburg.

Lamphear, John E. 1976. *The Traditional History of the Jie of Uganda.* Oxford: Clarendon.

Liyong, Taban lo. 1970. *Eating Chiefs: Lwo culture from Lolwe to Malkal.* London: Heinemann.

Malo, Shadrack. 1953. *Dhoudi Mag Central Nyaza* (Clans of Central Nyanza). Nairobi: Eagle.

Mboya, Paul. 1938. *Luo Kitgi gi Timbegi* (Luo customs and traditions). Nairobi: East African Standard.

Northcote, G. A. S. 1907. "The Nilotic Kavirondo." *Journal of the Royal Anthropological Institute of Great Britain and Ireland* 36: 58–66.

Ochieng, William R. 1974. *An Outline History of Nyanza up to 1914.* Nairobi: East African Literature Bureau.

———. 1975. *A History of the Kadimo Chiefdom of Yimbo in Western Kenya.* Nairobi: East African Literature Bureau.

Odhiambo, E. S. Atieno. 1992. "The Worlds of Ojiji: Luo Women, 1900–1990." In *Issues in Resource Management and Development in Kenya: Essays in Memory of Professor Simeon H. Ominde,* ed. R. A. Obudho and J. B. Ojwang. Nairobi: East African Educational Publishers.

Odira, A. n.d. *A History of Kanyada People up to 1914.* Nairobi: Kenyatta University.

Odiyo, E. Onyango. 1991. *State Formation among the Luo: The Case of Alego, 1500–1920.* M. Phil. thesis, Moi University.

Ogot, Bethwell A. 1950. "Social and Economic History of the Luo of Kenya, 1870–1910." Arts Research Prize essay. Kampala: Makerere University Library.

———. n.d. "Spirit Possession among the Luo of Central Nyanza." Typescript. Kampala: East African Institute of Social Research.

———. 1967. "Luo Songs." In *Introduction to African Literature: An Anthology of Critical Writing from* Black Orpheus, ed. Ulli Beier, 50–56. London: Longmans, Green.

————. 1996. *The Jii-Speaking Peoples of Eastern Africa*. Kisumu: Ayange.

Okola, Z., and M. Were. 1936. *Weche Moko Mag Luo* (Luo traditions, customs, and folklore). Nairobi: Church Missionary Society Bookshop.

Olang', D. A. D. 1972. "A History of the Karachuonyo, c. 1500–1900." B. A. graduating essay, University of Nairobi.

Oloo, P. C. 1969. "History of Settlement: An Example of Luo Clans in Alego (1500–1918)." B.A. graduating essay, University of Nairobi.

Ominde, S. H. 1952. *The Luo Girl from Infancy to Marriage*. London: Macmillan.

Onyango-Ogutu, B., and A. A. Roscoe. 1974. *Keep My Words: Luo Oral Literature*. Nairobi: East African Publishing House.

Opinya, Ondere J. 1969. "History of Kano: A Study of the Stranger Elements of Wang'aya, Sidho, and Kasagam." B. A. graduating essay, University of Nairobi.

Owen, W. E. 1932. "Food Production and Kindred Matters, Amongst the Luo." *The Journal of East Africa and Uganda Natural History* 11: 45–46.

Owuor, Henry A. 1951. *The Place of Folk Tales in the Education of Luo Children*. Arts Research Prize essay. Kampala: Makerere College.

Pender-Cudlip, P. 1973. "Encyclopedic Informants and Early Interlacustrine History." *International Journal of African Historical Studies* 6: 198–210.

Routledge, W. Scoresby, and Katherine Routledge. 1910. *With a Prehistoric People: The Akikuyu of British East Africa*. London: Arnold.

Schapera, I. 1947. Letter to the Chief Native Commissioner, Nairobi, on social anthropologists posted to Kenya. Personal archives of Bethwell Ogot.

Schiller, Lawrence D. 1977. "Gem and Kano: A Comparative Study of Stress in Two Traditional African Political Systems in Nyanza Province, Western Kenya, c. 1850–1914." Seminar paper, Department of History, University of Nairobi.

Southall, Aidan. 1952. *Lineage Formation among the Luo*. Memorandum 26. London: International African Institute.

Stam, Rev. N. 1910. "The Religious Conception of the Kavirondo." *Anthropos* 5, nos. 2–3: 359–62.

Tosh, John. 1978. *Clan Leaders and Colonial Chiefs in Lango: The Political History of an East African Stateless Society, c. 1800–1939*. Oxford: Clarendon.

Vansina, Jan. 1990. *Paths in the Rainforests: Toward a History of Political Tradition in Equatorial Africa*. Madison: University of Wisconsin Press.

————. 1994. *Living with Africa*. Madison: University of Wisconsin Press.

Wagner, Gunter. 1949. *The Bantu of North Kavirondo*. 2 vols. London, New York, and Toronto: Oxford University Press for the International African Institute.

Waligorski, A. n.d. "Soil Selection among the Luo." Unpublished paper. Kisumu: District Archives.

Webster, J. B., and D. Denoon. n.d. "A History of Uganda." 2 vols. Unpublished.

Webster, J. B., and Onyango Ku Odongo, eds. 1976. *The Central Lwo during the Aconya*. Nairobi: East African Literature Bureau.

White, Luise, Stephan F. Miescher, and David William Cohen. 1996. "Words and Voices." Position paper for the Bellagio conference. Unpublished.

Wilson, G. M. 1955. *Marriage Laws and Customs*. Report to the Kenya Government, Nairobi.

————. 1961. *Luo Customary Law and Marriage Laws and Customs*. Nairobi: Government Printer.

2

Reported Speech and Other Kinds of Testimony

Megan Vaughan

I begin my story of reported speech with a testimony. In 1794 a criminal court in Isle de France (now Mauritius) heard the case of Jupiter, a slave accused of *marronage* and of theft.[1] This "hearing," like all others, begins with a series of questions to the accused: "What is your name? what is your age? who is your master? which 'caste' do you belong to?" Jupiter is being asked to testify as to who, exactly, he is. He is being asked to name his ancestry. Perhaps never an innocent question, in the context of a slave society it may also have been a hard one to answer. Indeed, sometimes slave suspects and witnesses hinted at their difficulties by adding detail and uncertainty—"In my own country," they might say, "I was known as Marambe, but now I am known as Vincent." Or—"I belong to the succession of the Widow Verger, but I am rented out to the citizen Roblet." On the question of "caste" or ethnic origin, there were only a small number of allowable answers. "I am a Mozambique," said Jupiter. Other slaves appearing in the Isle de France courts answered that they were "Malgache," "Bengali," "Wolof" (this more likely earlier in the century), or, indicating that they had been born on the island, that they were "Creole." These were, of course, generic terms, covering a multitude of traumas and transitions already experienced. When Jupiter replied that he was a "Mozambique," this did not mean that he had necessarily forgotten who else he was or had been, but that in the here and now of Isle de France society, and most particularly in this courtroom, a "Mozambique" was what he was.

A witness to Jupiter's alleged misdemeanors was "called." He was called Mercure. It was Mercure who led to my almost falling off my chair in the National Archives of Mauritius. Mercure, though labeled a "Mozambique," like Jupiter, was found to speak little French and therefore required, as the law demanded, an interpreter. Mercure was, it transpired, of the "Maravi" caste, and so was Thomas his interpreter. Through Thomas, Mercure spoke. He did not, in fact, say a great deal—only that he had seen Jupiter with another slave, Azor, and that Jupiter carried his stolen goods in a great white sheet, whilst Azor had his in a sack. But this was certainly the first time I had ever heard a Maravi speak, albeit indirectly. If the pursuit of "History" is both rationalist and romanticist, romance was certainly in the ascendant at that moment. The history which this moment testified to was less that of the African experience of slavery than a history which linked me to those nineteenth-century audiences of abolitionists who had "itching ears to hear a colored man speak, and particularly a slave" (Radano 1996: 513). For though I had heard many a slave speak through similar documents, I had never before heard a Maravi—an eighteenth-century subject of a Central African polity—speak. It seemed that, though I had not known it before, my ears had long been "itching" for this bit of reported speech.

THE MARAVI IN MALAWI: ORAL TRADITION AND THE HISTORIANS

"It is commonly accepted," writes Matthew Schoffeleers, "that the name Maravi (or its modern equivalent, Malawi), denotes 'fire flames'" (Schoffeleers 1992: 41). Sometime in the fifteenth century, Schoffeleers and others argue, an emergent Maravi political culture began to make itself felt in present-day Malawi and in eastern Zambia. In oral traditions, the Maravi polity was associated with immigrants from the north, the Phiri clan. From their origins (as some traditions have it) in the Shaba Province of what is today the Democratic Republic of Congo, the Phiri brought not only fire but "a new order, which was both politically and culturally superior to the old order" (Schoffeleers 1992: 42). The Phiri, according to the traditions, some written documents, and the historians who interpret them, ushered in a new kind of "law and order"—Maravi chiefs had no standing armies, but they were judges and arbiters, whose deaths were followed by periods of ritualistic disorderliness. Maravi religious organization reflected the new political order, or at least its aspirations. Existing territorial shrines, with their spirit wives, pythons, and sacred pools, were opposed by new hierarchies of spirits of dead chiefs from ruling lineages. With the memorialization of a line of dead men, History in a Hegelian sense had begun—the succession disputes, the pushes and pulls of centralization and fission, the machinations of matrilineal relatives and, as Schoffeleers demonstrates in his remarkable account of the Mbona cult, the repression of pre-Maravi institutions and the resistance that this generated. Certain practices, here as elsewhere, showed an extraordinary persistence.

In the eighteenth century, the Maravi Empire, as it is sometimes called, was in decline. When the last great Maravi chief, Undi, died, things, it seems, fell apart, though what exactly was falling apart has always been something of a mystery to me. The evidence for the Maravi "system" seemed, in some ways, to have been deduced from tales of its decline. Mary Tew (later Douglas) suggested this in her (1950) ethnographic study of the peoples of the Lake Nyasa region, when she wrote that "[t]he degree of political unity achieved over this wide area is also uncertain, but it is probable that early accounts which hinted at a Maravi empire exaggerated the real degree of internal cohesion. Most probably the term Maravi was the generic title of a number of petty chiefs, sharing a common language and culture" (Tew 1950: 34). By the mid–nineteenth century a kind of nostalgia had set in. When Livingstone passed through in 1856 he was told that formerly "all the Mang'anja were united under the government of their great chief, Undi, whose Empire extended from Lake Shirwa to the River Loangwa; but after Undi's death it fell to pieces" (Livingstone and Livingstone 1865: 198). "Maravi" was unlikely to have been the primary identity of either Mercure or Thomas—perhaps they were Mang'anja or Nyanja, who became "Maravi" in the course of their transition into slavery, only to become "Mozambique" when they landed on Isle de France. Until I encountered Mercure in the Mauritian archives, I had never imagined the Maravi Empire to have speaking subjects. Nevertheless, when Nyasaland at independence took the name of Malawi (or Maravi), this marked the beginnings of a new imagining of the history of this region.

Under the rule of Hastings Banda the Malawian past and Malawian identity were constructed around a central core of Chewa ethnicity, all in the name of "nontribalism." Though Banda occasionally referred explicitly to the glorious past of the Maravi Empire (not least to make territorial claims to parts of eastern Zambia and northern Mozambique), it was around a version of Chewa culture and language that Banda pursued his project of nation building.[2] The notion of "Chewa" came to mean "Maravi," and hence "Malawi": a fragment of the Maravi Empire had, in fact, taken over the nation discursively. Some elements of this process mirrored what the historical accounts told us about the political struggles and machinations of the earlier version of the Maravi nation. It seemed, in an odd way, that the Maravi Empire had to be not only put back in its rightful place, but also recolonized internally, and this time around by the Chewa. For, like its predecessor, the new Malawian nation was in fact the product of a long history of movement and migration, sedimentation, give and take between many ethnic and cultural groups—a process which had become yet more complex through the eighteenth, nineteenth, and twentieth centuries with the impact of long-distance trade, of slavery, of both peaceful and violent invasion, and of colonialism.

One of the tasks of the academic historian in this context was to get things straight. There was, in fact, quite a bit of confusion around as to who was or was not "Chewa" in the modern state of Malawi, just as there may have been confusion earlier as to who was a "Maravi." A Chewa Language Board was set up to impose order on the linguistic front, and in the University of Malawi an oral history project was inaugurated. This latter project, in which I was involved, has been described by Leroy Vail and Landeg White as one contribution to the making of a "usable past" for the Banda regime. The message of the history we "found" in oral tradition and then reproduced was, wrote Vail and White, clear: "the Chewa people and Chewa culture was the core of modern Malawi by right of being the most ancient and least compromised by colonialism, and Malawi culture would be considered synonymous with Chewa culture" (Vail and White 1989: 182).[3] Though, in general terms, I agree with Vail and White's conclusion, my interest here is in exploring the particular route by which we arrived at this end, and whether the oral traditions we collected could have been used to tell a different set of stories.[4]

The Zomba History Project was set up in the University of Malawi in 1977, at the height of one of the Banda regime's fits of ethnic paranoia, during which "Northerners" in particular were targeted for arrest and detention, and when the president addressed the nation on the question of the "confusionists" who were infiltrating the country and creating, well, confusion. I was in the country teaching and attempting to begin my research on late precolonial and early colonial economic and social history (Vaughan 1981). My problem was that obtaining research permission was extremely difficult in a political climate in which expatriate historians and social scientists were frequently accused of being "confusionists" themselves, and in which the president himself took a very personal interest in all things historical.[5] My repeated applications for research permission and for permission to consult the National Archives (up to 1920) were repeatedly turned down. On the very first application, as I later saw for myself, the president had written in his large emphatic italic hand *NO,* and signed himself, equally emphatically, *HKB.* With this historic document in my file, it was more than anyone's life was worth to put the case to him again.

I was therefore more than happy to participate in the new oral history initiative at the University's Department of History, headed, nominally, by Dr. Zimani Kadzamira, a historian who was also a member of the ruling elite. Whilst he obtained the research permission, the real intellectual drive behind the project came from a newly arrived expatriate, Professor Bertin Webster, with a wealth of experience in the collection of oral traditions in different parts of Africa, and a strong personal commitment to the retrieval of the African precolonial past.[6] A powerful romantic attachment to the "real" Africa was allied to an equally powerful commitment to the science of historical research—every tool in the book (which was Jan Vansina's *Oral Tradition*) would have to be carefully studied and applied. Excitement at the possibilities of retrieval was mixed in equal quantity with anxiety, for it was clear to anyone who had studied the problems of the collection and analysis of oral traditions in Africa that truth was an elusive thing, that distortion was rife (as was forgetfulness), and that getting things straight, even at the level of the simplest chronology, was not going to be easy. Armed with the right tools, however, and with an appropriate degree of skepticism, we and our students headed off into "the field."

The implications of this kind of approach to the collection of oral traditions in Africa for the kind of history produced have been well rehearsed and I shall not repeat them all here, except to say that, indispensable and valuable as it is, in less able hands than those of Vansina it could have a deadening effect on the whole making of histories.[7] When, not so very long ago, I realized that the distortions were the body of the history whose skeleton we had been so painstakingly unearthing, I felt that a veil had been lifted from before my eyes. Only a historian would have had this problem in the first place. There were, however, some specific features of the methodology we followed in the Zomba History Project which, perhaps, compounded the more general problems with oral historical research at the time.

Professor Webster was passionately committed to the truth of the precolonial past—to the recovery of the time before the colonial intrusion and everything which went with it. Extraordinary as it now seems, our students were, therefore, instructed to turn off their tape recorders the moment the first white man entered the oral testimony. I had read my Vansina and knew this injunction to be a serious distortion of the biblical truth, and so I ignored it, as in fact did most participants in the project, but the exclusive interest in all things purely precolonial inevitably had its consequences. One was that the project as a whole was unable to address the question of how colonial and postcolonial political struggles were integral to the telling of the precolonial past—in spite (or perhaps because) of the fact that we were *living* this fact daily in Banda's Malawi. Second, and related to this, was an implied if not explicit association between chronological depth, spatial location, and authenticity—the longer a group of people had been in the area, the more genuinely representative of the old Africa they were held to be; the longer the genealogy, the more valuable it was. It was this association between geographical space, chronological depth, and authenticity (rather than any deliberate political manipulation) which led us to the "Chewa" bias to which Vail and White refer. There was no real need for the Malawi Congress Party to police our activities since, with our tools of rationalism and with our romanticism, we were, in fact, policing ourselves.[8] Third, we interviewed, if not exclusively, then almost exclusively, men. This was in part an outcome of our preconceptions as to what history was, and our preoccupation with a certain sort of "tradition," as well as being, if not imposed, than at least encouraged, by the formality of the interview process in a situation of political oppression and anxiety. With our male bias we also created problems for ourselves, since this was a predominantly matrilineal society, and one in which uxorilocal marriage was the norm, so that, infuriatingly, many men turned out to be incomers who knew little about the area (and, with some exceptions, we did not stop to explore their own histories). Women students were carefully steered away from oral history projects for their dissertations, fieldwork being regarded as "unsuitable" for them, and when I wrote a paper for our staff/student seminar speculating on the gender bias in our approach to oral history (titled "Old Wives' Tales: Women and Oral History"), I was told that I could not present it. Finally, we were working in an area which, not untypically for many parts of Africa, had an immensely complex history of movement and migration, especially in the eighteenth and nineteenth centuries, which went along with an equally complex history of ethnic creation and assimilation. These were the days (now hard to imagine) before we knew that all identities were "complex," "shifting," and "multiple." If we had only known that, we would have been saved all that digging deeper into clan histories, poring over genealogies, and all the historical unraveling. We could simply have written into our narratives that identities were "complex, shifting, and multiple," and that would have been enough. But we were pre-linguistic when it came to poststructuralism and worked with an idea that there were originary identities out there which could be uncovered and re-covered. Our opening questions to our informants were, then, very similar to those asked of Jupiter before he delivered his testimony to the court—they were about genealogy and ancestry and identity: what is your name, how old are you, and to which ethnic group and clan do you belong? In this case, it was not so much that our informants had difficulty in answering this last question (though some, I think, did), but that they frequently gave us the wrong answer. As time went on, it seemed that many people in the area did not really know who they were, or rather, who they thought they were was not what we, with our tools of enquiry, discovered them to be. This was another route through which we reinscribed Chewa dominance and recreated the Maravi Empire. It worked like this:

According to preexisting historical accounts the area we were working in was "originally" settled by Nyanja people (a former component of the Maravi, and a group which, in the modern Malawian nation, was being claimed as "Chewa"). From the late eighteenth century, but particularly in the mid- to late nineteenth century, the area had been subject to waves of immigration, both peaceful and warlike, from modern-day Mozambique by people calling themselves "Yao," important players in the long-distance ivory and slave trades. Yao chiefly dominance had been established in the area in the nineteenth century and had been reinforced by colonial policy. The exact fate of the Nyanja in all this was not known for certain, though written sources told us that they had suffered at the hands of slavers and had been scattered or taken refuge in the swamps surrounding Lake Chirwa, while later anthropological studies confidently described their location, social organization, and culture.[9]

The oral historical traditions collected by the project both filled out and complicated this picture,[10] proving that our tools of research and the intellectual direction of Professor Webster, though they had their limitations, could at least allow us to glimpse the complexity of nineteenth-century ethnicities. It emerged that Yao identity was rather slippery. Indeed, the more one probed back into Yao oral history the less substantial the Yao appeared.[11] Not only did it appear that at least some of the "Yao" were really, originally, "Lomwe" (this was a whole other problem), but many who now identified themselves as "Yao" were, as their own traditions testified, "really" Nyanja.

The Yao, in the nineteenth century, had assimilated (both peacefully and less peacefully through the institution of slavery) increasing numbers of Nyanja, and thus reduced their numbers and influence as a separate group. Our historical researches could be read as reversing this process. Whilst the Yao had proceeded by incorporating the Nyanja, we proceeded by stripping away Yao identity to reveal the Nyanja lurking underneath. In the nineteenth century Nyanja had become Yao; in modern Malawi, historians appeared capable of turning Yao into Nyanja (though since little of this work was published, its political influence should not be exaggerated).

Meanwhile, whilst we could find a Nyanja lurking under most Yao, finding Nyanja who were self-consciously Nyanja was less easy. This was the task assigned to myself and my colleague, Dr. Kings Phiri.[12] After weeks of scouring the Phalombe plain looking without success for "the Nyanja," we began to despair. Finally we were led to two Nyanja headmen: Bimbi and Nyani, modest men, rather surprised by the attention we paid them.[13] They told us that they were Nyanja of the Mwale clan and they told us where their ancestors had come from, beginning with the Tower of Babel; they told us of Nyanja custom and ritual, of the waves of Yao immigration, their intermarriage with the Nyanja and their usurpation of Nyanja chieftaincies. Since we did not turn off our tape recorder at the entrance of the first white man, we also learned from them, and from others, of the power of inscription. How, we asked another Nyanja informant, did a Yao like Malemia, fleeing from war with his kinsmen, come to be regarded by the British as their chief?

> By the time the first white man came into the area, Mpoto [a Nyanja chief] was under this "house arrest." This first man was David Living'istonia and he slept for only two days in Zomba and continued northwards. A few days later there came Buchanani [John Buchanan—one of the first white settlers], who we thought was Makanani. All the Yao chiefs and headmen went one after the other to greet him at his place near the Mulunguzi stream. The first to do so was Malemia. Buchanani asked Malemia "Who are you?" "I'm Malemia, the chief of the Mnjale area." Buchanani wrote down that, and gave the chief cloth, blankets and salt as gifts.[14]

Buchanan's first question, Who are you? (and the inscription of the answer), was also our first question as we followed the Nyanja trail, just as it was the first question asked by the Isle de France judge of the slaves before him. Sometimes, as I now remember with embarrassment, our interrogations began and ended with this question. Our task was to uncover the precolonial history of the area and, in particular, to clarify the process by which the Yao immigrants had come to dominate in the nineteenth century. But the Yao immigration was by no means the last to make its mark on this area. In the early years of the twentieth century thousands of families had made a similar east-to-west journey from Mozambique into colonial Nyasaland. Collectively known as the "Lomwe" (the very same "Lomwe," you will remember, who appear to have been at the source of some of the "Yao"), they were fleeing from one colonialism to another, from forced labor under the Portuguese to *thangata,* a milder form of the same thing, in Nyasaland.

Despite the changed conditions (much of the area had now been demarcated as white estates and taxation was being exacted by a colonial state), the "Lomwe" immigration proceeded in ways which were familiar from earlier periods. Access to resources and integration were effected through intermarriage with Nyanja and Yao, and facilitated through shared clan identities. Many "Lomwe," then, had become "Nyanja" and "Yao" in the twentieth century, just as (or so our researches were indicating) in the eighteenth century "Lomwe" had become "Yao," and in the nineteenth "Nyanja" had become "Yao." But the first few questions of our interviews had the power to reveal which of our informants were recent "Lomwe" immigrants, even if they thought of themselves (as some, but not all, did) as either "Nyanja" or "Yao." For reasons of politics, and because of our strong bias in favor of long settlement and "authenticity," we did not stop to interview those whose histories, from our point of view, began in the twentieth century (and who were at the bottom of the political and cultural heap in both the colonial and the postcolonial order of things). Landeg White was later to write one of the best pieces of social history written on this part of Africa on the basis of interviews with people who would have been our "rejects" (White 1987).

This, then, is how we went about producing historical texts which might later have been (but in fact to my knowledge never were) used for the recreation of Maravi history and the writing of the Chewa nation. Though political oppression and censorship were ever-present realities, they operated, not in the foreground, but in the background of this story. Furthermore, most of our Nyanja informants appeared unaware of the political uses (but see below for an exception to this) to which they could have put the history which they related to us. Or, if they were aware of them, they were not interested in them, for none of them seemed concerned to emphasize their links with the Chewa and the ruling elite. We lost out to the Yao, many said, because really we deserved to lose—we didn't have our wits about us.

The "Chewa" bias of the texts, then, was the product of things other than our informants' political ambitions or the presence of the local party leader at our interviews. It was produced by our own views of what constituted historical testimony and "real" history, of what were, and were not, "real" African identities, and of the relationship between space, time, authenticity, and ancestry. It would also have required a certain kind of reading, analysis, and rewriting to turn these texts into the Chewa nation's meta-narrative. On their own they appear to speak to a number of other things. They are lyrical (in their treatment, for instance, of the beginnings of human time and the role of the Nyanja Bimbi shrine) and prosaic (about, for example, the coming of the British). They are full of hesitancy, incomprehension (at our lines of questioning), and forgetfulness, as well as sometimes displaying a remarkable individual and collective recall. In this way (and this even after the deadening effects of transcription and translation) they show a capacity, maybe not to subvert, but certainly to circumvent a rigid and narrow-minded historical agenda. For despite all our efforts, we did not produce a set of traditions which (like those collected by Matthew Schoffeleers in the Lower Shire Valley) could be set side by side and compared and contrasted, dated and minutely analyzed. The testimonies which we collected leave open and unanswered a number of issues which would be only inadequately captured in either the meta-narrative of the Chewa nation, with its sense of long durée, authenticity, and essentialist identities or, for that matter, the postmodernist narrative of fragmentation, multiplicity, and complexity. We, and our informants, were still struggling with the difficulty of translating "knowing" (something, albeit fragmented) into "telling" (White 1987: 1). Their and our narratives were, perhaps fortunately, far from masterly.

In Banda's Malawi, then, the technical tools developed for the collection and analysis of oral tradition did little to guard against the really big "biases" in the production of history. Nevertheless, a set of oral texts was produced which are far from closed and which, perhaps despite themselves, shed light on complex processes of ethnic creation and recreation, in addition to giving us a glimpse of the historical consciousness of at least some members of the community. My own narrative, above, is of course greatly dependent on them. Future generations of historians, when reinterpreting them and reflecting on the Malawian historical consciousness of the late 1970s, may well be struck by the relative indifference which these testimonies show toward current political concerns. These are histories, remembered and told, no doubt, for a purpose, but perhaps not always for a purpose which is consciously known, and certainly not with the understanding that they might be used in the production of a larger, more encompassing and less open History of the Nation. Yet, in Malawi as elsewhere, there were attempts to produce local histories with a purpose—histories which would be inscribed, not by the academic historians, but by the people with the memories. These histories, which have all the attributes of the chronicle,[15] locate themselves in the space between oral testimony and the meta-narrative of the nation's History.

THE "BOOK OF MY CLAN"

The "Book of My Clan" is one such chronicle. It was shown to me by Village Headman Chingondo (Kustacio John Kanchewa) and had been written, he said, by his uncle, Andre Tambalika, who had died in 1968. Kustacio Kanchewa had copied out the work of his uncle and had added comments of his own, including accounts of recent land disputes and disputes over the village headmanship.[16] Though some of Kanchewa's additions were dated, it was impossible to be certain which parts of the Book had been written by

Kanchewa and which by his uncle, since the original text had been "borrowed" and never returned by an expatriate academic historian who had now left the country (reminding us that Banda's hostility to "foreign" historians was not simply nationalist paranoia). The "Book of My Clan" is the story of a Nyanja group of the Mwale clan, and it is told and written in the context of land shortages and local political disputes in order to "get things straight" for future generations. The Book begins with an account of the origins of the Mwale clan, their migration from Kaphirintiwa, and their first encounters with the Yao. Thus far, the "Book of My Clan" is indistinguishable from many of the Nyanja oral traditions collected by the Zomba History Project. But the tellers of those traditions, though alive and physically present, were far less intrusive in their tales than was the narrator of this written account. On the second page of the Book, the narrator interrupts his account of early Nyanja history with a diversion into more recent events—a diversion with a clear purpose:

> In 1915 Chaweza told the Whites at the Boma that his land extended to Matandwe which was a lie. When the Whites accepted this there arose a case which was resolved in favour of us, and not of Chaweza. The land was returned to us in 1915. . . . Today this land is in my hands.

1915 was the year of the Chilembwe Rising, and the date recurs throughout the Book as one around which the politics of land and chieftainship pivot.

In the aftermath of the Rising the British invested heavily in the Yao as their political agents—seen as loyal, traditional, Islamic (and thus unaffected by the radicalizing effects of Christianity), Yao headmen were elevated above Nyanja throughout the area, and land, already in relatively short supply, was placed under their control.[17] Chingondo's Book is in part, then, an account of the local Nyanja attempt to put right this perceived wrong, and it does so by moving back into the remote past of origins and migrations, and forward into the 1970s.

Yet, although the heart of the Book is the 1915 Rising, the story is far from being a straightforward one. It is hard, as the narrator tells us, to remember everything; it is hard to get things straight; it is hard in fact to know exactly who is who:

> I have explained the names because they are known by the people today. There are still many names which I have not written down for lack of space. Having mentioned this people might remember many other names, but those I have mentioned are our main names which those of you coming in the future should keep. You should not be misled by other people. There are a lot of Mwale people but they belong to different groups. When you lack a leader ask Nambaiko and Kamfani, explain all I have written, they understand and keep you.

One of the things the Book reveals, in a winding sort of way, is that the politics of identity in this area are a great deal more complex than a simple opposition between the "owners of the land" and inheritors of the Maravi Empire (the Nyanja), and the immigrant (and, in the context of colonialism, traitorous) Yao. Attempting to decipher the Book (as I did in the late 1970s, supplementing it with further interviews) was and is hard, in part because the narrator himself is struggling with the same uncertainties. He tries, but ultimately fails, to write a history which will straightforwardly serve the interests of his descendants, because the boundary of the group his history is designed to serve remains indeterminate. Not only do Yao and Nyanja share clan names (many Mwale, the narrator warns, are Yao who had been invited in by the Nyanja on the basis of their shared clan identities, but then turned against them), but even within the Mwale clan of the Nyanja there is the inevitable uncertainty created by a past permeated by the institution of slavery: "All those close to Chingondo belong to the Mwale clan but I cannot say that they are all of the same mother as me. Long, long ago they were slaves in the hands of *azimbili andala Chilewani.*"[18] Slavery, then, complicates the picture—some now claiming land and political status do so on the basis of an ancestry which is not legitimately theirs, the author argues, for those of slave origin can only be said to have been "carried in the basket" of the real ancestors. No genealogy, we are reminded, can ever be completely certain. To confuse matters further, claims to authenticity can be, and are, made in a number of different ways within the text. In his additions to the text, for example, Kustacio Kanchewa makes it clear that his case against the claims of others rests on their slave ancestry and his status as the descendant of slave owners. The fact that these slave owners were "Zimbili" (and hence "Lomwe") rather than Nyanja seems unimportant at this point. His identity as a Nyanja is, under certain circumstances, dispensable.

In an attempt to put some order into this confusing and contradictory picture, I wrote that the "Book of My Clan" demonstrated an appeal to

> a variety of historical facts, which though taking place over centuries, all hold weight. Alliance and legitimacy appear to depend on a) clan origins, b) slave or free origins and c) behaviour during the colonial period. The last has entered into "tradition" and is treated in the book as being of equal importance to more distant events. (Vaughan n.d.)

Whilst, in a sense, this analysis still holds, it is also, manifestly, an attempt to put order into what is, in some ways, a far from orderly account. Both Tambalika and Kanchewa are historians, and not simply recounters of histories, in the sense that they see events in the future as being linked to those in the past—at various points the "Book of My Clan" "remembers forward,"[19] it moralizes and grapples with questions of authority. Yet in most ways, the "Book of My Clan" chronicles events rather than tells them. At many points the narrators are only too evident, interrupting the flow of the account to make sure that we, the readers, have got the message: "When Iseek died [writes Tambalika of distant but still powerfully relevant events], who shaved? And where did he die? If I was a slave how could Chingondo raise an unknown man without enquiring who he was? The grandfather of Nanthambwe was Ntawa." If, as Barthes argued, we can distinguish between a discourse that looks out on the world and reports it, and one which "feigns to make the world speak itself and speak itself as a story," then the "Book of My Clan" falls into the former category. At many moments we are told about events which can have only one interpretation and whose relevance to contemporary land and chieftaincy disputes is spelt out for us didactically. At other points the Book resembles a chronicle of events, represented as existing in time, but whose meaning in relation to earlier and later events appears not to have been forced. The Book lacks narrative closure, and tells its story at times too openly, at others too distractedly. It lacks that integrity of the well-crafted story which conveys its message by producing in us a desire to know what happens next, and then lulls us to sleep.

TELLING IT ANOTHER WAY: "VOICES," DRUMS, AND "EMBODIED" HISTORIES

Despite our efforts in the Zomba History Project, and those of Tambalika, Kanchewa, and others like them, we did not produce a very easily "usable past" for the Banda regime. We are left, instead, with sets of "traditions," with unanswered questions, and with locally written histories which combine a retelling of "tradition" with attempts to tell the future, but whose lessons are often either too obvious or too obscure (to both the reader and the author) to allow us to easily negotiate the border between "knowing" and "telling." We were not saved by being "good" historians, acutely aware of the manipulations of our informants, of our context, and of our own craft; we were saved rather by being "bad" historians, unable finally to create the seamless narrative which would link the past events of the Maravi Empire with the present and the future of the Malawi nation in a way which would allow, within the telling, for the desire of the readers to find their own meaning. We did not, in fact, tell a very good story. We transformed other peoples' stories (the journey from the Tower of Babel, the origins of fire) into skeletal chronologies and wooden political genealogies. We had no Mercure or Thomas to enliven our accounts. We may have been memorializing the histories of lines of dead men, but they were certainly very dead after, if not before, our telling.

In Malawi in the late 1970s, then, whilst our collection and analysis of African oral historical traditions combined a hard-headed rationalism and skepticism with a heavy dose of romanticism for the precolonial past, we could not be accused of foregrounding individual exploits of historical agency.

Our African subjects were collective subjects, and our analysis was a structuralist one. Though great chiefs and warriors featured in the oral traditions we collected and in our accounts, we were aware that they might sometimes be "mythological" or at least the product of a great deal of "telescoping," merging, and backward projection of wishful thinking.

Meanwhile, in history departments of other African universities, attempts to radicalize the practice of oral historical research were underway. The new social history of Africa was a recovery history of a different sort than the one in which we were engaged through our collection of oral historical traditions. It shifted the emphasis from bodies of "tradition" to personal histories and reminiscences and, crucially, from kings and chiefs and dynasties to "the common man." As early as 1978, Terence Ranger was critiquing some aspects of this populist shift and its pretensions to radicalism (Ranger 1978).

Whilst there were pitfalls, there were also great possibilities in this turn toward a different kind of oral historical research. The Lomwe villagers whose histories I and my colleagues had rejected as "shallow" could now be listened to by a historian like Landeg White, who could see not only that these were stories of ordinary people, worth telling in themselves, but that they were embedded in longer histories and ways of recounting and remembering (L. White 1987). As such, their histories could tell us not only about history, but about how it was made. In this I refer not so much to the "African agency" which this new work aimed to demonstrate, but to the related dimension of the making of an account, or sets of accounts, which linked the past and present to the future, and the individual to the collectivity. Above all, with these new, more varied, less schematized and "democratic" sources, professional historians were much better able to produce "usable" histories through narratives which really worked. These new sources were the raw material for sophisticated historical accounts which would employ both diegesis and mimesis, would both "narrate" the unfolding actions of time and interrupt this narration, often with the sound of "the voice." A new kind of reported speech was foregrounded—not the collectively conserved "tradition" which was told as much in its form as in its explicit content, but the "voice," often disembodied, but immediately heard.

"Voices" are voices, not choruses; they cry in the wilderness of history and speak, apparently directly, to experience. They represent another kind of fantasy of authenticity, our access to the "real thing." And they can be immensely powerful, which is why the "voices" of Mercure and Thomas, speaking through the eighteenth-century court records, were enough to send me into a reverie on the Maravi Empire. Inserted into our texts at appropriate moments, "African voices" could also help the historian, especially the non-African historian, to negotiate the politics of the production of knowledge, for through these "voices" we could feign "to make the world speak itself and speak itself as a story." Completely inadequate as this was as a response to certain postcolonial criticisms, it has shown a capacity to fend off a few of the tamer wolves, for if you gave space to "voices" of the Africans oppressed in your text, then you were also "giving voice," or so it seemed to some. "Voices" gave prominence to a different kind of orality than that of "oral tradition." African "voices" in the text purport to be spontaneous, interrupting the flow of the historian's narrative. In fact, their spontaneity is likely to be part of a (conscious or unconscious) stage-management, which goes far beyond anything which can be achieved through the manipulation of "tradition." If President Banda had really wanted a usable past, one which linked the past of the Maravi Empire to the present of the Malawi nation, he should have employed the strategies of those very "radical" social historians whose motives and methods he found so suspect.

Though "oral traditions" and "voices" were a world apart, historians employing these sources shared the assumption that the history of a largely nonliterate people and time could best be captured through an analysis of what was said about it—through the word. In the case of oral traditions this was a kind of collective speech or chorus, often transmitted through the mouthpiece of a local expert; in the case of the African "voice," it was the individual's spoken word, which seemed to speak immediately to experience. In both cases, however, speech or reported speech was heard as both history (what had happened in the past) and as historical consciousness. This emphasis on a particular kind of spoken word entailed a neglect of the other forms in which individuals and communities carry forward the past.[20]

This neglect has operated at different levels. Unspoken practices of one sort or another are constitutive of history—what we do constantly exceeds, in some sense, our awareness of what is done. History is a sedimentation of practices which work on the human landscape, not all of which are "voiced" or invested with specific meaning by individuals at the moment at which they are performed.

In our study of the shifting agricultural system of Northern Zambia, *citemene*, Henrietta Moore and I argued that people's everyday "practices" in this area were as constitutive of "African agency" and of history as were their "voices" and more explicit self-interpretations (Moore and Vaughan 1994). Clearly this raises important questions of what we mean by "consciousness" and, specifically, by "historical consciousness," to which I shall return. Furthermore, when individuals and groups *are* apparently more directly creating meaning from what they do, there are many different ways in which this meaning can be created and transmitted.

Social anthropologists and historians of memory have told us of the many ways in which historical memory, both conscious and unconscious, may be carried forward, linking the past and the future in ways which are very different from those exemplified in the oral tradition or the narrativized "voice."[21] So, as Paul Connerton and others have argued, the social conventions of the body may carry a social memory—the way we sit, wield a hoe, carry our babies, and curl up or stretch out to sleep are social creations which either endure or change through social action. They distinguish "us" from others, and therefore form part of a collective (small or large, family or ethnic) identity and history—"stories," temporal sequences of events, are not the only "elements of memory that can be drawn from the storehouse of memory" (Mitchell 1994: 194).

For example, we know that the historical experience of colonialism can be carried forward and understood through the "mimetic embodiment" of spirit possession.[22] And you don't have to be possessed yourself, by the spirit of an ancestor or an invading foreigner, to experience the history and the future of which they speak—as Paul Stoller argues, the theatricality of spirit possession is about power and about transformation, and has the power to connect the spectators with their embodied memories, like an electrical current that "jolts bodies as they are charged and recharged by the social memories that define and redefine our being-in-the-world" (Stoller 1995: 198). Stoller argues, in the case of the Hauka, that spirit possession rituals can be seen as a form of "indigenous historiographic memory" which can be counterposed against the oral traditions and epics. Arguably Stoller falls into the trap of feeling he has, through them, access to "the real" when he goes on to argue that "the way of the text and epic are decidedly disembodied paths to Songhay history. Such disembodiment constrains their messages. . . . Whereas the text and the epic speak to the consciousness of the nobility, the bodily practices of possession speak to . . . 'conscious'" (Stoller 1995: 34),[23] but nevertheless, his and others' exploration of the nondiscursive historical conscious is persuasive. Ritual performance surely need not necessarily be regarded as a kind of "counter-history" to the narratives of oral traditions and epic tales. Connerton (upon whom Stoller draws) argues in fact that ritual can be viewed as another kind of "master narrative," one, like any other, which must be persuasive for it to work, and which in this case relies for its persuasiveness on the habituation of the bodies of its participants and spectators. Habituation and repetition are central to the work of ritual performance—you may not be able to "say" why it works, but you can certainly "feel" it working.

Steven Friedson's work on Tumbuka healing (in Malawi), like that of Stoller, draws on phenomenology to take this argument further (Friedson 1996). The role of the ritual specialist here, one might argue from a reading of his account, is to continually realign competing sets of historical memories in their manifestation as spirits. This realignment is effected in and through the transformation of the bodies of individuals and through their suffering. But before he or she can effect this realignment, the ritual specialist must first "see" (or divine) which spirit he or she is dealing with—must ask, in effect, "who are you?" and only when an answer is made manifest will the specialist be able to "hear" (or understand). Whereas historians have tended to listen or hear before they divine, the Tumbuka healer must divine before she or he can hear. *Vimbuza* spirits, as they manifest themselves in individuals, are a kind of roll call of Tumbuka history in the world. They manifest "otherness" as experienced historically by the people of this region: the ivory trade, the Ngoni invaders, the Europeans. This is an otherness which, it seems, has been literally incorporated (as in the Hauka case described by Stoller), but as with other kinds of incorporation, it can become uncomfortable. In particular, the vimbuza spirits, lying horizontally, come up against those of the individual's and group's ancestors, lying vertically. Whereas the vimbuza are an open-ended category of spirits, the *mizimu*, the spirits of the ancestors, are not. Most of the time these different sets of historical memories[24] live together compatibly, but on occasion (perhaps induced by the presence of a third element—witchcraft) they get out of line, vying with each other for space and causing illness. To realign the spirits and to make peace, the healer must first divine which vimbuza and which of the mizimu spirits he or she is dealing with. This "calling" is effected through the drum, through sound and rhythm, for each vimbuza can only be made manifest and brought to the surface if, in effect, he or she is called by the right name. Recognition is effected through a specific drumming rhythm—get it wrong and the spirit refuses to answer. In one sense, then, it is the drummer and not the ritual specialist who has access to the language which brings to the surface and makes manifest the past—it is he that knows, and can enact the code of, each spirit, and so can call him or her by the right name. But the drumming rhythm is not "merely" a code or a name—it works on and through the bodies of the participants and through the vimbuza "material" which lies latent in all of them. Unlike the drummer himself, they may "forget" the rhythm, but its memory has become embodied and can be called forth on a future occasion.[25]

To explore the nonverbal ways in which memory may be carried forward is not to privilege "embodiment" over the word as somehow more authentic, more real, and closer to experience, but rather to reflect that, as Elizabeth Tonkin says, "people do not need discursive accounts to represent themselves as historical entities" (Tonkin 1992). In addition, however, it may bring us back to "oral tradition" and oral performance with a somewhat different perspective. The non-narrative Yoruba *oriki* which Karin Barber (1991) has described and analyzed so illuminatingly are composed of words which, like the Tumbuka drumming, have the function of naming and calling forward. Like the vimbuza spirit world, the world of the words of oriki is incorporative: "Its mode is to subsist by swallowing other texts" (10). Words, we should also remember, are also composed of sounds and may sometimes, like the drumming, evoke their meaning and differences through their physicality (Moore 1996). Words used during ritual performance may work metonymically as much as they work metaphorically. The very sound of the word may work to evoke memories and meanings beyond the immediate one. When anthropologists (and ethnomusicologists) such as Friedson remind us that the texts of songs often appear less important as conveyors of meaning than the music to which they are sung, we might also add that in some cases the formation and utterance of those words is part of the musical experience.

Neither the 1970s analysis of oral traditions nor the 1980s recovery of voices exhausts the potential of "oral" sources of African history and African historical consciousness, even before we consider the nonverbal ways in which memory is carried forward and history made manifest[26]—social anthropologists and students of oral literature take this fact for granted. But the use of this wider repertoire of cultural productions (rhythms, dreams,[27] riddles, and speaking in tongues) raises rather large questions concerning our definitions of historical consciousness—it may be history, but is it History?

MERCURE, ROLAND, AND THE CREOLE MEMORY

Mercure and Thomas, subjects of the Maravi Empire, spoke (as "voices"), not through oral tradition, but through the rich written records of eighteenth-century Isle de France. We have no equivalent records for eighteenth-century Malawi. Slavery incorporated Mercure and Thomas into a world system of inscription and turned them into a certain kind of historical subject, with names (albeit newish ones), ages (albeit approximate), and voices (albeit muted). But slavery also violently interrupted the transmission of certain kinds of collective identity and memory. To be a slave in Isle de France, as elsewhere, and survive depended on swift learning of the ways of others, and on a certain amount of forgetting. Just how much forgetting is hard to know, but in present-day Mauritius (in contrast to present-day Malawi), the descendants of Mercure and Thomas appear not to have an "oral tradition" of the kind recognized as "history" by historians, or (more importantly) by other ethnic groups on the island.[28] The Maravi slaves of the eighteenth century had already been "creolized" to some degree before they touched Isle de France soil. They had already become "Mozambiques." This violent rupture was, of course, different in degree and kind from the transformations which were simultaneously taking place in the region which they had left—"Lomwe" were becoming "Yao," "Nyanja" were becoming "Yao," and new languages, new religions, and new ways of being were making their way up the caravan routes from the coast. In Isle de France Mercure would have to learn much faster the ways of being of his fellow slaves (from East Africa, West Africa, Madagascar, and India) and of his masters. Crucially, he would have to learn the island's language—a French Creole—very fast, for although Thomas could translate for him as he gave his testimony in court, in everyday life he would have to make himself understood.

The process of "creolization" in eighteenth-century Isle de France involved cultural compromise, enrichment and loss, on the part of everyone, but some clearly lost more than others.[29] African slaves were at the losing end of this process, but it was a long and complex process nevertheless. Slaves here, as elsewhere, created a world which was livable out of the pieces which they had brought with them and those which they had learned and made their own. The "mimicry" practiced by slaves, and much remarked upon by white nineteenth-century observers, was an essential practice in such a situation—one which allowed "foreignness" to be incorporated (just as foreign elements were incorporated by the Tumbuka as vimbuza spirits), and difference to be simultaneously marked out.

By the time of the abolition of slavery, descendants of African and Malagasy slaves, and of their unions with non-slave others (Indian immigrants of the eighteenth and nineteenth centuries, "French" settlers, and other "Europeans" or East Asians), had come to be known as the "Creoles," a nomenclature originally reserved for those of French descent born on the island. This category persists in today's "rainbow nation" of Mauritius. It is, in fact, a residual category within a "multicultural" nation in which all other groups have clear (if invented) historical origins and cultural practices.[30] The Mauritian cultural categories of "Hindu," "Muslim," "Tamil," "Chinese," and "Franco" are, of course, troubled and divided (not least by caste and class), but they are held together pretty well by two things—firstly, reasonably coherent accounts of "origins" in other places and the narrative histories which follow from them; and secondly, a visible celebration of difference through dress, bodily comportment, and religious beliefs and practices. Though all Mauritians are creoles, only a minority are Creoles. There are Creoles who have Indian, Chinese, or European "blood" in them, along with their slave "blood," but who will nevertheless be Creoles rather than creoles because they are not culturally identified as Hindu, Muslim, Tamil, Chinese, or European. Creoles are Creoles because they have, in the words of one Hindu intellectual I talked to, "no history, and no culture." They do not, in Mauritian terms, know "who they are," and knowing who you are is essential in Mauritius if others are to accord you respect.

Mauritians are rightly proud of their "rainbow nation," but it is one which shares all the drawbacks of multiculturalism. In effect, to be a real member of the Mauritian nation, you must first have a "culture" (preferably with origins elsewhere in an "ancient" civilization) to contribute to the multicultural cooking pot. For a variety of reasons relating to the specific history of slavery in Mauritius and to the politics of the Creole community, the African and Malagasy origins of the Creoles appear extremely muted. Creole intellectuals make the very valid point that their history begins on the island—their origins lie in *métissage,* in *créolité* itself, and not in a mythic originary moment which came before. And yet, making up (and believing) their stories of origins, looking to their roots, and constructing narrative histories which explain how "they" got from there to here is what every other group in Mauritius does, and it is this which constitutes, politically, a culture and a History. It is hard, then, to avoid at least asking the question of Creole people—do you know where your ancestors came from? With the few exceptions of individuals who would point out to sea and say "Malgache" or "Mozambique," those of whom I have asked this question shake their heads and say, "no, we don't know," though they may, indeed, be able to tell you that the "Hindus" came from India, and that a certain lady in the village has a French ancestor. Other people, then, have origins, but not them.

Of course, there are many ways in which a historian can turn disadvantage into advantage in the struggle to produce a narrative account. Forgetting does have a history, or rather, more than one possible history, and language can turn spaces into substances. Forgetting is a familiar subject in the historiography and literary representation of the experience of slavery. The nineteenth-century North American slave narrative was testimony to both memory and forgetting: Frederick Douglass's narrative, we are reminded, began with the sentence "I do not remember to have ever met a slave who could tell of his birthday" (quoted in Mitchell 1994: 186). Furthermore, we have to allow for the possibility that the violence of slavery, like (in this respect) other violences, could produce "a blankness in memory so radical that it cannot be described as forgetting, amnesia, or repression, but as the absolute *prevention* of experience, the excision not just of 'memories' as a content, but the destruction of memory itself, either as an artificial technique, or a natural faculty" (Mitchell 1994: 186). Memory is not only the recollection of past experience by an individual, but its "telling" or passing on to another. Remembering, we also know, can be a way of putting a distance and letting go (or "forgetting"), as when we remember and memorialize the dead, whilst we may "forget" precisely those things which we hold on to most deeply (Phillips 1994, chapter 2). It could be, then, that the slave population had, in some sense, not only forgotten how to remember, but forgotten how to forget.

A history of forgetting, or of forgetting to forget, may well be part of the history of the Creole population of Mauritius. But the forgetting has been selective. In the late nineteenth century a Franco-Mauritian folklorist, Charles Baissac, was bemoaning the disappearance of what he saw as "true" Creole culture with its African and Malagasy origins (Baissac 1888). He put the forgetting down, not to slavery, but to its abolition, to the epidemics of malaria which had wiped out a proportion of the Creole population, to the influx and cultural influence of Indian immigrants, and, broadly speaking, to a process of modernization. But at least some of the oral culture described and recorded by Baissac does survive today in Creole communities. Whilst Creole people may not have an oral historical tradition, they certainly do have an oral tradition of riddles and storytelling, and whilst folklorists have done considerable research into the origins and diffusion of these stories and riddles in the Indian Ocean (Haring 1991), there is doubtless a great deal more that could be said about them. I have not analyzed Mauritian Creole riddles and would need help in doing so, but as far as I can see they are assimilative and expansive, encompassing new experiences and cultural influences in an enduring form. They are not about origins, then, but they may be "about" the history of creolization. Though there may not be an oral historical tradition of an African kind in the Creole community, there certainly is an oral culture which, with some pushing and shoving and manipulation from the historian, may be made to yield historical content and provide an insight into historical consciousness. And, of course, there are the other ways in which this culture might be bringing forward its memories and making manifest its history. Armed with insights from the social anthropologists and historians of memories (but, I should add, with few of their professional skills), I moved from asking people the "who are you?" questions, which drew blanks, to asking them about their practices. I moved from reported speech to reported practice.

Monsieur Roland (or Lolo, as he is known) is an elderly fisherman living on the far south of the island.[31] I have interviewed him several times because he seems to be knowledgeable about various aspects of "Creole ways," and because he is quite different from other elderly Creole people I have met. Roland lives alone in a small hut in considerable poverty. He fishes a bit, and begs the rum and bread to go with his fish. He has no television (many Creole people do) and no radio; he cannot read, and he is very definitively not a practicing Catholic (unlike most of the other members of this community). He has an unusual knowledge of the construction of "traditional" creole instruments, and has something of a reputation as a raconteur and singer of *sega* songs. He was even once featured on television—less surprising than you might think on this small island where, according to a Mauritian friend of mine, "even a rat coming out of a hole makes it onto television."

Roland, like everyone else I have interviewed, is more than a little vague about his ancestral history and his slave origins. He shrugs his shoulders when asked where his ancestors came from, and gestures across the sea. He says he only knows one story about slavery (this is the same one which I have heard repeated all over the island and which features in tourist brochures), and is sure that I will not find anyone who can tell me any more. Not unreasonably, he gets bored answering questions which he cannot answer and in which, or so it appears, he has very little interest. But when asked, not about the ancestors, but about the spirits of the ancestors (les grands dimounes), Roland has a great deal more to say. There are spirits, he says, which have to be "called," addressed in a strange foreign language ("They talked Greek," he says, and gives a demonstration). Perhaps these spirits will do harm to your family, make your child ill, in which case you have to call a specialist, a "traiteur" who will sacrifice a cock like this: "the cock is not cut with a knife, the head of the cock is put directly in the mouth and he cuts it with his teeth. He drinks the blood also . . . the cock will take the child's illness with him." Do the spirits have names, I ask. "Yes," says Roland, "perhaps Alfred or Roland . . . Yes, supposing I Roland died and being a spirit I enter someone, so the spirit is Roland." So the spirits take the names of the deceased in the family, rather than others? "Yes," replies Roland, "even a cousin's name—alliances are very important."[32]

Roland can go on with these stories for some time, interspersed with bouts of sega singing and improvised drumming. The Creoles, it seems, do have ancestors after all, but they are made manifest, not in oral historical tradition, but through the drumming of the healing event. Listening to Roland I make frenzied connections. The vimbuza healing rites of the Tumbuka feature an animal sacrifice very similar to that described by Roland—the cock's neck is broken by the teeth and the blood is drunk. Perhaps Roland is really a Tumbuka, descended perhaps from one of those "Maravi" slaves, Mercure or Thomas. But Roland does not seem to be worried about his roots, and is not the slightest bit interested in the cultural practices of Africa or Madagascar, from which some of his bodily memory, his memory of rhythm, may originate. He bemoans instead the shortage of fish, and the price of rum. Perhaps he prefers to leave his ancestors in peace, and more importantly, to be left in peace by them. He will "remember" them on All Saints' Day, but will try and "forget" them otherwise.

Conscious and Consciousness

It is possible (but of course it would be extremely hard to demonstrate) that Roland, and others like him, do hold very deep, unvoiced memories of the practices brought to the island two hundred years ago by their ancestors from Africa and Mozambique. Is this what Stoller means by a "conscious" rather than a "consciousness," and if so, what are we to do with it, if anything? It is clear that the kind of historical "conscious" or "consciousness" which has been described to me is of a different kind than that expressed through African "oral traditions," through the writings of historians like Tambalika and Kanchewa, and certainly than narrative histories. Perhaps the rituals described by Roland do constitute the endogenous historicity of the Mauritian Creole people, for, as Jean and John Comaroff argue, "the policies of history lie also in mute meanings transacted through goods and practices, icons and images dispersed in the landscape" (Comaroff and Comaroff 1992: 35). Roland's version of history does not claim anything beyond what it demonstrates directly. It has no "origins," its "authenticity" lying within its lived practice, rather than in any claims to go beyond, or to come from a "before." Roland's ancestors are not a long line of memorialized men but "les grands dimounes," who, in order to be "forgotten" from day to day, must be remembered and fed on certain occasions.

By describing Roland's account in this way, I have already, of course, inserted it into another sort of "history." Perhaps Roland's ancestors should be left alone by historians like myself. As Johannes Fabian has argued (1983), by translating the experience of others into our own measures of being-in-time, we are laying down the terms in which they may be represented. I have argued earlier in this paper that it was perhaps fortunate that our attempts to so translate the histories of southern Malawi in the late 1970s were so flawed and incomplete. And yet, it is hard to escape the conclusion that, within a nation-state such as Mauritius, we cannot afford to leave Roland's ancestors alone in their endogenous historicity. To represent them in a way which would allow the Mauritian Creole community to be seen, heard, and recognized would inevitably involve the insertion of Roland's practices into a narrative which, if it does not invent "origins," must at the very least create a kind of coherence; which transforms Roland's "knowing" into a very specific kind of "telling," a telling which recognizes the existence of the state and expresses the conflict between "desire and the law."

NOTES

This essay was previously published in the *Journal of Historical Sociology*, August 2000. © Blackwell Publishers. It appears here with the permission of Blackwell Publishers.

1. This case is recorded in the National Archives of Mauritius, JB 80: Case of Jupiter.

2. For the politics of the Banda regime, see Lwanda 1993; AfricaWatch 1990; Williams 1978; Englund 1996.

3. More prominent in their account than the work of the project I was involved with is the published work of both Ian Linden and Matthew Schoffeleers. I feel that they may have also overstated their case in regard to these two historians. For a "revisionist" account, see Harri Englund's work (1996). Leroy Vail's recent death is a great loss to students of Malawi's precolonial history.

4. At this point my narrative becomes overtly autobiographical. Like any other "personal reminiscence" it needs to be read with care.

5. Hastings Banda's interest in "History" would make an interesting study in its own right. He gave speeches regularly on such historical subjects as the colonial past of the British (a history of colonization by the Romans), and on Welsh place names.

6. Professor Webster had already acquired wide experience in the practice of oral history during his time in East Africa, before arriving in Malawi. He had also published a well-received work on African Christianity. See Webster 1964, 1973, 1976.

7. For a full discussion of "oral tradition" and its uses by historians and others see Tonkin 1992; Hofmeyr 1993.

8. The only direct policing which I was aware of was that to which we had all grown accustomed—the frequent presence of a local Malawi Congress Party branch chair at our interviews. Of course, there may have been more control of the larger intellectual enterprise than I was aware of, but my impression was that though everyone knew that history was "political" and potentially "dangerous," there were no very clear directives from above. There were always government "spies" amongst our students, but they were often confused as to their exact mission.

9. Perhaps not so confidently—see Tew 1950. Nyanja were, however, "counted" in the colonial censuses and therefore deemed to exist, even in areas dominated by "Yao" and "Lomwe."

10. All the Zomba History Project interviews are deposited in the Library of Chancellor College, University of Malawi, Zomba.

11. See the interpretation in Webster 1977.

12. Dr. Phiri is a historian of precolonial Malawi, trained in the United States by Jan Vansina.

13. Roderick Graham Chipande (village headman, Nyani Village, T. A. Malemia, Zomba District) and Arnold Frederick Bimbi (group village headman, Bimbi Village, T. A. Malemia, Zomba District), interviewed on 23 November 1977 by Kings Phiri and Megan Vaughan, Zomba History Project: Amachinga Yao Traditions, Vol. 2.

14. Interview with Morgan Sawali, Sawali Village, T. A. Msamala, 31 August 1977: Zomba History Project, Amachinga Yao traditions, Vol. 2.

15. For the attributes of the "chronicle" I have again drawn on White (1987), though his discussion does have the drawback of being directed primarily at understanding the nature of narrative through an examination of non-narrative forms. In other words, the chronicle is viewed primarily as an incomplete or imperfect narrative.

16. "The Book of My Clan," written by Chingondo I (Andre Tambalika) and copied out by Chingondo III (Kustacio Kanchewa), translated by Ellias Chakwela. Copy in my possession. See also the following interviews: with Granger Matengula, Chingondo Village, T. A. Mwambo, 19 July 1978; with Gravelo Njala, Njala Village, T. A. Kuntumanje, 15 July 1978; with Clement Palira, Saima Village, T. A. Mwambo, 8 September 1978; and with Kustacio John Kanchewa and Tipa January, Chingondo Village, T. A. Mwambo, 6 September 1978.

17. For the Chilembwe Rising and its political consequences, see Vail and White 1989; L. White 1987; Shepperson and Price 1958.

18. The *azimbili* were probably "Lomwe" slave traders.

19. Barthes's term (1977: 115), drawing on Lacan and Nietzche and referring to the capacity to assimilate stories, to tell them, and to be capable of "making promises."

20. Of course, historians of Africa have always, of necessity, engaged with other kinds of nonverbalized histories—through, for example, their use of archaeological evidence and art history—but this engagement has been for the purpose of securing alternative, "supporting" evidence, rather than reflecting on the nature of historical consciousness.

21. See Connerton 1989; Hutton 1993; Matsuda 1996; Stoller 1995.

22. For mimesis and memory, see Stoller 1995; Kramer 1993; Taussig 1993.

23. Perhaps there is a danger of overprivileging "the embodied" here—clearly this point relates to a large literature on the nature and meaning of embodiment.

24. I am loosely interpreting these spirits as "memories," but of course there is a great deal more to them than this, and Friedson does not himself make this argument as crudely as I am putting it here.

25. Ronald Radano's work on the transcription of slave spirituals is suggestive here. The songs, working as a "sound text," continually exceeded their transcription. The transcribed text could only ever be partial (Radano 1996: 525).

26. Historians of Africa have much more readily explored the (also important) interaction between written texts and oral culture.

27. See Achille Mbembe's (1991) use of dreams as an historical source.

28. A note of caution here: I am not clearly in a position to pronounce that no such "tradition" exists, and, for reasons which will become evident in the following discussion, am reluctant to do so. It is clear, however, that the kind of collective traditions of an ex-slave society found by Richard Price (1983) in Surinam do not exist in Mauritius. More research on the African diaspora in the Indian Ocean may well uncover a "hidden history." See Alpers 1997.

29. On "creolization" as a continuum, see the interesting discussion in Burton 1997.

30. For what I regard as a rather partial account of Mauritian multiculturalism and nationalism, see Erikson 1992.

31. Interview with Idesse Rolo (Lolo), Le Morne, Mauritius, 12 September 1995. Transcribed and translated by Mr. Pavi Ramhota.

32. Here my research assistant, Pavi Ramhota, remarked in his transcription of the interview that "amongst the Creoles, kinship among the dead seems stronger than among the living." Creoles have a reputation amongst other groups for having "unstable" families.

BIBLIOGRAPHY

AfricaWatch. 1990. *Silence Rules: The Suppression of Dissent in Malawi.* New York: AfricaWatch.

Alpers, Edward A. 1997. "The African Diaspora in the Northwestern Indian Ocean: A Reconsideration of an Old Problem, New Directions for Research." *Comparative Studies of South Asia, Africa, and the Middle East* 17, no. 2: 62–81.

Baissac, Charles. 1888. *Le Folklore de l'Ile Maurice.* Paris: Maisonneuve et Ch. Leclerc.

Barber, Karin. 1991. *I Could Speak until Tomorrow: Oriki, Women, and the Past in a Yoruba Town.* Edinburgh: Edinburgh University Press.

Barthes, Roland. 1977. *Image, Music, Text.* Trans. Stephen Heath. London: Fontana.

Burton, Richard D. E. 1997. *Afro-Creole: Power, Opposition, and Play in the Caribbean.* Ithaca: Cornell University Press.

Comaroff, Jean, and John Comaroff. 1992. *Ethnography and the Historical Imagination.* Boulder: Westview.

Connerton, Paul. 1989. *How Societies Remember.* Cambridge: Cambridge University Press.

Englund, Harri. 1996. "Between God and Kamuzu: The Transition to Multi-party Politics in Central Malawi." In *Post-colonial Identities in Africa,* ed. Richard Werbner and Terence Ranger, 136–57. London: Zed.

Erikson, Thomas Hyland. 1992. *Us and Them in Modern Societies: Ethnicity and Nationalism in Mauritius, Trinidad, and Beyond.* Oslo: Scandinavian University Press.

Fabian, Johannes. 1983. *Time and the Other: How Anthropology Makes Its Object.* New York: Columbia University Press.

Friedson, Steven M. 1996. *Dancing Prophets: Musical Experience in Tumbuka Healing.* Chicago and London: Chicago University Press.

Haring, Lee. 1991. "Prospects for Folklore in Mauritius." *International Folklore Review* 2: 83–95.

Hofmeyr, Isabel. 1994. *"We Spend Our Years as a Tale That Is Told": Oral Historical Narrative in a South African Chiefdom.* Portsmouth N.H.: Heinemann.

Hutton, Patrick. 1993. *History as an Art of Memory.* Hanover and London: University of New England Press.

Kramer, Fritz. 1993. *The Red Fez: Art and Spirit Possession in Africa.* London: Verso.

Livingstone, David, and Charles Livingstone. 1865. *Narrative of an Expedition to the Zambezi and Its Tributaries, and the Discovery of Lakes Shirwa and Nyasa, 1858–1864.* London: John Murray.

Lwanda, John. 1993. *Kamuzu Banda of Malawi: A Study of Promise, Power and Paralysis.* Glasgow: Dudu Nsomba.

Matsuda, Matt K. 1996. *The Memory of the Modern.* New York and Oxford: Oxford University Press.

Mbembe, Achille. 1991. "Domaines de la nuit et autorité onirique dans les maquis du sud-cameroun, 1955–1958." *Journal of African History* 31: 89–121.

Mitchell, W. J. T. 1994. *Picture Theory: Essays on Verbal and Visual Representation.* Chicago and London: University of Chicago Press.

Moore, Henrietta. 1996. "Sex, Symbolism, and Psychoanalysis." Audrey Richards Memorial Lecture, Queen Elizabeth House, Oxford.

Moore, Henrietta, and Megan Vaughan. 1994. *Cutting Down Trees: Gender, Nutrition, and Agricultural Change in Northern Province, Zambia, c. 1890–1990.* Portsmouth, N.H.: Heinemann.

Phillips, Adam. 1994. *On Flirtation.* London: Faber and Faber.

Price, Richard. 1983. *First-Time: The Historical Vision of an Afro-American People.* Baltimore: Johns Hopkins University Press.

Radano, Ronald. 1996. "Denoting Difference: The Writing of Slave Spirituals." *Critical Inquiry* 22, no. 3: 506–44.

Ranger, Terence. 1978. "Personal Reminiscence and the Experience of the People of East Central Africa." *Oral History* 6, no. 1: 45–78.

Schoffeleers, J. Matthew. 1992. *Rivers of Blood: The Genesis of a Martyr Cult in Southern Malawi, c. A.D. 1600.* Madison: University of Wisconsin Press.

Shepperson, George, and T. Price. 1958. *Independent African: John Chilembwe and the Origins, Setting, and Significance of the Nyasaland Native Rising of 1915.* Edinburgh: Edinburgh University Press.

Stoller, Paul. 1995. *Embodying Colonial Memories: Spirit Possession, Power, and the Hauka in West Africa.* New York and London: Routledge.

Taussig, Michael. 1993. *Mimesis and Alterity: A Particular History of the Senses.* New York: Routledge.

Tew, Mary. 1950. *The Peoples of the Lake Nyasa Region.* Ethnographic Survey of Africa, East Central Africa, Part 1. London: Oxford University Press.

Tonkin, Elizabeth. 1992. *Narrating Our Pasts: The Social Construction of Oral History.* Cambridge: Cambridge University Press.

Vail, Leroy, and Landeg White. 1989. "Tribalism in the Political History of Malawi." In *The Creation of Tribalism in Southern Africa,* ed. Leroy Vail, 151–92. London: James Currey.

Vaughan, Megan. n.d. "Local Politics and 'Tradition': Chingondo's 'Book of My Clan.'" Unpublished paper.

———. 1981. "Social and Economic Change in Southern Malawi: The Shire Highlands and Upper Shire Valley." Ph.D. dissertation, School of Oriental and African Studies, University of London.

Webster, J. B. 1964. *The African Churches among the Yoruba, 1888–1922.* Oxford: Clarendon.

———. 1973. *The Iteso during the Asonya.* Nairobi: East African Publishing House.

———. 1976. *The Central Luo during the Aconya.* Nairobi: East African Literature Bureau.

———. 1977. "From Yao Hill to Mount Mulanje: Ivory and Slaves and the Southwestern Expansion of the Yao." Seminar paper, Department of History, Chancellor College, University of Malawi.

White, Hayden. 1987. *The Content of the Form: Narrative Discourse and Historical Representation.* Baltimore and London: Johns Hopkins University Press.

White, Landeg. 1987. *Magomero: Portrait of an African Village.* Cambridge: Cambridge University Press.

Williams, T. D. 1978. *Malawi: The Politics of Despair.* Ithaca: Cornell University Press.

3

John Bunyan, His Chair, and a Few Other Relics

ORALITY, LITERACY, AND THE LIMITS OF AREA STUDIES

Isabel Hofmeyr

As a number of voices in different disciplines are starting to demonstrate, African studies has been haunted by the ghost of orality (Barber 1995; Finnegan 1990; Hofmeyr 1995; Julien 1992). The idea of orality has become an implicit last redoubt where Africa's "difference" lurks. As the terms "developed" and "undeveloped," "modern" and "traditional," "urban" and "rural" have been uncoupled, the dyad of literacy and orality has acquired an afterlife in which it doubles for these terms and for their supposed progenitors, namely Europe and Africa. As Eileen Julien has shown, the atomic clusters of Africa/orality and Europe/literacy still shape much thinking. Is it possible to unbundle these clusters? Can any new energy be sparked in this splitting?

This essay tries to bring to life some possible answers to these questions in relation to John Bunyan's *The Pilgrim's Progress*. A thoroughly transnational and globalized text, strongly streaked with "European" orality, it suggests various lines of approach to the issues posed above. One could, for example, focus on how the twentieth-century reception of this seventeenth-century text (produced by a first-generation literate in a paraliterate world) has sidelined the text's orality. One could equally trace how the text was received in the numerous quarters of the imperial world to which it traveled along the highways of nineteenth-century evangelical mission activity. An interesting template for combining oral and literate traditions, the book often provided a reference point for graduates from mission schools who in their own literary work were grappling with just these issues.

These are not the subjects of this paper. Instead, the paper considers the massive nineteenth-century popularity of the text. In brief, it argues that the scope and nature of this popularity has attracted only fitful interest despite the massive scale of Bunyan scholarship. It argues that this situation can be understood as part of the indirect effects of the Africa/orality, Europe/literacy split set out above. This analytical balkanization means, firstly, that Bunyan's nineteenth-century reception has been analyzed in terms of a historically contingent and narrow notion of reading which screens out the oral, performative dimensions through which the text's success was secured. Secondly, this division of Africa from Europe means that reading and reception are largely understood as activities restricted by national boundaries. The paper attempts to demonstrate that the reading and reception of this book depended as much on the imperial presence of the text as on its dissemination in Britain (Spargo 1997: 102–104).

⁕ ⁕ ⁕

If remembered at all today, John Bunyan is usually recalled as a rather cranky religious writer of the olden days who wrote a book about a pilgrim. Those who know slightly more will think of him as a Nonconformist writer of the English Revolution who after centuries of neglect rose to prominence in the nineteenth century and whose text *The Pilgrim's Progress* traveled to many parts of the world via the arteries of mission proselytization. Read in today's secular climate, when biblical language is no longer commonly used, the book appears turgid and at times incomprehensible, and it is probably difficult for modern readers to envisage how it could ever have been so popular.

Yet popular it was, in some instances inspiring a cultish devotion which is hard to imagine. Macaulay, for example, in his 1854 entry on Bunyan for the *Encyclopaedia Britannica,* noted that austere Puritans were known to display Popish emotionalism when it came to the subject of Bunyan: "Many Puritans to whom the respect paid by Roman Catholics to the reliques and tombs of saints seemed childish and sinful, are said to have begged with their dying breath that their coffins might be placed as near as possible to the coffin of the author of the *Pilgrim's Progress*" (Macaulay 1910: 806).

This strong sense of emotionalism was widespread. Readers of *The Pilgrim's Progress* talked of reading it with "heart palpitant" (Law 1927: 50). Others spoke lovingly of the characters as friends, familiar as those "on the Front at Brighton" (Birrell 1927: 152). This sense of emotional investment operated at both a personal and a national level. At the unveiling of Bunyan's statue in his home town of Bedford, the dean of Westminster, speaking of *The Pilgrim's Progress,* said,

> It is one of the few books which has struck a chord which vibrates alike amongst the humblest peasants and amongst the most fastidious critics. Let us pause for an instant to reflect how great a boon is conferred upon a nation by one such uniting element. How deeply extended is the power of sympathy, and the force of argument, when the preacher or the teacher knows that he can enforce his appeal by a name which, like that of an apostle or evangelist, comes home as if with canonical weight to every one who hears him; by figures of speech which need only to be touched on in order to elicit an eclectic spark of understanding and satisfaction. (Stanley 1874: 52)

In effect the book became a national institution and, for many, one of the key symbols of an increasingly racialized patriotism. One commentator on Bunyan's work compared all Britons to Bunyan's pilgrim. "It is the fact, that every man, whether a seeker for God or not, comes into the world inseparably connected with his Race. He is born a member of a great society, so that already at his birth he is under certain laws, and subject to influences beyond his control. . . . in the language of modern science, the pilgrim is deeply affected from his birth by the solidarity of his Race" (Stevenson 1912: 7).

In addition to being a national symbol, Bunyan also assumed a strong imperial presence. One commentator claimed that there were more copies of *The Pilgrim's Progress* in existence than of any other English book save the King James version of the Bible. In its English version and in numerous translations, the text was seen as a key link in imperialism, a book to "mitigate the antipathies of race [by sailing] across estranging seas" (Birrell 1928: 79).

Attempts to explain this extraordinary popularity have generally centered on the changing fortunes of Nonconformist and Dissenting traditions. These moved from being radical underground movements in the seventeenth century to respectable middle-class organizations by the mid–nineteenth century. The way in which Bunyan's text became the beneficiary of these shifts has, like all aspects of Bunyan's work, been extensively documented (Greaves 1983; Keeble 1988).

In broad outline, this scholarship tells a story of a text which in the century after its publication in 1688 was both sneered at and revered. For the eighteenth-century Anglican intelligentsia, the book was lamentably vulgar. For many ordinary people—particularly Nonconformists—the text became, as E. P. Thompson has shown, the "book of books," second only to the Bible and a source for radical meditation on social inequality (Thompson 1975: 34).

This divergence of opinion narrowed as both the evangelical revival, which lauded Bunyan's theology, and Romantic thinking, which hailed the text for its untutored genius and spontaneous creativity, brought Bunyan into the mainstream. A series of influential editions of *The Pilgrim's Progress,* entries in encyclopedias, and literary histories ensured that Bunyan became a ubiquitous nineteenth-century presence. The growing respectability of Nonconformism augmented the cultural authority of Bunyan's work.

By sketching some of the broader intellectual developments which occasioned his parabolic rise, these accounts of Bunyan's reception have fixed a crucial framework in which our understanding can be located. Yet these accounts give little sense of *how* this popularity was secured. How, for example, was the book disseminated? How was it used? What reading contexts could ensure its evident affective power? How could the book become a cult object of such national importance? These questions are taken for granted; one comes away with the feeling that the book's popularity simply spread like ink in blotting paper.

These silences around distribution may in some instances be seen as mere empirical oversights: a matter of filling in detail. I would like to take a stronger position and argue that the silence grows out of a prior set of assumptions regarding the term "reading." The first assumption derives from an ahistorical conception of reading in which present-day reading practices are rolled back into the past. Reading is envisioned as a noiseless interaction of brain and text. The broader supporting institutions, performances, landscapes, and social networks which make reading possible are not considered. In short, reading is construed as a narrowly "literate," silent, and decorporealized activity. The dimensions of oral performance and reenactment which accompany reading are erased from view.

The second assumption is that the meanings extracted from "reading" are largely limited to national boundaries: the reception of Bunyan is consequently imagined as if it were only a matter of examining what happened within the borders of the United Kingdom or, at times, Europe. The idea that the power of reading may precisely revolve around its ability to enable instantaneous and imaginative transnational "travel" is not contemplated. I do not mean only that we can read about far-away places, but that very often our sense of one place is tied up with many others. As a reader of Bunyan said, "I was born nearly 500 miles from Bedford, but, in my boyhood, [I] used to read the 'Pilgrim's Progress' and think of Bunyan and Elstow [the village near Bedford where Bunyan was born] . . . in the same way . . . as I thought of the Holy Land where the prophets wrote and spake" (Wylie 1974: 38). In addition, the way in which Bunyan came to be seen by his readers was inseparable from his circulation in the British Empire.

These ideas of reading circumscribed by nation and medium can be glimpsed from Q. D. Leavis's discussion of Bunyan's success. "[H]ow is it," she asks, "that Bunyan was able to write the most popular book of his age and the most popular of subsequent ages?" (1939: 101). For her the answer lies in Bunyan's use of language heavily implicated with the register of the Authorized Version: "the characteristic effect of reading a passage of Bunyan is a stirring of the blood—the Biblical phrases and cadences evoke overtones, and the peculiarly thrilling quality of the prose is due to this technique which enables a precise particular occasion to draw on the accumulated religious associations of a race. Bunyan's work could no more then Shakespeare's have been done in any other language" (101).

The passage assumes that Bunyan's power derives from a Protestant Englishness (which the passage naturalizes as being synonymous with nationality) and that it depended on his actually being read. This essay questions both of these assumptions. It will argue, firstly, that Bunyan's success depended as well on people who didn't read him, and secondly that part of Bunyan's popularity depended on his construction as a quintessentially English writer. This construction cannot, in turn, be separated from the propagation of the text in the Imperial world and the contemplation of its reception back in the metropolis (Spargo 1997: 102–104).

◦ ◦ ◦

In the Bunyan museum at Bedford, there is a replica of Bunyan's chair. Alongside it is a reproduction of an advertisement from a nineteenth-century

Nonconformist newspaper offering the chairs for sale. According to this advertisement, "No Nonconformist minister can be without one!"

If one is looking for clues to explain the success of *The Pilgrim's Progress*, Bunyan's chair—and the museum in which it is housed—is a good place to start. Located in the church buildings on the site of Bunyan's church, the one-room museum is filled with display cases containing all manner of Bunyan relics and regalia. Pictured in the introductions to any number of editions of *The Pilgrim's Progress*, the relics form a minor canon of their own. Bunyan's stick, "wrought by the cunning hand of an Indian workman" (Thompson and Robjohns 1900: 20); Bunyan's apple corer; Bunyan's ale jug; Bunyan's fiddle—pictures of these routinely punctuate texts about Bunyan. Other display cases contain Victorian objects—jigsaw puzzles, items of crockery, playing cards—commemorating the "Bedford tinker." Framed prints on the walls represent canonized moments from Bunyan's life (such as Bunyan's blind daughter Mary visiting him in prison). Also hanging on the walls are various wooden doors. One is the door of the Bedford jail, in which Bunyan spent twelve years. Another one comes from the church in which he was christened. It contains within itself a smaller opening said to represent the wicket gate of *The Pilgrim's Progress*. The museum also includes a display of translated editions of *The Pilgrim's Progress* opened to reveal their various illustrations. After being conducted around the cramped room, one is taken to the adjoining church to see the commemorative stained-glass windows and door with alto-relievo panels representing episodes from the book (*Souvenir Guide* 1992).

This provincial museum usefully summarizes some of the ways in which one can start thinking about the reception of *The Pilgrim's Progress*. The Congregational church which houses the museum points to the Nonconformist tradition in which the text arose and was subsequently nurtured. Within this tradition, Bunyan's text stood second only to the Bible and was often read in the same devout and intensive way. Yet, as the relics and regalia remind us, the text's meaning and popularity did not depend solely on its being read. One could participate in the idea of the book through making jigsaw puzzles, drinking from commemorative teacups, playing a card game, and adorning one's house with pictures of the author and scenes from the book. At the same time, by looking at pictures from translated foreign editions of *The Pilgrim's Progress* (often made available by mission organizations), one could nurture the assurance that one's own beliefs and tastes were proving ineluctably popular throughout the globe.

Let us expand briefly on these different ways of "consuming" the text. This could be done through many forms of reading. As indicated above, one way of absorbing the text involved intensive, devout reading strategies, since the book was a kind of "shadow" Bible. This could include daily study of selected excerpts, using books like *Half-Hours with Bunyan's Pilgrim's Progress* (Burbridge n.d.) or *Some Daily Thoughts on* The Pilgrim's Progress

(1917). Or one could learn sections off by heart, and reread the text often over many years. The book itself, in its original version and in most evangelical editions, contained marginalia indicating Biblical verses appropriate to the section of text being read. In some instances, these marginalia could mean that one read from two books simultaneously, pausing when necessary in *The Pilgrim's Progress* to page through the Bible to locate the reference given in the margin. More commonly, though, Nonconformist readers would instantly have recognized the verse, which would then have echoed in their heads as they continued their reading (Hancock 1994). This "double-decker" reading could also occur in relation to the songs quoted in the texts. At least one of these subsequently became a famous hymn ("He who would valiant be") and, particularly when the text was read aloud, the songs might be sung. Serious devotees of the text could attend lecture series, acquire commentaries, and, in the latter half of the nineteenth century, read a range of biographies of Bunyan. Introductions to the text often assumed familiarity with these biographies and commentaries and, like other traditions of scholarship, Bunyan books endlessly plagiarized each other in that process through which "commonsense" knowledge becomes established. For the aficionado, *The Pilgrim's Progress* existed at the center of a web of texts stretching at times to the ends of the earth.

Another favored strategy for consuming the text was through reading aloud. While such reading was often directed at children in the home, the widespread institution of Sabbath reading provided an opportunity for adults and children to absorb the text as a family. School and Sunday school were other places where children would have encountered the text in a range of media, such as tracts, wall charts, magic lantern slides, songs, and in one instance a cantata written especially for children. Many would also have received the book as a Sunday school prize or as a gift. For many, *The Pilgrim's Progress* entered the deepest warp and weft of their existence. Robert Blatchford, subsequently editor of *The Clarion* (an early and important Labour newspaper), described Bunyan as "the friend and teacher of my childhood; *The Pilgrim's Progress* was my first book. . . . in my tenth year I knew it almost by heart" (Blatchford 1900: 191). Like many other children, he amused himself enacting scenes from the text. To do this he equipped himself with a two-foot broken stage sword-blade, a paper helmet, and a breastplate. Thus prepared,

> I went out as Greatheart and did deeds of valour and puissance upon an obsolete performing poodle, retired from Astley's Circus, who was good enough to double the parts of Giant Grim and the two lions.
> The stairway to the bedroom was the Hill Difficulty, the dark lobby was the Valley of the Shadow, and often I swam in great fear and peril, and with profuse sputterings, across the black River of Death which lay between kitchen and scullery. The baby also, poor, unconscious mite, played many parts. Now

it was Christiana, and had to be defended against the poodle at the point of the sword; now it was Faithful being tried for his life; now it was Ignorance crossing the Black River in a cradle boat rowed by myself as Vain-Hope; and anon it was Prudence and Charity buckling on my harness before I went out to fight and vanquish Carlo [the poodle] (as Apollyon) in the Vale of Humiliation. (192–93)

This pleasurable internalization of the text meant that many people carried intense and abiding memories of the book. In 1927, one journalist recalled, "I remember with special vividness—I was a little under six years of age—the Sunday afternoon when my father gave me a large volume, bound in green half-morocco and containing 'The Pilgrim's Progress' and 'The Holy War' by John Bunyan with outline illustrations by H. C. Selous" (Roberts 1927: 15).

This recall of the illustrations points to the crucial role that pictures—both in the text and beyond—played in propagating the text's popularity. For many, pictures became mnemonics for episodes in the story. For others, pictures *were* the story. Or, as one nineteenth-century reader said, "If you had ever seen our 'Pilgrim's Progress' with its thumbed, tousled and tattered pages, you would have sworn that it had been read by generations of children, but all torn pages and creases did not really mean that we had read it; they only meant that we were never tired of looking at the pictures" (Birrell 1927: 151).

These pictures—often reproduced outside the text as postcards, framed pictures, and magic lantern slides—in turn became a way in which people could participate in and own a story they might never have read themselves. "I fancy that if the question were put in the next census paper, 'Did you as a child read "The Pilgrim's Progress" or have it read to you?' most honest men and women would have to answer 'no'" (Birrell 1927: 151).

These pictures also provided a vehicle through which translated editions could be interpreted for a "home" audience. Translations had quickly followed the first appearance of the book. They appeared still more rapidly in the nineteenth century, as missionaries prepared translations in conjunction with evangelical literature societies. At first these texts simply included British illustrations. Later they were "indigenized." These pictures were often reproduced in mission literature and the reports of evangelical literature societies. They also formed part of missionary exhibitions. Since the book and all of its episodes were so intimately known, the pictures were generally recognizable to British viewers. This recognition in turn nurtured the notion that others were reading the same story and subscribing to the same ideas: "Even the Caffrarian and Hottentot, the enlightened Greek and Hindoo, the remnant of the Hebrew race, the savage Malay, and the voluptuous Chinese—all have the wondrous narrative in their own language" (Offor 1847: xxv).

What readers in other parts made of these pictures—particularly the early British ones containing "late romantic landscapes, idealized Puritan maidens, abundant lace, and steeple-crowned hats" (Sharrock 1980: 50)—it did not occur to British readers to wonder. In their minds, these pictures signaled that everyone read the same story, with characters "whose names and faces are familiar to the whole world" (Stanley 1874: 51). Japanese illustrations could hence be considered "very characteristic, especially the portraiture of Mr Worldly Wiseman who appears before us as the very ideal of a smug, self-satisfied Pharisee" (Brown n.d.: n.p.). Another commentator spoke of "Apollyon giving a truly Japanese conception of that great enemy" (Green 1899: 172).

Yet each translation occasions a different text. Even a quick glimpse at some translated titles—*The Book of Bunyan, The Traveller, A Heaven's Pilgrimage*—reminds us that there was no one fixed story. (These are the English renditions of the titles of Zulu, Swahili, and Somali versions.) But because the meaning of the text was so tied up with its pictures, many British readers were able to sustain the illusion that one of their most beloved texts could cross untouched the lines of language, culture, and national boundary.

The nature of this British readership was of course not static. In the early part of the nineteenth century the most ardent Bunyan readers would have been Nonconformists, although as a classic among the poor, the book had long since become infantilized and was read by British children of all classes. By the end of the century, Bunyan's status had shifted considerably. He had become a firm symbol of Englishness. His readership had also spread beyond its initial Nonconformist core, although an element of prejudice against this artisan writer never quite disappeared from the upper reaches of society (Bishop of Durham 1928).

This shift in Bunyan's fortune is in turn linked to the nation-building craze of the late 1800s. Driven by a quickening imperial beat, this new sense of national belonging based itself in stronger forms of racialized citizenship underwritten by nostalgic—and often rural—models of history, culture, and lineage (Colley 1992; Colls and Dodd 1986). In addition, the civil disabilities which Nonconformists had experienced also began to disappear, allowing them to participate more enthusiastically in the spectacles of nationality. With his cross-class appeal, Bunyan lent himself admirably to this project of national harmony and soon became a national obsession (Sellers 1977; Binfield 1977).

The unveiling of Bunyan's statue in Bedford in 1874 gives some insight into this growing interest in Bunyan. The idea—and capital—for the statue came from the Duke of Bedford, prompted by his "pious regard" for the memory of the first book given to him as a child by his mother (Wylie 1874: 22). There was a considerable build-up to the event. Special sermons were preached in all Nonconformist and some Established churches (24). Several thousand people attended the unveiling and four thousand children received memorial illustrated copies of *The Pilgrim's Progress* in addition to being fed a ton-and-a-quarter of cake and six hundred gallons of tea. Bunyan relics were on display.

Two related themes dominated the numerous speeches: Bunyan united the nation, and therefore he could claim to be the most quintessentially English writer. *The Pilgrim's Progress* spoke to "peer and peasant" (Wylie 1874: 119), to the "least instructed and the best instructed" (54), to "the humblest peasants and . . . the most fastidious critics" (52), and to Churchman and Dissenter (113–20). The dean of Westminster described his work as "a well of English language and of Christian thought, pure and undefiled" (Stanley 1874: 54).

This theme of Englishness cropped up in other speeches. Bunyan was "more spontaneous than Shakespeare" (Stanley 1874: 36); his language, described elsewhere as "hardbitten, clean-cut Saxon English" (Blatchford 1900: 219), was celebrated as being "of the soil" and "steeped to the very heart in the genius of the people among whom it was born" (Wylie 1874: 77).

This compound sense of Christian Englishness was of course not limited to Britain alone. Through the spread of *The Pilgrim's Progress* this concept had spread across the world. Or, as one speaker at the unveiling said, "Travel whether you choose, along the stream of the Ganges—through the rich groves of Ceylon—by the sparkling shores of Polynesia—or under the broad-leaved bananas of New Zealand, you shall meet thousands who rejoice and tremble over the vicissitudes of 'Christian'" (Birrell 1874: 108).

This theme of Bunyan in the world was taken up by the dean of Westminster: "And when I speak to you of Bunyan in . . . his world-wide aspect, I speak to you no longer as a stranger to the men of Bedford, but as an Englishman to Englishmen; no longer as a Churchman to Dissenters; but as a Christian to Christians, and as a man to men throughout the world." It all amounted to a sense of nationality so extravagant that it overflowed its national limits. Or, as the dean continued, "It is one of the few books which act as a religious bond to the whole of English Christendom. It is, perhaps, [one of the books] which, after the English Bible, has contributed to the common religious culture of the Anglo-Saxon race" (Stanley 1874: 51).

If a sense of nationality could be bigger than the nation, it could also be smaller. One of the subthemes at the unveiling was Bunyan's nature as a man of Bedford. The dean expressed the idea thus: "It is the strength of a country and of a town to have its famous men held in everlasting remembrance. They are the links by which you are bound to the history of your country, and by which the whole consciousness of a great nation is bound together. In your Bedfordshire lanes he doubtless [finds] the original of his 'Slough of Despond.' In the halls and gardens of . . . Haynes and Woburn [stately homes] he may have snatched the first glimpse of 'House Beautiful'" (Stanley 1874: 48).

This allegorical logic in which the local could stand in for the national was to become a crucial plank in the wider reinvention of Bunyan as a national institution. In some instances, this localism was propagated by Bedford citizens keen to extend the cult of Bunyan further afield. In others it arose in tandem with the patriotic notions of ruralism modeled on the landscape of South England and the South Midlandshires, an area into which Bedford just fell. Numerous books were produced which illustrated the extent to which *The Pilgrim's Progress* reflected the landscape and features of Bedford. This in turn led to a guidebook genre describing how one could walk, cycle, and subsequently motor to view the sites of Bunyan and the features of the landscape which appeared in the story (Foster 1907; Thompson and Robjohns 1900; Crockett 1946).

Yet when one turns to the text itself there is surprisingly little description of landscape. What there is relies mainly on stylized and often Biblical descriptions of the environment. This lack of description deterred few. Blatchford, himself an active propagator of ruralism in his books *Britain for the British* and *Merrie England*, said,

> We remember many of Bunyan's scenes because he tells us so little about them. Of the Hill Difficulty he tells us nothing but that it was a hill and steep; of the footpath across the Giant Despair's demesne he tells us little but that it ran hard by a hedge; and we remember these things because we have all seen steep hills and hedgerow paths, and because we at once adopt a hill or a path from the pictures in our memories. (1900: 213)

In another guidebook—Foster's *Bunyan's Country: Studies in the Bedfordshire Topography of* The Pilgrim's Progress (1907)—almost anything can be construed as typically Bedford. At one point, Foster notes that Bunyan observed and loved "Bedfordshire streams, and Bedfordshire roads and lanes and footpaths, Bedfordshire mansions and gardens, and Bedfordshire hills" (29). This love is then linked to a passage in *The Pilgrim's Progress:* "at a great distance he saw a most pleasant mountainous country, beautified with woods, vineyards, fruits of all sorts, flowers also, with springs and fountains, very delectable to behold." Bedford is, of course, an area with few mountains and no vineyards. But few were detained by such minor impediments in their quest to "write" the meaning of Bunyan into the landscape.

This sense of localized nationalism was to expand like concentric ripples from its center. By 1948, another guide book, *Bunyan's England: A Tour with the Camera in the Footsteps of the Immortal Dreamer* (Crockett) speaks of Bunyan's grave in London: "he rests in the Metropolis of the British Commonwealth . . . one of the noblest creations of the British race" (2).

This image of Bunyan—one of the key nodes of English culture—radiating out from the Midland shires into the imperial world was a common one. Elsewhere he was referred to as "a light [shining] forth . . . to enlighten the habitable globe" (Offor 1847: xxv). This spreading sense of Englishness in turn allowed many to think of Bunyan as being both English and universal at the same time.

This sense of Bunyan's English reputation's linkage to his imperial presence has largely been lost. Today many studies of Bunyan consider him only within national boundaries. His presence in the wider world is recognized, but it remains cut off from the mainstream of Bunyan studies. This paper has attempted to reestablish that link, to remind us that the reinvention of Bunyan as a national institution is inseparable from his dissemination into the Empire.

In this sense, the paper has attempted to demonstrate what we lose if we continue to think in area-studies pockets. If we think of Bunyan only in Europe, an entire dimension of his reception disappears. If we think of him in both Africa and Europe, that dimension is restored. Such ringfencing of the world has further consequences in that particular topics are prioritized for different regions. Hence questions of orality are seldom deployed in relation to recent European cultural history, being seen as a topic which "naturally" belongs in African studies. However, if we refuse this logic, we can gain new insights into the factors which secured Bunyan's extraordinary success. By doing so, we will also begin to liberate words like "read" and "reception" from their current imprisonment in narrow conceptions of literacy and nationality. The beneficiaries of such a move will be those with an interest in seeing knowledge released from what Gyan Prakash has called its "disciplining as area-studies" (1995: 12).

BIBLIOGRAPHY

Barber, Karin. 1995. "Literacy, Improvisation, and the Public in Yoruba Popular Theatre." In *The Pressures of the Text: Orality, Texts, and the Telling of Tales,* ed. Stewart Brown, 6–27. Birmingham: Centre of West African Studies, University of Birmingham.

Binfield, Clyde. 1977. *So down to Prayer: Studies in English Nonconformity, 1780–1920.* London: Dent.

Birrell, Augustine. 1927. "John Bunyan Today." *The Bookman* 73, no. 435.

———. 1928. "Links of Empire—Books (IX)." *The Empire Review* 47, no. 235.

Birrell, C. M. 1874. "Bunyan's Personal Pilgrimage." In *The Book of the Bunyan Festival: A Complete Record of the Proceedings at the Unveiling of the Statue,* ed. W. H. Wylie, 13–21. London: James Clarke and Christian World Office.

Bishop of Durham. 1928. "An Anglican Reflection on Bunyan's Career." In *The Review of the Churches,* n.s. 3.

Blatchford, Robert. 1900. *My Favourite Books.* London: Walter Scott.

Brooker, Peter, and Peter Widdowson. 1986. "A Literature for England." In *Englishness: Politics and Culture, 1880–1920,* ed. Robert Colls and Philip Dodd, 116–63. London: Croom Helm.

Brown, John. N.d. *Bunyan's Home.* London: Ernest Nister.

Burbridge, John. N.d. *Half-Hours with Bunyan's Pilgrim's Progress.* Liverpool: J. A. Thompson.

Colley, Linda. 1992. *Britons: Forging a Nation, 1707–1837.* New Haven: Yale University Press.

Colls, Robert. 1986. "Englishness and the Political Culture." In *Englishness: Politics and Culture, 1880–1920,* ed. Robert Colls and Philip Dodd, 29–61. London: Croom Helm.

Colls, Robert, and Philip Dodd, eds. 1986. *Englishness: Politics and Culture, 1880–1920.* London: Croom Helm.

Crockett, Bernard C. 1948. *Bunyan's England: A Tour with the Camera in the Footsteps of the Immortal Dreamer.* Luton: Leagrave Press.

Finnegan, Ruth. 1990. "What Is Orality, If Anything?" *Byzantine and Modern Greek Studies* 14, 130–49.

Foster, Albert J. 1907. *Bunyan's Country: Studies in the Bedfordshire Topography of* The Pilgrim's Progress. London: H. Virtue.

Greaves, Richard L. 1983. "Bunyan through the Centuries: Some Reflections." *English Studies* 64, no. 2, 113–21.

Green, Samuel. 1899. *The Story of the Religious Tract Society for 100 Years.* London: Religious Tract Society.

Hancock, Maxine. 1994. "Bunyan as Reader: The Record of *Grace Abounding.*" *Bunyan Studies* 5, 68–84.

Hewitt, Gordon. 1949. *Let the People Read: A Short History of the United Society for Christian Literature.* London: Lutterworth.

Hofmeyr, Isabel. 1995. "'Wailing for Purity': Oral Studies in Southern African Studies." *African Studies* 54, no. 2, 16–31.

Howkins, Alan. 1986. "The Discovery of Rural England." In *Englishness: Politics and Culture, 1880–1920,* ed. Robert Colls and Philip Dodd, 62–88. London: Croom Helm.

Julien, Eileen. 1992. *African Novels and the Question of Orality.* Bloomington: Indiana University Press.

Keeble, N. H. 1988. "Of Him Thousands Daily Sing: Bunyan and His Reputation." In *John Bunyan: Conventicle and Parnassus: Tercentenary Essays,* ed. N. H. Keeble, 241–63. Oxford: Clarendon.

Law, Alice. 1927. "Some Aspects of *The Pilgrim's Progress.*" *Empire Review* 46, no. 318, 22–36.

Leavis, Q. D. 1939. *Fiction and the Reading Public.* London: Chatto and Windus.

Macaulay, T. B. M. (Lord). 1910. "Bunyan, John." In *Encyclopaedia Britannica,* 11th ed., vol. 4, 803–806. New York: Encyclopaedia Britannica.

Offor, George, ed. 1847. *The Pilgrim's Progress from This World to That Which Is to Come,* by John Bunyan. London: Haddon.

Prakash, Gyan. 1995. "After Colonialism." Introduction to *After Colonialism: Imperial Histories and Postcolonial Displacements,* ed. Gyan Prakash, 3–17. Princeton: Princeton University Press.

Roberts, Ellis. 1927. "Bunyan in His Times." *The Bookman* 73, no. 435, 715–20.

Sellers, Ian. 1977. *Nineteenth-Century Nonconformity.* London: Edward Arnold.

Sharrock, Roger. 1980. "Life and Story in *The Pilgrim's Progress.*" In The Pilgrim's Progress: *Critical and Historical Views,* ed. Vincent Newey, 49–68. Liverpool: Liverpool University Press.

Some Daily Thoughts on The Pilgrim's Progress. 1917. London: Churchman.

A Souvenir Guide to the John Bunyan Museum, Library, and Bunyan Meeting Free Church. 1992. N.p.: Fidelity Colour.

Spargo, Tamsin. 1997. *The Writing of John Bunyan.* Aldershot: Ashgate.

Stanley, A. P. 1874. "The Character of Bunyan: Local, Ecclesiastical, Universal." In *The Book of the Bunyan Festival: A Complete Record of the Proceedings at the Unveiling of the Statue,* ed. W. H. Wylie, 22–31. London: James Clarke and Christian World Office.

Stevenson, Robert Louis. 1912. *Expositions from* The Pilgrim's Progress *with Illustrative Quotations from Bunyan's Minor Works.* London: A. and C. Black.

Thompson, Edward P. 1975. *The Making of the English Working Class.* Harmondsworth: Penguin.

Thompson, John, and Sidney Robjohns. 1900. *Bunyan's Country.* Bedford: J. Thompson.

Venables, Edmund. 1888. *Life of John Bunyan.* London: Walter Scott.

Wylie, W. H., ed. 1874. *The Book of the Bunyan Festival: A Complete Record of the Proceedings at the Unveiling of the Statue.* London: James Clarke and Christian World Office.

4

The Dialogue between Academic and Community History in Nigeria

E. J. Alagoa

The history of oral historiography may be completing a circle in Nigeria. After the halting efforts in the eighteenth century of the Efik trader Antera Duke in Calabar, and of the Igbo ex-slave Olaudah Equiano in Britain, oral histories by Nigerians flowered from the end of the nineteenth through the first half of the twentieth century. In northern Nigeria, the *Kano Chronicle* exemplifies the genre of *tarikh* that featured the transcription of the oral tradition in the Islamic tradition of historiography. Sometimes the writers were Christian missionaries or had been influenced by them, such as the Reverend Samuel Johnson of the Yoruba (1921). Often, as with Jacob Egharevba of Benin, the initial narrative was in the local language. Egharevba's history of Benin, first written in Edo in 1934, was only translated into English in 1956 when it was published by the historians at the University of Ibadan, who went on to award an honorary doctorate to the author. In 1956, Professor Dike's pioneering academic history of European commercial impact on the Niger Delta city-states was published, followed closely by Biobaku's powerful history of the Egba in 1957.

These works opened a period of expansion of academic historiography in the western tradition, in the context of Dike's and Biobaku's strong advocacy of the use of oral sources. The process was aided by the big government- and foundation-funded interdisciplinary research projects started by Dike and Biobaku for Benin and the Yoruba respectively. But these projects yielded less fruit than had been expected. From the 1970s through the 1980s, government and other funding for research into oral traditions declined disastrously. The circle has begun to close, however, as the communities being studied have partially taken over the funding of academic oral history research and writing. Thus, Professor Okon Edet Uya's history of the Oron people in 1984 was substantially funded largely by the Oron Development Union. Okon acknowledged the efforts of local nonacademic professional historians from the 1920s on, to whom he dedicated his work.

This essay attempts to report and analyze, in some detail, my own recent experience of writing the history of an ethnic community from research over a period extending thirty years, with the backing and participation of the community. I believe that we must learn something about relevance and other matters of interest to all academic oral historians from this exercise in the open discussion of community history all the way from research to publication.

I

The process of narrowing the gap between academic history and local community history has not yet been fully appreciated in Africa, and is even less acknowledged outside. Ignorance of the growing accommodation between academia and the community partially accounts for some of the criticisms of African historiography by Ranger (1976) and Jewsiewicki (1986), among others. Ranger discovered "a widespread disenchantment with African historiography inside Africa itself; a widespread feeling of its artificiality and distance from real issues" (17). Ranger's "real issues" were defined from outside Africa by "historians of Europe, America and the rest of the world" (21), and from inside Africa by "younger students and intellectuals" (22). The urban and rural populations who constitute the largest audience and consumers of oral historiography were not included in this critical analysis of African historiography. The focus of this essay, in contrast, is specifically to discover the views of this popular audience on what constitute real issues, and what is a usable African past.

Jewsiewicki too believed in "essential questions," the counterpart of Ranger's "real issues," but, in his case, the questions were conceived as having been raised by "the African peasant." The questions were also conceived as addressed to "university historians," who took no notice, and the result was a "dialogue of the deaf" (1986: 10–11). Rather than deal with these essential questions, the "university historians" were busy constructing "monuments of African academic history." Accordingly, university historians were unfavorably compared to "historical narrators" who perform in city bars and village squares for "historical actors" (9–10). Jewsiewicki, in contrast to Ranger, placed the urban and village population at the center of the historical enterprise. The problem was that he observed no dialogue between the academic historians of Africa and this audience of peasant community actors. Indeed, he was skeptical of the ability of the African academic historian to "maintain a discourse responsible to local needs and demands" (17).

The Nigerian case suggests to me that the seeds of genuine dialogue between academic historians and local communities have already been sown in Africa, although academic historians have yet to replicate, and perhaps cannot replicate, the communication tool kit of the traditional narrator (Alagoa 1989). Academic historians may be expected, in time, to develop the words and messages appropriate for the consciousness of those with whom they are locked in critical dialogue.

The possibilities of a fruitful dialogue between university and community historians, the depth and nature of such a dialogue beyond the outward transfer of funds from the community to the academic, are among the questions that may be answered by the story of my encounter with the Okpoama community of the Niger Delta. In what ways and to what extent did the community desire to influence the scholar's account, and was it able to do so? How can the scholar remain faithful to professional canons of objectivity while maintaining a discourse responsible to local needs and demands? I plan to tell a story first from the point of view of the academic, and second from that of the community, in order to derive conclusions about and understandings of the practice of African oral historiography.

II

My umbilical links to the Okpoama community provide my best qualifications to serve as historian of the community. My mother went to her mother's home in Ewoama for the delivery of her second son, just as she had done for the first. Her father, then chief of the royal house of Obasi, was not far away, at Okpoama. Indeed, Ewoama lies at the roots of Okpoama history, the site of Saikiripogu, on which Ewoama is located, being one of the principal ancestral settlements of the founders of Okpoama. The name Ewoama, "New Town," itself derives from its current inhabitants' migration back to the ancient site from Okpoama as recently as 1873. Accordingly, my links to the Okpoama community are strong, deriving as they do from both maternal grandparents. Some of my earliest knowledge of Okpoama and Ewoama history came from my grandparents while I was a child. I could, in fact, trace my credentials as a local historian to my grandmother in particular, a priestess, midwife, and herbalist, who was recognized within the community as an expert in oral historical traditions and religious lore and as an accomplished teller of folk tales.

My paternal affiliation is to the larger Nembe community, to which Okpoama is linked by linguistic, cultural, and ambivalent historical ties. However, the founder of my paternal lineage, Chief Joseph Alagoa, was the nephew of King Obasi of Okpoama, at whose court he had been nurtured before returning to Nembe to assume leadership of his matrilineage. Since, as an adult, I have principally borne a paternal identity, I may be identified negatively as an outsider, as well as positively as an insider, in Okpoama. In my practice of local historiography, my instincts, roused at Ewoama by my grandmother, were fed by the instruction of a Nembe history teacher at the elementary school in Nembe. My first book, *The Small Brave City-State: A History of Nembe-Brass in the Niger Delta*, acknowledged this teacher (Alagoa 1964b: vii). My authorship of a local history from a Nembe point of view at the beginning of my academic career was, in fact, one of the acts that gave me an image as an outsider among the younger elements in Okpoama. What these youths do not realize, however, is that my first publication in an international journal, *Africa*, was my account of the unique *idu* creator festival of Okpoama (Alagoa 1964a), before I wrote a history of Nembe.

My research on the history of Okpoama, then, began at the beginning of my academic career in the early 1960s. My first informant and guide was the late James Berena, who bore the title of town clerk or secretary. Through him I had direct and easy access to the political and religious leadership, collecting traditions from the king (*amanyanabo*), chiefs, priests, and cultural leaders. The tapes and information base I created during the period of my field research in 1964—my base then was Madison, Wisconsin—are clearly identified in my book *People of the Fish and Eagle: A History of Okpoama in the Eastern Niger Delta* (Alagoa 1996).

My second period of research was 1967–1976, based in the Institute of African Studies, University of Ibadan, with full funding from sources outside the community. During the Nigerian civil war (1967–1970), information was gathered outside the community from refugees in Ibadan and Lagos. After 1970, it was possible to carry out research in the field, and a most fertile occasion for cultural research was provided by the idu festival organized at my urging (and with my partial funding) in 1972. This festival is now known in the community as *beke idu* (the white idu) because of its recording on film and tape by a team of researchers from the Institute of African Studies, University of Ibadan, as well as by a European visitor.

The third and final period of research was in 1988, with principal funding from the Okpoama Development Union, Port Harcourt, an association of Okpoama men and women living and working outside the community, but with a home branch located in Okpoama. The president and secretary of the Union approached me at the University of Port Harcourt in 1987, asking me to consider writing a history of Okpoama. I explained my commitment to the task, as evidenced by my earlier research program, which was stalled for the moment by the drying up of public funding for academic research. Eventually it was agreed that the Union would fund the final phase of field research. I eventually met with a six-member History Committee of the Union, which supplied a list of informants, funds for their transportation and entertainment, a cassette tape recorder with tapes and batteries, and stationery. The home branch provided material and moral support.

It may be noted that the first and third periods of research were both carried out within the community. Informant historians were selected through community sources such as the Development Union. Recorded interviews with individuals were watched by interested audiences, or even by authorized spokesmen of lineage or cultural groups. No secret sessions were held. The process of recording remained as open as possible throughout the first and third periods of research. It was only in the second period that informant historians were largely on their own, during interviews separated from the community and its direct influence.

By the close of 1988, the major field research had been completed, and the manuscript was finished in the course of my 1993–1994 sabbatical leave at the University of Ibadan. A copy was handed over to the History Committee in September 1993. A banker member of the community, Chief Banigo-Ogbulu, offered to underwrite the cost of publication by the Isengi Communications Ltd. Press of his All States Trust Bank. It was at this stage that all the latent hostilities and suspicions of the project came out into the open, leading to delays in the publication process. Only after the issues raised by community activists had been resolved through three public symposia, bringing me together with community leaders and interest groups at Okpoama in May 1995, could the publication process be resumed.

III

What were these community fears and suspicions, and what their sources? And how were they allayed until publication became imminent? How deep and effective were the channels of communication and the processes of dialogue?

The History Committee of the Okpoama Development Union operated effectively only up to a point. The members were full-time workers and could not always attend meetings. I had hoped that the committee would assist in the process of data collection, but this proved unworkable in practice. During field visits, however, the home branch members attended recording sessions and even accompanied me on trips to outlying villages. Since the Port Harcourt committee was unable to keep in constant touch with me, they were apparently unable to provide the Union with the monthly briefs required; the only reports the Union received may have been the ones I submitted after every field trip. In July 1992, the Union requested a report, since "no report has been received from the committee" and the Union had "lost track of progress made so far." It was only after I submitted the completed manuscript in September 1993 that the Union again wrote, in December, asking to review the manuscript. Similar requests came from the Okpoama Youth Movement, from the Okpoama Development Union (Home Branch), from a chief, and from a professor of engineering and former president of the Okpoama Development Union (Port Harcourt Branch). Those from the Youth Movement and the Home Branch were couched in particularly offensive language, even threatening court action if their demands were not met!

There were many overlaps in the objections raised to the manuscript and the demands made. Complainants insisted that the histories and the list of kings of neighboring communities included in the text and appendices be expunged. The former president concluded that "only the Okpoama versions of these [histories] ought to be mentioned" and "the Okpoama viewpoint is what is to be emphasized" in every other instance. Resistance to these parallel histories derived from the many territorial disputes dating from the colonial period, and still subsisting in courts, between these neighboring communities and Okpoama. The fear was that the appearance of versions different from the Okpoama account would result in "irreparable damage . . . to the interests of Okpoama."

Second, all community representatives resented any statement remotely capable of being interpreted as conferring a leadership role on Nembe. The youth loudly denounced me, accusing me of "insulting, humiliating and relegating Okpoama to the 'dust,' suppressing her legitimate rights." One communication stated as a corollary that I had represented Nembe in "an upgraded capacity." These violent feelings against Nembe were understandable in the light of recent events that had led to the withdrawal of Okpoama from the Brass Divisional Council of Chiefs. Dominated by Nembe chiefs, the council had proceeded to recognize certain persons from Ewoama—presented to it by a small faction in that community—as chiefs, against the wishes of Okpoama. This matter has, in fact, resulted in violent confrontations, leading to the destruction of a large part of the Ewoama community and to a government commission of inquiry. The Okpoama community considered the action of the Nembe chiefs in this matter most insulting, and became hypersensitive to any historical reference to Nembe leadership.

Third, I was accused of underrating and suppressing the heroic deeds of the ancestors. This complaint came from one member of the King Goli and King Obu lineage group. He complained that I had not given sufficient prominence to these kings, who had fought wars in the eighteenth and nineteenth centuries, the last being against the British in 1895.

Fourth, one letter complained that I should be held responsible for the fact that the Rivers State government had not yet accorded official recognition to the king of Okpoama in its classification of chiefs. My alleged responsibility derived from my membership in a government panel commissioned to report on the chieftaincy institution, and from my book on the history of Nembe (Alagoa 1964b).

Fifth, the former president wished to see a history which devoted primary attention to the activities of development unions and similar associations and the Christian religion, a history that would pay little or no heed to the role played by the traditional religion, in spite of his own admission that this religion had "shaped the destiny of Okpoama"—in his view, for ill.

The symposia arranged by the publisher, under the auspices of the Okpoama/Ewoama Council of Chiefs, including representatives of every lineage and house, youth associations, and other groups, proved an ideal forum for these and other views to be openly debated, after the manuscript had been made available to each group in advance.

Each of the three symposia was moderated by the chairman of the Ok-poama/Ewoama Council of Chiefs, a retired officer of the colonial Nigerian army. He made opening addresses in which he appealed for fairness and decorum. My opening addresses merely stated my professional liability for views and interpretations based on evidence fully cited in the manuscript, and my readiness to accept correction when superior evidence was presented. After this, the chairman called on each lineage and house leader, association, and other recognized interest group to raise issues in a systematic manner, going through the manuscript from beginning to end.

It proved surprisingly easy to convince the chiefs and community leaders that stating only the Okpoama viewpoint on issues was not in the best interests of Okpoama: that community interests were better served by an account able to persuade a third party of the author's commitment to objective standards through the inclusion of all known versions of events. However, all statements that the complainants considered derogatory or insulting were removed. Most charges of suppressing the heroism of particular ancestors were set aside by the majority of participants. In fact, there were counter-protests alleging exaggeration of the achievements of certain ancestors in accounts that had been derived from their descendants. The fourth accusation, holding me responsible for government inaction and injustice, was not brought up in any of the symposia. Earlier correspondence had made clear that the panel on which I served had presented to the government all the evidence necessary to classify chieftaincies in all communities in the state, including those in Okpoama. Indeed, the youth proved much less vocal in the presence of the legitimate community leaders than they had been in their letters to me.

The balancing of differing group expectations and viewpoints resulted in relatively few corrections or additions. References to the "Nembe kingdom" were changed to "Nembe area," "Nembe people," etc. The section on the history of the traditional religion proved acceptable to the majority of the home-branch population. The Christians, however, updated the list of church agents in the appendices. New lists of presidents of the Okpoama Development Union, and of new chieftaincies and their incumbents, were added. The histories of neighboring communities, supplied by their own informants, and the lists of their kings were retained. These symposia proved instructive and corrected some factual errors that would have been embarrassing had they been left to appear in print.

IV

What, then, were the issues and questions of interest to the community? I will first outline my own views, followed by those of the community as they were presented in the memorandum from the professor of engineering and long-time president of the Okpoama Development Union, as those views were moderated by the participants at the symposia. Professor Beredugo did, in fact, represent community views rather than those of academia. He had been appointed official spokesman for the Okpoama community at the government commission of inquiry into the disturbances at Ewoama, although he was unavoidably absent from both the commission hearings and the symposia.

People of the Fish and Eagle: A History of Okpoama in the Eastern Niger Delta was designed to be "an exercise in the definition of identity" (Alagoa 1996: ii). The use of community totems in the title was intended to penetrate community consciousness directly and immediately. The fish identifies the community at its economic base, the eagle at its religious; both succeed in distinguishing Okpoama from its neighbors in the Nembe area. The definition of identity at the community level was expected to reach down to the individual, whose identity and confidence derives, at least in part, from group identity. Accordingly, I conceived of the history of Okpoama as something in which I was deeply implicated, as a part of my self-identification and the self-definition of "many individual men, women and youth" of Okpoama (ii). I believed it was possible to define identity by "defining the character of the community" and delineating its "beliefs, hopes, aspirations and frustrations" (ii). This ambitious agenda was to be accomplished in seven chapters, eight appendices, three maps, and six photographs.

Chapter 1, "Old Images—The Heritage of the Past," outlined the images that the community has created over the years to identify itself, contrasting them with images of the community used by its neighbors to identify it. The community drum praise poems identify it as the town of "vigilant fisher folk," tough as the bite of the "red snapper," and the people refer to their guardian deity as the "god of Fishtown." The eagle, of course, is the totem of the god *Kalaorowei* and therefore sacred to all Okpoama people. These two symbols—the fish and the eagle—appear in color on the front cover of the book.

Chapter 2, "Movements and Settlements," set out the traditions of origin and migration. A summary of archaeological excavations at the ancient site of Saikiripogu was provided, along with the radiocarbon dates that form the basis of the early chronology of Okpoama history. But chapter 2 became the focus of controversy, since the histories of other settlements on the same island had to be given to indicate the relative antiquity of human habitation there.

Chapter 3, "Elders, Priests, and Kings," was a straight account of the historical development of the political system. The traditions indicated that the earliest names on the list of kings were, probably, the oldest men, in a gerontocratic system; they were followed by rulers who achieved their positions through the hierarchy of priests of the guardian god. In the mid–twentieth century political leadership was clearly distinguished from the religious hierarchy, under pressure from youth educated by Christian missionaries.

Chapter 4, "Houses," presented a social and political history of the lineages and groups constituting the community. It was the section of the book in which individuals would hope to be able to locate themselves and identify their ancestors.

Chapter 5, "Culture, Customs, and Institutions," covered in historical perspective the major religious, social, and artistic institutions and associations peculiar to the Okpoama people in the Nembe and Niger Delta environment.

Chapter 6, "Economy and Environment," related the history of the community to its environment and outlined the ways in which the Okpoama have been able to make a living from the resources of the land and water. The excavations at Saikiripogu provided evidence for taking the reconstructions back to about A.D. 1000.

Chapter 7, "New Images—Impact of the External World," summarized the changes effected by the arrival of the Anglican mission along with European trade in the nineteenth century, by the introduction of Western Christian education, which created a new elite responsible for the development of youth associations and other organizations in recent times, and by the operations of the multinational oil corporations within the tough Nigerian political system.

The appendices listed rulers of Okpoama and of the neighboring communities, the members of various priesthoods, leaders of the elite Sekiapu Masquerade Association and of the new chieftaincies, and presidents of the Okpoama Development Union. A list of "plants and their uses" illustrated community knowledge of the environment and how to use it. There were maps of Okpoama town, of the immediate area, and of the Nembe District. Photographs showed ancient bronzes recovered from the Christian mission site, regalia, a chief's chinaware from the period of the Atlantic trade, and a variety of cultural artifacts.

To what extent were the issues and questions covered by this narrative considered relevant, usable, or adequate by the community? We have the summary prepared by Professor Beredugo as a convenient enumeration of community expectations of an adequate history. Chapter 2 was the first target of attack, as containing inappropriate or irrelevant material in the form of the histories and lists of kings (appendix 2) of neighboring communities. This was also a common objection at the symposia, but was eventually resolved by my arguments in their favor. Second, the professor objected to the degree of attention given to traditional religion—"Juju worship" or "Jujuism," as he termed it. This position was not shared by the majority of participants at the symposia. Indeed, additional details of rituals and festivals were offered for inclusion. It stands to reason that Professor Beredugo, who is also a knight of the Anglican Church of Nigeria, would take the position he took. Third, he demanded expanded treatment of the history of unions and associations that have spearheaded the movement to situate Okpoama in the modern world. Fourth, he demanded enhanced attention to the following:

Okpoama's participation in the overseas slave and palm-oil trade; its contribution to the war of 1895, in which the Nembe-speaking peoples combined to fight the British in a last-ditch effort to ward off colonial rule; the migration to Ewoama from Okpoama in 1873; and litigation against neighboring communities for rights to land, "as a way of putting the record straight." Finally, he demanded a listing of persons who played a significant role in the development of the community. This was intended to "provide role models for the younger generation."

As a community spokesman, Professor Beredugo derived this listing of issues and questions suitable for a community history from his concept of history as "a veritable tool, which can be used to unravel the crisis of identity in a people." My appeal to the community at the symposia was to consider my narrative in its totality, not in bits and pieces, in the light of this same commitment to the definition of community identity.

V

My dialogue with the Okpoama, Niger Delta, Nigeria, taught me a number of lessons out of which I wish to offer a few general insights and inquiries, the majority of them derived from discussions at Bellagio and Ann Arbor.

1. A mutually rewarding dialogue between the African academic historian and his or her community is possible, and is already going on within Africa at varying levels of effectiveness. The degree of effectiveness would rise, and the dialogue would receive greater notice, if the academic historians, African or Africanist, would acknowledge the expertise of local historians and the basic rationality, diversity, and wisdom residing within the communities they study. This calls for a greater measure of humility among scholars than is normally evident in their patronizing eagerness to lay down universal laws.

2. Both African historians and their communities work with issues and questions which they consider relevant to their contemporary conditions and circumstances. These issues and questions are not always articulated, but it would be presumptuous to prescribe particular issues and questions as appropriate to all communities or all historians. It would be best to accept the general principle of dialogue, so that each situation throws up the relevant issues and questions. Here, again, the underlying value of humility appears. The academic historians of Africa, insiders and outsiders, must realize that they have not mastered everything about African historiography; we are still learning.

3. By what standards or principles was "truth" determined in this dialogue? I believe my earlier definition, derived from proverb texts, applied (Alagoa 1994: 20): "direct eyewitness testimony," "confirmation by a second witness," and "the probability of the account or claim from 'the nature of things.'" In a crunch, the consensus of those assembled carried the day.

4. The meaning of silence must be considered. There were matters which some community interests wished passed over in silence. The lineage claiming King Akirigbo as progenitor asked that references to his sobriquet "the wife-beater" be removed, but was overruled by the majority, who had heard it passed down for generations in the traditions. Dialogue brought several such instances into the open, through the interpretation of material objects in ancestral shrines or of fixed literary texts (such as proverbs, drum praise poetry, etc.). The academic historian generally seeks ways of breaking silences, but must remain sensitive to them.

5. Does dialogue reveal the academic historian to be impartial, partial, or just ignorant? Dialogue provides academic historians with opportunities to negotiate their position on the basis of the stature accorded them by the perceived authority of the written word they represent. So much stature may accrue to the historian that the community may be seen to be trying to recruit him or her as an agent for communicating its perspective of the past: hence the violence of some of the controversy, which was fed also by latent suspicion and fear of the written word.

6. Might the insistence on dialogue be a form of idealization? Is it possible for all scholars to engage in dialogue? Is it, for example, possible for junior or female scholars to engage in dialogue with a community? Is the potential for violence not excessive, considering the high stakes for which some of the interest groups contend?

The advocacy of dialogue cannot resolve all the problems of oral historiography. It is intended simply to return history to its owners and close the gap of communication between the academic historian and the community to which the history he or she writes belongs. The method cannot be bound by age or by sex, depending as it does principally on the skills of empathy, persuasion, and communication. There is, of course, a potential for violence, in the face of which the scholar must be prepared to operate. Dialogue is not an easy or risk-free enterprise.

7. Controversy does not cease after a dialogue establishes an "approved text." It continues, proving the limitations, even fallacy, of the view that the written word is authoritative, permanent, and final, in total opposition to the oral tradition. Indeed, the approved text is an oral text reproduced in a new form. I wish to acknowledge, finally, that the "approved" authoritative text of *People of the Fish and Eagle: A History of Okpoama in the Eastern Niger Delta* remains a contested text within the Okpoama community.

BIBLIOGRAPHY

Alagoa, E. J. 1964a. "Idu: a creator festival at Okpoma (Brass) in the Niger Delta." *Africa* 34, no, 1: 1–8.
———. 1964b. *The Small Brave City-State: A History of Nembe-Brass in the Niger*

Delta. Madison: University of Wisconsin Press and Ibadan: Ibadan University Press.

———. 1989. "Communicating African History." *Storia della Storiografia* 15: 75–89.

———. 1994. "An African Philosophy of History in the Oral Tradition." In *Paths towards the Past: African Historical Essays in Honor of Jan Vansina,* ed. Robert W. Harms et al., 15–25. Atlanta: African Studies Association Press.

———. 1996. *People of the Fish and Eagle: A History of Okpoama in the Eastern Niger Delta.* Lagos and Port Harcourt: Isengi Communications.

Biobaku, Saburi O. 1957. *The Egba and Their Neighbors, 1842–1872.* Oxford: Clarendon.

Dike, K. Onwuka. 1956. *Trade and Politics in the Niger Delta, 1830–1885: An Introduction to the Economic and Political History of Nigeria.* Oxford: Clarendon.

Egharevba, J. U. 1969. *A Short History of Benin.* 3rd ed.; first published 1934. Ibadan: Ibadan University Press.

Equiano, Olaudah. 1967. *Equiano's Travels: His Autobiography; The Interesting Narrative of the Life of Olaudah Equiano or Gustavus Vassa the African.* 1789. Reprint, ed. Paul Edwards, London: Heinemann.

Jewsiewicki, Bogumil. 1986. "One Historiography or Several? A Requiem for Africanism." Introduction to *African Historiographies: What History for Which Africa?* ed. Bogumil Jewsiewicki and David Newbury, 9–17. New York: Sage.

Johnson, Rev. Samuel. 1921. *The History of the Yorubas from the Earliest Times to the Beginning of the British Protectorate.* Ed. O. Johnson. Lagos: C. M. S. Bookshops.

Ranger, T. O. 1976. "Towards a Usable African Past." In *African Studies since 1945: A Tribute to Basil Davidson,* ed. Christopher Fyfe, 17–30. London: Longman.

Uya, Okon Edet. 1984. *A History of Oron People of the Lower Cross River Basin.* Oron: Manson Publishing.

The Birth of the Interview

THE THIN AND THE FAT OF IT

Abdullahi A. Ibrahim

Once upon a time there was an Igbo man called Okonkwo. He ardently desired to make it big in his community, and succeeded in earning titles and respect. Okonkwo's success was remarkable for a son of a poet, a worthless category among the Igbo. His father died of an abominable disease and was buried in the Evil Forest, the dumping ground of failures and the diseased. In strictly observing the hard and fast rules of his culture in his difficult path to success, Okonkwo was blinded to his culture's core values. Against the advice of his closest friend, he participated in the ritual killing of his adopted son, whose death had been signaled by the oracles. Okonkwo's own son was alienated by this heartlessness.

Okonkwo was banished to his mother's lineage for committing another murder, a "female" crime: killing a relative inadvertently. He was counting the days until he could return to his community and continue his rise to glory. Just before his return, the British advanced from the African coast into the interior of modern-day Nigeria, imposing colonial rule. Missionaries came in their footsteps to spread Christianity. The administrative and spiritual impact of this invasion precipitated a political crisis in Okonkwo's village. While Okonkwo pushed for confronting the occupiers, others, who recognized that the Igbo were no match for the British, were inclined to give up. Okonkwo's son even converted to Christianity. Okonkwo called these hesitators "women." He was unrelenting in his insistence on the Igbo's need to defeat their enemies. Realizing that most Igbo were inclined to resign themselves to their fate as subjects of the new colonial power, Okonkwo took the fight upon himself. He ended up killing a messenger working for the British district commissioner. Forlorn, he committed suicide.

When the district commissioner, not knowing of Okonkwo's suicide, came to arrest him for murder, Okonkwo's friend took him to the tree from which his body was dangling. Another friend asked the district commissioner to do them a favor by burying Okonkwo, because, he said, the Igbo were forbidden by their culture to bury a man who had taken his own life. Amused, the district commissioner took note of this Igbo custom with the idea of including it in his projected book, titled *The Pacification of the Primitive Tribes of the Lower Niger.* In recording this custom as a pristine Igbo practice, he wrote himself and the powers he represented out of a situation they had brought about. Okonkwo's death and burial can only be understood if the British invasion is taken into consideration. In a typical case of "imperialist nostalgia" (Rosaldo 1989: 70), the district commissioner established his innocence at the same time that he recorded for posterity what he had destroyed. Through this nostalgia, a guilty colonial agent was transformed into a blameless bystander.

Sixty years after the events described above, an Igbo writer, Chinua Achebe, wrote *Things Fall Apart,* a novel about Okonkwo's trial and tribulations. The book was an immediate success. In the novel, Okonkwo's death is depicted as a "compulsory suicide," which, in Norma Field's words, suggests the dark mixing of coercion and consent (1991: 67).

In the light of this preamble, this paper investigates the ethnographic interview as a data-generation technology that installs a regime of truth (Foucault 1980) for the governance of people. In other words, the interview will be viewed as a technique designed to map the political body "so as to render it knowable and amenable to social regularization" (Bennett 1995: 64). Briefly, the paper seeks to address the wider concern of the governmentalization of culture.

The paper will consist of three parts. First, it will discuss an array of views on fieldwork and interview which underline the relation of power and knowledge in ethnography. It will demonstrate that ethnography, an enterprise that started on the heels of colonialism, so that the will to know and the will to surveil and administer intertwined at its birth,[1] used the interview as a technique for the regulation of data in order to better know and govern the colonized. Second, the paper will argue that by using the interview technique, whose origins in the governmentalization of culture rendered it a bad conductor of information, ethnography became a process of "learned ignorance" (Bourdieu 1977: 19).[2] Drawing on recent ethnographic breakthroughs and some of my own fieldwork,[3] I argue that the indigenous "interpretive practices" are lost to ethnography due to its insistence on using the interview technique unreflectingly and unquestioningly.

THE INTERVIEW AND THE THEATRICS OF POWER AND KNOWLEDGE

As late as 1986, Charles Briggs was disheartened by the fact that we still knew very little about the nature of the interview as a communicative event (3). Instead of researching the ubiquity of the interview in the human sciences and its use as a way of generating data, scholars have either addressed interview technicalities such as rapport-building, sampling, etc. (2–3), or looked at the interview as a cultural encounter without presenting an in-depth statement of how it can be undertaken (10). This "mystification" (6) of the interview, a device of "communicative hegemony," a subtle form of scientific colonialism (121), lies in "[b]oth our unquestioned faith and our reluctance to adopt a more sophisticated means of analyzing its findings[, which] emerge from the fact that the interview encapsulates our own native theories of communication and realities" (3).

One of the popular and most intelligent pieces on the interview as a technique for colonial interrogation, James Clifford's (1988) study of Marcel Griaule's "dramaturgy of ethnographic control" skirts the hegemonic constitution of the Griauleian interview routine. Instead, the piece admirably argues for salvaging the ethnographic encounter and ethnography as a genre from even the fanaticism of a practitioner like Griaule. And Griaule had macabre methods: In his belief that his role as an ethnographer was to sniff out social facts like a detective or examining magistrate (73), Griaule was out to bring the sly informants to their knees and information to his coffers:

> We would be able to make asses of the old hesitators, to confound the traitors, abominate the silent. We are going to see mysteries leap like reptiles from the mouth of the neatly caught liars. We would play with the victim; we would rub his nose in his words. We'd make him smile, spit up the truth, and we'd turn out of his pockets the last secret polished by the centuries, a secret to make him who has spoken it blanch with fear. (77)

To argue for the intrinsic good of ethnography, Clifford attributes this Griauleian reign of terror to Griaule's malign French ethnographic theatrics, that fly in the face of the benign Anglo-Saxon method of participant observation (75).[4] He also faults Griaule for his "penchant for the dramatic" (77). Clifford would even blame the terrorized informants for their plight. Griaule's pacification campaign, Clifford says, can be accounted for by the idiosyncrasies of the Sudanese societies of West Africa, which jealously guard their occult traditions (67).

Despite Clifford's argument to the contrary, Anglo-Saxon participant observation is not a perfect realm of ethnographic liberalism. For instance, James Faris (1973), in Talal Asad's celebrated *Anthropology and the Colonial Encounter*, drew attention to the "bullying" interview technique S. F. Nadel had expounded in 1939. Like all interviewers, Nadel was concerned to detect lies as both culturally and personally constituted social facts. In interviews bearing on secret, forbidden topics, Nadel found that "divide and conquer" was his best strategy:

> I have found it most profitable to stimulate the emotionality of a few chief informants to the extent of arousing almost violent disputes and controversies. The expression of doubt and disbelief on the part of the interviewer, or the arrangement of the interviews with several informants, some of whom, owing

to their social positions, were certain to produce inaccurate information, easily induced the key informants to disregard their usual reluctance and to speak openly, if only to confound his opponents and critics. (Nadel 1939: 323)

The professional ethics of ethnography discouraged the use of leading questions in interviews, but Nadel would rather have risked being caught in ethnographic malpractice than have forgone the revelations garnered by these theatrics.

Participant observation has also had to come to grips with the traumatic field experiences of some of its founding fathers. Maddened by the tropics, these lucid practitioners of participant observation were pushed to the edge and became verbally violent. E. E. Evans-Pritchard came up with the pun "Nuerosis" to name the symptoms of craziness one displayed as a result of Nuer reluctance to cooperate with ethnography (1940: 11–12).[5] Several practitioners succumbed to this tropical pathology. Previously, Bronislaw Malinowski (1967), a victim of the same pathology, had written "brutes" in his *Diary in the Strict Sense* to get back at the sly natives (Clifford 1988: 105). The embarrassment caused in the field of anthropology by this revelation was considerable. Ethnographers were disheartened to learn that the apostle of getting the "native's point of view" had turned against his informants.

Clifford has perceptively mapped the many ways in which Malinowski fashioned his diary after Conrad's *Heart of Darkness,* where the phrase "exterminate the brutes" is first uttered by a maddened-by-the-tropics Kurtz. Malinowski's ironic invocation of the "b" word, according to Clifford, provided him with a fictional grasp of the stresses of fieldwork and the violence of his feelings. Facing the inseparability of discourse and power, Malinowski had to struggle for control in the ethnographic encounter (Clifford 1988: 105).

Clifford Geertz (1988) suggests an approach to this fusion of discourse and power in the ethnographic encounter that holds much promise for understanding the hegemonic nature of the interview situation, as well as other fieldwork routines. He sanctions the "diary disease," the flow of fieldwork experiences written by returning or veteran ethnographers that has been gathering momentum in the field lately, as a necessary complement of the classic ethnography. Whereas ethnographies, he argues, have always presented us with the ethnographer as the "Absolute Cosmopolite" who turns native out of a liberality of soul that endows him or her with agility in adaptation, the erstwhile dearth of diaries has allowed that presentation to stand unchallenged (1988: 80). Diaries, in which the theatrics of control are played out, will undoubtedly shed more light on the ethnographer as a "Complete Investigator." Far from causing embarrassment or consternation, revelations like the ones in Malinowski's diary will turn ethnography into a two-stranded creature. In coming out of the closet, the "Complete Investigator" will no longer be threatened by a dormant scandal.

"WE TOO KNOW THE PAST, BECAUSE WE CARRY OUR NEWSPAPERS IN OUR HEADS": WHY THEY DIDN'T GET IT

It is regrettable that a scholarly concern such as African oral historiography, born in performance and an ardent desire to grant informants authority equal to that of Western investigators, should turn its back to these origins by suspecting performance and denying informants that authority (Fabian 1983: 31).[6] Jan Vansina describes oral historiography's birth one day in the spring of 1953 among the Kuba of Zaire. It was a sunny day; the fierce sunlight shimmered off the pale sand in Mbop Louis's courtyard. Mbop, a mature Congolese Kuba, was patiently giving well-considered answers to questions asked by his sister's son on behalf of the "exotic-looking" Vansina.

> Suddenly Mbop interrupted the leisurely pace of his speech and exclaimed rhetorically as he addressed me, the stranger: "We too know the past, because we carry our newspapers in our heads." Full of enthusiasm, he recited as proof a number of short poems. . . . In a burst of insight, half-forgotten [medieval] dirges [on which Vansina had written his master's thesis in history] . . . surged through my mind. These Kuba poems were just like these medieval dirges. They were texts and hence just as amenable to the canons of historical method. Once one could assess the value of tradition, it could be used as a source like any other: one could then use such poems to reconstruct at least a part of a "real" Kuba history. (Vansina 1994: 16)

Oral historiography denied coevalness to informants,[7] the historians of the field, by turning them into a "walking reference library" (Vansina 1985: 37), that is, "an image overshadowed by what is left of their ancient culture," "a reenactment of a debris of the past" (Fabri 1995: 142). These local historians, who synthesized traditions into historical narratives, came to be known in the literature as the "encyclopedic informants" (Vansina 1965: 192, 1985: 65). Vansina took a dismal view of them, even against the best judgment of his disciples (Hartwig 1971; Irwin 1982; Pender-Cudlip 1973). He has, however, relieved us of the duty to stop this "othering" of historians of the field by his recent heartfelt confession that his long-held suspicion of encyclopedic informants was unjustified. He regrets the fact that it took him many years to realize that these informants "are my confreres, historians just as I was. . . . Only recently have I come to appreciate their crucial role in the fashioning of the historical consciousness of their communities" (1994: 16).

Suspecting informants of embellishing traditions led to a lack of attention to the performative, dialogic, and discursive properties of oral tradition. A positivist-minded methodology prevailed, in which traditions were interrogated to cleanse them of falsehoods and accorded the respectability and reliability of historical evidence that had long been enjoyed by written documents. In focusing on the referents of traditions—stories of past events, or, in Benveniste parlance, *historie*—this methodology slighted *discours,* the aspects of narrative performance which pertain to the process of communication, the relation between the speaker and the hearer (Babcock-Abrahams 1976: 178).[8]

Scholars of oral tradition have been busy sifting the referents from the additions made by informants (Vansina 1965: 21). Intelligent informants are the worst, because they are the most artistic and therefore corrupt the referent most in discourse (108–10). In a quest to rescue the referent from the process of communication, historians are encouraged to reconstruct an archetype of a testimony: the hypothetical wording of the original composition (137).

MONSIEUR PAUL: WHAT LIES HAVE TO DO WITH IT

Clifford felt the need for a history of fieldwork that took into consideration its indigenous side, which is responsible for making ethnography a form of "plagiarism" (1988: 44). This history would concern itself partly with how both cooperative and uncooperative informants influenced the research process. I can see Clifford's point, having myself written an ethnography of Sudan Rubatab inspired by rebellious and reluctant informants (1994). They argued with my mission, which they described as the collection of old, irrelevant stuff, and dismissed my request for interviews as a waste of time. But with the trickster charm typical of men of words among the Rubatab, they made my mission by subverting it. A instance of this constructive criticism will be discussed shortly.

Clifford's call for a history of fieldwork as a plagiarized enterprise will bring us even closer to ethnography based in "manufactured information." In their obsession with cleansing ethnography of lies, unacceptable "social facts" (Comaroff and Comaroff 1992: 22), ethnographers distilled the interview into a technique of interrogation, as we have seen in the extreme cases of Griaule and Nadel. The way in which ethnographers take "lies" as professional as well as personal insults is best illustrated by Paul Stoller's description of how he shuttled between two informants who, he realized, had exaggerated the number of languages they spoke. Stomping back to the shop of the informant who "lied" first, Stoller complained,

> "Abdou [the other lying informant] tells me that you speak only one language. But you just told me that you speak three languages. What is the truth?"
> "Ah, Monsieur Paul, Abdou is telling you the truth."
> "But how could you lie to me?"
> "What difference does it make, Monsieur Paul?" (Stoller and Olkes 1987: 9)

Stoller confesses that he considers himself lucky for discovering early in the field that informants "lie to their anthropologists" (1989: 9). He was fortunate, as well, for being advised to forsake his methodological interview fundamentalism and adopt a far more mellow attitude toward learning about the Songhay of the Niger. After the lie episode, an old Muslim cleric told him,

> "Monsieur Paul, you will never learn about us if you go into peoples' compounds, ask personal questions, and write down the answers. If you remain here one year, or two years, and ask us questions in this manner, we would still lie to you."
>
> "Then what am I to do?"
>
> "You must learn to sit with people, Monsieur Paul. You must learn to sit and listen. You must learn the meaning of the Songhay adage: One kills something thin in appearance to discover that inside that it is fat" (1989: 10–11).

We will see shortly how a host of fieldworkers have been blessed by similar advice that inspired them into writing first-class thick—or fat—ethnographies.

Interviews apparently invite lies. In their grip, an informant has to throw in a lot of nonsense to feed this colonial, alien, hungry, and powerful apparatus. A researcher has to accept that the interview is a breeding place of lies. Attempts to turn it into a lie-detector are misguided.

As early as 1920, R. Davis, an enlightened district commissioner and an authority on the Kababish nomads of Sudan, suggested that the Seligmans' ethnography of these nomads had drawn on information from people too close to or dependent on the paramount chief to be trusted as representative of the range of the nomads' social experience (1920: 283). While visiting the Kababish in 1931, C. A. E. Lea, a shrewd district commissioner, wanted to check out the story of the Kababish who lied to the anthropologist. District commissioners, of course, were resourceful in finding ways to pass time in cultureless lands. Two of the Seligmans' informants whom Lea met said that they had been fond of Seligman when "they had got over his habit of sitting down and asking things like 'What are your customs on the bridal night?' and such-like intimate questions and then promptly writing down the answers in his note book like a policeman at an accident" (Lea 1994: 56). In calling an interview an interrogation, the Seligmans' informants admitted that they had stuffed them with a lot of nonsense. An informant said he was only a boy under the Mahdist state in Sudan (1885–1898) and wondered why the Seligmans expected him to remember those times accurately and answer their questions about that past. Furthermore, he was confused by their questions on the customs of the nomads, for they were too many and varied for one to know them all (56).

Recent seminal and award-winning ethnographies have come to us through remarkable field plagiarism. Steeped in a training that prepared them to prey on thin themes, ethnographers were forced by their consultants and the community at large to pursue a more worthy game. Renato Rosaldo's *Ilongot Headhunting* (1980) was conceived after the end of his fieldwork on Ilongot social structure and drew on oral history genres that the Ilongot forced him to listen to over his objections (Clifford 1988: 44). Similarly, Robert Launay's work (1992) was based on Muslim sermons in Ivory Coast which he was invited to record, although by and large he had declined the invitations, preferring to focus on his set themes of trade and marriage. After returning from the field, he wrote, biting his finger, "I looked back with horror at what I had done, or rather, not done. I had been offered data on a plate, and I had turned it away" (1992: ix). It took Launay a second trip to the field to make up for his "occasion manquée" (ix–xi). Finally, Lila Abu-Lughod's *Veiled Sentiments* (1986) would have been a different, but surely poorer, ethnography had she stuck to her guns and followed her original plan to study Awlad Ali's interpersonal relations rather than the "sad-sounding short poems" she kept hearing and ignoring. Gradually the songs took the center stage of her ethnography, and the rest is history—and a success story (1986: 23–27). All the ethnographers I have discussed above were, like Stoller, humbled by their hosts into looking their ignorance in the face and learning the way their communities wanted them to learn, rather than the anthropologists' way. Whereas the latter ask questions when they are ignorant, the Songhay, for example, first learn how to ask the right questions (Stoller and Olkes 1987: 31).

An appraisal of Launay's occasion manquée, that is, "what dropped out of sight" (Clifford 1988: 39) due to ethnographic hegemony, is an exercise in writing the history of things that do not happen. The effort is worth our while because it illuminates these hegemonic methodologies "by recording alternatives that were no less real because they were submerged or silent" (Lears 1985: 585).[9]

According to Clifford, current ethnography is seeking new ways to restore to informants the authority they lost in the post-Malinowski era. Culture, in that era's prevailing view, was "an ensemble of characteristic behaviors, ceremonies and gestures susceptible to recording and exploration by a trained onlooker" (1988: 45). Ethnographers thus trusted their own powers of observation rather than the speculative and doubtful interpretations of indigenous authorities (45). This singular usurpation of cultural authority resulted in two major deformations in ethnography as a mode of cultural translation. First, the various idiosyncratic voices of indigenous consultants were smoothed over into the "expository prose of more-or-less interchangeable informants" (49). Second, in writing culture as a bounded (homogenous, coherent, and timeless) artifact, ethnographers depicted informants as robots programmed with "cultural rules." Abu-Lughod's call for "writing against culture" stems from a conscious attempt to subvert such a bounded, perfect culture by "polluting" it with the vagaries of time, fuzziness, and particularity (1991: 154–58).

Taking stock of the wastefulness of the Western "will to knowledge" (Abu-

Lughod 1991: 148) may not, God forbid, reveal ethnography as "colonial nonsense" (defined by Homi Bhabha as the "loss of the narrative of cultural plurality" [1994: 126]), endlessly failing to completely translate culture into the dominant Western idiom. This failure occurs because the colonial "custom of power" stands in the way of ethnographers' perfecting their knowledge of non-Western cultures (Bhabha 1994: 129–30).

Salvaging Indigenous Interpretive Practices, or, Bypassing the Interviewer: "It Isn't for You This Time. It Is for My Sister There"

In the late seventies and the early eighties folklorists were excited by Dell Hymes's concept of the "breakthrough into performance," which was seen as effectively deterring ethnographers from reading texts over the shoulder of the folk (1975: 69). Simply stated, the concept celebrates the redundancy of the interviewer-as-collector whose informant has decided to put his or her traditions to better use than mere collection. In breaking through into performance, the tradition's bearer assumes responsibility for these traditions, not merely before a collector, but also before an indigenous audience.

I was fortunate enough to witness a breakthrough into performance as early as 1967, while collecting and studying the traditions of the nomad Kababish of west-central Sudan, whose absolute nomadism is cleverly described in Asad's *The Kababish Arabs* (1970). This momentous "disruption" of my fieldwork stands out in my fieldnotes as a rich, puzzling turn of events. I only found an English name for it fifteen years later when I came to Indiana University to pursue a doctorate degree in folklore.

Tirayh (1897–1970) was my principal informant on the traditions of the Kababish. He entered my tent one noon in the summer of 1967 completely depressed and wrapped up in his thoughts. His encouraging, confidence-inspiring, and vigorous old face was troubled. At the entrance of the tent he threw me alternately injured and vague looks. I hastened to welcome him, offering him a seat. He knew that that was the prelude to one more of our interviews, which had begun in December of the previous year. He suddenly fixed his eyes on an elderly woman who was visiting my host family. He seemed for a moment to be working out something in his mind. He pointed at the elderly woman and said to me,

—It is not for you this time. It is for my sister there. l compose this poem in praise of Chief Ali at-Tom [d. 1938] and Chief at-Tom Ali at-Tom [reigned 1930–1945]. I will remind her of their blessed days and make her weep.

He then recited his poem "Alas, ephemeral is [life], and time is beguiling." On finishing his recitation he asked the woman:

—Are my words true or false?

The woman replied:
—True.

Tirayh continued, reciting a number of other poems by older poets. I had recorded most of the poems delivered in this momentous session in previous interviews. However, by opting to speak in the first person, by directing his recitation of his own poems to an audience of his choice, Tirayh imbued the poems with rhetorical and sentimental strategies undreamed of in collection routines.

To understand this emergent reshuffling of tradition, one needs to plumb the ethnographic and biographic, as well as historical, contexts of the performance. Ethnographically speaking, discontent was rife in the *dikkah* (the moving capital of the Kababish and the summer camp of the chiefly lineage) at the time I was doing my fieldwork. Everybody was complaining about everybody else. The chiefs resented the desertion of their slaves to hired work, leaving their families for the chiefs to maintain. The chiefs were also apprehensive about the central government's intention to review the status and authority of tribal administrations. Furthermore, the people of the dikkah were dissatisfied with the wheeling and dealing going on between the merchants and their herdsmen behind their backs. Clients were complaining that they were no longer fed or clothed by their patrons. A woman even rebuked "today's girls" for their individualistic attitude toward what used to be communal activities.

The dikkah was thus going through tumultuous and traumatic times. Its restlessness and anxiety stemmed mainly from loss of confidence in the chiefs, whose periodic competition over administrative offices and resources had divided the chiefly lineage into two antagonistic camps. The chiefs' loss of control over their internal affairs shook the faith of those around them. Disillusioned, the people of the dikkah began to idealize the reigns of Ali at-Tom and his son At-Tom as periods that had perfectly respected traditional political and social mores.

In the context of this generalized agony, Tirayh's anguish centered on two things: the paramount chief's obligation to reward him for the testimonies he had been called on to record for me, and the lack of sympathy the chiefs showed him in a dispute over a well.

Tirayh and the chiefs belonged to the Nurab clan. Tirayh took pride in his descent from an ancestor of the present chiefs just five generations back. Historically built around the office of chieftainship, the Nurab clan has, over the years, shown a tendency toward progressive segmentation (Asad 1970: 194). The pressing claims of the chiefs' immediate kin for limited offices and resources have resulted in the progressive exclusion and estrangement of the distant kin.

This segmentation has created two models for identification among the Nurab. An idealized model is accessible to all Nurab by right of birth, emphasizing the ancestor chief from whom the segmentary line sprang and at whom the division arose between power and kinship. A second, more realistic model makes clear that the scarce political resources are available only to the lineage of the ruling chief.

One can see why it was hard for someone like Tirayh, left with only the idealized model, to reconcile himself to his estrangement from power and its perks. He could understand why segmentation would exclude him from the highest prizes of power, but was reluctant to give up hope of lesser manifestations of *mahannah,* defined by Asad as a "relationship of mutual goodwill, accommodation and help" (1970: 75–76). In other terms, mahannah is having one's kin's interests at heart. It therefore gives rise to a form of preferential democracy, in which the viewpoints of one's kin are sought first and are favorably considered. Before his breakthrough from "interview" into performance, Tirayh had visited one of the chiefs. No doubt the chief hurt him by denying him his residual power of mahannah. That did it for him, and he went out campaigning for traditional mores. He was voting by his performance.

Rhetorically speaking, the three poems strung together in Tirayh's performance shared a lucid structure of sentiment. They all originated in tumultuous times in which ethos and norms were in jeopardy. Each poem consisted of two distinct parts: the "vicissitudes of fate or change of fortune" part and the "alas" part. In the "vicissitudes of fate" sections, life *per se* was decried for being treacherous. In the "alas" parts, the poets nostalgically depicted the past of the Nurab as a bright era of kin solidarity. One of the wronged poets was approached by Ali at-Tom and they were reconciled. I remember Tirayh reciting the same poem with which he began his unique performance for the visiting lady to the deputy chief at one point during the dispute over the well. The deputy chief was callous and listened impatiently to its message of mahannah. The chief was incapable of modeling his actions on the perfect example of his father as described in the poem. The poem was wasted on him. Tirayh broke through into performance that day to prove that there was something rotten in the kingdom of the Kababish.

KABABISH HISTORIANS AND THEIR SCHOOLS

I was struck by another discursive property in the Kababish history I researched in the late sixties that I could name only after I had read Mikhail Bakhtin, well into the eighties. In discussing the early Kababish migrations with informants, I was made acutely aware of their division into two distinct historical schools. These two crystal-clear sets of individual voices and positions defied my attempt to smooth them into a *historie* cleansed of lapses of memory, falsehoods, and biases, the kind of flattened ethnography whose sources are reduced to "more-or-less interchangeable informants" (Clifford 1988: 49).

Neat divisions of oral historical accounts (or guild accounts, for that matter) into schools are, of course, risky. Obviously, my Kababish consultants freely merged elements from the two schools. Even my key informant, Tirayh, who was very partisan when it came to drawing the line, borrowed episodes from the seminal narrative of the other school without perceiving any inconsistency. Each group of Nurab historiographers is aware of the views of the other group. However, each group exerts a conscious effort to keep its basic narrative intact.

When asked about the seminal story of the rival school, Tirayh said he did not *yastandafah* (know it well enough to tell it). He referred me to representatives of the other school to get it directly from them. Furthermore, a member of one of the schools accused the competing school of plagiarism for drawing on a narrative which had the signature of a distant, archaic, nomadic community. Finally, an informant vehemently contradicted the record of the rival school. When asked if the Kababish ever fought with Shukriyyah (a nomadic community living on the east bank of the Nile in central Sudan), he replied, "They fought with neither the Shukriyyah nor the Shaiqiyyah [a riverine community]," in anticipation of the sequence of events told by the other school. The following excerpts from my field notes indicate the intensity of the disagreements between the two schools of Nurab historiography:

1–6 May 1967: I asked Tirayh to tell me the core story of the rival school. He first denied any knowledge of it. He then narrated it along the lines set by the school that espouses it. Two days later I asked him to record it for me on tape. He refused and advised me to get it straight from its originators. After we both visited one of the originators, Tirayh willingly told the story, not changing any of the elements we had heard a day before.

29 December 1969: I was told that one of the Kababish chiefs, who belonged to the school opposing that of Tirayh, would like to listen to what Tirayh had narrated about the Nurab migrations. Was he worried that I heard an unapproved version?

30 December 1969: Another informant, who had learned his traditions from some of the same sources as had Tirayh, reported that he had heard Tirayh tell the seminal story of the other school only once: in 1961. Evidently my key informant was ill disposed to retain this story. He heard it repeatedly and occasionally repeated it on request. But it suited him best either to forget it or to pretend to have forgotten it.

These contestations bring forth the dialogic nature of oral tradition as a discourse. "Dialogic" is used here after Bakhtin and is understood to mean, paraphrasing Bakhtin, how one testimony of a historical discourse builds on other testimonies and polemicizes them (Bakhtin 1981: 69). The issue here, to paraphrase Bakhtin again, is not how these testimonies are derived from the event of Nurab migration, but rather how they record that event while reacting to one another (91).

"Text-Hungry" Ethnographers

Oral tradition texts, as collected by ethnographers, are the site of one of the most significant excisions of indigenous interpretations. Justified by an unrelenting search for the ur-form, the collectors view narrators' commentaries as uncalled-for and disruptive. Wendy James was taken aback by the way her Sudanese Uduk informant "desecrated" the myths he was delivering to her by interjecting mundane comments (1979: 60, 77). Unknowingly, she became part of this desecration when the narrator, mistaking her for a descendant of the kind white people in his story, incorporated her own field trip into his myth (84).

In order to break the custom of privileging text over commentary, folklorists embraced Alan Dundes's call in 1966 to elicit "oral literary criticism," the meanings attributed to folklore texts by the people who use them (Narayan 1995: 243). Raconteurs' asides were recognized as crucial to gauging folk interpretive practices. But the power of habit is difficult to break. Narayan (1995) laments the fact that three decades after Dundes's insight "[we] still cannot locate enough cases where scholars have patiently sought out and respectfully produced extensive exegeses of particular texts" (243).

My study of the evil eye as a largely verbal behavior (1994) was considerably nuanced thanks to a nugget of Kababish literary criticism. Viewed largely as a gaze event, the evil eye is rarely recognized as a speech behavior. The utterances that go into the constitution of the event, if not ignored, are glossed as intimating generalized admiration or envy. A culture like the Middle Eastern one is classified as evil-eye culture because praise is disapproved of, whereas American culture is deemed free of the evil eye because praise is socially expected and culturally prescribed. Analysts have hardly stopped to ask themselves why Middle Eastern culture, supposedly intolerant of expressions of admiration, is simultaneously hospitable to long and varied traditions of high and folk praise poetry.

The crucialness of speech genres (and their conventions) to a refined understanding of the concept of the evil eye was brought home to me by a line from Kababish folk criticism. In the nineteenth century, a poet had praised a chief by saying, "When he lifted the keg of beer and put it on his feet / He caused the leather strap of his amulet on his arm to burst." The chief interjected, "What a lousy praise this is . . . you just keep smiting me with the evil eye. Call Shabat [his favorite poet] instead." Shabat responded,

> He [the chief] called to attendance Shiraym [a slave]
> Yet he sounded like calling Manduf [another slave]
> When night guests came to his place
> They would find an ox and sheep slaughtered in their honor. (Ibrahim 1999)

Evidently, it was not praise that posed a threat to the chief's well-being. Rather, it was the source of that praise. When praise is expressed from sub-alterns, it is well received and rewarded. Thanks to an embedded nugget of Kababish literary criticism, one is able to access the intriguing intertextuality of the two poems.

Lack of interest in local interpretive practices struck me as pervasive and wasteful during my work among the Rubatab of Sudan in 1984. A poet and consultant bedecked her delivery with astute asides and commentaries. Unfortunately, she was interviewed for me by a "text-hungry" (Dundes 1966: 512) assistant who would stop recording whenever the informant "derailed" from the text into asides. However, the few asides that persisted in the record allowed me to argue that, contrary to the suspicions of positivist ethnographers, the Rubatab's claim to be both ethnic Arabs and good Muslims should be taken as ethnographic reality (Ibrahim 1991).

The surviving asides subscribe to a concept, similar to one found in textual Islam, of the poet as a liar (Shahid 1983). After delivering the lines

My love of her began before her weaning
And till *Israfil* [an angel] blows the horn for the Day of Judgment

she commented laughingly, "He is a liar, boy. Would it enter your mind that he would love her till *Israfil* calls, "Hey you!" In repeating these lines later on she said, "What a liar! Are you going even to hear what *Israfil* would say?" In another song, a poetess said she had seen the galloping horses of a lineage she was praising. The informant said, "She is the one who saw them. I did not," clearly refusing to be held accountable for the veracity of the line because she merely repeated it after the poetess (Ibrahim 1994: 75–76).

PERSPECTIVES ON THE INTERVIEW

Is the interview reformable? The power/knowledge paradigm holds out no hope of salvage and improvement. The most this paradigm can suggest to ethnography is that we forsake *renovating* the interview and continue *interrogating* it (Gordon 1980) by basically denying it even the hope of ever being fair and representative. These calls for interrogation may sound too deconstructionist to serve a pragmatic enterprise. But good ethnography emerges from such a deconstruction. Lila Abu-Lughod, for instance, was humbled by her vulnerability as a woman in a strict Arab patriarchy into recognizing that she could not impose her research agenda through interviewing. She settled for less imposing techniques for conducting her research (1986: 23–24). Jeanne Favret-Saada (1980: 9–12) presents us with a more radical interrogation of the interview. In pursuance of the practice paradigm, she concludes that practices like witchcraft are more than objects of ethnographic enquiry. In recognizing that practices can only be known through practices, anthropologists should prepare themselves to engage in a totally different ethnography. The interview, I would assume, would be the first victim of this emergent ethnography.

More importantly, we need to question the belief that good ethnography is a progressive process, and that by repairing the interview we can arrive at good ethnography. Bad ethnography would still constitute ninety percent of the literature, whatever we may do, according to Sturgeon's Law, which stipulates that 90 percent of everything is crap (Fine 1993: 279).

Furthermore, a progressive view of ethnography fails to explain why we have always had some good ethnographic studies. Although they were written by a government anthropologist for a colonial authority that was having a hard time pacifying and administering a colonized community, the undiminished appeal of Evans-Pritchard's *Witchcraft, Oracles, and Magic among the Azande* (1976) and *The Nuer* (1940) defy the humanist notion that "once someone gains power he ceases to know" (Foucault 1980: 51). The reverse is also true: more power does not translate into good knowledge—or good ethnography. Perhaps what saved *Witchcraft, Oracles, and Magic* and *The Nuer* from being boring colonial readings was Evans-Pritchard's admission that, even in the prime of colonial power, he took to heart the realities that interested his "people." He was interested in neither witchcraft nor cattle when he embarked on his research among the Azande and Nuer, respectively. The Azande prevailed upon him to cherish what fascinated them: magic. Similarly, he had no interest in cattle "but the Nuer had, so willy nilly I had to become cattle-minded" (1940: 242).

My care to bring out the local interpretive agents and practices which interviews suppress is not intended to provide dos and don'ts for reforming the interview. By pointing to these practices I hope to shed some light on a rather vague call to reinvent the interview as a bonding between the interviewer and the interviewee. I would personally like to see the participants bond by engaging in "conversations" which are in no way or fashion interviews (Briggs 1986). A meaningful conversation is only feasible when informants/consultants are granted their long-denied expertise and acknowledging their mastery over local frameworks of interpretation. Engaging in ethnography as conversation, however, would, of course, require engaging in a different kind of ethnography.

News from the feminist quarters in anthropology about engaging in this different ethnography is, however, discouraging. Feminist interviews have not become the "passionate scholarship" about women that was originally projected. Bonding was trivialized by researchers' lying through their teeth to informants about their marital statuses, identities, and class backgrounds (Wolf 1996: 11). Also, women ethnographers ended up controlling the creation of knowledge, much as in the rest of ethnography.[10] Like all conscientious anthropologists, feminist ethnographers have instead challenged the structure of academia in light of their field encounters with a marginal group—women like them (2–4).

This return of the gaze—the pinnacle of good ethnography—has lucidly engaged Akhil Gupta and James Ferguson in *Anthropological Locations: Boundaries and Grounds of a Field Science* (1997). In their book they question the normalization of the idea of "the field" in light of its anthropologically significant premises and assumptions. To denaturalize "field," they identify it as a triumphant, Malinowskian, "hegemonic" tradition that displaced other traditions more sensitive to informants (23–24), more attentive to history, or less fanatic about the "ethnographic present" (52).[11] Also, they trace the denial of informants' authority and the exoticization of subjects to the natural-history traditions in anthropology requiring that subjects be directly observed in their natural surroundings (7) and to the implied distinction between "field" and "home" and the resultant hierarchy of purity by which some places are more "anthropological" than others (13).[12]

Anthropology's newfound interest in the state (Herzfeld 1997) will further disrupt the localization of the field practice. This localization has falsely bifurcated indigenous knowledge into "field" knowledge and knowledge not essential to the field. A belligerent informant brought the absurdity of this division home to me during my fieldwork among the Rubatab in 1984. This hardworking, angry farmer did not like my "folkloric" inquisitiveness into his culture. He took me to task:

"What good do these ways of olden times contain to deserve your attention?" he said.

Laughingly, I said, "I want their *bud'* [amusement]."

"These discourses are worthless in this time of ours. What really matters are today's discourses," said the farmer. "The discourses of people of the past are futile. They are like someone narrating a folktale. I just cannot stomach such a narration because it is like waking from a dream. These discourses have no *zubd* [butter]."

"Pardon?" I said.

"Milk produces butter when it curdles. Nay, the stuff of old days."

He turned to those around him, who were having the time of their lives watching an encounter in which a representative of the "authentic" national elite was grilled and contradicted. It struck me later that those villagers were using this research situation to protest the very idea of the "field." I felt injured by this (veiled and unveiled) aggression when the man continued, saying, "Discourses of the past are nonsense. Or isn't that so?"

I asked with a suppressed anger, "But where do you think the *zubd* lies now?"

"In the discourses of today, which are sound, pointed, and pragmatic. Past discourses lack *siyasa* [politics, acumen], shrewdness, discernment. You will find even the average person today adept, pragmatic, and discriminating."

This counter-governmentalization of culture may have been occurring more often than ethnographers cared to report it. Francis Deng, my compatriot, had a really bad experience when his southern Sudanese Dinka informant, his "tribesman," perceived him to be representing the law, that is, the national government dominated by the northern Sudanese. Deng, a Dinka scholar, was asked by Chief Ayeny Aleu to reveal his research identity, to say whether he was doing his research as a Dinka or as a "representative of the law" of the northern Sudanese state:

> I ask you because our country is still in the hands of the Northerners and, as you know, our country has remained far behind the North. Today as I talk to you, are you after the words of your people, the people of your father, Deng, and your grandfather, Kwol, or do you want these words from us as the representative of the law? That is the first thing I must ask about before I talk any further. I must understand; If you are a Northerner, then frankly, some words will remain unspoken. (Deng 1978: 43–44)

These interviews are dramatically different from the one the district commissioner of *Things Fall Apart* conducted for his projected book on the pacification of the primitive tribes of the lower Niger. In these interviews, unlike the district commissioner's, the informants interrogated the silent ethnographer and admonished him to "spit up the truth," in Griaule's terms.

AFTERTHOUGHTS

Sherry Ortner is less disheartened by the chance that the critique of representation underway in scholarship may throw doubt on the possibility of ethnography itself. She argues that the ethnographic stance—an attempt to understand another life world using the self as the instrument of knowing—will remain with us, with its ideals of thickness, implying exhaustiveness and holism, and contextualization (1995). And for thickness and contextualization local practices of interpretation, what the Comaroffs call "the endogenous historicity of local worlds" (1992: 27), are indispensable.

I hope I have made it clear, though, that these techniques can still lead to bad ethnography. Recall Sturgeon's Law, according to which excellence may certainly exist, albeit in short supply. Intuitive ethnographers can perform miracles with few or none of these field techniques. Rosaldo has advised against taking the doctrine of field preparation, knowledge, and sensibility too much to heart; it can lead to a false sense of security hinging on obtaining a greater number of verbal elaborations from informants or on using another analytical level. His loss of a brother and wife enabled him to fathom the loss and rage of his Ilongot. This breakthrough in his Ilongot research came through his own loss rather than any "systematic preparation for field research" (1989: 3, 8).

In putting this much faith in ethnographic miracles and idiosyncrasies, I am encouraged by Althusser's appreciation of Freud's miracle. Althusser was awestruck by the paradox that Freud's thought could open so many paths in the psychoanalysis of children, psychotics, homosexuals, and perverts even though it was based on therapy with ordinary adult subjects (1996: 100–102). With their arresting lack of logic, miracles, no wonder, are few and far between.

NOTES

1. Nicholas Dirks has usefully developed Edward Said's notion of the slippage of "administer, study, and reconstruct" into "occupy, rule, and exploit" (Said 1983: 222) to argue that "culture was what colonialism was all about" (Dirks 1992: 3).

2. I am still stalked by a memory of an episode of "learned ignorance" in my fieldwork. My informant kept saying *sokari,* which I thought to be his ignorant corruption of *'askari,* the Arabic and Swahili word for "soldier" or "policeman." I won't even try to guess what sokari means. Suffice it to say that when textual scholars later argued about its meaning, I felt empty and ashamed for having denied them a rare oral perspective on the term through sheer ethnographic arrogance.

3. For full descriptions of these ethnographic encounters, see Ibrahim 1983, 1987, 1991, 1994, and forthcoming.

4. Renato Rosaldo built on Clifford's evaluation of Griaule to contrast the latter's "pacifying" field techniques to the American tradition of fieldwork in which an ethnographer yearns to be accepted by the host community as one of them (1989: 205–206).

5. Fieldwork pathology is treated in Howell 1990.

6. Denial of this coevalness may be taken to literally deadly extremes. Ed Rutsch, an anthropologist, was quoted by the Chicago *Tribune* (11 November 1991) as saying that skeletons, in the view of anthropologists, are wonderful informants. "They are quiet, they do not go anywhere and they don't talk back."

7. Jan Vansina argues that historical field research, although different from its anthropological counterpart, took off from the latter. Anthropological fieldwork, he says, remains the model for oral historians (1996: 128).

8. David William Cohen and E. S. Atieno Odhiambo make the point that genealogies constructed by guild historians for preliterate communities are cleansed of the debates and nuances they contain in their oral, discursive mode (1989: 32). Isabel Hofmeyr graciously highlighted the *discours/historie* dyad by admitting that her incompetence to deal fairly and squarely with some "native" texts made her veer away from their performative aspects to the regular historical narrative (1994: 22).

9. Luise White 1993 is an amusing take on the history of things that did not happen.

10. For revelations of the limitations of the interview as bonding in feminist ethnography, see Hale 1997.

11. The triumph of this Malinowskian concept of the field left undeveloped Paul Radin's notion that socially aloof Ph.D. holders are poorly equipped to interview working-class subjects. Instead, local intellectuals should be assigned these interviews. Gupta and Ferguson find it useful to ask how the relation between professional researcher and local expert might have been theorized if Radin's argument had been accepted (1997: 23–24). They also discuss the separation of history from anthropology, a Malinowskian feat, as a loss not unique to anthropology; prior to Malinowski

history and anthropology, at least in the study of nonliterate peoples, had comfortably coexisted. Adenaike and Vansina (1996) is a useful discussion of historians' fieldwork research.

12. Richard Shain and Janet Ewald, historians, have an interesting take on the continuum of field and home. In view of his long fieldwork in Nigeria, Shain is inclined to see researchers as a category of "exiles." His treatment of the concept is both angry and educational (1996). Ewald defines fieldwork primarily by the work rather than the worker. Historians, in her view, find the field where evidence remains subject to people who continue to change it. She adds,

> Fieldwork thus represents a particular moment in a particular place: a moment in the middle, bracketed by what precedes it and what follows it. Historical knowledge based on evidence from the field emerges not from the moment of the fieldwork, but from the stages before and after it. (1996:94)

BIBLIOGRAPHY

Abu-Lughod, Lila. 1986. *Veiled Sentiments: Honor and Poetry in a Bedouin Society.* New York: Oxford University Press.
———. 1991. "Writing against Culture." In *Recapturing Anthropology: Working in the Present,* ed. Richard G. Fox, 137–62. Santa Fe: School of American Research Press.
Adenaike, Carolyn K., and Jan Vansina, eds. 1996. *In Pursuit of History: Fieldwork in Africa.* Portsmouth, N.H.: Heinemann.
Althusser, Lois. 1996. *Writings on Psychoanalysis: Freud and Lacan.* New York: Columbia University Press.
Asad, Talal. 1970. *The Kababish Arabs: Power, Authority, and Consent in a Nomadic Tribe.* New York: Praeger.
Babcock-Abrahams, Barbara. 1976. "The Story in the Story." *Studia Fennica* 20, 177–84.
Bakhtin, Mikhail M. 1981. *The Dialogic Imagination: Four Essays.* Trans. C. Emerson and M. Holquist. Austin: University of Texas Press.
Bennett, Tony. 1995. *The Birth of the Museum: History, Theory, Politics.* London: Routledge.
Bhaba, Homi. 1994. *The Location of Culture.* London: Routledge.
Bourdieu, Pierre. 1977. *Outline of a Theory of Practice.* Cambridge: Cambridge University Press.
Briggs, Charles. 1986. *Learning How to Ask: A Sociolinguistic Appraisal of the Interview in Social Science Research.* Cambridge: Cambridge University Press.
Clifford, James. 1988. *The Predicament of Culture: Twentieth-Century Ethnography, Literature, and Art.* Cambridge, Mass.: Harvard University Press.
Cohen, David William, and E. S. Atieno Odhiambo. 1989. *Siaya: The Historical Anthropology of an African Landscape.* London: James Currey.
Comaroff, John, and Jean Comaroff. 1992. *Ethnography and the Historical Imagination.* Boulder: Westview.
Davis, R. 1920. Review of *The Kababish, a Sudan Arab Tribe,* by C. G. Seligman and Brenda Z. Seligman. *Sudan Notes and Records* 3, no. 4, 281–86.
Deng, Francis. 1978. *Africans of Two Worlds: The Dinka in Afro-Arab Sudan.* New Haven: Yale University Press.

Dirks, Nicholas B., ed. 1992. *Colonialism and Culture*. Ann Arbor: University of Michigan Press.

Dundes, Alan. 1966. "Metafolklore and Oral Literary Criticism." *The Monist* 50: 505–16.

Evans-Pritchard, E. E. 1940. *The Nuer*. New York: Oxford University Press.

———. 1976. *Witchcraft, Oracles, and Magic among the Azande*. Abridged ed. Oxford: Clarendon.

Ewald, Janet J. 1996. "A Moment in the Middle: Fieldwork in the Nuba Hills." In *In Pursuit of History: Fieldwork in Africa*, ed. Carolyn Keyes Adenaike and Jan Vansina, 94–103. Portsmouth, N.H.: Heinemann.

Fabian, Johannes. 1983. *Time and the Other: How Anthropology Makes Its Object*. New York: Columbia University Press.

Fabri, Antonella. 1995. "Memories of Violence, Moments of History." In *Labyrinth of Memory: Ethnographic Journeys*, ed. Marea C. Teski and Jacob J. Climo, 141–58. Westport: Bergen and Gravey.

Faris, James. 1973. "Pax Britannica and the Sudan: S. F. Nadel." In *Anthropology and the Colonial Encounter*, ed. Talal Asad, 153–70. New York: Humanities, 1973.

Favret-Saada, Jeanne. 1980. *Deadly Words: Witchcraft in the Bocage*. Cambridge: Cambridge University Press.

Field, Norma. 1991. *In the Realm of a Dying Emperor*. New York: Vintage.

Fine, Gary. 1993. "Ten Lies of Ethnography: Moral Dilemmas of Field Research." *Journal of Contemporary Ethnography* 22, no. 3, 268–82.

Foucault, Michel. 1980. *Power/Knowledge: Selected Interviews and Other Writings, 1972–1977*. Edited with an afterword by Colin Gordon. New York: Pantheon.

Geertz, Clifford. 1988. *Works and Lives: The Anthropologist as Author*. Stanford: Stanford University Press.

Gordon, Colin. 1980. Afterword to *Power/Knowledge: Selected Interviews and Other Writings, 1972–1977*, by Michel Foucault. New York: Pantheon.

Gupta, Akhil, and James Ferguson, eds. 1997. *Anthropological Locations: Boundaries and Grounds of a Field Science*. Berkeley: University of California Press.

Hale, Sondra. 1997. *Gender and Politics in Sudan: Islamism, Socialism, and the State*. Boulder: Westview.

Hartwig, Gerald. 1971. "Oral Traditions Concerning the Early Iron Age in Northwestern Tanzania." *International Journal of African Historical Studies* 6, no. 1, 93–113.

Herzfeld, Michael. 1997. *Cultural Intimacy: Social Poetics in the Nation-State*. New York: Routledge.

Hofmeyr, Isabel. 1994. *"We Spend Our Years as a Tale That Is Told": Oral Historical Narrative in a South African Chiefdom*. Portsmouth, N.H.: Heinemann.

Howell, Nancy. 1990. *Surviving Fieldwork: A Report on the Advisory Panel on Health and Safety in Fieldwork, American Anthropological Association*. American Anthropological Association, 26.

Hymes, Dell. 1975. "Breakthrough into Performance." In *Folklore: Performance and Communication*, ed. Dan Ben-Amos and Kenneth Goldstein, 11–74. The Hague: Mouton.

Ibrahim, Abdullahi. 1983. "Kababish Discourse: The Lunch Politics." *Sudan Notes and Records* 64: 95–112.

————. 1987. "Things Are Falling Apart in the Kababish *Dikkah*." *Al-Mathurat al-Sha'biyah* 5, no. 1: 104–11.

————. 1991. "*Sahir* and Muslim Moral Space." *International Journal of Middle East Studies* 23, no. 3: 387–98.

————. 1994. *Assaulting with Words: Popular Discourse and the Bridle of Shari'ah.* Evanston: Northwestern University Press.

————. 1999. *Firsan Kanjarat: Ayam wa Diwan al-Kababish fi alqarnayn al-Thamin 'Ashar wa al-Tasi' 'Ashar* (Kanjarat knights: The days and rhetoric of the Kababish in the eighteenth and nineteenth centuries). Khartoum: Khartoum University Press.

————. Forthcoming. "Debating Kababish: Historians Like Us." *Sudan Notes and Records.*

Irwin, Paul. 1981. *Liptako Speaks: History from Oral Tradition in Africa.* Princeton: Princeton University Press.

James, Wendy. 1979. *'Kwanim Pa: The Making of the Uduk People: An Ethnographic Study of Survival in the Sudan-Ethiopian Borderlands.* Oxford: Clarendon.

Launay, Robert. 1992. *Beyond the Stream: Islam and Society in a West African Town.* Berkeley: University of California Press.

Lea, C. A. E. 1994. *On Trek in Kordofan: The Diaries of a British District Officer in the Sudan, 1931–1933.* Oxford: Oxford University Press.

Lears, T. J. Jackson. 1985. "The Concept of Cultural Hegemony: Problems and Possibilities." *American Historical Review* 90, no. 3, 567–93.

Malinowski, Bronislaw. 1967. *A Diary in the Strict Sense of the Term.* New York: Harcourt, Brace and World.

Nadel, S. F. 1939. "The Interview Technique in Social Anthropology." In *The Study of Society: Methods and Problems,* ed. F. C. Bartlett et al., 319–34. New York: Macmillan.

Narayan, Kirin. 1995. "The Practice of Oral Literary Criticism: Women's Songs in Kangra, India." *Journal of American Folklore* 108, no. 249: 243–64.

Ortner, Sherry. 1995. "Resistance and the Problem of Ethnographic Refusal." *Studies in Comparative History and Society* 37, no. 1: 173–93.

Pender-Cudlip, P. 1973. "Encyclopedic Informants and Early Interlacustrine History." *International Journal of African Historical Studies* 6: 198–210.

Rosaldo, Renato. 1980. *Ilongot Headhunting, 1883–1974: A Study in Society and History.* Stanford: Stanford University Press.

————. 1989. *Culture and Truth: The Remaking of Social Analysis.* London: Beacon Press.

Said, Edward. 1983. *The World, the Text, and the Critic.* Cambridge, Mass.: Harvard University Press.

Shahid, Irfan. 1983. "Another Contribution to Koranic Exegesis: The Sura of Poets (xxvi)." *Journal of Arabic Literature* 14: 1–12.

Shain, Richard A. 1996. "A Double Exile: Extended African Residences and the Paradoxes of Homecoming." In *In Pursuit of History: Fieldwork in Africa,* ed. Carolyn Keyes Adenaike and Jan Vansina, 104–12. Portsmouth, N.H.: Heinemann.

Stoller, Paul, and Cheryl Olkes. 1987. *In Sorcery's Shadow: A Memoir of Apprenticeship among the Songhay of Niger.* Chicago: University of Chicago Press.

Vansina, Jan. 1965. *Oral Tradition: A Study in Historical Methodology.* Chicago: Aldine.

————. 1985. *Oral Tradition as History.* Madison: University of Wisconsin Press.

————. 1994. *Living with Africa.* Madison: University of Wisconsin Press.

————. 1996. "Epilogue: Fieldwork in History." In *In Pursuit of History: Fieldwork in Africa,* ed. Carolyn Keyes Adenaike and Jan Vansina, 127–40. Portsmouth, N.H.: Heinemann.

White, Luise. 1993. "Cars out of Place: Vampires, Technology, and Labor in Central Africa." *Representations* 43: 27–50.

Wolf, Diana L. 1996. *Feminist Dilemmas in Fieldwork.* Boulder: Westview.

PART II

African Lives

6

Conversations and Lives

Corinne A. Kratz

He did ever love to converse with old men as Living Histories.
—*John Aubrey (1626–1697), describing himself*[1]

Aubrey's enthusiasm for oral history has not always been shared by professional historians, but accounts of the past are a staple of conversations everywhere. They are told in various forms and circumstances, and some of the
most compelling accounts narrate the past as personal experience. Beyond
showing his delight in these encounters, Aubrey's comment also implies a
process of canonization that raises a question: when and how do people become Living Histories through conversation? My own questions in this essay
are related to this one, but are more rudimentary. I want to ask, how does
conversation become "a life"? And how do conversational lives become "life
histories" or "life stories," a scholarly canonization conferred on the account
rather than the conversationalist?

Both these questions involve the definitions and dynamics of verbal and
written genres, which are particularly vexed in situations of cultural translation. Issues of epistemology and multiple moments of reflexivity also come
into play. What and how can we know as people talk about aspects of their
lives, their selves, their memories, and the events and relations they have
experienced in various ways? Narrators and their interlocutors reflect on all
these topics as they talk, as well as on their own interactions, relationships,
and present communicative situation. Conversations that are recorded, transcribed, and turned into written life accounts are subject to further reflection
by those who effect these transformations. Some accounts begin as written
documents or combine oral and written versions in various ways. I concentrate in this essay on those that begin verbally, in order to consider their
conversational groundings and some of the critical practices of orality involved in their study.

Personal anecdotes about particular incidents and events are common,
often told and exchanged spontaneously in the course of conversation.[2] Accounts that span an entire life in some detail, however, are told less often,
only in particular kinds of situations. The terms "life history" and "life story"
usually refer to these fuller accounts. They are sometimes told in therapeutic
or legal settings, at ritual investitures, at high school reunions, or during inti-

mate moments that help establish close friendships, but those that become published accounts are most often elicited by researchers.

As a scholarly category and genre, life histories/stories index changing intellectual interests, research practices, and writing conventions. They have been used in a range of fields and treated as sources providing evidence for historical and cultural analysis and access to personal experience and attitudes; as means of constituting and expressing various identities, selves, and social relations; and as narratives that demonstrate artistic creativity worthy of literary analysis. Life histories/stories can be all of these, but proponents of different approaches and emphases have sometimes drawn battle lines over which is best suited or truest to the material, as discussed below. Contentions also arise about the very name to use. Since this paper is addressed equally to scholarship that uses "life history" and "life story," I use a range of terms, alternating among "life history," "life story," "life account," and "life history/story."[3]

Whatever their differences, each of these approaches draws a life history/story away from its moment and context of production, where it begins as communicative exchange and situated interaction. Indeed, their emphases help define what is most important for analysis and shape the account's published forms by providing criteria for editing the content or form of the exchange. Editing often includes deleting repetitions and false starts, rearranging sections thematically or chronologically, removing side remarks or other material judged peripheral, and deleting questions, comments, rejoinders, and exclamations made by others present. When some questions and comments are included, they often serve as signs of presence and authenticity that promote an "image of intertextual transparency" (Briggs 1993: 396, 419), but rarely are they taken as material for explicit analysis. Issues of translation can also be central when creating a written life history/story. A life history/story's conversational moorings in the interactions and settings where it is produced are reduced, then, but minimal attention is given to this movement from the moment of production to moments of analysis, presentation, and publication.

This inattention does not mean that all life histories/stories have been badly done or fundamentally flawed. Rather, it simply mirrors the primary interests and goals of researchers who worked on them: to represent the content of the lives narrated and illuminate them through historical, cultural, psychological, and literary commentaries. Nor is it the case that scholars have totally ignored the situations and interactions in which the life-tellings are embedded. Most life histories/stories provide some discussion—more extended in recent works—of the relation between researchers and the people who tell their lives;[4] most also note whether or not an interpreter was involved or others were present. This is presented as context, a kind of preliminary material to summarize before presenting and examining the life history/story itself.

The character of life history/story as verbal communication, however, has received surprisingly little attention, though this too is constitutive of the situation where it is told. How do life stories incorporate diverse conversational forms, communicative repertoires, and conventions of interaction? To what extent are these communicative features expunged as life histories/stories become texts and books? Several people have noted that the life history/story is an artificial or hybrid genre, an artifact produced through the interaction between researcher and interlocutors (Mintz 1979; Keesing 1985: 32; Gal 1991: 191). But what precisely is the nature and form of such a product before it is written in a way that resembles our notion of autobiography? This paper will address some of these questions by considering my several attempts to ask Okiek men in Kenya to tell me life histories/stories.

The broad similarity of published life histories/stories contrasts with the varied specifics of social action and communicative resources in each such situation. The constitution of the genre begins anew in each telling but clearly proceeds afterward, in many ways and places. The continuity of this process, stretching across different settings, highlights some of the recently identified problems in conventional distinctions between text and context (Bauman and Briggs 1990: 66–72; Duranti and Goodwin 1992). Text is typically understood as a separable discursive product, while context is rather vaguely defined as relevant material that must be provided, but can be bracketed as background (as in life history/story summaries of researcher-narrator relations).

Scholars in the 1970s emphasized relations between text and context as part of their critique of approaches that emphasized ideal, "authentic" texts or analyzed language structure in isolation from language use. Subsequent work showed increasingly how text and context grow out of one another. The notion of context was reformulated to a verbal noun—contextualization—to acknowledge these close ties and stress the processual, ongoing, and changing character of text/context relations.[5] More recently, Bauman and Briggs (1990: 72–78) and others have turned this concern on its head to ask instead what makes certain discursive products *separable* from ongoing social process (Briggs 1993, 1996a; Silverstein and Urban 1996: 15)?[6] This reorientation draws attention to entextualization, ways of "rendering discourse extractable, of making a stretch of linguistic production into a unit—a text—that can be lifted out of its interactional setting. A text, then, from this vantage point, is discourse rendered decontextualizable" (Bauman and Briggs 1990: 73).

This perspective at once raises questions about interrelations and tensions between contextualization and entextualization, processes that simultaneously anchor discourse in its setting and make it extractable. It reaches beyond any particular setting to ask how texts are reconfigured as they are resituated in other social settings through corresponding processes of decontextualization and recontextualization. For life history/story scholars, these notions focus critical attention on what sections of communicative exchanges are taken as part of a life, what is left behind, and why. They might also encourage analyses of the constitution of life histories/stories that bridge elicitation, telling, translation, editing, and publication and include a broader political economy of the production of knowledge through the form and content of life histories/stories. Part of the background to that political economy is an understanding of the history of life history/story research itself and the different ways life accounts have been invoked in various disciplines at different times. After reviewing some key aspects of this history, I consider conversations that might have become Okiek life histories/stories.

Lives as Method, Testimony, and Creative Process

Life histories/stories engender knotty questions of definition for scholars. These have been taken up in a range of fields—including anthropology, history, literary studies, psychology, sociology, and women's studies—as scholars recognize life accounts as valuable for various reasons. Annals of life history/story usually begin early this century. Written autobiographies and critical studies of autobiography in English increased in the late nineteenth and early twentieth centuries (Smith 1987: 4),[7] roughly the same period with which Langness (1965) begins his review of life history in anthropology. According to him, biography and autobiography had expanded before 1925 to include popular, literary accounts of Native American subjects (though few other non-Euroamericans),[8] but life histories were not yet taken seriously as cultural documents for analysis. American anthropologists were among the first to do so. Paul Radin's 1926 *Crashing Thunder* is generally recognized as pioneering such study, though he published two shorter, preliminary life histories/stories in 1913 and 1920. Crashing Thunder used Winnebago syllabary script to write the text that Radin (and others) translated and edited,[9] but orally related life histories became the norm as scholars recorded them throughout the world in many places where people were not literate.

Langness's next period, 1925–1944, is characterized by growing acceptance and use of life history/story in anthropology in ways that stressed Radin's concern—both humanistic and analytical—to "place individuals in time and in life trajectories" (d'Azevedo 1997), as well as by methodological attention to life stories in both anthropology and sociology. Langness marks the start of his final period, 1944–1965, with Kluckhohn's 1945 review of life history work for the Social Science Research Council (Gottschalk, Kluckhohn, and Angell 1945)[10] and a range of other 1944–45 publications that emphasized growing interest in psychological anthropology and in the relation between culture and personality.[11] During this time life histories/stories were used to address a number of anthropological interests and became more common in psychological studies as well. Langness's bibliography also shows broader geographical coverage, including some early African life accounts (e.g., Fosbrook 1955, 1956; Huddle 1957; Smith 1954; Winter 1959).[12]

Langness's review ends at 1965, noting attenuating interest in life history/story in anthropology (1965: 19). At about this time, historians were finally starting to recognize oral sources as legitimate, particularly in African history.[13] Vansina's programmatic volume promoted oral sources but paid almost no attention to life accounts, devoting only two paragraphs to personal recollections (1965: 160). Since then life histories/stories have experienced a new resurgence, corresponding to changing interests in the humanities and social sciences more generally. Smith describes two shifts in interest in autobiography in literary work after 1970: first from a focus on a text's historicity and factual basis to questions of identity and self-representation, and later an increasing turn to the poetic and literary nature of the narratives (1987: 5–7). Not limited to written autobiography or literary studies, these developments were widespread in life history/story research.

A surge of writing about life histories/stories in the 1980s places the start of this renewed interest in life accounts in the mid-1970s (Smith 1987: 3; Crapanzano 1984: 953; Heilbrun 1988: 12, 26; Geiger 1986: 342).[14] It was sustained by greater interest in social history and "history from below,"[15] by rising sociological interest in the phenomenology of everyday life (Berger and Luckmann 1966), and by reflexive trends in anthropology that included more hermeneutic approaches, critical attention to the politics of research and representation, and greater concern for questions of identity and agency (Scholte 1971, 1972; Fabian 1971, 1983; Hymes 1972; Asad 1973; Watson 1976; Karp and Kendall 1982; Karp 1986). One sign of this attention is Vansina's extended 1980 discussion of life history as personal reminiscence in relation to history, memory, and reliability. The growth of feminism and women's studies at this time provided a further, particularly strong impetus to life history/story studies. Studies of women's lives dominated the field through the 1980s. The "his" in life history studies declined even as they came to be called life stories. Major studies of men's lives have only reappeared fairly recently (Keegan 1988; van Onselen 1996).

This broad-based interest in life histories/stories consolidated in the 1980s. Like many of their predecessors, these scholars stressed the significance of life histories/stories as expressions of personal experience, keys to understanding individuals in cultural and historical context, and important representations of under- (or un-) represented perspectives, particularly those of women.[16] However, this work added particular emphases on the role life histories/stories can play in critiques of broad historical and cultural generalizations, the constitution of selves and identities through narration, and the narrative forms of life history/story. The alternative term "life story" is a product of this last concern, intended to stress creative and fictional aspects (Titon 1980).

Though widely accepted, life history/story research remained a subject of ambivalence, caught in a number of dichotomies: literary/scientific, personal/general, historical/artistic, subjective/objective (Crapanzano 1984: 954; Swindells 1989: 25; Geiger 1986: 337; Peacock and Holland 1993: 367). Young (1983: 479) notes a "general prejudice against life histories, which have a disconcerting tendency to say both more and less" than researchers want.[17] This Janus-faced blending may be one source of life histories/stories' appeal and interest, but these antinomies also establish different ideas about how life accounts should be treated and what kinds of analysis are most appropriate.

This essay is not intended as an overview, so I will not consider these differences in detail, but the following quotations give the flavor of the contrasts and issues involved:

• The life history is the mother lode out of which flow the data for all other genres of history (Vansina 1980: 265). As a general rule of thumb one can say that the more artistic any narrative is, the less it probably reflects a succession of events or an accurate rendering of an historical situation (Vansina 1965: 78).

• The life story need not be "used" for anything, because in the telling it is a self-sufficient and self-contained fiction (Titon 1980: 291).

• What does it mean to confirm a [life] account? . . . naive empiricism (Crapanzano 1984: 955). Narratives of the self are more than a story, a chronology, a history of the self (however defined); they are taken as a means of knowing the self (Crapanzano 1996: 108).

• Precisely because they are subjective documents, life histories exhibit integrity (Geiger 1986: 338).

• With something as alive and vital as a life history document, however, where the individual stands revealed to us by his own choice, we have a natural, self-contained source of information about subjective experience that cries out for understanding (Watson 1976: 98).

• These texts are not transparencies; they are dense with their own sound even as they invite us to glimpse the world within which they take place (Patai 1988: 165).

As these suggest, one major division lies between a) those who treat life histories/stories primarily as a source of evidence about history, social relations, cultural meaning, or psychological processes, as a series of synecdoches for extrapolation, and b) those who emphasize the creativity, particularities of expression, and self-constituting nature of life history/story narration. Titon, for instance, draws a strict line between history and story: "A story is made, but history is found out. Story is language at play; history is language at work" (1980: 278). Behar makes a similar distinction. She draws on Walter Benjamin's contrast between storytelling and information, she claims, in order to avoid "colonization of the act of telling a life story" and problematic oral/textual contrasts; this leads her to assimilate her own editing and writing to an act of retelling (1990: 228–29). Of course, there is no such either-or choice here, but rather a question of how these aspects of life history/story relate to one another, to the interests and values promoted in different academic fields, and to the dynamics and different understandings in play when life histories/stories are told.

These false dichotomies[18] fuel debate that seeks to prioritize the uses of life histories/stories. Similar contrasts inform attempts to define life history/story in relation to other genres familiar in European and American settings. Contrasts with biography, autobiography, memoir, oral history, and case history are drawn in terms of oral-written, first person–third person, perspective, and intention. Some definitions combine the way life history/story is produced with such attributes. Langness introduces his 1965 survey by saying, "*Life history* will be used in this book to refer to an extensive record of a person's life as it is reported either by the person himself or by others or both, and whether it is written or in interviews or both," and adds, "I can see no reason for restricting the term to only first person accounts" (4–5 and n.). Geiger paraphrases this and changes the original emphases, but still presents it as a direct quotation: "a life history is generally distinguishable from other kinds of oral documentation as 'an *extensive* record of a person's life told to and recorded by another, who then edits and writes the life as though it were autobiography'" (1986: 336). As a result, her definition is much narrower than his; Langness recognized that life histories are sometimes written rather than narrated, or combine writing and oral narration (as in Radin's classic studies).

Other characteristics of life history/story are oft-noted but not usually taken as definitional. These include moments of critical reflection by the narrator and the creation of different characters or personae identified as "I" in different episodes (complexly related to one another and to the "I" of present narration)[19] (Watson 1976: 99; Titon 1980: 287; Personal Narratives Group 1989: 99–100; Crapanzano 1996: 111; Tonkin 1992: 57; cf. Ochs and Capps 1996: 23; Urban 1989). These are not unique to life histories/stories, but they do figure in them regularly.

For me, these reflexive passages present fundamental questions for life histories: how and when are they introduced? which episodes and topics seem to call for such comment? what kinds of reflection are included? In some cases, they focus on the narrator's sense of self—consistency in character or values over time, important changes in self-understanding, conversions and epiphanies that result in transformation, or general developmental processes and retrospective teleologies. They might address key relations in similar ways. Others might be revealing metacommentary on the life story narration and situation itself.[20] Further, people often take themselves and their lives as signs of the times, musing on and appraising social and historical changes.[21] These last sorts of reflections may, in fact, be the more common ones in non-Western life histories/stories. As Keesing notes, "we need constantly to remind ourselves that [life histories/stories] are likely not only to represent the co-creation of a nonexistent 'genre' but also to reflect different folk models of self and person than those we take for granted" (1985: 33). And given that the people who relate life histories/stories are often those whom researchers come to know well, they may be accustomed to researchers' questions and interactions that call on them to formulate social and historical descriptions and generalizations.

Closer examination of these reflexive passages would provide a sense of the cultural meanings and paths of "a life" as well as of what kinds of stances narrators take toward historical process.[22] These questions return us to the situations in which life histories/stories are initially produced and their different goals and meanings for those present. Efforts to define life history/ story as a genre remain vague and variable in part because they try to be comprehensive; life histories/stories take diverse forms in different times and places. They have varied beginnings, related to different verbal or written genres relevant to their narrators (cf. Tonkin 1992: 49, 55). With this broader purview, defining what makes a life history/story is more a matter of exploring how life histories/stories are made. This requires looking at the uneven and uncertain correspondences between life history/story conversations, local genres, later written (and edited) presentations, and other written genres, such as autobiography. Even if narrators are not familiar with Euro-American versions of autobiography or life history/story, certain features or topics might be encouraged in the course of the conversation, later emphasized in the transformation to written form. Questions of contextualization, entextualization, and de- and recontextualization are central to this.

Also central is the conversations' relation to research. Some are more obviously like interviews, with specific questions or topics posed to guide the talk, more interjections that explicitly shape its course, and distant relations between researcher and narrator.[23] Others are more open-ended but have nonetheless been framed, given some direction, and had their purpose explained, even if in general terms.[24]

For instance, Keesing writes that "[m]ost of the Kwaio women we talked to assumed that their task was to tell us about women's virtues, their paths to prestige, the ancestral rules governing their lives, and their appropriate roles vis-à-vis watchful and potentially punitive ancestors, their daughters, and their husbands and affines. Most told us about themselves as commentaries on these more general ideologies about paths and responsibilities and rules of life" (1985: 31). Both formal, interview-like conversations and more open-ended ones may include episodes told with elaborate performative features (dramatization of characters and voices, quoted speech, dialogue, extensive scene-setting, etc.), though we expect these to a greater extent in more open-ended conversations. Researchers might develop warm friendships during their work, but it is probably misleading to think that their "role is mainly that of a sympathetic friend" (Titon 1980: 276) when they only ask occasional questions.[25]

Most life history/story conversations probably include an interplay among more and less directive interview styles and other kinds of conversational exchange, but these exchanges and patterns have rarely been considered. Researchers offer less direction when they perceive conversations as proceeding smoothly, somehow approximating their sense of "the story of a life." As sequences, topics, transitions, questions, and sessions themselves are negotiated, the shape of that story may change. Patai notes, "Marialice . . . transforms my questions in ways I could not have foreseen" (1988: 147). When we remember that many life histories/stories are told in multiple sessions over hours, weeks, or months, the potential complexity of this communicative negotiation becomes clear.[26]

Scholars have noted puzzled responses when they first ask people to tell their life history/story, and have described ways the request has been interpreted. These suggest various understandings of the task, interpreted through genres familiar to the tellers.

• "[T]he conventional form of 'a life' as a self-centered passage through time was not familiar [to Awlad 'Ali Bedouin]. Instead there were memorable events, fixed into dramatic stories with fine details" (Abu-Lughod 1993: 46).

• "Although the endless and repetitive lists of taboos and rhetorical appeals to virtue are frustrating and redundant to the ethnographer, our subjects construed them to be the central part of their task, in relation to which their autobiographical accounts took moral force" (Keesing 1985: 34).

• "*Miya ana ifufu* ('life its story') is not an indigenous genre and there are few narrative expectations about the form it should take. (Iyahalina recited his myths when I asked him for his life story; another man sang the drum songs of his lineage; yet another centered his account on the suicide of his father)" (Young 1983: 482–83).

• "Kru people of all ages and experience [were] willing and able to give a sequential account of their lives, often tied at some points to Western dates. A few hundred miles to the north west, in Sierra Leone, Michael Jackson found that 'spontaneous biographies are almost impossible to elicit from Kuranko individuals'" (Tonkin 1992: 132).

• Crashing Thunder wrote his life account in two parts. The first, called "The Story of My Life," is told in the first person. The second, "My Father's Teachings," is the "system of instruction used among the Winnebago and forms a unit by itself. The Indian regarded it as part of his autobiography inasmuch as it represents what he remembered to have heard from his father when he was a young boy" (Radin 1963: 2).

While many note that life history/story is not everywhere recognized or narrated in the form we know, there has been little effort to consider exactly what *is* told and presented, and how it might be produced and shaped through these conversational encounters.

At their start, then, most life histories/stories are conversational hybrids, a kind of research genre that remains in the making. In such situations, "what we make of them and their talk, what they make of us and our talk, comes loose from the anchors of their cultural understandings, and ours" (Keesing 1985: 32–33). This communicative negotiation is always also simultaneously a negotiation of micropolitics in the community (Keesing 1985; Mbilinyi 1989) and "the several levels of unequal power and privilege that characterize the ethnographic encounter and which also determine who is able to talk and what it is possible to say" (Gal 1991: 191; cf. Briggs 1986: 90–92).[27] All involved may agree to produce "a life" and understand that it will be retold again elsewhere, perhaps in different form.[28] But that production is far from seamless. A request for a life history/story is also a request for entextualization, but life history/story is not a uniform or universal genre. Conversations tack between different notions of what it should be and how it should be told, and include shifts of form and tone responsive to the situation and episodes related. They include various forms of personal narrative and may have reflexive sections as bridges, transitions, interruptions, or codas. These are contextualized and entextualized in diverse ways, facilitating or hindering later extraction, rearrangement, and re-presentation.

My focus here is not on what is altered, lost, added, or gained in the transformations of decontextualization and recontextualization, but on situations where life histories/stories are told. One example, however, can illustrate some of the issues and problems attendant on those processes, e.g., how different conversational tones may affect the way recontextualized life histories/stories are understood.[29] How does one start a life history/story? That beginning often includes signs of what genres are invoked, how narrators see and feel about their role, their task, and their relation with the researcher, and entextualizing shifts as other imagined audiences become relevant. Behar presents the start of Esperanza's life story in two articles, but in somewhat different ways, thereby illustrating some of the differences possible in recontextualization.

In the first, she begins a new section with Esperanza's beginning: "'*Comadre*, what a life, the life I've lived. My life is such a long history. My life has been very sad, very sad. Black, black, like my mother's life.' With these words, Esperanza begins her narrative, going on to recall her mother's life" (Behar 1990: 237). With no indication that these sentences had been excerpted from a longer exchange and combined, this struck me as earnest and rather dramatic, framing the tale to come with sorrowful regret and resignation. In the later article, however, Behar includes a fuller sense of the situation. The passage above comes in separate pieces, embedded in an interchange between Esperanza and Behar that gives a very different impression. The two renditions also show the slightly different translation choices Behar made in each case. Behar does not identify these words as "the start" in the second; the evocative sentences are almost buried in a teasing prefatory negotiation. Esperanza and her children laugh heartily when Behar asks her to tell her life.

> As the laughter died down Esperanza said, "Comadre, what a life, what a life I've had. No, my life is a very long history." The persistent ethnographer, I replied, "No, well, tell me your history." Esperanza laughed again. "Ay, comadre. Ay, the chewing gum is falling out of my mouth! No, my life has been very sad. Sad. Dark, dark. Like my mother's life. Look, do you want me to tell you from the time I was born?" Unaware that this was a joke, I responded, "Yes." There was more laughter. "I'm very scandalous about laughing, talking. My sister says to me, 'Ay, woman, what do you say? Laugh calmly. Laugh seriously. Calm down. You get too excited.' 'That's the way I am. You because you are bitter. Not me.' Despite the fact that I've had some dark times in my life." . . . [break for sodas] After a pause Esperanza turned to me, suddenly serious. "Look, comadre, why would you like me to tell you about my life since childhood?" I said, hoping to sound convincing, "It seems very interesting." Esperanza was laughing again. I added, encouragingly, "And you speak very well," and after a pause, "I like to hear you tell stories." She still found all this quite funny. But she soon became serious and started. "Well, look. Since I was born, well, God knows. My mother says that I was born at three in the afternoon." (Behar 1992: 111–12)

Placed in the fuller conversation, the same comments seem more like a laughing ploy or rebuff to Behar's request than like the striking, melancholic preface they formed in the first article. Their very different tones and presentations result from Behar's different recontextualizations. The conversational turns and glitches, intermissions, missed cues, and multiple possibilities of the longer quotation are not unique to Behar's situation but part of the character of life history/story as verbal communication. Sections that are awkward, false starts "irrelevant" to the life story or too closely tied to the immediate situation to be understood elsewhere, should not simply be deleted without further thought. They, too, can instructively clarify what understandings of a life, life history, and other ways of speaking were in play. Understanding the contexts in which life accounts start can surely lead to a clearer understanding of how these conversations become lives and life histories/stories.

CONVERSATIONAL PATTERNS AND SHIFTS: FRAMES, GENRES, EPISODES, ASIDES, ETC.

In negotiating life narratives, these conversations also address questions about what counts as history. We might expect first-person accounts that focus on individual actions and experience, if not also on psychological self-reflection. But narrators may not offer this as appropriate. Even if they do, the choices of topics, episodes, sequence, and mode of narration are not automatic. They all draw on ideas about what matters in recounting the past, what should be remembered and why. The Sunjata epic, for instance, offers intricate and elaborate descriptions of war preparations, but has very little about actual battles. These narrative choices are closely bound up with Mande notions of history and personhood (Bird and Kendall 1980). Further, ideas about history are varied; different aspects and perspectives are perceived as relevant in different settings. When asked about the history of initiation ceremonies, Okiek in Kenya usually give a broad account of tradition and continuity. In other situations, however, they tell a complex account of gradual elaboration that incorporated and adapted new ritual events and elements (Kratz 1993).

Choices and negotiations over topic, form, turn-taking, and even how to start and stop the story continue throughout life history conversations, involving the researcher, the narrator, and any others present.

I turn now to my own attempts at life history/story with Okiek in Kenya.[30] I cannot consider them fully in this essay, but they can nonetheless illustrate misunderstandings that can arise from different expectations, the conversational grounding of life history/story, its shifting modes of communicative exchange, aspects of entextualization and contextualization, and various reflexive passages. In November 1974, as a young student doing my first research with Okiek, I approached Simpole Mapelu, father of my research assistant, about recording his life history. What I had learned about the use of life histories/stories as an anthropological method suggested that that of an old man with whom I had established "good rapport" would be ideal. I also knew I was not to "lead" him, but to let him tell his own story.[31] My Okiek language skills were still rudimentary, so we worked with the help of his son, Joseph.

The narrative that resulted that day was extremely short—just over five minutes long—and bore little resemblance to other life histories/stories I knew. It was more like by-then-familiar generalized accounts of past Okiek life (Kratz 1993; 1994: 58–60). Beginning with their hunting and honey-gathering life, Simpole named honey flowerings and animals, went on to mention the start of Okiek farming and herding and the coming of non-Okiek to the area through colonial influence, and ended with a declaration of how Okiek now pursue a variety of economic activities, especially farming, so that they can enrich themselves like other people. I tried again in January 1975. Simpole again began with general description of important Okiek practices (how to make bows and spears and arrange marriages; the whole was just over four minutes long). When I asked about several specific events in his own life, he told three brief personal narratives (about working for Maasai as a child and returning home, a serious hunting injury that crippled his hand, and working on early colonial road crews in the Narok district; about eleven minutes total).

In February 1985, a decade later and much more linguistically able, I asked Kirutari Meitukut to tell me about his life.[32] This attempt produced a series of personal narratives interspersed with other exchanges—conversation, joking, and gossip. Kirutari also included generalized passages describing the past, though with different foci than Simpole's. However, Kirutari incorporated them in ways that arose out of his personal narratives or in response to my questions and comments. Later still, in 1993, I worked with Kirutari to transcribe and discuss our earlier session.

I will concentrate on my discussion with Kirutari, but Simpole's narration is also of interest.[33] In the first session, Simpole spoke quickly, in a high-pitched voice, giving a kind of monologic recitation. Listening to it again after some years, what struck me was the very *lack* of conversational engagement. No one provided the phatic responses that punctuate virtually all Okiek conversation and storytelling. No one asked questions or made comments. My comprehension was not good enough, and Joseph sat silently. At one point, Joseph shushed some children and another man joined us and commented on the unusual task; Simpole responded, "Yes, it's tiring." When he finished, Simpole remarked, "Isn't that the way it's done?"; others assured him, "You really did it well."

Simpole saw the sessions as additive, ending the second group of general descriptions with "Those are the words I remember, together with the ones I told you the other day." He spoke more slowly the second time; in addition to being significantly longer, his personal narratives also included more expression, gestures, and quoted speech in specific interactions. These could have been part of a more natural conversation, though there were still no phatic agreements to indicate engagement and interest, no spoken interactive responses to what he said.

How was this life history? Simpole had clearly planned topics he felt were central; the start and finish of each general commentary are explicitly marked and transitions between topics are smooth. He understood the life account I requested as a testimony to the fundamental social and historical changes he had lived through. Before talking about the start of Okiek farming, he situates himself relative to the hunting and honey-gathering he describes: "Those are the things people were doing when I became clever." He situates farming in relation to age-sets following his. He turns to the influx of other ethnic groups by noting that Maasai were not there when he and his age-mates were children; the Maasai came and formed friendships with their fathers. These practices and changes *are* his life's circumstances and experiences, then, but Simpole did not regard personal incidents and perspectives as an appropriate way to relate them. The broad sweep was what mattered, not his personal location and experience within it, particularly when he thought the testimony should be brief.

Kirutari's account is also clearly framed. In fact he marks the end twice, because I continued past his first declaration and tried to continue past the second one as well. We were alone; I taped over two hours of our interaction that afternoon. Our discussion turned away from the life story during the last half hour, but it is full of conversational exchanges, phatic responses, and mutual interruption. The broad structure of the discussion is as follows (disregarding for now many brief shifts, asides, and comments). After initial fiddling with the tape recorder and negotiation of how to start, Kirutari tells a life history/story with four major episodes: early childhood (with an emotional reunion with his brother as the dramatic focus), advanced boyhood (which brings him to stay with his brother), initiation (the longest, most elaborate and dramatic), and adulthood (featuring Mau Mau and his government service). Each ends with a summarizing coda and three include a reprise that further elaborates key events.

Just after Kirutari first ends, he responds to a question and then we explicitly negotiate whether to stop there or continue until the tape finishes. Kirutari adds another episode, in which he tries to spear his father, they are jailed, and later they make peace. He follows with an extended evaluative recap of his past and present situation, ending in advice to me about marriage. Following this, I try three times to elicit other episodes, asking about matters that I know have affected him or are important in Okiek life. I first ask about his health problems,[34] taking off from his own mention of them, then about early hunting experiences, and finally about marriage. Each time, our discussion begins on topic, then veers in another direction—explanations of certain concepts or insistent tests of my language ability when I falter. His extended evaluative coda was intended as the end of the session. His comments on marriage included concern for his dead brother's children, leading us finally into extended discussion of current land politics and sales, price comparisons relating acres and cars, a challenging riddle,[35] and other matters far from Kirutari's life history.

Kirutari's account was far closer to my own understanding of life history/story, a series of narratives about his own experience over time. But it still skipped much that I thought would be told (some of which I asked about at the end) and began before his own birth, by situating his mother.[36]

C: [initial discussion about the tape recorder] So won't you remember?
K: If I think-is-i (hmm), there are some I remember and some I don't remember.

C: So won't you tell me what you remember?

K: I'll tell you. (yes) So, um— Mother was— Should I [start by] remember [ing] Mother? (yes) Mother was—she was of Kap Lerimo [family]. (yes) [The one] of Sang'olung'ola. Mother. (yes). She was sister to Sang'olung'ola. (yes) She was born by Kesenoi. (yes) *Basi*. So Kausa had Kesenoi [as his wife]. It's him that we named my son Kausa after.

He continues with an abbreviated genealogy that includes his parents' marriage and the birth of their first children. I interrupt several times seeking elaboration, specific place names, etc. Kirutari's own birth is treated simply as a chronological marker within his mother's unfortunate marriage:

K: *Basi*. So then they up and, um—came and gave Mother to this family [in marriage]. So didn't she come and stay? (yes) and had this many children [makes sign for two]. (yes) So she had the first and it died.

C: Yes. What happened to it?

K: I don't know, illness. Was I born? Illness. I don't know. She stayed until she had another baby, um—Nemboko's father. (yes) *Basi*. So she stayed, and then Papa up and chased Mother away then.

C: Why? [We discuss what the situation was like, how he treated her, then Kirutari returns to the story line.]

K: So Mother went to that house—to her father's house. (hm) So she went and stayed. And when she left-i (hm), she was pregnant with another child who follows me. She was pregnant (yes) because I was born here, along with Nemboko's father. (yes) *Basi*. So when we had become two-i, he chased her off. And she went carrying me on her back. (You?) Yes. (yes) *Basi*. So we went then. Nemboko's father stayed in this country. (yes) That's what brought me back here myself.

Kirutari himself is a minor player in these early scenes, still a young child, but he assembles the cast of siblings that will punctuate the rest of his story (two younger brothers by a different father, living elsewhere, and his older brother) and sets in motion the domestic drama that determined at least the first fifteen years of his life: his mother dies suddenly while he is still young; he is separated from his siblings;[37] his father abandons and ignores him, even when Kirutari later comes to live with him, joining his older brother. This also provides effective dramatic structure for the life history/story and a varied and vivid scenario of hardship that becomes thematic.

Kirutari was a skilled speaker. His thematic linkages and dramatic structures lend coherence and vitality to the sequence of incidents, giving a simple temporal sequence emotional texture and intensity. Regardless of whether or not a life history/story is told with talent and flair, however, its structure is episodic.[38] This may be an obvious point, but it has several important implications. As Simpole indicated, telling a life history/story is an additive process; more episodes can be included, initial versions can be expanded. Episodes represent narrative chunks that can be rearranged, even combined, through later editing (by a narrator's comments as well as by a researcher). This expandable nature is the foundation of life history/story as methodology. In repeated conversations, narrators go back and add episodes or fill in sections. In the process, a life history/story's form is negotiated; researchers (and others) ask questions and suggest topics, though they may not be taken up. Just as I asked Simpole and Kirutari about particular events after they had finished their own renditions, for instance, Shostak also "mentioned some of the topics I hoped to cover . . . asked for expansion of topics . . . [and] [i]f a woman found it difficult to sustain a topic or to start a new one, I suggested alternatives" (1981: 21–22).

Treating life history/story as a method means encouraging these recursive and additive aspects in systematic ways,[39] but they are already part of conversational practice. Kirutari himself introduces reprises, returning to his story after an explanatory interlude with a recap or retelling certain incidents with greater elaboration. He retells the story of his mother's death, for instance, after he realizes that he left out her remarriage. The episodic nature of life history/story is related to its conversational grounding in other ways as well. Episodes are usually marked, verbally or in other ways. They effect shifts in conversational turn-taking, giving the floor over for an extended narration, and may mark the assumption of a performative frame (Bauman 1977). Often, marked episodes are sections of interaction entextualized for export and retelling. One simple example of marking is the word "basi," which appears in the selections from Kirutari's life account. A multipurpose conjunction and exclamation, "basi" can mark a return to narration after interruption, the start of a new episode, the structural segments within an episode, and the passage of time (when combined with other phrases).[40] Life history/story episodes create natural breaking points where other comments, issues, activities, and questions intervene—though of course they intervene at other times as well.

Life history conversations are not only memory in action, but the configuring of perspective in action. Narrators combine episodes in sequences based on particular notions of time, social relations, and self. Assumptions about historical causality inform episodes and sequences, suggesting which episodes are included and elaborated, how events are related, what forces and incidents are influential, and how individuals figure in larger sociohistorical currents. All episodes are not equal, however, and the structure, elaboration, and order of episodes are also related to particular cultural concerns, conventions, and genres of speech. Both Simpole and Kirutari, for example, tell four-part life accounts initially. This may be coincidence, but it might also suggest a nexus between composing an unfamiliar narrative genre and the performance of both ritual action and other, familiar verbal genres. Four is an auspicious (*esiny'a*) number for Okiek and part of several generative poetic schemes. Ritual actions are often repeated four times and draw on a set of auspicious places, plants, and substances (Kratz 1994: 136–37, 148–61). Okiek formulate ritual solutions for novel situations with these resources. Fours are also part of the poetic patterning of Okiek blessings, in line structure, development, and thematic repetition (166–75).

The four-part structure is put to quite different use by the two men, however. Simpole is an economic and political historian in his four brief parts. Kirutari emphasizes social processes and cultural concepts in an account whose four parts correspond to Okiek notions of the life cycle: two sections devoted to different stages of childhood,[41] a major segment about initiation into adulthood (the most significant ritual occasion and change of personhood [Kratz 1994]), and a final episode that combines several adult experiences.[42] Changing conceptions and circumstances of the family, work, the body, childhood, and so forth—important topics of cultural history—can be encoded not only in the content of life histories/stories, but in their structural form and organization as well.

Kirutari does not ignore Simpole's concerns, however; the same economic and political transformations are the backdrop of his story. Several of his general descriptive passages focus on similar themes, and reflexive passages (discussed below) sometimes draw contrasts between times before and after Okiek began farming. Early on, when I ask where his parents were living when his brother was born, Kirutari gives a general description of Okiek residence patterns and migration, key circumstances of hunting and honey-gathering life. Later on, listing foods shared in his grandmother's home, he comments on the absence then of *ugali*, the current maize-based staple food, and includes a commentary on the introduction of maize with a wonderful short description of maize from a child's perspective:

> Grandfather and them brought it. (yes) Grandfather and them brought it. (From where?) I don't know what country it came from, where they went to bring it. I don't know if—do I remember? I just saw maize.
>
> So if you were given some, you didn't eat it. You'd go and sleep and you put it here [just under the blanket near your head], (CK laughs) so you can feel at night where it is. If you were given a roasted cob, you didn't finish it. You eat one kernel, you eat one kernel. Later you eat another, later you eat another, later—and it was good! Very good! At that time we were frightened to see it [the first time].
>
> So if millet was made—porridge, because we weren't making ugali. Well, we didn't want it. (yes) We said, "Should we eat food that looks like shit, and says pe-pe-pe-pe?" (CK laughs). It was only maize that we liked.

The structure of episodes—punctuated with general descriptions, comparative comments, and reflections—and various kinds of elaboration among and within episodes also create and convey different emphases, perspectives, and cultural values. Kirutari's initiation episode might illustrate the occasion's significance for Okiek, but this does not mean that most Okiek would tell lives with similarly extensive descriptions. His initiation is dramatic and striking for other reasons as well. For one thing, it is unusual. Kirutari "stole" initiation at a young age; he successfully planned a way to secretly join initiates before his time, gaining approval from ritual leaders, without his family's knowledge. It is also dramatic, however, because of its relations to previous episodes.

The hardships of Kirutari's childhood are one relevant dramatic feature, combined with his relation with his older brother. Forsaken by his father even before his mother's death, Kirutari describes his time with his grandmother and uncle as one of poverty. The second part of his childhood episode depicts an emotional reunion with his older brother. They no longer knew one another, but soon became inseparable. Though the boys lived near their father, he ignored them. They fended for themselves, building small houses, following young men to the forest to ask for honey or meat, coming home in late evening only to go fetch their own water. Describing how close they lived to their father by pointing to houses in the area, Kirutari finishes his boyhood episode with a summary and begins the initiation episode with emphases on these difficulties:

> We lived in this house now, (yes) and that woman and Father lived in that house right there (yes) with her children. We just saw them. (hee-ya) We just saw them. It was very bad trouble, very bad, very bad. [clucks][43] If this illness hadn't gotten me, friend, this illness that got me and made me all bent up— Basi. We staaaayed. Otherwise I would have been able to find something for myself, if it were cured. I would still live in my place, and do my things until all these people saw [how much I did]. (hm) So we staaaaayed. And I was no longer there [at my grandmother's], (yes) it became [the case] that I was just here. (Here) Here. (yes)
>
> Basi. So we stayed and stayed and lived with trouble, being mistreated, mistreated, mistreated, until it came time to circumcise our age-set. (yes)

Kirutari's older brother is initiated. Kirutari is not only alone again, but a boy that secluded initiates can harass.

> Basi. So I went about alone then indeed. And these initiates would call me. (yes) So wasn't my brother sick [i.e., recovering from circumcision]? (yes) So those other ones started to persecute me. (yes) They beat me because I saw their penises.[44] [CK laughs] They yelled at me this many days [makes a sign for a number] (yes) and the next day they were planning to circumcise Araap Semeri here nearby again, at Cakaayua.

Physical persecution and the sudden social gulf that initiation introduces between the brothers is too much. Kirutari sneaks off to be initiated as well, becoming a man at the same time as his older brother. Kirutari's trouble with the initiates further exacerbates the difficulties of his childhood, but initiation proves the watershed. This long, stirring episode ends with resolution of the hardship:

> We came and staaaayed and didn't concern ourselves about anythiiiiing. Until our heads were shaved [to end initiation] and we became *murenik* and came and stayed. We didn't see any more trouble then. (yes) Hmm-mm. We had [become big enough] to take care of ourselves. (yes) We went eating our honey, and went and killed our giant forest hog, and farmed.

Narrative and dramatic structure are tied up with psychological and cultural patterns and with historical memories in life histories/stories.[45] Any element or incident may be multiply implicated, overdetermined by these overlapping dynamics, just as the significance of initiation, brotherly solidarity, a nightmare polygynous household, and a cruel father become entwined emphases in Kirutari's account of his 1940s initiation.

The foundations of such continuity, cohesion, and dramatic momentum and the ways of creating them vary (e.g., Young 1983: 489ff; Rosaldo 1980: 177ff.), and some narrators weave these ties more tightly than others. Structural marking and segmentation into episodes, among other techniques, may facilitate entextualization by identifying potentially extractable and rearrangeable parts, but narrative ties simultaneously render segments more difficult to separate and reorder.

This is a tension within entextualization itself, concerning the relative tightness of textual coherence and discourse-internal connections: just how independent of one another are various stretches of entextualized and decontextualized discourse? At the same time, there are also contradictory tendencies to entextualization and contextualization, between making discourse extractable and embedding it in its communicative circumstances. As distinct portions of life history/story conversations are more clearly defined and abundantly marked, they may be elaborated internally, perhaps cast in genre forms. Segmentation and separation from conversational interaction might thus become easier, but more elaborate rendering and development can simultaneously draw on performative features that tie episodes more closely to their contexts. This might provide significant cultural and historical details and create more compelling stories, but at the same time render translation and recontextualization more difficult.

Kirutari's initiation episode is a good example. I cannot even begin full analysis of that section here, but when Kirutari moves into his own initiation, he begins a markedly more elaborate performance. The action moves slowly, following the chronology of ceremonial sequence in some detail over twenty-four hours. The episode is dense with quoted speech, building drama, characters, and relationships. Kirutari used quoted and reported speech occasionally in earlier episodes—with a briefer, less dense cluster of such speech during the reunion scene[46]—but much of the initiation is told in dialogue. He goes beyond reporting and quoting speech to take on characters' voices in dialogue. There are no quotative frames ("I said," "He replied") in these sections, but Kirutari speaks in the high-pitched voice that signals quoted speech paralinguistically.

Reported speech, quoted speech, and dialogue are extremely versatile and interesting resources, used in many forms and ways (Bakhtin 1981; Lucy 1993; Kratz 1994: 193–94, 205–209).[47] Together they may create a continuum that is one indicator of narrative distance or the extent of performative immersion and involvement (Hymes 1975). To enacted dialogue and quoted speech, Kirutari adds sound effects, snatches of song, gestures, and exaggerated facial expressions. Some of the very features that make the initiation episode an effective, well-developed, and compelling personal narrative and performance—even without the rest of the life history/story—also embed the episode in its setting and tie it to nonverbal modes of communication possible there. Further, quoted speech often builds on communicative assumptions and background knowledge that remain unspoken but would require extensive explanation in another context.

Life history episodes are told in ways that reach in several directions at once, constituting them as self-contained but at the same time situating them thoroughly, simultaneously entextualized and contextualized. I have noted a few aspects of this double process that have to do with the narration of episodes themselves, as if they were always uninterrupted, but that is certainly not the case. Just as markers such as "basi" can signal shifts from conversational dialogue back to extended personal narrative, so too narrators interrupt or divert their own narratives or can be diverted by questions, comments, and actions, breaking *out* of performance. This possibility of moving in and out of dialogic and narrative modes is ever-present in the phatic agreements that punctuated Kirutari's life account but were conspicuously absent from Simpole's. Maintaining conversational interaction, functioning as signs of surprise, sympathy, and simple attention, these responses encourage and in subtle ways shape the telling. Asides and explanations also punctuate life history/story episodes, responsive to the knowledge, interests, and relations of those present. These conversational groundings are part of the same double process, contextualizing life history/story conversations yet rendering them partially decontextualizable.

Modes of interaction shift over the course of the conversation, as expectations and understandings of life history/story are negotiated. During the first episode of Kirutari's account, for instance, we are both seeking suitable roles and ways in which to approach the telling of his life. After his opening disclaimer about the limits of his recollection (quoted above), Kirutari makes three further comments about memory and knowledge.[48] All occur in sections responding to my questions. Kirutari also interrupts himself when he remembers an important event (his mother's remarriage) and corrects his account accordingly. This period was indeed at (or beyond) the limits of his personal memory; the absence of such remarks in the rest of the conversation may simply reflect Kirutari's confidence in memories that were closer in time. But it also seems that he was not quite sure of our goal yet. He also includes two unsolicited asides in this episode, explaining his situation at his grandmother's with examples that placed me in the role of the mother.[49] Kirutari probably sensed from my questions that our understandings did not quite match; these asides attempted to clarify the matters that he thought confused me. This kind of aside is also absent in the rest of the conversation.

Kirutari's shifts, of course, were related to my own as well. I interrupted him many times as he began the first episode, seeking details of setting that would have been provided in narrative forms more familiar to me.[50] Kirutari's opening—the skeletal genealogy and the chronology of his parents' marriage—seemed vague and unlocated. As in interviews about Okiek history, culture, and social relations, I sought to clarify specific times, places, people, and chains of events. As Kirutari continued, his narrative began to take clearer shape; my questions became fewer, intended mainly to elicit details of events and his age. By the second episode, we had both settled into the situation. My turns were fewer and focused on Kirutari's descriptions. During the initiation episode, Kirutari spoke for long stretches with only phatic responses from me.

In the final episode, Kirutari begins to break his own narration, for example by first asking me if I remember Mau Mau (leading to discussion of my age) and then making jokes about sex. We also get into several asides about the meanings of words, as Kirutari searches for the word for "nursery school" and I fail to understand Okiek pronunciation of military terms and ranks. The end of the life account shows negotiation similar to that at the start. As noted above, Kirutari says he is finished, but continues at my request, adding another episode. He then provides a second ending, a series of broad evaluative comments. After describing the wealth and hospitality of his younger siblings, whose house remained a second home to him, he goes on:

I don't remember others. (hm) There are those ones I don't remember from when I was born. So you remember? (hmm-mm, I don't remember those ones.) That thing I remember indeed is all those troubles (hm) that I saw. I saw— When Mother died, then came trouble, trouble, trouble. (hm) Here you see that I'm not staying with anyone. And when I thought to stay with someone [his mother's co-wife] I had trouble. (yes) Otherwise—otherwise we would be people today.[51] If this illness hadn't gotten me? Look at these people. They have cows. Mine were—before I became sick I had a lot of goats. . . . [continues about how people taking care of his goats cheated him]. . . . Even if they are Okiek, Cory, don't think they are all good [people]. Different tribes of people are the same. (They're the same.) They're the same because if a man marries you now and goes and bothers you, do you think you will stay [with him]? (no) Better just [get] the one that—you see likes

you-e, (yes) and you stay. One that doesn't annoy you and bully you, and usually—usually brings you things—buys you clothes, and buys you good food.
(yes) That's the only one that's a person [i.e., a real husband]. And that one
that you see is just [interested in] screwing-i that-i (is bad), that bothers you-
i, is just worthless. There is no need [of yours] that he sees to.

Kirutari's advice to me, of course, is based on his mother's hapless situation. His second summation draws lessons for me and expands them philo-
sophically. Immediately afterward, I ask the first question eliciting further
episodes: "When did this illness first get you?" In response to each of my
three final questions, Kirutari turns his answers into explanations, not personal narratives. Just as I fell into a question-and-answer format resembling
directed interviews at the beginning, when Kirutari's narrative form jarred
my expectations, Kirutari transforms my efforts to continue the life history
into an undirected interview. In the conversation following my second question, I first confuse two similar-sounding Okiek words and later stumble
over the right morphological form of a verb. A hard linguistic taskmaster,
Kirutari turns these errors into occasions for language lessons and takes us
still further from the life story. When I rephrase my sentence, he insists that
I keep trying, and I offer four morphological variations (all wrong!). By returning to some of our other regular, structured conversational modes, Kirutari ends the life history/story section for good and our conversation becomes
more casual.

While Kirutari told his life history/story in episodes that could be decontextualized and retold in transformed versions elsewhere in speech or print,
the particular shape of those episodes emerged out of the conversational
grounding of our interaction. Some of his reflexive comments were also tied
to our interchanges, such as his remarks on memory mentioned above. Others may have been evoked by the very life history/story endeavor, reflecting
on connections seen in retrospective overview. While considering patterns
in Kirutari's asides, explanations, and other reflexive passages would further
illuminate the interactive, conversational creation and structuring of his life
history/story, I will remark here on only one such kind of comment.

Kirutari seasons his account a number of times with comparative evaluations, relating past and present in ways that emphasize their contrasts. From
one perspective, these might be just the kind of statements against which
Vansina warns: "one must be distrustful also of statements about former
norms or general rules. . . . Since informants have a strong tendency to gen-
eralize and often speak in terms of 'norms' (to be contrasted, of course, with
today's norms!), this caveat applies often" (Vansina 1980: 269). Vansina would
probably agree that these comparisons can be seen as moral statements and
indicators of contemporary concerns, even if they are not accurate statements about specific historical facts. His main concern is to assess the factual
basis of individual statements, seeking criteria by which to ferret out histori-

cal truth and discarding the rest as chaff. But such statements might also suggest ways that social and historical trends are perceived from different perspectives, and broader topical patterns might also point to other visions of history and historical representation.

At different times, for instance, Kirutari compared past and present in terms of foods eaten, garden sizes, crops, government administration (in relation to hunting), wildlife abundance, ceremonial organization, respect between different age-sets, and children's experience and knowledge. Comparisons were drawn with several points in the past, considered in relation to Kirutari's age during the events recounted. His comparison of garden sizes and crops, for instance, concerned the time just after his initiation; during earlier episodes, a more general prefarming past was the contrast. Recalling hunting during his childhood, Kirutari noted the past absence of Game Department intervention, described the general absence of government and *cumpeek* (white Europeans) then, and went on to talk about the shops of red cumpeek (Asians) who were in the area at the time.

Apart from remarks on respect (on the decline according to elders everywhere, it seems), Kirutari's comparative comments concern Okiek economic diversification and ceremonies (particularly, ceremonial aspects related to that diversification). These topics dovetail with the general descriptive passages included in Kirutari's childhood episode (on migration patterns within the forest and early encounters with maize and millet) as well as with the themes of Simpole's condensed account. I have argued elsewhere that Okiek represent historical change in several ways, with a notion of "tradition" serving as a kind of shared, public historical narrative. Yet Okiek do not represent "tradition" in a broad, undifferentiated way; they concentrate on and valorize two particular domains: their hunting and honey-gathering life and their initiation ceremonies (Kratz 1993). It may not be surprising, then, that Kirutari's and Simpole's explicitly historical comments also flow from and address these domains. People narrate their lives in ways informed by conceptions of time and history and indeed might reflect on memory, narrative, and historical process as they do so. This does not make people into Living Histories or simple repositories of useful historical facts, but it does mean that life histories/stories are one important way that history and historical understanding live and are produced in different guises and situations.

As I found during my work with Simpole and Kirutari, there is no obvious, naturally occurring model for how life accounts should be told or what they should include. Each of us brought to the encounter notions of relevant topics, narrative forms, appropriate presentations, and our ongoing relationships, all shaping the conversation in specific ways in a mutual attempt to figure out what these particular life accounts would be. Many scholars have observed that life histories/stories are hybrid genres, but I have tried here to explore the contingent nature of that hybridity, how it comes about and is developed through conversational interaction. Taking account of the contexts and ways in which oral life histories are produced may challenge claims of the "integrity" of life histories/stories and their status as representing "authentic voices," but it does not challenge the value of exploring life experiences and narratives.

A GENRE ITSELF?

Conversations that produce a life history/story are the start of a process that might yield a written text. The conversations can move in many directions, shaped through ongoing, situated interaction. Interlocutors include and allude to different frames, genres, topics, attitudes, and tones and incorporate a variety of expressive communicative resources as they move into and out of episodes, questions, asides, reflections, and other exchanges. Various kinds of narrative are embedded in and fashioned through life history/story conversations. They often include personal narratives,[52] experiences told in the first person, but lives can certainly be told in other ways. Each conversational situation and range of available communicative resources holds both possibilities and constraints,[53] for critical practices of orality are always social practices as well.

Such practices are characterized by subtle communicative negotiations of social relations, power, knowledge, and identities. A life told at different times and settings may present different selves and emphasize different themes. Speaking of a Sumbanese man, for instance, Hoskins notes, "During the course of my work with him, he outlined his life history to me on three different occasions, each time in a totally different way" (1985: 153). First he featured his involvement with missions, government, and travel, then emphasized his family life and marriage, and finally presented his life through the lens of ritual history and training. Historicizing lives, verbally constructing their sequences and trajectories, creates understandings of particular perspectives and meanings, what Ricoeur calls "seeing as" (1979: 133).[54]

In this paper I have considered life history/story as method, as data, as composite "genre," and as scholarly category, but I have emphasized life history/story as told in conversation, i.e., as complex communicative interaction and exchange. My own attempts to "do life histories" with two Okiek men, Simpole Mapelu and Kirutari Meitukut, illustrated some of the issues and processes involved. They also demonstrated the variable forms that these conversations can take, from Simpole's terse ideal history told in awkward monologic dialogue to Kirutari's more extended mixture of personal narrative, commentary, advice, and general historical description and comparison, developed more interactively and with different modes of elaboration and performance.

Life history/story conversations always hold surprises. Apart from taking unanticipated forms and directions, they often mention unexpected events, involvements, and connections as well. Though I knew Kirutari had brothers elsewhere and that he had been in colonial service, I did not know about his dire childhood circumstances, the extent of his travels during his employment, that he learned Kiswahili while living in Ololunga center for a time as a child, that he attended school for a few months, or that he had stolen initiation![55] Methodologically, then, life history/story conversations can be a valuable and humbling discovery procedure that should urge researchers to reflect critically on their own assumptions about and expectations of life trajectories, cultural and historical knowledge, forms of communication, and research practice itself.

Jan Vansina was not the first or last to observe that "'life history' as a genre itself is ill-understood at best" (1980: 265). This paper suggests some of the sources of this perennial obscurity and ambiguity, including the very expectation that life history is a "genre itself." Life histories/stories are multiple and variable in form, quite indeterminate in content, and entail multiple settings and situations. Oral life histories/stories usually begin as conversational hybrids, genres-in-the-making at best. As they are entextualized, recontextualized, and retold, they are reshaped and re-presented in ways that other audiences will understand. From variable beginnings all over the world, these processes may make them more alike as accounts and produce a written genre of life history/story known in some parts of the world. These diverse origins and multiple processes of translation and transformation cannot but spawn ambiguities and fruitful puzzlement, as different understandings of self, life, society, and history come into contention.

NOTES

I would like to thank colleagues who commented on an earlier draft and offered kind encouragement: David Anderson, Mark Auslander, Carla Freeman, Ivan Karp, Steve Kaplan, Tom Spear, and participants at the marvelous "Words and Voices" conference in February 1997. I dedicate this essay to the memory of Kirutari Meitukut, a dear friend who died in April 1994.

1. Quoted by Samuel (1994: 11), who draws Aubrey's self-description from Tylden-Wright (1991: 15–16). Aubrey wrote little about himself; when he did, he sometimes described himself self-effacingly in the third person (Tylden-Wright 1991: 12–13).

2. A number of scholars have considered when and how personal narratives are told in conversation, and how "spontaneity" is produced and negotiated through considerable social and communicative work (Bauman 1986; Gumperz 1992; Jefferson 1978; Sacks, Schegloff, and Jefferson 1974; Sacks 1972, 1992).

3. In an earlier draft, I used "life hi/story" as an abbreviation combining the two main terms. However, most readers assumed that this was intended to make a point about the gendered nature of life accounts or scholarship about them. A number were confused, put off by, or simply weary of the presumed implications of the slash-form. While the rise of women's studies does intersect with the history of the terms "life history" and "life story" and the way such scholarship has developed in recent

decades (as discussed below), gender is not the only or even primary aspect of relevance here. Accordingly, I dropped the original abbreviation and use this plurality of terms, including the longer, but more neutral, combination form "life history/story." Peacock and Holland (1993) briefly survey approaches to life history/story; they emphasize psychological and anthropological concerns but give no attention to historiography.

4. Behar's recent book *Translated Woman* (1993) makes her own background and her relation with Esperanza, whose story she tells, as important as the story itself. The terms used for people in these situations can be quite interesting. In a searching and frank treatment of her working relation with Rebeka Kalindile and the process of producing Kalindile's life history, for instance, Mbilinyi (1989) refers to Kalindile as the life historian and herself as the producer, perhaps drawing on a cinematic model. She also refers to Kalindile as coauthor of the life history and concludes with a careful discussion of different models for attributing authorship and copyright in published life histories/stories (223–25). Behar, on the other hand, reserves the term "life historian" (or "life historian/author") for the researcher and refers to the person whose life is told as "the native" (1990: 224–27).

5. This shift was also part of broader shifts toward processual analyses of how social relations, culture, and history are constituted.

6. See also Duranti and Goodwin 1992. Tedlock and Mannheim (1995) explore how ethnography and culture both emerge in communicative interaction and is relevant to life history/story work more generally.

7. According to Lionel Trilling, autobiography developed somewhat earlier as a confessional kind of narrative, e.g., with Rousseau's *Confessions* (Rosaldo 1976: 148).

8. Of roughly eighty references in his bibliography for this period, only three deal with other geographic areas (Australia and Melanasia). Langness did not include slave autobiographies, which also burgeoned during the late 1800s (Geiger 1986: n. 30), but their inclusion does not belie the European and American focus of autobiographies of the period.

9. Radin says this quite clearly in the introduction to the 1920 *The Autobiography of a Winnebago Indian*, but the book's 1963 Dover reprint has a back cover blurb that describes the study in terms that later became more conventional: "Originally taken down in the field, in Winnebago, from the dictation of the Indian known as S.B." Crashing Thunder was actually the name of the older brother of the narrator in the 1920 and 1926 books; Lurie discusses this choice of pseudonym (1971: 92–93, 96–100).

10. Kluckhohn's essay has a substantial section on written and narrated life histories, biographies, and autobiographies. Angell's review of personal documents in sociology includes oral life history as a useful method and source. Gottschalk's chapter on "The Historian and the Historical Document," however, focuses entirely on written documents. He includes written autobiographies and diaries, but remarks that narrated testimony is rarely available to historians (Gottschalk, Kluckhohn, and Angell 1945).

11. Langness's intellectual interests as a psychological anthropologist may have influenced this periodization as well.

12. Griaule's work in France during this period singled out Ogotemmêli as an individual sage but focused on his knowledge and exposition of Dogon cosmology rather than on his life.

13. Samuel (1994: 4) notes that oral history was only recognized as a valuable source by guild historians in the late 1960s and 1970s.

14. Geiger identifies 1960 as the turning point but justifies that date neither in terms of the chronology of feminism and women's studies nor in relation to published work on life history/story. In fact, the works she cites would seem to support 1970 instead (Geiger 1986: 342–46).

15. Ginsburg notes, for instance, that he "stressed, against the undifferentiated notion of 'collective mentality,' the importance of the development of specific beliefs on the part of single individuals" (1993: n. 43).

16. These aspects of life accounts have been "discovered" repeatedly through the years, much as Steiner (1996) finds that African art has been "discovered" roughly once each decade since early this century.

17. The absence of an article on life history/story in the *Annual Review of Anthropology* series (1972–present) or the preceding biannual reviews (1959–1971) may be one sign of this unsure footing, which Crapanzano characterizes as "somewhat of a conceptual—and an emotional—embarrassment" (1984: 954). The latest volume (1996) includes an essay on "Narrating the Self," but it centers on narrative theory and developmental approaches to narrative. Though it gives little consideration to life histories/stories specifically, the essay addresses relevant issues and places them in a broader framework (Ochs and Capps 1996).

18. Inadequate political dodges accompany both Titon's and Behar's work. Recasting her writing and editing as just another retelling likens Behar to Esperanza and portrays them as women in similar situations doing similar things. Using this analogy to reposition herself, however, allows Behar to obfuscate the way their different situations inform the telling to frame their relation in the best light. Titon suggests that life stories—by which he means any personal narrative, not necessarily covering an extended period—are the result of research friendships, recorded through nondirective methods. He dismisses life histories as "the interview that comes to masquerade as a life story" (1980: 277), seeming to exempt his own work from the political negotiations of research. Most literature on life history also advises researchers to be nondirective and not to do life histories too early, but to wait until their relations in the communities have developed.

19. The complexity of this last characteristic is not captured by simply calling life accounts "subjective." Smith's definition of autobiography points to this feature: "written or verbal communication that takes the speaking 'I' as the subject of the narrative, rendering the 'I' both subject and object" (1987: 19).

20. See Briggs on various kinds of metadiscursive practices (1996b: 19, 23–25).

21. These seem to be the kind of reflections that Vansina warns historians not to take at face value, since they frequently construct past golden ages and other idealizations (Vansina 1985: 31–32). See Kratz (1993) on Okiek constructions of the past.

22. Rosaldo (1976) discusses what "a life" is for Ilongot. Menon and Shweder (forthcoming) consider Oriya Hindu women's understandings of life cycle stages and personal growth. Briggs (1996b: 26–27) notes some of the ways narrators create and indicate different stances.

23. When the conversation is presented later in written form, different kinds of interjections must be juggled. A number of authors discuss the ways they chose to present their own various "I"s in writing: the "I" who was present when the life history/story was told, the present authorial "I," and the "I" who may write in generalizations and the third person to provide background needed to understand what is said (Shostak 1989; Behar 1990: 224; Crapanzano 1996: 111).

24. The following excerpts provide examples of this broad framing, quite similar from one case to another. When information is available, I also include the researcher's assessment of how the life history/story's narrator understood what she or he was doing:
"I explained that I had come to learn about the past, and especially about the history of women in the colonial days. . . . I did not formally state at the beginning that I wanted to produce her life history." "I gradually realized that she perceived the narrative as both a testimonial about the oppressions experienced by women in the context of family and community, and a way of preserving Nyakusa tradition and culture and handing it down to others" (Mbilinyi 1989: 212, 214).

"One evening I asked Tukbaw to tell me the story of his life. He looked puzzled. I was perplexed; I explained it was really quite simple. He should tell me the first thing he could remember, then the second thing, and go on from there in chronological order." "He conceived of his lifetime as a progressive realization of his culture's design for adult manhood" (Rosaldo 1976: 133, 149).

"When I told Esperanza that I thought her life narrative would make a very good book, she completely agreed. . . . I began by saying, 'Comadre, I'd like you to tell me about your life. From your first memory.'" "Esperanza describes her story, at the end of our conversations in 1985, as a confession" (Behar 1992: 111, 112).

"First of all I knew John very well before I ever started this project. I discussed with him what I wanted to do and he agreed to 'have a go.' So we sat down with an empty tape on the recorder and began. I first asked a very general question—'Tell me about your early life.' I always asked general questions except when I wanted something explained in more detail. Once I had asked a question I sat quietly and let John talk. Even when he seemed to have finished I sat with an expectant look in the hope that he would continue, as he often did. Only when he seemed to have nothing more to say did I continue with a subsidiary query, or go on to a new area altogether" (Morton, quoted in Titon 1980: 286).

25. Titon's sense of "life story" does not cover the span of a life; rather he seems to refer simply to any personal narrative, whenever someone relates an episode of personal experience. Such stories may indeed be told "spontaneously" in interactions with a researcher, but his examples are usually cast as responses to a broad question that he posed. This may not be like a closely monitored, directed interview, but the friendships developed during research also include growing knowledge of what interests both parties have and the development of shared communicative conventions that might accomplish interview-like exchanges in more informal ways. Watson notes specifically that people directed their conversation toward interests that they had come to associate with him (1976: 116). When McGovern (1996: 7–11) tried to circumvent the interview format by asking pedestrians to tape personal commentary as they walked down Forty-Second Street in New York, he found that they spoke in dialogic monologues that nonetheless assumed the interview frame.

26. Some examples: Watson 1976: four months; Behar 1992: several three–four hour sessions; Mbilinyi 1989: roughly seventeen one-hour interviews; Lurie 1971: five weeks; Winter 1959: fifty-five hours. Geiger (1986: 340) notes that *Baba of Karo* was narrated in meetings held over six weeks.

27. Life history/story was called a "feminist method" when women's studies advocates first embraced it because the extended speech of the narrator presents an image of "overcoming the hierarchical relationship between the researcher and the researched" (Geiger 1986: 350). Clearly, giving the floor over for extended description is not the same as giving up control; in some cases it would actually seem to underline power differences. A more critical stance toward these efforts to declare methodological equality has brought out the complexities of these questions (Harding 1986; di Leonardo 1991; Gal 1991; Abu-Lughod 1993: 3–6).

28. At times, Okiek laughingly described one notion of what my presentation might be like in the United States. Okiek life, culture, language, and history are referred to in general as *ng'aleek aap Okiek,* the "words" of Okiek. Capitalizing on the ambiguity between the literal meaning of "words" or "language" and the more general sense of customs and history, they would imagine coming upon a school somewhere in the U.S. where a company of white people were chattering away in the Okiek language.

29. Patai (1988) shows how certain affective and rhetorical aspects of verbal form can be maintained and emphasized in written re-presentations. Paredes' 1977 article remains a classic on how superficial knowledge of colloquial language usage and missing the cues that signal the joking key of a conversation can derail understanding in ways that researchers may never catch.

30. Thanks to all who supported the research over the years: the Anthropology Department, Wesleyan University; the Fulbright-Hayes program; the Institute for Intercultural Studies; the National Science Foundation; Sigma Xi; the Social Science Research Council; the University of Texas at Austin; and the Wenner Gren Foundation. A John Simon Guggenheim Memorial Foundation Fellowship provided time to write this paper. I also thank the Sociology Department, University of Nairobi, for academic affiliation; the Office of the President, Government of Kenya, for permission to conduct research; and the people with whom I live and work in Kenya.

31. In fact, my impression of how to do life history was close to Rosaldo's caricature: "place a tape-recorder in front of Mr. Non-literate Everyman and he will tell the 'real truth' about his life. . . . if only he were asked, Tukbaw would reveal his authentic life story" (1976: 145–46).

32. Kirutari was about fifty at the time. Keenly intelligent and articulate, he could also be prickly and irascible. When I returned to Kenya in 1982, he was living alone in the Kaplelach area that was one focus of my research. Okiek there were moving to places where they wanted to claim title when group land holdings would be subdivided, a kind of homesteading process. Through regular visits and long discussions, Kirutari taught me much about Okiek culture and history. Over the years, we became fast friends.

33. I concentrate on Kirutari's account in part because it is fuller and in the first person, but also because I taped the full session, stopping mainly to change tapes. During the early work with Simpole I had not yet learned to tape framing conversation and the entire exchange. Only brief conversational excerpts are captured at the end of several of his narratives; pauses in recording mark discussions in which I asked him about specific incidents.

34. Kirutari began to suffer from rheumatoid arthritis in the early 1970s or so. For nearly twenty years he suffered only intermittent serious attacks, but he became less mobile as the illness progressed. He was unable to walk during the last few years of his life.

35. Kirutari challenged me to decide which is more precious: land or vagina. When I guessed right, he went on to elaborate a philosophy of value and fecundity that equates the two.

36. Excerpts show my ongoing phatic responses and short questions or comments in parentheses. Explanatory material is included in brackets. Since I am not attempting extensive poetic or discourse analysis of Kirutari's account in this paper, I have quoted excerpts in English translation. However, I leave in the translations several expressive aspects of Okiek discourse that mark narrative sections or modes of delivery. The word *basi*, discussed below, serves many structural roles. In several later examples, I indicate the lengthening of a vowel that shows a process done over time (e.g., so we staaaaaayed = so we kept staying for a long time). I also include the pragmatically important suffix -i, which is used when listing things or actions, to create a slight dramatic pause at the end of a clause, and in the interactive structuring of conversation. A clause ending in -i usually evokes a phatic response.

37. Kirutari had been separated from his mother, too, for a period just before her death. Given in marriage again, she left Kirutari with her mother when she first went to the home of her new husband. She was pregnant at the time and eventually bore another son. She had come to see her relatives and take him to live with her when she was urged to go on a honey-gathering trip to Mau, where she died. After his mother's death Kirutari was separated from his younger siblings as well. His mother's second husband took them as his own, but left Kirutari with his mother's mother and his mother's brother.

38. This is characteristic of narrative more generally, not simply life history/story. "Narratives transform life's journeys into sequences of events and evoke shifting and enduring perspectives on experience" (Ochs and Capps 1996: 20). Ochs and Capps

review literature that considers temporality and point of view as the basic dimensions of narrative, including Labov and Waletzky's "definition of narrative as two or more temporally conjoined clauses that represent a sequence of temporally ordered events" (quoted, 23).

39. This includes the later work of transcribing and interpreting a life account with the narrator or others as well. Researchers or writers who attempt to define their work as simply capturing and presenting subjects' "voices" deny its communicative and intersubjective foundation.

40. "Basi" is a word from Kiswahili (shared with Arabic), but it is virtually ubiquitous in Kenyan languages, used in similar ways.

41. Okiek have two specific names for a grown girl approaching initiation, *mepayt* and *melyaat;* a boy of this age is usually just described as a "big boy" (*weeriit inka oo*).

42. Kirutari's initiation section includes and ends with the post-initiation age grade that Okiek call *muran* (young man, often translated as "warrior" though it has always included more than martial activities). His final section explicitly begins with entry into the age grade *paayaat* (mature man, plural *paaiik*) "We came then and became paaiik, until the trouble of Mau Mau. Do you remember that?" A muran becomes a paayaat when the age-set following his begins initiation.

43. The cluck is an emotional sign (cf. Kratz 1994: 193). Upset by the memory, Kirutari interrupts himself to swear how much he would do if he were able. His hard work and prosperity would contrast with his boyhood poverty and distress.

44. Genitals were often uncovered while the initiates were recovering.

45. These interconnections are not limited to life stories, but may be particularly noticeable when they involve first-person narratives. In terms of dramatic structure, Kirutari's account has two linked highlights. First, Kirutari's reunion with his brother after physical separation leads to solidarity in childhood hardship. The second and more elaborate, initiation, is effectively another reunion with his brother. When they are joined in adulthood, all their childhood problems evaporate. After this, Kirutari's adulthood episode is rather anticlimactic.

46. All speech quoted in that scene is by adults, directed to Kirutari or his brother. The first quoted speech by either of them occurs later, as the boyhood episode starts. Kirutari's brother tells him, "I say, friend. Let's stay together. Don't go [back] to a place where boys beat you anymore."

47. In a Kalauna life story, for instance, Young describes how a woman puts evaluations of her worth and statements of moral values into the mouths of others (1983: 495–97). He relates this attribution of speech to questions of agency and gender. See Kratz (2000) on gender, agency, and discourse patterns in Okiek marriage arrangement.

48. For instance, Kirutari finishes his general explanation of forest migrations during the time of his mother's marriage with "Do I know about that time? I don't know. When I hadn't been born yet? I just grew up and saw that that's what was being done." Or when I ask what caused his mother's sudden death, "Do I still remember [what happened to Mother]? I just remember that that is when she died."

49. "I was with Grandmother myself. It's like if you had left your child yourself, you left it for your mother [to look after]."

50. Labov and Waletzky (1967) discuss the structure of narrative and elements usually expected and included. Kratz (1991) discusses skeletal narratives and narrative transformation in another Okiek context.

51. When Kirutari clarified this comment later, he said he was alluding to the fact that because of his illness he was not married and had not become prosperous.

52. Scholars of life history/story sometimes use "personal narrative" as a virtual synonym, but personal narrative is actually a much broader category that includes life history/story. The Personal Narratives Group (1989) never explicitly considers the question of all that is included, taking the category almost as a given and including

only a few of the possible forms. Ochs and Capps provide a good sense of the range: "Personal narratives comprise a range of genres from story to novel, diaries and letters to memoirs, gossip to legal testimony, boast to eulogy, troubles talk to medical history, joke to satire, bird song to opera, etching to palimpsest, and mime to dance" (1996: 19). In the *Annual Review* article where it appears, this definition is dense with citations (omitted here) that discuss each of these examples.

53. Crapanzano (1996) discusses an interesting case of narrative constraints in a written nineteenth-century French life history. Barbin, the protagonist, grew up as a girl but at age twenty-one was legally declared male. Crapanzano considers Barbin's use of tense and pronominal forms as s/he tries to constitute narrative personae and tell the story of a life that does not fit conventional forms.

54. Some perspectives and attitudes are explicitly expressed or marked; others are conveyed by juxtapositions, progressions, hesitations, or silences. Patterns of tense, person, aspect, and modality can play a particularly important role as well. See Bauman for a cogent analysis of "the management of point of view in personal experience narratives" (1986: 33–53).

55. "Stealing" initiation is a matter of great interest and drama when children attempt it, but it does not remain a source of regular narrative interest long after. Later attempts to steal initiation might provide occasions to recall and recount earlier ones, but I had never heard of Kirutari's (even though some girls planned to steal initiation in 1983—including Kirutari's daughter [Kratz 1994: 113]). This is also the case in marriages in which a woman "came out for" a man, i.e., avoided an arranged marriage by going to someone she chose herself. Though it is a sensation at the time it happens, if the marriage does take place these initial circumstances are not often remarked on years later. Marriage arrangement among the Okiek has changed in many ways, and this practice has largely been replaced by elopement (Kratz 2000).

BIBLIOGRAPHY

Abu-Lughod, Lila. 1993. *Writing Women's Worlds: Bedouin Stories.* Berkeley: University of California Press.

Asad, Talal, ed. 1973. *Anthropology and the Colonial Encounter.* New York: Humanities.

Bakhtin, M. M. 1981. *The Dialogic Imagination: Four Essays.* Trans. C. Emerson and M. Holquist. Austin: University of Texas Press.

Barnet, Miguel. 1991. *Rachel's Song.* Trans. W. Nick Hill. Willimantic, Conn.: Curbstone.

Bauman, Richard. 1977. *Verbal Art as Performance.* Rowley, Mass.: Newbury House.

———. 1986. *Story, Performance, and Event: Contextual Studies of Oral Narrative.* Cambridge: Cambridge University Press.

Bauman, Richard, and Charles Briggs. 1990. "Poetics and Performance as Critical Perspectives on Language and Social Life." *Annual Review of Anthropology* 19: 59–88.

Behar, Ruth. 1990. "Rage and Redemption: Reading the Life Story of a Mexican Marketing Woman." *Feminist Studies* 16, no. 2: 223–58.

———. 1992. "A Story to Take across the Border: Inscribing a Mexican Woman's Life." In *Storied Lives: The Cultural Politics of Self-Understanding*, ed. George C. Rosenwald and Richard L. Ochberg, 108–23. New Haven: Yale University Press.

———. 1993. *Translated Woman: Crossing the Border with Esperanza's Story.* Boston: Beacon.

Berger, Peter, and Thomas Luckmann. 1966. *The Social Construction of Reality: A Treatise in the Sociology of Knowledge.* New York: Anchor.

Bird, Charles S., and Martha Kendall. 1980. "The Mande Hero: Text and Context." In *Explorations in African Systems of Thought,* ed. Ivan Karp and Charles S. Bird, 13–26. Bloomington: Indiana University Press.

Briggs, Charles. 1986. *Learning How to Ask: A Sociolinguistic Appraisal of the Interview in Social Science Research.* Cambridge: Cambridge University Press.

———. 1993. "Metadiscursive Practices and Scholarly Authority in Folkloristics." *Journal of American Folklore* 106, no. 422: 387–434.

———. 1996a. "The Politics of Discursive Authority in Research on the 'Invention of Tradition.'" *Cultural Anthropology* 11, no. 4: 435–69.

———. 1996b. Introduction to *Disorderly Discourse: Narrative, Conflict, and Inequality,* ed. Charles L. Briggs, 3–40. Oxford: Oxford University Press.

Crapanzano, Vincent. 1984. "Life Histories: A Review Essay." *American Anthropologist* 86: 953–60.

———. 1996. "'Self'-Centering Narratives." In *Natural Histories of Discourse,* ed. Michael Silverstein and Greg Urban, 106–27. Chicago: University of Chicago Press.

d'Azevedo, Warren. 1997. Personal communication.

di Leonardo, Micaela, ed. 1991. *Gender at the Crossroads of Knowledge: Feminist Anthropology in the Postmodern Era.* Berkeley: University of California Press.

Duranti, Alessandro, and Charles Goodwin, ed. 1992. *Rethinking Context: Language as an Interactive Phenomenon.* Cambridge: Cambridge University Press.

Fabian, Johannes. 1971. "Language, History, and Anthropology." *Philosophy of the Social Sciences* 1: 19–47.

———. 1983. *Time and the Other: How Anthropology Makes Its Object.* New York: Columbia University Press.

Fosbrook, H. A. 1955. "The Life of Justin, Part 1: An African Autobiography Translated and Also Annotated." *Tanganyika Notes Record* 41: 31–57.

———. 1956. "The Life of Justin, Part 2: An African Autobiography." *Tanganyika Notes Record* 42: 19–30.

Friedrich, Paul. 1979. *Language, Context, and the Imagination.* Stanford: Stanford University Press.

Gal, Susan. 1991. "Between Speech and Silence: The Problematics of Research on Language and Gender." In *Gender at the Crossroads of Knowledge: Feminist Anthropology in the Postmodern Era,* ed. Micaela di Leonardo, 175–203. Berkeley: University of California Press.

Geiger, Susan. 1986. "Women's Life Histories: Method and Content." *Signs* 11, no. 2: 334–51.

Gengenbach, Heidi. 1994. "Truth-Telling and the Politics of Women's Life History Research in Africa: A Reply to Kirk Hoppe." *International Journal of African Historical Studies* 27, no. 3: 619–27.

Ginsburg, Carlo. 1993. "Microhistory: Two or Three Things That I Know about It." *Critical Inquiry* 20: 10–35.

Gottschalk, Louis, Clyde Kluckhohn, and Robert Angell. 1945. "The Use of Personal Documents in History, Anthropology, and Sociology." Bulletin 53. New York: Social Science Research Council.

Gumperz, John J. 1982. *Discourse Strategies.* Cambridge: Cambridge University Press.

Harding, Sandra. 1986. *The Science Question in Feminism*. Ithaca: Cornell University Press.

Heilbrun, Carolyn. 1988. *Writing a Woman's Life*. New York: Norton.

Hoppe, Kirk. 1993. "Whose Life Is It, Anyway? Issues of Representation in Life Narrative Texts of African Women." *International Journal of African Historical Studies* 26, no. 3: 623–36.

Hoskins, Janet. 1985. "A Life History from Both Sides: The Changing Poetics of Personal Experience." *Journal of Anthropological Research* 41, no. 2: 147–69.

Huddle, J. G. 1957. "The Life of Yakobo Adoko of Longo District." *Uganda Journal* 21: 184–90.

Hymes, Dell. 1975. "Breakthrough into Performance." In *Folklore: Performance and Communication,* ed. Dan Ben-Amos and Kenneth S. Goldstein, 11–74. The Hague: Mouton.

———, ed. 1972. *Reinventing Anthropology*. New York: Vintage.

Jefferson, Gail. 1978. "Sequential Aspects of Storytelling in Conversation." In *Studies in the Organization of Conversational Interaction,* ed. Jim Schenkein, 219–48. New York: Free Press.

Karp, Ivan. 1986. "Agency and Social Theory: A Review of Three Books by Anthony Giddens." *American Ethnologist* 13, no. 1: 131–37.

Karp, Ivan, and Martha Kendall. 1982. "Reflexivity in Field Work." In *Explaining Human Behavior: Consciousness, Human Action, and Social Structure,* ed. Paul F. Secord, 249–73. Beverly Hills: Sage.

Keegan, Timothy. 1988. *Facing the Storm: Portraits of Black Lives in Rural South Africa*. Cape Town: David Philip.

Keesing, Roger. 1985. "Kwaio Women Speak: The Micropolitics of Autobiography in a Solomon Island Society." *American Anthropologist* 87: 27–39.

Kratz, Corinne A. 1990. "Sexual Solidarity and the Secrets of Sight and Sound: Shifting Gender Relations and Their Ceremonial Constitution." *American Ethnologist* 17, no. 3: 31–51.

———. 1991. "Amusement and Absolution: Transforming Narratives during Confession of Social Debts." *American Anthropologist* 93, no. 4: 826–51.

———. 1993. "'We've Always Done It Like This' . . . Except for a Few Details: 'Tradition' and 'Innovation' in Okiek Ceremonies." *Comparative Studies in Society and History* 35, no. 1: 30–65.

———. 1994. *Affecting Performance: Meaning, Movement, and Experience in Okiek Women's Initiation*. Washington, D.C.: Smithsonian Institution Press.

———. 2000. "Forging Unions and Negotiating Ambivalence: Personhood and Complex Agency in Okiek Marriage Arrangement." In *African Philosophy as Cultural Inquiry,* ed. Ivan Karp and D. A. Masolo. 136–71. Bloomington: Indiana University Press.

Labov, William, and J. Waletzky. 1967. "Narrative Analysis: Oral Versions of Personal Experience." In *Essays on the Verbal and Visual Arts,* ed. June Helm, 12–44. Seattle: University of Washington Press.

Langness, L. L. 1965. *The Life History in Anthropological Science*. New York: Holt, Rinehart and Winston.

Lewis, Oscar. 1969. *A Death in the Sanchez Family*. New York: Random House.

Lucy, John, ed. 1993. *Reflexive Language: Reported Speech and Metapragmatics*. Cambridge: Cambridge University Press.

Lurie, Nancy, ed. 1971. *Mountain Wolf Woman, Sister of Crashing Thunder: The Autobiography of a Winnebago Indian.* 1961. Reprint, Ann Arbor: University of Michigan Press.

Mbilinyi, Marjorie. 1989. "'I'd Have Been a Man': Politics and the Labor Process in Producing Personal Narratives." In *Interpreting Women's Lives: Feminist Theory and Personal Narratives,* ed. Personal Narratives Group, 204–27. Bloomington: Indiana University Press.

McGovern, Michael. 1996. "Discourse Analysis." Unpublished manuscript.

Menon, Usha, and Richard Shweder. Forthcoming. "The Return of 'White Man's Burden': An Encounter between the Moral Discourse of Anthropology and the Domestic Life of Hindu Women." In *Welcome to Middle Age (and Other Cultural Fictions),* ed. Richard Shweder. Chicago: University of Chicago Press.

Mintz, Sidney. 1979. "The Anthropological Interview and the Life History." *Oral History Review* 7: 18–26.

———. 1989. "The Sensation of Moving, While Standing Still." *American Ethnologist* 16, no. 4: 786–96.

Ochs, Elinor, and Lisa Capps. 1996. "Narrating the Self." *Annual Review of Anthropology* 25: 19–43.

Paredes, Americo. 1977. "On Ethnographic Work among Minority Groups." *New Scholar* 6: 1–32.

Patai, Daphne. 1988. "Constructing a Self: A Brazilian Life Story." *Feminist Studies* 14: 143–66.

Peacock, James L., and Dorothy C. Holland. 1993. "The Narrated Self: Life Stories in Process." *Ethos* 21, no. 4: 367–83.

Personal Narratives Group, ed. 1989. *Interpreting Women's Lives: Feminist Theory and Personal Narratives.* Bloomington: Indiana University Press.

Pollitt, Katha. 1996. "A Mother's Memoir." *The Nation,* 16 December, p. 9.

Radin, Paul. 1963. *The Autobiography of a Winnebago Indian.* 1920. Reprint, New York: Dover.

———, ed. 1926. *Crashing Thunder: The Autobiography of an American Indian.* New York: Appleton.

Ricoeur, Paul. 1979. "The Function of Fiction in Shaping Reality." *Man and World* 12, no. 2: 123–41.

Rosaldo, Renato. 1976. "The Story of Tukbaw." In *The Biographical Process: Studies in the History and Psychology of Religion,* ed. Frank E. Reynolds and Donald Capps, 121–51. The Hague: Mouton.

———. 1980. *Ilongot Headhunting, 1883–1974: A Study in Society and History.* Stanford: Stanford University Press.

Sacks, Harvey. 1972. "On the Analyzability of Stories by Children." In *Directions in Sociolinguistics: The Ethnography of Communication,* ed. John J. Gumperz and Dell Hymes, 325–45. New York: Holt, Rinehart and Winston.

———. 1992. *Lectures on Conversation.* Ed. Gail Jefferson. Oxford: Blackwell.

Sacks, H., E. Schegloff, and G. Jefferson. 1974. "A Simplest Systematics for the Organization of Turn-Taking in Conversation." *Language* 50: 696–735.

Samuel, Raphael. 1994. *Theatres of Memory.* Vol. 1, *Past and Present in Contemporary Culture.* London: Verso.

Scholte, Robert. 1971. "Discontents in Anthropology." *Social Research* 38: 777–807.

———. 1972. "Toward a Reflexive and Critical Anthropology." In *Reinventing Anthropology,* ed. Dell Hymes, 430–58. New York: Vintage.

Shostak, Marjorie. 1981. *Nisa: The Life and Words of a !Kung Woman.* Cambridge, Mass.: Harvard University Press.

———. 1989. "'What the Wind Won't Take Away': The Genesis of *Nisa: The Life and Words of a !Kung Woman."* In *Interpreting Women's Lives: Feminist Theory and Personal Narratives,* ed. Personal Narratives Group, 228–40. Bloomington: Indiana University Press.

Silverstein, Michael, and Greg Urban. 1996. "The Natural History of Discourse." In *Natural Histories of Discourse,* ed. Michael Silverstein and Greg Urban, 1–17. Chicago: University of Chicago Press.

Smith, M. F. 1954. *Baba of Karo: A Woman of the Muslim Hausa.* London: Faber and Faber.

Smith, Sidonie. 1987. *A Poetics of Women's Autobiography: Marginality and the Fictions of Self-representation.* Bloomington: Indiana University Press.

Steiner, Christopher. 1996. "Discovering African Art . . . Again?" *African Arts* 29, no. 4: 1, 4–8.

Swindells, Julia. 1989. "Liberating the Subject?" In *Interpreting Women's Lives: Feminist Theory and Personal Narratives,* ed. Personal Narratives Group, 24–38. Bloomington: Indiana University Press.

Tannen, Deborah, and Muriel Saville-Troike, ed. 1984. *Perspectives on Silence.* Washington, D.C.: Georgetown University Press.

Tedlock, Dennis, and Bruce Mannheim, ed. 1995. *The Dialogic Emergence of Culture.* Urbana: University of Illinois Press.

Titon, Jeff Todd. 1980. "The Life Story." *Journal of American Folklore* 93: 276–92.

Tonkin, Elizabeth. 1992. *Narrating Our Pasts: The Social Construction of Oral History.* Cambridge: Cambridge University Press.

Tylden-Wright, David. 1991. *John Aubrey: A Life.* London: Harper Collins.

Urban, Greg. 1989. "The 'I' of Discourse." In *Semiotics, Self, and Society,* ed. Benjamin Lee and Greg Urban, 27–51. Berlin: Mouton de Gruyter.

van Onselen, Charles. 1996. *The Seed Is Mine: The Life of Kas Maine, a South African Sharecropper, 1894–1985.* New York: Hill and Wang.

Vansina, Jan. 1965. *Oral Tradition: A Study in Historical Methodology.* Trans. H. M. Wright. Chicago: Aldine.

———. 1980. "Memory and Oral Tradition." In *The African Past Speaks: Essays on Oral Tradition and History,* ed. Joseph C. Miller, 262–79. Hamden, Conn.: Archon.

———. 1985. *Oral Tradition As History.* Madison: University of Wisconsin Press.

Watson, Lawrence. 1976. "Understanding a Life Story as a Subjective Document: Hermeneutical and Phenomenological Perspectives." *Ethos* 4, no. 1: 95–131.

Willis, Justin. 1996. "Two Lives of Mpamizo: Useful Dissonance in Oral History." *History in Africa* 23: 319–32.

Winter, Edward H. 1959. *Beyond the Mountains of the Moon: The Lives of Four Africans.* Urbana: University of Illinois Press.

Young, Michael. 1983. "Our Name Is Women; We Are Bought with Limesticks and Limepots: An Analysis of the Autobiographical Narrative of a Kalauna Woman." *Man* 18, no. 3: 478–501.

7

The Life Histories of Boakye Yiadom
(Akasease Kofi of Abetifi, Kwawu)

Exploring the Subjectivity and "Voices" of a Teacher-Catechist in Colonial Ghana

Stephan F. Miescher

Over the last ten years, historians of colonial Africa have explored life histories in order to give "voice" to people subjected to the colonial project. A few scholars have revisited biographical portraits recorded by colonial missionaries (Wright 1993; Alpers 1983). Since most documents remain silent about the experiences of women, rural dwellers, migrant laborers, and other disadvantaged groups—and rarely provide insight from an African perspective—oral research has been used as a method to supplement the shortcomings of the colonial archives. Historians have asked African men and women to talk about their personal lives, to share their tales and memories of repression and resistance experienced within the colonial context. Listening to these oral accounts, some researchers, especially those focusing on women, developed a genre of African history written through the collection and publication of life histories.[1] This methodology was borrowed from anthropologists, who have published life histories since the 1920s.[2] Some scholars have chosen to present life histories as "unmediated voices" in the form of edited first-person accounts kept separate from interpretation and historical contextualization (Mirza and Strobel 1989; Davison 1989; cf. Keegan 1988). Others have taken a different approach by extensively citing the interview transcripts enmeshed with their interpretations, while also supplementing these oral accounts with written archival records.[3]

My work, exploring notions of masculinities among people of Kwawu in colonial Ghana, has been indebted to this scholarship, especially to the work of Belinda Bozzoli (1991) and Charles van Onselen (1996). Like these scholars, I have organized accounts by men and women along the life cycle (Miescher 1997a). But there are also significant differences between their work and mine. Unlike South Africa's, Ghana's colonial history was not dominated by white settlers and forced removals from the land. Instead, many

Ghanaians, at least those in the cocoa-producing areas, among them Kwawu people, enjoyed relative prosperity for most of the colonial period. Moreover, my objectives have been dissimilar. While Bozzoli (1991: 7) presents collective biographies and social identities, revealing "otherwise hidden forms of consciousness," I am interested in subjectivities, reading and presenting my interview transcripts as evidence of self-representations, moments of subjective reflection about the past.[4]

Charles van Onselen (1990, 1996) explores the rich and long life of the sharecropper Kas Maine in order to reflect on major changes in the South African countryside which often contradicted the periodizations of rural transformation suggested by recent South African historiography. My work shares with van Onselen's the retelling of men's lives in order to correct certain assumptions in, in this case, Ghanaian historiography. In the foreground of my endeavors has been the task of reading these accounts in order to reconstruct the modes of promotion and negotiation of different masculinities. Further, oral accounts of interviewed men's lives are not merely used to complement the silences of the archives—hence treated like written documents; rather, they are listened to, and read as transcripts, to explore these men's self-presentations. I argue that these men's selves, their subjective experiences, are being reconstituted in narrating episodes about their lives.

In a provocative article, Luise White (1994: 80) has deplored the fact that "research into colonial subjectivities by historians is rare." When historians, following their colleagues in anthropology departments, have written about the Kwawu people, or the Asante, they have referred to these men and women (often without any gender distinction) as monolithic categories. Supposedly, all Kwawu men had the same understanding of their "customs," of the norms and expectations of their lives. Moreover, White asserted that "voices" captured in interviews do not represent historicized selves. Rather, in the course of the interview process a self is being reconstructed and selectively presented to the interviewer.[5]

In a review article on life histories, James L. Peacock and Dorothy C. Holland (1993) have identified two common approaches. One, more positivist, understands the narration as a mirror of reality. In this view, life histories become immediate windows into historical realities and complement omissions of the archives (Mirza and Strobel 1987; Davison 1989). The other approach has focused on the narration as the presented reality, which defines and constructs the self (Crapanzano 1980). In my work, which is modeled on Peacock and Holland's intervention, I take a middle road. While I still consider self-narration to be primary data, the "self and other experiences narrated are also accorded ontological status" (Peacock and Holland 1993: 371). The life histories provide insights into historical processes and cultural practices, such as childhood and marriage as well as the introduction of formal education and colonial rule, but they are affected by the situation of the narration. In this approach, the "telling of life stories" becomes important.

The intersubjectivity, the transforming relationship between elicitor and narrator, is crucial to the presentation of the account; hence the narrative can be "envisioned as a product of the interaction and desire of understanding between teller and listener (372f.).["6] Still, the importance of the researcher in the production of the narration should not be overemphasized. Narrators of life histories have their own agenda and are involved in a "myriad of processes involving numerous relationships" (376), in addition to the one with the researcher.

NARRATIVE GENRES

This chapter focuses on the life histories of Kofi Boakye Yiadom, a retired teacher-catechist. I explore competing notions of masculinity referring to expectations and prescriptions of proper male behavior, as well as lived practices reflected in Boakye Yiadom's accounts. Further, I present Boakye Yiadom's multiple identities, his shifting self-representations in different narratives, and seek to historicize his subjectivity.

In March 1993, I was introduced to Boakye Yiadom by his younger brother, Emmanuel Anim, who thought he would be helpful in my research. Although we had a very good initial conversation, I did not follow up with formal interviews, since I had already organized my research. Only after Boakye Yiadom pursued me did we continue our work and start to spend more time together.

Boakye Yiadom's life histories, as presented here, are based on different oral and written texts: transcripts of taped interviews and various autobiographical texts, some in diary form. I heard stories about his life in informal meetings around Abetifi as well as in extended, taped interviews. Since the language of the formal interviews was mainly English, all quotations from the interview transcripts are in their original language, reflecting Boakye Yiadom's word choice and style of speech. This adds an immediacy to these transcripts which is often lost in translation.[7] During my second stay in Abetifi, in 1994, Boakye Yiadom shared with me his personal papers, among them two autobiographies: one titled "Autobiography: My Own Life," written in the form of a diary, primarily in English, over the period 1946–1981 (n.d.a);[8] the other, "My Life History: The Autobiography of Akasease Kofi Boakye Yiadom," written in Twi after he retired in 1978 (n.d.b). Excerpts from these autobiographical writings and the interview transcripts permit one not only to identify his oral and written self-presentations, but also to illuminate tensions among conflicting notions of masculinity and to educe a precise historicization of his self. These texts show how he experienced certain episodes in his life, how he wrote about them from different vantage points, and how he presented them *ex post facto* to a Swiss historian. Other scholars, like Pat Caplan (1997) in her study of a Swahili peasant in Tanzania called "Mohammed," have asked informants to keep a diary during the research process. Acting as Caplan's ethnographer, Mohammed provided her with a description of his environment. His text, produced for Caplan, contains "few personal entries" (64) and lacks the historical dimension of an autobiography written in diary format over decades.

Boakye Yiadom formulated his texts, oral and written, for distinct audiences. The brief autobiography "My Life History," offering a flawless biography, was mainly written for his church congregation and perhaps for outside readers beyond Abetifi. The narrative presents a trajectory of his life from an industrious youth at the Presbyterian schools of Abetifi to his retirement as a senior catechist and head teacher of a primary school. In this idealized version, all rough edges and ruptures in his biography are either smoothed over or omitted entirely. The text features Boakye Yiadom as a model Christian who has embodied all the values acquired in his mission education.

In the interviews, Boakye Yiadom is addressing me as a European friend and scholar, interested in learning about his life and about the past in Kwawu. During our taped conversations, Boakye Yiadom was aware that he was speaking to a larger audience beyond the boundaries of Ghana, since I had explained my intentions of writing a book about men in Kwawu.[9] The relation to his audience is more fluid in the interviews than in "My Life History," because our relationship changed from one conversation to the next, altering their content.

In the two volumes of "Autobiography: My Own Life," Boakye Yiadom addressed mainly himself. He wrote the text like a diary and used it as a mnemonic device. The volumes are an attempt at preserving moments of his life for an explicit audience of his wife and children, other close relatives, and friends. The accounts are personal and sometimes reflective. The entries cover his migrations and his relationships with his wives, girlfriends, and children, as well as conflicts at work and with his extended family. They contain notes on his family background and on private, inner experiences, such as dreams, prayers, and pledges to himself. Boakye Yiadom also read a draft of this essay, made a few factual corrections, and commented on my representation of his life (Boakye Yiadom 1997).

Boakye Yiadom's oral and written recollections represent different narrative genres. According to Elizabeth Tonkin (1992: 51), genre may be understood as "patterned expectancy." The phrase refers to a sense of agreement in a dynamic process "between speaker or writer, reader or listener on what sort of interpretation is to be made." This definition builds on that of Mikhail M. Bakhtin (1986: 61), who distinguished between "primary (simple)" and "secondary (complex) speech genre[s]." The former reflect oral and written everyday communication, including letters and journals, while the latter refer to literary production and scholarly writing (including interpretations of life histories) which "absorb and digest" various primary genres (62). Boakye Yiadom's oral and written texts provide contrasting maps for exploring his life, especially ideals and values which constitute his understanding of being a man; through them, we can compare divergent identities chosen for different life situations. Because there is never one truth, one version, in a person's accounting of his or her life, personal narratives must be seen as meta-dialogues between the author and his imagined audiences, interplays between desired effects, anticipated responses, and perceived understanding. Or, using Bakhtin's formulation, this dialogic situation determines the choice of genre.[10] Thus, Boakye Yiadom's narratives, rendered in written and oral texts, reveal different shades of his self. Since his narratives can only be relied on to a limited extent in reconstructing historical experiences, the conditions of their production need to be problematized and unpacked. Boakye Yiadom's oral and written texts, explored in this chapter, offer a unique chance to reintroduce a historicized subjectivity into Akan historiography.[11]

CHILDHOOD

Kofi Boakye Yiadom was born in 1910 at Apedwa, Akyem Abuakwa, the offspring of a cross-cousin marriage, abusua-wareɛ. Both his parents came from Kwawu, an Akan state wedged between Akyem Abuakwa and Asante, about one hundred miles north of Accra. During the nineteenth century Kwawu was part of greater Asante, the dominant power in precolonial Ghana. In 1875, after breaking with Asante, Kwawu chiefs welcomed the Basel Mission, which established a church and school in Abetifi, one of the main towns on the Kwawu ridge. The missionaries were crucial in negotiating a protectorate treaty with the British in 1888, gradually incorporating Kwawu into the Gold Coast Colony (Haenger 1989). Kwawu people, who practice matrilineal descent, are well known for their trading activities. In the nineteenth century, Kwawu traders frequented the northern markets of Salaga and Atebubu, exchanging kola nuts, imported fabric, and glass beads for hides, metal goods, and slaves. At the beginning of the twentieth century, they reoriented their trading activities toward the emerging commercial centers of southern Ghana (Garlick 1967; Arhin 1979).

Boakye Yiadom's mother, Afua Ntoriwah, belonged to a secondary branch of the royal Bretuo abusua (matrilineage) of Abetifi. His father, Kwabena Somua, worked as a trader with his own store in Apedwa. Like many Kwawu people, Somua had moved south, to the growing towns of Akyem Abuakwa, seeking to profit from the new trading possibilities created by the cocoa boom. In 1923, Somua was forced to leave Apedwa by an order of the paramount chief, Ofori Atta I, expelling all Kwawu traders from Akyem Abuakwa.[12] Somua returned to Kwawu and started his own cocoa farm, becoming one of many Kwawu traders who invested their profits in cash crops, launching a cocoa industry within Kwawu, and erected cement buildings in their hometowns to demonstrate their newly acquired wealth (Garlick 1967).

As a child, Boakye Yiadom first lived with his parents in Apedwa; then he was sent home to stay with his maternal grandmother, Adwoa Antie, in his hometown of Abetifi. At the age of ten, he was taken to the smaller town of Akwasihu, where the new Accra–Kumase railway was under construction. Boakye Yiadom lived with and served his maternal grandfather, Nana Kwasi Ampomah, the chief of Akwasihu. In his recollections, Boakye Yiadom often mentioned Ampomah, who was wealthy and well respected throughout Kwawu. Boakye Yiadom recalled that Ampomah had fathered seventy-seven children and was considered an *ɔbarima pa*, a valiant and successful man. He was of unique importance for Boakye Yiadom. Since his grandmother, as a "stranger" to Kwawu, had married Ampomah, she and her children had become part of her husband's matrilineage. Hence Ampomah was not only Boakye Yiadom's maternal grandfather, but also the head of his abusua. Staying with his grandfather, Boakye Yiadom was exposed to life at the *ahenfie* (chief's palace), learning how to drum and to play the elephant-tusk horn. His responsibilities were fetching water, sweeping around the house, and helping on his relatives' farm. Although boundaries between work and play were fluid, Boakye Yiadom feared his powerful grandfather and did not dare to play too late in the evening. Whenever he had a chance, he visited Abetifi, where he was less supervised (Boakye Yiadom 1993: 2f; 1994a: 6; 1994c: 6, 15; n.d.b).

Boakye Yiadom recalled his visits to Abetifi as times for play. He especially liked competitive games with other boys. He talked about mock military parades through town:

> BY: There were outside games, [we played] with our friends, we called it "army." We tie our cloths and hang it over the shoulder (gets up, calls his wife and uses her cloth to demonstrate) and put some stones into the cloth and tie it. Then we march in the night, let's say from seven o'clock going, we march from street to street. (starts singing) "*Pii, pii, yɛnsuro obiara, pii, pii, yɛnsuro obiara, yɛrekɔ Asante yeato tuo, poo . . .* " [Piff, piff, we don't fear anybody, we don't fear anybody, we go to Asante to shoot, bang . . .] So, we march, when we meet other children from this side and go to the end of the street, then those boys there also march. When we meet them, we take them [stones wrapped in cloth] and start beating up one another.
> SM: That can be painful.
> BY: Yes, very painful! And sometimes those other boys run away, or we will run away, being defeated. (1994a: 10)

The strongest boy became the leader; Boakye Yiadom often claimed this position for himself. The soldier game took place exclusively in *Manem*, in the old section of Abetifi. Boakye Yiadom kept a distance from *Abarem*

(Christian Quarters), the settlement built at the edge of town by missionaries.

> SM: Did you also fight against the children from Abarem, from Christian Quarters?
> BY: We don't go to Christian Quarters, because at that time, those who were there were white men and we were afraid to come to the Quarters, they would drive us away. So only in the town did we operate and play our army game.
> SM: And the children from Abarem would not participate in the games?
> BY: No, they would not go there, people at the Quarters they would not allow them to go to town, because immediately, you come to this side [Christian Quarters, where Boakye Yiadom now lives] as a Christian, you become isolated and you don't go to any place again. These people are not your friends. (1994a: 10)

Since their arrival in Abetifi, the Swiss and German missionaries of the Basel Mission had made a deliberate effort to separate their followers from local people. They offered plots to converts to build houses within the boundaries of Christian Quarters (Schlatter 1916, 3: 72ff, 116ff.). There, converts were expected to live according to a set of rules that intervened in every aspect of daily life and reframed gender relations by promoting new notions of masculinity and femininity. According to these guidelines, and contrary to Akan practice, husband and wife were expected to live with their children under one roof. For boys, schooling was compulsory; for girls, it was optional, though recommended.[13] Expelled in World War I, the Basel Mission was succeeded by the Scottish Mission. Although the latter granted the mission church more independence, reorganizing it as Presbyterian in 1926, separate Christian communities continued and expanded during the interwar period.[14] Boakye Yiadom had little contact with the world of Christian Quarters until he entered school.

BECOMING A *Krakye*

In colonial Ghana, formal education was mainly organized by mission churches, especially the Presbyterian Church of the Basel Mission and the Scottish Mission, and the Methodist Wesleyan Mission (Foster 1965). A student who completed school and passed the Standard VII exam was called a *krakye* (plural *akrakyefoɔ*) in the Akan-Twi language, commonly translated as "scholar." Akrakyefoɔ were trained to work as clerks, accountants, storekeepers, primary school teachers, and, if they pursued their education, as certified teachers and pastors. During their education, they were exposed to gendered norms of marriage, parenthood, sexual behavior, and wealth which often conflicted with those of their hometown communities. Presbyterian schools sought to shape their male students into hard-working and law-abiding colonial subjects, as well as monogamous husbands, who would privilege their wife and children over lineage members. Becoming part of a new social group, while remaining members of extended families and other communities, akrakyefoɔ developed distinct social and subjective identities. They navigated among different, and at times conflicting, notions of masculinity, one promoted in missionary schools and others expressed by hometown communities and employers, as well as colonial officials.[15]

At the age of sixteen, after his older brother had received some formal education, Boakye Yiadom was sent in his place to the Presbyterian primary school of Abetifi. Despite missionary presence in Kwawu since the 1870s, it was still quite unusual in the first quarter of the twentieth century for a child to attend school. Boakye Yiadom recalled,

> During our time we did not go to school in time. I stayed at home for sixteen years. . . . I was accepted, because they wanted children to come to school. Our parents did not understand schooling, so they let the children stay at home to serve. But they were begged by missionaries, they came to your house and they ask you: "What is this boy doing here? Let him come to school tomorrow."[16]

The European missionaries' request for children is probably more a topos than an actual occurrence in Boakye Yiadom's case. From 1924 on, missionaries only occasionally lived at the old Basel Mission station. Still, as a child Boakye Yiadom must have witnessed the colorful scene of missionaries, accompanied by the African pastor, presbyters, and an evangelist, going from house to house, engaging in street preaching. Striking their omnipresent bell, at times supported by a brass band, the missionaries gathered the people of Abetifi and encouraged them to attend church and send their children to school. Then the missionaries visited elders at home. For the year 1915, the Abetifi pastor reported,

> Nearly all our members; men and women, old and young feel the pleasure—are anxious—to attend Street preaching. But the question, whether they attend in order to Christianize the heathen, or to show their clothes, and singing with brass instruments, is very difficult to answer. I am of the strong opinion, that most of them do not even pray for the conversion of the heathen while they attend Street Preaching; and one would scarcely preach the word of God to the heathen, from his own free will, unless he is called to do so.[17]

Later Boakye Yiadom corrected himself and spoke about "teachers and ministers [who] used to go from house to house" (1994a: 4). Probably it was Rev. C. M. Adu who, in his position as the local pastor and manager of schools, made the initial contact that led to Boakye Yiadom's two *wɔfanom* (maternal uncles), Kwadwo Opong and Kwabena Mensa Opong, becoming the driving force behind their nephew's education. They went to see Kwasi Ampomah, Boakye Yiadom's grandfather in Akwasihu, and pleaded with the old man to let his grandson go. Boakye Yiadom noted how his wɔfanom also had to overcome the reluctance of his father, Kwabena Somua:

> My uncles paid my school fees, because my father told my uncles not to send me to school, instead I should work with my father. But my uncles said no: "This is our nephew and we have the power over him. . . . We know that when we send him to school, it is better for the child." So, my father let me in the hands of my uncles. (1993: 4)

Looking back at his school days, on many occasions Boakye Yiadom emphasized the importance of his late start and declared that these days children begin formal education too young, since they had not "well matured yet." There were thirty-six pupils in his class, and he was "truly . . . the first," as he notes in "Autobiography: My Own Life" (Boakye Yiadom 1994a: 4; 1993: 1; n.d.a, 1: 2). After one year, he was able to skip one class, which gave him much pride.

In the 1920s, Abetifi had the best schools of Kwawu; the inspecting district commissioner called them "above average" and "situated in very fine grounds."[18] The primary and middle schools were located next to the old mission station, overlooking the town, the Kwawu hills, and the plains to the north. Going to school brought many changes to Boakye Yiadom's life. Ascending daily the path to Christian Quarters removed him from his boyhood context and introduced him to different values, giving him a new identity as a scholar. Boakye Yiadom recalled how he was admired by other children, how he seemed different from his age-mates not enrolled in school. This sense of difference was formative for those who later joined the ranks of the akrakyefoɔ. Wearing school uniforms, being exempted from work on parental farms, pupils were reminded that their weekdays were organized by a different schedule. Going to school brought new obligations. Every morning pupils' physical appearance and personal hygiene were examined; on Sundays they were expected to attend church. If they failed to do so, or their clothes were considered inadequate, teachers used the stick or sent them home (Miescher forthcoming).

After completing primary school (Standard III), Boakye Yiadom entered the closed environment of the Abetifi Boys' Boarding School (middle school). There he experienced a greater separation. Boarding schools, where students were isolated and lived under the close supervision of missionaries and teachers, were a principal component of the educational system established by the Basel Mission in its efforts to reshape individual personhood. Boakye Yiadom has vivid memories of his life as a boarder, and how it changed his value system. He was exposed to a modern concept of time, since every hour of the day was organized on a rigid schedule. He belonged to one house, with its specific hierarchies, rules, and group identity. He was taught to compete against his classmates in academic subjects, as well as in sports and other outdoor activities, such as planting the most productive cassava garden.

Still proving his physical prowess, Boakye Yiadom had replaced the violent army games with more controlled activities like sports and Boy Scout events, in which he excelled.[19]

In 1933, Boakye Yiadom was baptized and confirmed. According to "My Life History," he was attracted to the church and imagined himself becoming a minister. He often preached to his classmates, so skillfully using his knowledge of Akan proverbs that "some of his friends called him Reverend" (Boakye Yiadom n.d.b:3). But such ambitions could not be realized upon his leaving school in 1935, since he lacked financial support for training college.[20] Like most Standard VII leavers, he initially tried his luck as a clerk. Those of his colleagues who had access to cash paid the security deposit to run a store for one of the European companies. After Boakye Yiadom had approached his uncles in vain for capital, he went to live with his mother in Kurofa. He took a position as a second assistant clerk to a United Africa Company (UAC) cocoa buyer in nearby Konongo, the first six months without pay. Working as a clerk, Boakye Yiadom earned some money that enabled him to buy furniture, clothes, shoes, hats, greeting cards, and soap and other toiletries. These products aided in the public display of his new status as a krakye (1993a: 5).

During Boakye Yiadom's employment as a clerk, the cocoa industry was brought to a standstill by the "cocoa hold-up" of 1937–38. Cocoa producers, in a coalition with brokers and chiefs, challenged a buying agreement among the major European firms. The hold-up was a reaction by cocoa producers and their allies against falling prices, which they ascribed to market manipulation by the large buying firms. Launching this protest, cocoa farmers sought to improve the conditions under which their product was sold. This is not the place to reevaluate this cocoa hold-up and its impact on various social groups within colonial Ghana.[21] But Boakye Yiadom's memory of the event forty-five years later reveals a great deal about his identity as a krakye. He took an intermediary position between cocoa farmers and buying companies:

> BY: I remember, we were at the office when one of the cocoa brokers came to tell the big man, my master, Mr. Neizer, "We are not bringing you any cocoa." And he asked, "Why?" And he said, "The money given to us farmers is too small, so we are not bringing any cocoa." And he said, "What I have received, I will rail it to Takoradi." He had received about 250 bags, more than that, 300. . . . He railed them, because one van takes about 310 bags, and he had more than that.
>
> SM: And one bag is about sixty pounds?
>
> BY: Yes.

Although Boakye Yiadom's voice expressed a certain admiration for the "brave" cocoa farmers who were destroying their crops, he did not share their cause. Rather, he was unaware of their agenda.

SM: Did you understand why the farmers stopped bringing the cocoa?
BY: No, *we* did not understand.

Here he spoke for the group of akrakyefɔɔ employed by the buying firms. Then, changing perspective, he explained the farmers' strategies:

> But what the farmers would do, they would go to a meeting, a special meeting, and write resolutions to the cocoa factors, and through the factors to the cocoa head office of UTC, UAC, Ollivant and the cocoa buyers that . . . cocoa should be increased to this price. If we . . . , you don't do that, say in two or three months, but the farmers did not do that. They just said, "We don't want to sell our cocoa."

Assessing the attitudes and power of Europeans, Boakye Yiadom described why the producers were forced into the hold-up.

> And you know the Europeans, the white men, they would not mind you too much, if you don't impress them harshly. They want everything to . . . If you say you are trying to do something harsh to them, they will consider you. . . . [The farmers] said: "We are not bringing you our cocoa." So the farmers . . . , the factors, the agents of the cocoa dealers, they did not mind, they [just] kept it.

In Boakye Yiadom's analysis, however, the cocoa farmers lost the struggle for higher prices, since they were stuck with their crop.

> BY: After all the farmers failed, they could not. . . . Because you don't know what the cocoa beans will do for you, they all dried, I mean spoiled.
> SM: You can't eat them . . .
> BY: You can't eat them, you can't do anything with them. So they came forward to sell their cocoa; they got about one shilling and a sixpence for a load of cocoa, . . . [prior to the boycott] they were paid about five shillings. (1994c: 1)

The cocoa farmers had also called a boycott of imported European goods. Boakye Yiadom recalled respecting the boycott but added, qualifying his support, that he had done so more out of necessity than political solidarity, since he himself "had no money" during the hold-up.

Although Boakye Yiadom's oral recollections were quite vivid about how the hold-up placed him, as a krakye, in the middle, in his "Autobiography: My Own Life" the disruptions caused by the cocoa hold-up are not mentioned. It appears that during the late 1930s and early 1940s the cocoa farmers' political action for higher prices was not his principal concern; at least he did not feel compelled to write about it. Instead he noted his "grand luck" in receiving a salary increase and, the following year, a promotion to first assistant weighing clerk (n.d.a, 1: 11). This raises the question of whether the silence in "My Own Life" concealed a tension around Boakye Yiadom's conflicting loyalties in his position as a krakye. He was close to the cocoa producers, since many members of his abusua made their living in the cocoa industry, and he was impressed by the bravery of cocoa farmers who resisted the power of the European firms. Later in the conversation, he explicitly identified bravery as an important male virtue.[22] At the same time, as a kra-kye, he had moved away from farm labor. Economically, he depended on his employers' goodwill and on an uninterrupted cocoa industry, in order to draw a regular salary that allowed him to consume material goods appropriate to the status of a krakye. This discrepancy between Boakye Yiadom's autobiographical writing at the time and his *ex post facto* accounts points to uneven layers of his subjectivity that were crucial in organizing his life and negotiating his identity as a krakye.

Becoming a Soldier

Boakye Yiadom's employment as a krakye for the UAC was only a temporary occupation. In 1940, he volunteered and enlisted as a signaler in the Gold Coast Regiment. Becoming a soldier affected his notion of self as a man and strengthened his identity as a krakye, since his literacy fitted him for certain positions. In January 1940, when a train filled with soldiers of the Gold Coast Regiment stopped en route from Accra to Kumase in Konongo, Boakye Yiadom closely observed the spectacle.

> My house was very near the railway station, so I went there to watch them. The train waited there for about thirty minutes, and they made a parade at the railway station . . . in Konongo, wishing to get more soldiers. Every big station they stopped for about thirty minutes and then they paraded. So I watched them, that parade. They were blowing their whistles, singing, marching, then I said, well, I will go to the soldiers too.[23] (Boakye Yiadom 1994b: 18)

In becoming a soldier, Boakye Yiadom fulfilled a dream. Already during his school days he had been attracted to uniforms. Joining the army, Boakye Yiadom made a break with at least three responsibilities and obligations in his life: his employment, his marriage, and his involvement with the emerging Presbyterian Church of Konongo. According to "My Own Life," leaving his employment with the UAC came as a great relief. He noted that, "owing to the hard and strict discipline of my master," he was more than willing to quit his clerical work (n.d.a, 1:11). He was living with his customary wife from Kurofa, Yaa Ntiri Frempomoah, who had borne his first child, Yaw Obeng, in 1936. He recalled,

> So I came home and made all my preparations. During that time I was staying with this woman, Yaw Obeng's mother, so I told her to go to Kurofa and go to collect some food. I did not tell her that I wanted to join the army, otherwise

she would have wept, she would [have] cried and [would not have] let me go. So I told her to go to Kurofa and collect some food stuff and come [back]. She went there on the seventeenth of January, 1940.

The exact dates of this event are deeply ingrained in his recollections:

> So on the eighteenth, I made all the preparations in my room and put them there and I locked the room. I wrote a letter on the table, and I wrote another letter to the house owner, so when my wife comes, he can tell her I had gone to Kumase to the army and I would not come back. So on the eighteenth, I left for Kumase. On the nineteenth, we were taken to the senior officer, the commanding officer of the army, and we were sworn in. So, I wrote another letter to my wife that she should marry, because I was going overseas. That's all. I did not come until we were [discharged] . . . So, it came to me as *a man going to the front to fight*. So it was in my power to go, *it came to me as a dream*. (1994b: 19, my emphasis)

Boakye Yiadom was willing to exchange his commitment to his wife and child for a life as a soldier. He was driven, at least in his memories, by a romanticized notion of going to war in order to prove his masculinity, his braveness as a "warrior" in the all-male environment of the Gold Coast Regiment, while also living out a boyhood fantasy. In this endeavor there was no room for marriage.

In making the transition from an assistant weighing clerk to a signaler in the Gold Coast Regiment, Boakye Yiadom acted very much as a krakye. He sat down at his table and wrote letters. This allowed him to communicate with his landlord and his wife from a distance, without directly confronting them, and without having to rely on messengers who would pass on his oral statements. Instead, the landlord, also literate, was designated to read the letter to Boakye Yiadom's illiterate wife, informing her of his decisions to leave and to end the marriage. In this communication the landlord, as the interlocutor, became the crucial link. How would he perform the letter? If he needed to translate from English into Twi, would he elaborate certain parts, or even omit a section? Although Boakye Yiadom had acquired literacy and distinguished himself by using that skill professionally, as well as in communication with his wife and landlord, his letter still needed to be performed orally, following a written script, in order to serve its purpose. Boakye Yiadom's written statement to his wife went through the filter of orality.[24]

Boakye Yiadom's practice of writing explains his surprising recollections of dates. He remembered the dates of leaving Konongo and joining the Gold Coast Regiment so well because he wrote them down, first by composing letters, second in recording this important episode in "My Own Life," which was rewritten in 1946 for that period, and third in reminiscing in his autobiography, "My Life History," some fifty years later. Being a krakye altered his sense of time. Certain events did not happen in some distant, unspecified past, but could be located as specific instances on the timeline of his life. These moments, connected to a precise date, could be recalled and contextualized with other events.

In retrospect, talking about his early years as a krakye, Boakye Yiadom emphasized his missionary zeal for the Presbyterian Church, demonstrated by his helping to found a congregation in Konongo. Curious about his writing habits, I inquired whether the church also received a letter:

> *SM:* You stopped the missionary work. Did you also write a letter?
>
> *BY:* No, [I left] without saying anything to the mission, because they were not paying me. . . . So I went without their knowledge. One day, they heard that their missionary had gone to the army. The one they got [as replacement] came from Abetifi, this man, Mr. Donko. . . .
>
> *SM:* When you left did they blame you?
>
> *BY:* No, no one blamed me. Because I was establishing the church, I was caring for the church for five years. So if I go, well, another person will come to control the church.

Because Boakye Yiadom was not compensated for his missionary work, he did not feel obliged to inform the church authorities. There was no employment. His relation with the UAC was different. After reaching Kumase, he contacted his employer, Mr. Neizer.

> *SM:* And you also wrote Mr. Neizer a letter that you were leaving?
>
> *BY:* At that time he was in Kumase too; so I went there, I dressed up as a soldier, I went to his house. When I [left] in January, the cocoa season was coming to the end. So we had no cocoa coming. He went to Kumase to rest for a while. I went to Kumase to see him. When he saw me in army attire, he said: "*Eh Kofi, woabɛdisoldier*—Eh Kofi, have you become a soldier?" I said, "*Ane*—yes." "*Hwan na bɛboa me adwuma no*—Who will help me now with the work?" I said, well, "*wobɛnya bi*— you will find somebody!" (laughter) He took another clerk. (Boakye Yiadom 1994b: 18f.)

Certainly finding another krakye was not very difficult, despite the military's recruiting among formally educated men.

Although Boakye Yiadom professed great enthusiasm for the male world of the military, he failed to become a hero on battlefields in far-away countries. After six months of training, divided between Kumase and Accra, Boakye Yiadom qualified as a soldier. During his service, he had relationships with women. "My Own Life" contains a brief entry about two "wives," one of whom became pregnant (n.d.a, 1: 12). After nine months, the martial episode ended; Boakye Yiadom was discharged on suspicion of tuberculosis. Although such a rejection on medical grounds, either during recruitment or while serving as a soldier, was quite common, the discharge was a disappointment for Boakye Yiadom, a blow to his ambition to excel as a soldier.[25] In the second autobiography, "My Life History," Boakye Yiadom preferred not to indicate his reason for leaving the army. Instead, he emphasized having been decorated and having extended the duration of his service to over two years (n.d.b:4). His love for uniforms and military settings was later gratified by his career as a Boy Scout leader. His identity as a former soldier, an ex-serviceman, became crucial in his self-presentation. The first pictures he showed me depicted him during his military service.

WORKING AS TEACHER-CATECHIST

Returning from the army, Boakye Yiadom chose the other option open to akrakyefoɔ, working as a primary school teacher, first for the African Universal Church in Abetifi, then for the Presbyterian Church outside of his home-town. Teaching mainly in small rural communities, Boakye Yiadom was in an ambivalent position. In one way, he remained an outsider, closely watched by the local people; on the other hand, due to his literacy and his position as a representative of the church, he had access to power, acting as mediator between local chiefs and the colonial administration.[26] Although Boakye Yiadom was quite engaged with local people as a catechist, his friends were other teachers, who formed close networks. At times of crisis, he felt isolated. In "My Life History" he recalled his loneliness after the death of his wife, Alice Safoaah, in Kumawu, where he only knew one person, a former teacher from his days in primary school.[27] Boakye Yiadom's relationships with women did not always match village elders' and church authorities' expectations of a teacher-catechist. After an accusation of adultery, he left the Presbyterian school and looked for other employment, first teaching in Catholic schools, then briefly working as a clerk (1994a: 11f.).

In 1950, at the age of forty, Boakye Yiadom returned to the Presbyterian school system and enrolled in the Presbyterian Training College, Akuropon, then in the recently opened St. Andrew's Training College at Asante Mam-pong. This institution was established to strengthen the education of previously untrained primary school teachers. Deliberately placed in a rural area, it focused on practical subjects, such as hygiene, gardening, agriculture, and citizenship, besides more academic ones: English, history, arithmetic, and one local language. After two years, Boakye Yiadom became a certified B teacher, profiting from the expansion of education during the postwar period. Attending the Presbyterian seminary at Abetifi for one year, he qualified as a catechist in 1953 (cf. Foster 1965: 169f.; Gold Coast 1942: 5f.).

Until his retirement in 1978, Boakye Yiadom worked as a head teacher and catechist in small towns and villages. Usually he was transferred every few years. But in one station, at Adamsu, Brong Ahafo, he stayed for ten years; this period became the high point of his professional career, documented by many photographs and oral, as well as written, recollections (1994a). In the second autobiography (n.d.b), he emphasized his achievements in opening or improving schools and churches, for example acquiring pews, a pulpit, and a baptismal basin in Kokofu in 1954, or building the chapel and a mission house in Adamsu in the 1960s. Boakye Yiadom placed himself in a Presbyterian tradition derived from nineteenth-century Basel missionaries who had started schools and erected buildings for church services.[28] In 1971, Boakye Yiadom gained certification as an A teacher, which entitled him to a full pension. He continued working as a catechist until he was sixty-eight years old and then returned to Abetifi to retire in Christian Quarters. In his long teaching career, living outside his hometown, Boakye Yiadom had carefully maintained social contacts with his extended family, by regularly visiting family members and attending funerals. The two volumes of "Autobiography: My Own Life" bear witness to the distances covered and expenses incurred fulfilling his obligations to his matrilineage as son, *wɔfa* (maternal uncle), and brother (n.d.a). Characterized by "cyclical migration" (Bartle 1980), Boakye Yiadom's teaching career exemplifies a migration pattern typical of many Kwawu people who made a living beyond the boundaries of their hometowns.

NEGOTIATING MARRIAGE AND SEXUALITY

Boakye Yiadom struggled to accommodate conflicting expectations of him as a man and competing notions about proper relations with women in different marriage arrangements. Since he spoke freely about his involvement with the sixteen women who gave birth to his twenty-seven children, and shared his two autobiographies, we have the opportunity to reconstruct how he negotiated different notions of masculinity, while arranging his marriages within the changing contexts of his life. These narratives provide a window onto how he recorded events in "My Own Life," written like a diary at the time, and how he presented them *ex post facto* to different audiences.

As a teacher and especially as a catechist, Boakye Yiadom was expected to live monogamously with his Christian wife following the regulations of the Presbyterian church. Church authorities frowned on extramarital relationships and demanded that members either have their customary marriage blessed by the Presbyterian church or enter an Ordinance marriage regulated by colonial statutory law.[29] In accordance with Presbyterian rules, Boakye Yiadom usually lived with one woman, with whom he had performed customary marriage rites—his unions with five of them, sequentially, were also consecrated by the church. He identified the woman residing under his roof as his spouse to church officials and tried to keep knowledge of his former wives and concubines away from them. This arrangement was for him neither problematic nor contradictory to his explicit aim of leading a life as a devout Presbyterian, since he claimed in his recollections to have compensated the extramarital mothers of his children and provided for all his children, in such ways as paying school fees up to Standard VII (1994b: 8, 12ff.).

There are discrepancies in Boakye Yiadom's representation of the organization of his marriages. In his second autobiography, "My Life History," he preferred to mention only two of his Christian wives: the first one, who died tragically in childbirth in 1945, and his current wife of over thirty years (n.d.b). Asked during the first taped conversation whether he had had any other wives or girlfriends besides these two Christian wives, Boakye Yiadom initially denied it and then avoided the question.

> SM: When did you marry your second wife?
> BY: I married in 1960.
> SM: In 1960? But you said before your wife died in 1945?
> BY: But then I went as no-wife.
> SM: Ah, then you did not have a wife for many years.
> BY: I stayed like that, wishing to get money, and then to have the go-ahead to go to the training college.
> SM: But you were then a man . . . Did you have a girlfriend then, I mean, so many years without wife?[30]
> BY: Yes (laughs), a good stay. . . .
> SM: You had a girlfriend then?
> BY: Yes . . . , any way. . . . (laughs).
> SM: Of course. Did you have any more children?
> BY: No, I did not have more children, but I had my wife here. In 1960, I married her. (Boakye Yiadom 1993: 6)

I did not pursue the question. More than a year later, Boakye Yiadom showed me a copy of "My Life History," which contained a list of his children but did not mention their mothers. This gave me the opportunity to inquire further. In the meantime we had become closer acquaintances, and he felt more comfortable sharing parts of his life which did not fit closely into a Presbyterian ideal of masculinity. Thus, in our later interviews, as well as in the two volumes of "My Own Life," Boakye Yiadom revealed how navigating through and around narrowly defined church regulations and expectations enabled him to organize his sexual relations in multiple ways (Boakye Yiadom 1994a: 1ff.; 1994b).

Working as a teacher, Boakye Yiadom encountered difficulties with superiors because of his sexual relations with women. In 1944, his first Christian wife, Alice Safoaah, accused him of adultery and was supported by church authorities. Two years later, when church elders of Kumawu pressed charges of sexual misconduct against him, he strongly denied any wrongdoing. Both parties attempted to settle the case before the senior pastor in Kumase, and finally at the local chief's court (Boakye Yiadom n.d.a, 1: 33f.; 1994b: 11f.). A few years later, in Adumasa, he stayed with a woman named Comfort Pomaah, with whom he had performed customary marriage rites in 1947 and received Christian blessing from a Methodist pastor; further, he had a girl-friend in the same town. Both women gave birth to his children the same year. Since there was no local Presbyterian church and he was not the church's employee, he was, as he stated, "free from Presbyterian authority." When Boakye Yiadom entered training college in 1950, he divorced Comfort Pomaah and presented himself as a single man without children, in an attempt to conform to the college's expectations.

> I saw I had to go to training college, but I can't go when I have a wife, I can't train myself while having children; so I had to compensate with little money, let's say, I buy her about two cloths, and about, let's say during that time, about £5 . . . to cover the children (Boakye Yiadom 1994b: 8).

Fatherhood is for Boakye Yiadom an important part of his self-conception as a man. Emphasizing his accomplishments as a father, having many children, enhances his own masculinity. He noted, "When you beget, you become a man yourself. I have become a man myself" (1993: 4). His strong identity as a father is reflected in various forms of self-presentation. During the interviews, he spoke at length about his children and gave detailed answers about the whereabouts of at least some of his sons and daughters. In his second autobiography, he proudly listed thirty-nine "living children," including his own nineteen surviving children and those of his three deceased brothers, whom he succeeded.[31] In the two volumes of "My Own Life" he meticulously recorded the birthdates and names of all his children, sometimes adding comments concerning the place of conception and the birth, such as the midwife's fee, or elaborating on the choice of a name. Occasionally, he listed the order and names of the children he had fathered so far; in 1968 he compiled a complete table with information about the children's mothers and hometowns. He took note of the upbringing and expenses of the sons and daughters who lived close to him.[32] "My Own Life" provides extended testimony to visits by his children, some accompanied by their mothers, and to conflicts. In 1966, Boakye Yiadom expelled his daughter Noble Akosua Obiyaah from his house at Adamsu, Brong-Ahafo Region, for being "lazy," not behaving according to his wishes, and scolding him with abusive language, hence challenging his paternal authority (Boakye Yiadom n.d.a, 2: 33ff.). His position as a father was acknowledged among his non-Christian relatives, because he had recognized and named his children after their births. This recognition carried weight whether he had actually entered customary marriages with their mothers or only compensated them. Needless to say, Boakye Yiadom was expected to provide for all his children by compensating their mothers and their *mmusua* (matrilineages); if he failed to do so, this must have caused serious conflicts and criticism.

Considering his moderate salary, it seems unlikely that Boakye Yiadom had the means to take care of all these children, and especially to pay their school fees up to Standard VII. It appears that he was more generous toward those whose mothers he had married, while the children of his "concubines," whose mothers were only compensated, probably received less support. In 1956, while stationed as head teacher and catechist in his second hometown, Kurofa, Asante-Akyem, his annual salary was forty-two pounds. At that time, seven of his children were old enough to attend school. If Boakye Yiadom had covered all their school fees, which he estimated, in retrospect, as approximately nine shillings and sixpence, he would have had to spend three pounds, six shillings, and six on school fees, amounting to almost one month's income. In 1967, ten of his children were enrolled in school. Further, Boakye Yiadom also noted that he had "three nephews and two nieces" who stayed with him, and that he paid for all "their school fees, together with [his] own children" (1994b: 13, 16). Boakye Yiadom's experience in fatherhood supports Jean Allman's (1997) argument for neighboring Asante that in the course of the twentieth century fathers were less likely to be persuaded or forced to meet the rising costs of childrearing.

Reconstructing his marriages, Boakye Yiadom especially mentioned two attributes which were important to him: entering a "Christian marriage" and finding a wife "at home" (1993: 11; 1994b: 6). Both wives mentioned in his second autobiography met these criteria. Selecting his first Christian wife, Alice Safoaah, he did not rely on mediation by his father or other relatives. According to his recollections, they met in 1943 during a funeral service in Bukuruwa, a town close to Abetifi. While Boakye Yiadom, as catechist, was preaching from the pulpit, he suddenly spotted a "particular woman" whose presence "touched" him. He considered it an act of God that, after the service, Alice Safoaah approached him and asked about his hometown. Then he learned that she was also from Abetifi, although her mother had married in Bukuruwa (1993: 11). Since they entered a Christian marriage, whenever he later mentioned Alice Safoaah in his autobiographical writings, he added the qualifier "Christian." For example, in 1944, upon the birth of his fifth child, he rejoiced in his diaries that his "real beloved and only Christian wife delivered a well symmetrical child, called Grace Ankomaah Yiadom."[33]

Presenting his married life during the interviews, Boakye Yiadom stressed the importance of husband and wife's living together under one roof.

> In Christian Quarters here, it is the law, Christian law, that every person stays with his wife so you can cooperate with your wife and everything. It is not good when you are living here and your wife is living in the town.

Then he added all the inconveniences, if husband and wife do not stay together.

> Your wife would come to this place in the night to sleep, she would have to take water from town for you to take your bath, and even, if she wants to consult a small matter with you, she should not have to travel up from the town. So, it is better if you stay with your wife.[34]

Discussing his ideas about marriage, Boakye Yiadom emphasized that his two Christian wives, featured in "My Life History," came from his hometown. He noted the economic advantages of this, since husbands and wives from different towns face additional costs attending funerals. He added that after his death, matters of inheritance and succession would be easier to settle if his abusua and that of his wife and children already knew each other.[35]

In the early 1960s, while stationed as teacher-catechist in Adamsu, Brong Ahafo, Boakye Yiadom married his last wife. He contacted his mother by letter, asking her to search for a suitable wife from Christian Quarters in Abetifi. In Susana Ansomaah his mother found exactly what he was looking for. Boakye Yiadom occurred wedding expenses of fourteen pounds, five shillings, and sixpence. He considered this marriage, which was "properly arranged by his relatives," as "much better" because his mother and his abusua had a chance to inquire whether his bride came from a "very good house," not from one of "thieves or robbers," and whether she was not a woman fond of "quarreling." Boakye Yiadom deplored the neglect of such scrutiny by the younger generation, who are, instead, following their "heart."

> SM: So it is not good that nowadays young people are choosing their own wives . . . ?
> BY: Their own wives . . . , that's not good. You have to tell your parents [about your marriage intentions], and your parents will find a suitable wife for you, or a suitable husband for a woman. That is better than finding yourself a woman, or finding yourself a husband; no, that's not good according to my spirit. (1993: 13)

In Boakye Yiadom's recollection, the account of his last marriage becomes a formulaic description of how Christian marriages should be performed, and how they should be emulated by younger generations. After taking many liberties throughout his life, arranging marriages and relations with a multitude of wives and concubines, he felt compelled, at least in his self-presentation, to arrange his final marriage precisely according to Presbyterian values and norms, fitting his self-image as teacher-catechist. In recalling his life Boakye Yiadom did not focus on the fluidity of his marriages' organizations and forms, but instead foregrounded the Presbyterian ideal he sought to achieve and hoped to be remembered for.[36]

BECOMING AN *Ɔpanyin*

In the Twi language, the term *Ɔpanyin* (elder) incorporates a broad semantic field. The linguist J. G. Christaller (1933) distinguished between two groups of meaning. The first, emphasizing age, depicted an *Ɔpanyin* as "an old person" and "an adult, a grown-up person" as opposed to *abofra* (child);

the second, expressing the status and achievements of an elder, depicted an ɔpanyin as a "gentleman, respectable man, person of rank, senior alderman, senator, elder." This second definition refers to an ɔpanyin as a figure of authority, "chief, master," or, in the plural, to the council of elders, *mpanyin-foɔ*, of a chief (375). These days, asking in Kwawu about the meaning and implications of the term "ɔpanyin" often triggers a lively discussion. Some people emphasize age, others maturity, experience, and honor. "Ɔpanyin" is not necessarily gender-specific, since men and women may occupy offices at a chief's court, sitting among the mpanyinfoɔ. Moreover, ɔpanyin status is not permanent. Someone respected as an ɔpanyin needs to continue proving his or her worthiness, since a person's conduct, behavior, and speech determine whether he or she will be referred to as an ɔpanyin. An elder who misbehaves may immediately lose status; once some people begin to ridicule an ɔpanyin, others rapidly lose respect for him or her as well (Miescher 1997a: chapter 7).

Boakye Yiadom summarized his understanding of ɔpanyin status while explaining a man's obligation to his wives, children, and abusua. After his declaration that over the course of the last few decades he had "become a man," I inquired,

SM: What makes someone a man?
BY: To make somebody a man, I used to say that you have a work to do, that you do it well and get some income from the work, from the business you do. Then, you have to marry; after you have seen that you got some little amount to cater for your wife and children, then you have to marry. When you marry and bring forth with your wife some children, you have to care for them until they are at the age of going to school, and you care for them when they are in school. And you care for your wife, you have to clothe your wife, you have to finance your wife to do something also to help you, the husband.

Boakye Yiadom included in this idealized presentation of a man's duties his responsibilities to matrikin and within the larger household:

BY: You must cater for the children and the family and your relatives [nephews and nieces]. You don't forget your relatives. Then you have become a man. When a case comes to your house, you have to sit down and settle the case amicably so that every person will say that you can rule your house well. Then you have become a man, and they call you a man of the house. And that man of the house we call ɔpanyin.
SM: And you are now an ɔpanyin?
BY: Yes, I am now an ɔpanyin. . . . Because I have a wife, I have children that I have looked for all the children, so I have become an ɔpanyin. And when they go to school, when they finish, I help to see that I sponsor them to some work, or to continue their education. (1993: 3f.)

For Boakye Yiadom, an ɔpanyin is the quintessence of a man who has fulfilled a number of expectations: to marry, to support a wife and give her some
capital for her economic activities, and to father children and provide them
with an education, as well as to meet his obligations toward his abusua and to
mediate conflicts. It is significant that Boakye Yiadom stressed an ɔpanyin's
responsibilities to his wife and children, as well as to his own matrikin. As
noted, Boakye Yiadom's Presbyterian training sought to strengthen the notion of a Christian (nuclear) family, privileging patrilineal ties, at the expense
of obligation to the abusua. By setting up the ideal of devoting the same
attention and support to nieces and nephews as to wife and children, Boakye
Yiadom raised expectations which were hard to meet with the limited financial resources of a teacher-catechist.

CREATING A LEGACY

Since his retirement, Boakye Yiadom has been active in shaping his personal legacy. In his second autobiography, "My Life History," he emphasized
his devotion as a missionary and catechist in the service of the Presbyterian
church as a major part of his life. In detail, he narrated his founding of a
Presbyterian church in Konongo in 1935 and responsibility for the expansion
of the congregation over the following five years. This accomplishment in
Konongo is framed as the beginning of his service to the church (n.d.b).
Notes in the earlier "Autobiography: My Own Life" about the first thirty-six
years of his life, written in 1946, present a different picture; there, his missionary activities at Konongo are not mentioned at all. The brief entry about
his stay in Konongo covers only his work for the UAC, documenting his promotion and raise and the birth of his first child (n.d.a, 1: 10f.). This omission
is striking, since he must have used these notes in composing the second
autobiography. With the exception of his missionary work in Konongo, these
notes correspond closely to "My Life History" and only sometimes provide
a few additional details. At least while he was writing "My Own Life," there
were more important occurrences in 1935 than the founding of the Konongo
Presbyterian Church.

In 1968, having worked as a trained catechist for fifteen years, Boakye
Yiadom applied for ordination, which was denied. He recalled,

> BY: I wanted to be a minister . . . I sent in my application to be a minister of
> the church. But according to my record, they say I am over-age. They have to
> ordain a person at the age of thirty or forty.[37]
> SM: You did not go to training college till forty.
> BY: When I went to training college, even when I came out of the training
> college [becoming a certified A teacher], I was more than sixty. But I estab-
> lished the Konongo Presbyterian Church in 1935. If you go there, you see my

photograph at the mission house. When I got out of the middle school in 1934, I went to Konongo to buy cocoa, as a cocoa produce agent. I saw that there was no Presbyterian church, and I made my mind that God may help me to establish the church. And I did, it is now flourishing. (1993: 9)

In this response, the immediate switch from being denied the ordination to the accomplishment in Konongo is significant. It shows how Boakye Yiadom considered the early missionary work in Konongo decisive in his work as a catechist and in his aspiration to become a minister. During the fiftieth anniversary celebration of the Konongo Presbyterian Church, Boakye Yia-dom made a public announcement pleading with the church authorities to make him a "special minister without salary." He declared, "[M]y greatest desire is to be made a minister and receive full ministerial burial when I die."[38] In 1994, this appeal was repeated in letters to the Synod Committee (church leadership). The biographical information he provided was adapted. He stated that he served in the army for five years, and that he had one wife and twelve children. Boakye Yiadom requested more than a position as an honorary minister; he suggested to the Synod Committee that they rename the Presbyterian chapel of Konongo after him, mount a plate with his name and picture at the back of the chapel, and allow him to be buried there.[39] The founding of the church at Konongo and the second autobiography's omissions concerning his multiple sexual relationships and marriages be-come crucial in Boakye Yiadom's self-presentation as a staunch, rule-abiding Presbyterian. His perception of the past has shifted. What may have been a brief involvement with the Konongo church at that time, or may not have happened as recalled, has moved to the center stage in his narrative.

After reading a draft of this chapter in 1997, Boakye Yiadom showed me another notebook with a more detailed history of the beginnings of the Ko-nongo Presbyterian Church. This version of the Konongo story was recorded in the 1970s, although, as he indicated, it was based on earlier jottings. Boa-kye Yiadom saved a printed program describing the "Laying of Corner Stones" for a new church building in 1955. To it, he added by hand that "Mr. B. Yiadom" presented a "History of the Kgo Presby, Church (15 min.)."[40] These different recollections of the founding of the Konongo Presbyterian Church show that for Boakye Yiadom his life history has been "an open text," subject to rearrangements and rewritings which reflect his shifting interpre-tations and objectives (Mbilinyi 1989: 225).

Boakye Yiadom's petition to the Synod Committee expresses his concern that future generations know and mention his name. These days, in Kwawu, names of ancestors are evoked in libations, carried on by children, or, as a colonial innovation, preserved by concrete memorials, the most notable of these being the large lineage houses. Practically all men and women who gain some wealth seek to construct a building for their matrikin so that they will be remembered by future generations. These houses, as mnemonic devices, will remind the deceased's descendants of his (or her) former physical existence, offering a way to transcend death by creating a space of afterlife in the memories of others.[41]

Boakye Yiadom failed to erect a building. He was constantly juggling demands from his wives and his many children. Members of his abusua expected support from their salaried relative, such as assistance with funeral expenses.[42] In 1997, Boakye Yiadom was living with his wife, Susana Ansomaah, in a house in Abetifi Christian Quarters. This house belonged to Susana Ansomaah's sister. When Boakye Yiadom reflected on his material wishes as an octogenarian, he emphasized that he did not desire to acquire luxury items, such as beautiful *ntɔma* (cloths worn by Akan men on festive occasions) that would allow him to present himself as an ɔpanyin of means, or a new suit adequate to his rank as a krakye. Nevertheless, Boakye Yiadom has not forgone his hopes of erecting a house.

> As far as my age is concerned, I am not wishing to get more properties, only one thing is in my mind: to make a building for my wife and children, but according to personal properties like cloth or dresses, I don't like [need] it. Because I can use already this cloth for one year, and one suit can last me about ten years, but now, if I am trying to get ten cloths, keeping them in a box, for what?

Boakye Yiadom elaborated his wish that some of his children would be in a position to support him in erecting a house.

> But I want to have a building. If God blesses me and my children are also coming up and get some business. . . . What I have told them is that they have to work properly without touching somebody's property. They have to go ahead with their own money, they have to keep part of it in the post office or bank. As Monkey says, "Soft, softly, you go ahead." They come to help me to make a building. And when they have given [me] a building, as my wife's sister has got one, then it is all right for them. (1993: 18)

Boakye Yiadom waited until he was over sixty years old to name a child, his last-born son, after himself. He has especially high expectations of this child, hoping that he will go to university and one day might study abroad in the United Kingdom, where, in Boakye Yiadom's youth, the few university graduates obtained their degree. The son, carrying the father's name, should achieve in his education what the father failed to do, and then erect a house on the father's behalf.

Finally, it appears that Boakye Yiadom's motivation in providing me access to the various oral and written representations of his life is connected to his wish to preserve his legacy beyond his lifetime. Commenting on this chapter, he insisted that the title should include his nickname, "Akasease Kofi of Abetifi, Kwawu," since "there are so many Boakye Yiadom at Abetifi," but only one person with this unusual name. He concluded that "everybody who sees this [essay] will know that I am the person."[43]

❖ ❖ ❖

The oral and written recollections of Boakye Yiadom presented in this essay are typical of those of many akrakyefoɔ in colonial Ghana. Mission education exposed him to a set of cultural values and behavioral patterns which proved to be problematic in his understanding of being a man. The imposition of such cultural values, the colonization of mind and body, is not a conscious process; rather, contradictory values can be played out in a person's life (cf. Comaroff and Comaroff 1991). Throughout his life, as reflected in the different narratives, Boakye Yiadom negotiated conflicting expectations of masculinity and developed multiple—social and subjective—identities appropriate to different contexts. In his life history accounts, he presents himself as a devout Presbyterian, devoting himself to his work as a catechist, who therefore should be ordained in recognition of his services. But he also portrays himself as a krakye, as a dedicated teacher, who felt that he had some rights because of his educational status and sought to keep a certain independence from church authorities. He sees himself as an ex-serviceman and scout leader who was prepared to defend the Empire and continues to serve the national government of Ghana. He emphasizes his fulfilled obligations as wɔfa to his matrilineage and stresses his identity as a father. In all accounts, he is certainly proud of having fathered many children. In his recollections, the arrangements of marriage and concubinage are shifting, at times contested, depending on the intended audience.

These multiple identities could be understood as a fragmentation of the self resulting from the colonial situation, as Frantz Fanon (1967) argues.[44] It appears, however, that Boakye Yiadom's identities are held together by his "perseverance"[45] in struggling to do the right thing as a man, to become an ɔpanyin of whom it might even be said by the other mpanyinfoɔ, his fellow elders, "ɔyɛ ɔbarima pa (he is a good, a real, valiant man)." Talking about the responsibilities of an ɔpanyin and about praise a man might receive for his deeds, Boakye Yiadom explained the expression "ɔbarima pa." He stated that the term is used for someone who, due to his "strong manhood," is responsible for the conception of many children, or for someone who is brave, like a warrior, in crisis situations, or for someone who shares his acquired wealth freely with the community.[46] Boakye Yiadom, who implied that the term might also be used for himself, sought to achieve all this, with variable success. He is obviously a potent man who produced many children. He tried to become a warrior by enlisting in the army and, after failing for reasons of health, by serving as a Boy Scout leader. He attempted to gather riches, which in Kwawu means trading, by twice seeking his fortune as a storekeeper; both times he lacked the necessary capital.

Boakye Yiadom's understanding of having overcome hurdles in his life is also reflected in a series of self-selected attributes, "honorary twelve descent titles," which he associated with the twelve letters of his name: "*B*rilliant, *O*bedient, *A*rdent, *K*een, *Y*outhful, *E*conomist" and "*Y*ieldy, *I*deologist, *A*cceptable, *D*utiful, *O*rderly, *M*artinet."[47] Boakye Yiadom gave me a copy of these "titles" when reviewing the manuscript; he suggested that they belonged to this representation of his life histories.

Whether, or to what extent, Boakye Yiadom and other akrakyefoɔ of this period succeeded in amalgamating conflicting models of ideal behavior in their own lives as they strove to be successful men depended upon their abilities, circumstances, and personalities. The differing emphases and omissions in Boakye Yiadom's representations of his life provide insight into his negotiation between distinct and sometimes contradictory ideals of masculinity. The texts in various narrative genres produced for specific audiences in different moments and contexts of his life reveal strategies and transformations in Boakye Yiadom's constructions of his self. A careful reading of these narratives allows us to historicize his subjectivity.

NOTES

I am grateful for financial support to conduct oral and archival research in Ghana (November 1992 to November 1993, and August to December 1994) from the Wenner-Gren Foundation (Gr. 5561), the John D. and Catherine T. MacArthur Foundation, the Janggen-Pöhn Stiftung, and Northwestern University. Bryn Mawr College enabled me to return to Ghana in July 1997. Many thanks for comments and inspirations by Kofi Anyidoho, Jim Campbell, Lane Clark, David William Cohen, Lisa Lindsay, Tom McCaskie, Steven Pierce, Ben Soares, Peter Seitel, Lynn Thomas, and Luise White, and by the participants of the two "Words and Voices" conferences in Bellagio and Ann Arbor.

1. See Mirza and Strobel 1989, Davison 1989, and Bozzoli 1991. For a discussion of this methodology, see Geiger 1986, Personal Narratives Group 1989, Hoppe 1993, and Gengenbach 1994.

2. See Radin 1926. Smith (1954) and Shostak (1981) published influential African life histories; Caplan (1997: 9–17) and Kratz (this volume) offer a history of the genre.

3. See Bozzoli 1991, van Onselen 1993, 1996, and Geiger 1997. Cf. Wright's (1993: 151–78) discussion of Bwanikwa's life, based on oral research conducted by an English missionary.

4. I often had the impression that the seventeen women at the center of Bozzoli's (1991) study do not receive individual selves in her text, but rather are cited as "voices" to illustrate other themes. Discussing recollections of urban gangsters, Bozzoli cited and identified Mahubi Makgale, then cited Ernestina Mekgwe without mentioning her name in the text, then cited and named Naomi Setshedi, and ended with another anonymous quotation of Ernestina Mekgwe (113f.). Only the notes reveal Mekgwe's identity.

5. See Tonkin's (1992) suggestions about the position of subjectivity in oral research; cf. Vaughan's (1991) discussion of making colonial subjectivities through and in response to biomedical discourse in British Africa.

6. In Crapanzano's (1980) study, the selves of Tuhami and Crapanzano are discovered through their participation in the narrations of the self; the narration becomes a cocreation of self and other. Cf. Prell 1989.

7. See Kendall's (1996: 166f.) comments about her decision to record and publish Mpho 'M'atsepo Nthunya's life history in English. All formal interviews with Boakye Yiadom were taped in Abetifi and transcribed verbatim. Our informal conversations in the course of other activities, such as attending funerals together and regularly exchanging visits, were conducted in Twi. I took notes, when possible, on our more spontaneous conversations. I am very grateful to Kofi Boakye Yiadom for speaking about so many aspects of his life and for allowing me to publish this essay.

8. Volume 1 of Boakye Yiadom's "Autobiography: My Own Life" (n.d.a, 1) begins with extended notes about the first thirty-six years of his life. I am thankful to Kwame Fosu in assisting me with translations from Twi to English.

9. Boakye Yiadom inevitably associated me with his former European supervisors. This became obvious while we were looking at his personal papers. He suddenly commented that it reminded him of the olden days when a European educational officer used to visit the school, sit down at his desk, and inspect his schoolbooks. When I asked him whether he would have shared the intimate volumes of "My Own Life" with an educational officer, he laughingly said no.

10. Bakhtin (1986: 95) argues, "Each speech genre in each area of speech communication has its own typical conception of the addressee, and this defines it as a genre." This insight complicates Caplan's (1997) presentation of Mohammed's life, particularly her inclusion of different textual genres.

11. See McCaskie 1995 for an attempt to historicize personhood in precolonial Asante.

12. For restrictions placed on Kwawu traders in Akyem Abuakwa, see the National Archives of Ghana (hereafter NAG), ADM 11/1/1639. Due to pressure from the colonial administration, Ofori Atta I and his council were forced to withdraw the order; cf. Simensen 1975: 108f. and Rathbone 1993: 58.

13. Basel Mission Archives, Switzerland (hereafter BMA), D-9.1c, 11a and 19b, *Ordnung für die evangelischen Gemeinden der Basler Mission in Ostindien und Westafrika*, 1865, revised 1902. For Basel Mission gender ideals, see Miescher 1997a: chapter 2 and Prodolliet 1987. Cf. Allman 1994.

14. Witschi 1965: 162ff. In 1926, some Basel missionaries were allowed to return: Witschi 1970: 306ff. Cf. Smith 1966: 155ff.

15. Cf. Miescher forthcoming. Emmanuel Akyeampong (1996b: 233), who has contributed to my thinking about *akrakyefoɔ* as a social category, translates the term "akrakyefoɔ" as "gentlemen."

16. Boakye Yiadom (1994a: 4). Opening government schools during the interwar period, colonial officials pursued similar strategies. NAG, ADM 34/5/2, District Record Book 1923, 152 (hereafter Record Book).

17. BMA, D-3.6, Rev. D. E. Akwa, annual report, Abetifi, 15 February 1916; cf. BMA, D-3.6, Rev. Martinson, annual report, Bompata (Abetifi), 11 February 1916, describing street preaching in the neighboring town of Bompata, Asante Akyem.

18. Record Book, 152f.

19. Boakye Yiadom n.d.b:2; 1993. On 5 December 1994, we visited together the grounds and buildings of the former Abetifi Boys' Boarding School, where Boakye Yiadom recalled his life as a boarder, especially the sporting competition among the four houses.

20. Due to the depression, the colonial government had drastically reduced expenditure on education, including scholarships, during the 1930s; cf. Austin 1964: 16.

21. See Southall 1978, Austin 1988, and Alence 1991.

22. Explaining the Twi expression "ɔyɛ ɔbarima pa [he is a valiant man]," Boakye Yiadom (1994c: 15) noted, "Sometimes, something has happened in this town that a *brave* man should go forward with a gun, or to do something, then we say, ɔyɛ ɔbarima pa."

23. Killingray (1982: 91) reports on recruitment efforts using modern media like mobile cinemas showing newsreels and aircraft dropping flyers.

24. For the interrelations between literacy and orality, see Hofmeyr 1994 and Barber 1995; cf. White 1995.

25. According to Killingray (1982: 88), the rejection rates on medical grounds were high. In the Eastern and Central provinces, these rates were over 40 percent up to March–April 1941. Only when the army urgently required more men were standards of health and height lowered.

26. For a discussion of the ambiguous position of village teachers, see Miescher forthcoming.

27. In "My Life History," Boakye Yiadom recorded the career paths of his former teachers (n.d.b).

28. Andreas Riis, who founded the first Basel Mission settlement of Akuropon, Akuapem, in 1843, is remembered as ɔsi adan [the one who builds houses]. See Reindorf 1895: 225.

29. BMA, D-9.1c, 13d, *Regulations, Practice, and Procedure of the Presbyterian Church of the Gold Coast,* 1929, 17ff. (hereafter *Regulations*). Cf. Miescher 1997a: chapter 6.

30. The interview transcript reveals my preconceived notions about Boakye Yiadom's understanding of masculinity, based on other conversations in Kwawu and on reading the ethnographic literature, such as Bleek 1975, 1976 and Bartle 1978.

31. Boakye Yiadom (n.d.b:12). After reading a draft of this chapter, he corrected some of the names and relative ages of his children (1997: 2).

32. Cf. Boakye Yiadom n.d.a, 1: 36, 71 for the expenses of his daughter Comfort Akosua Ankomaah. His children are listed in n.d.a, 2: 74–77 and n.d.b: 12.

33. Boakye Yiadom n.d.a, 1:19. The birth took place "by the help of Mrs. D. Riggs, a famous well known Government Certificated Midwife," who charged twenty-three shillings.

34. Boakye Yiadom (1993: 16) referred to *Regulations,* 19f. Tashjian (1995: 125) notes an "unusual reason for co-residence" by one married couple who moved in together after their marriage was blessed in a church of rural Asante. In towns with large Christian congregations, like Abetifi, and among teachers, there was more pressure to co-reside after entering a Christian marriage than in the two villages studied by Tashjian.

35. See Miescher 1997b for conflicts over inheritance in Abetifi Christian Quarters.

36. In 1999, Susana Ansomaah passed away unexpectedly.

37. In 1968, Boakye Yiadom was fifty-eight years old.

38. Boakye Yiadom's appeal was reported in *The Presbyterian* 1 (1985).

39. Letters to the Synod Committee, 2 May, 23 June, and 30 September 1994.

40. Boakye Yiadom, personal papers and 1997: 2f..

41. Cf. Bartle 1978: 115. For the practice of libations, see Yankah 1995: 172–80 and Akyeampong 1996a: 5.

42. In the two volumes of "Autobiography: My Own Life" Boakye Yiadom (n.d.a) meticulously recorded his funeral expenses and other responsibilities to his abusua.

43. Boakye Yiadom 1997: 1, 3). "Akasease" refers to the street in Manem, the old part of Abetifi, where he and his mother used to live.

44. Fanon's notions of alienation and the fragmented self have been important themes in postcolonial writing; cf. Vaughan 1991: 14f. and Bhabha 1994: 40–65.

45. The cover of Boakye Yiadom's "Autobiography: My Own Life" bears in bold letters the motto "Perseverance" (n.d.a).

46. Boakye Yiadom 1994c: 15f. I asked many men for an explanation of this expression. The answers are fascinating, all slightly different but agreeing on the aspects of physical and moral strength (reliability) and community-mindedness. They do not agree on whether this community-mindedness is expressed only in money or also in other ways. For the warrior ideal in precolonial Asante, see Arhin 1986; for a discussion of wealth, see McCaskie 1995: 37ff.

47. Boakye Yiadom's personal papers, and 1997.

BIBLIOGRAPHY

Akyeampong, Emmanuel Kwaku. 1996a. *Drink, Power, and Cultural Change: A Social History of Alcohol, c. 1800 to Recent Times.* Portsmouth, N.H.: Heinemann.

———. 1996b. "What's in a Drink? Class Struggle, Popular Culture, and the Politics of *Akpeteshie* (Local Gin) in Ghana, 1930–67." *Journal of African History* 37, no. 2: 215–36.

Alence, Rod. 1991. "The 1937–1938 Gold Coast Cocoa Crisis: The Political Economy of Commercial Stalemate." *African Economic History* 19: 77–104.

Allman, Jean. 1994. "Making Mothers: Missionaries, Medical Officers, and Women's Work in Colonial Asante, 1924–1945." *History Workshop Journal* 38: 23–47.

———. 1997. "Fathering, Mothering, and Making Sense of *Ntamoba*: Reflections on the Economy of Child-Rearing in Colonial Asante." *Africa* 67, no. 2: 296–321.

Alpers, Edward A. 1983. "The Story of Swema: Female Vulnerability in Nineteenth-Century East Africa." In *Women and Slavery in Africa,* ed. Claire C. Robertson and Martin A. Klein, 185–219. Madison: University of Wisconsin Press.

Arhin, Kwame. 1979. *West African Traders in Ghana in the Nineteenth and Twentieth Centuries.* London: Longman.

———. 1986. "The Asante Praise Poems: The Ideology of Patrimonialism." *Paideuma* 32: 163–97.

Austin, Dennis. 1964. *Politics in Ghana, 1946–1960.* London: Oxford University Press.

Austin, Gareth. 1988. "Capitalists and Chiefs in the Cocoa Hold-Ups in South Asante, 1927–1938." *International Journal of African Historical Studies* 21, no. 1: 63–95.

Bakhtin, Mikhail M. 1986. "The Problem of Speech Genres." In *Speech Genres and Other Late Essays,* trans. Vern W. McGee, ed. Caryl Emerson and Michael Hoquist, 60–102. Austin: University of Texas Press.

Barber, Karin. 1995. "Literacy, Improvisation, and the Public in Yoruba Popular Theatre." In *The Pressures of the Text: Orality, Texts, and the Telling of Tales,* ed. Stewart Brown, 6–27. Birmingham: Centre of West African Studies, University of Birmingham.

Bartle, Philip. 1978. "Urban Migration and Rural Identity: An Ethnography of a Kwawu Community, Obo, Ghana." Ph.D. dissertation, University of Ghana.

———. 1980. *Cyclical Migration and the Extended Community: A West African Example.* Leiden: Afrika-Studiecentrum.

Bhabha, Homi K. 1994. *The Location of Culture.* London and New York: Routledge.

Bleek, Wolf. 1975. *Marriage, Inheritance, and Witchcraft: A Case Study of a Rural Ghanaian Family.* Leiden: Afrika-Studiecentrum.

————. 1976. "Sexual Relationships and Birthcontrol in Ghana: A Case Study of a Rural Town." Ph.D. dissertation, University of Amsterdam.

Boakye Yiadom, Kofi. 1993. Interview with the author. Abetifi, 27 June.

————. 1994a. Interview with the author. Abetifi, 28 August.

————. 1994b. Interview with the author. Abetifi, 15 November.

————. 1994c. Interview with the author. Abetifi, 15 November.

————. 1997. Interview with the author. Abetifi, 23 July.

————. n.d.a [1946–1981]. "Autobiography: My Own Life." 2 vols.

————. n.d.b [after 1978]. "My Life History: The Autobiography of Akasease Kofi Boakye Yiadom."

Bozzoli, Belinda, with the assistance of Mmantho Nkotsoe. 1991. *Women of Phokeng: Consciousness, Life Strategy, and Migrancy in South Africa, 1900–1983.* Portsmouth, N.H.: Heinemann.

Caplan, Pat. 1997. *African Voices, African Lives: Personal Narratives from a Swahili Village.* London and New York: Routledge.

Christaller, Johann Gottlieb. 1933. *A Dictionary of the Asante and Fante Language, Called Tschi (Twi).* 2nd ed., revised and enlarged. Basel: Basel Evangelical Missionary Society.

Comaroff, Jean, and John Comaroff. 1991. *Of Revelation and Revolution.* Vol. 1, *Christianity, Colonialism, and Consciousness in South Africa.* Chicago: University of Chicago Press.

Crapanzano, Vincent. 1980. *Tuhami: Portrait of a Moroccan.* Chicago: University of Chicago Press.

Davison, Jean, with the women of Mutira. 1989. *Voices from Mutira: Lives of Rural Gikuyu Women.* Boulder: L. Rienner.

Fanon, Frantz. 1967. *Black Skin, White Masks.* Trans. Charles Lam Markmann. 1952. Reprint, New York: Grove Press.

Foster, Philip J. 1965. *Education and Social Change in Ghana.* Chicago: University of Chicago Press.

Garlick, Peter. 1967. "The Development of Kwahu Business Enterprise in Ghana." *Journal of African History* 8, no. 3: 463–80.

Geiger, Susan. 1986. "Women's Life Histories: Method and Content." *Signs* 11, no. 2: 334–51.

————. 1997. *TANU Women: Gender and Culture in the Making of Tanganyikan Nationalism, 1955–1965.* Portsmouth, N.H.: Heinemann.

Gengenbach, Heidi. 1994. "Truth-Telling and the Politics of Women's Life History Research in Africa: A Reply to Kirk Hoppe." *International Journal of African Historical Studies* 27, no. 3: 619–27.

Gold Coast. 1942. *Report of the Education Committee, 1937–1941.* Accra: Government Printer.

Haenger, Peter. 1989. "Die Basler Mission im Spannungsbereich afrikanischer Integrationsversuche und europäischer Kolonialpolitik. Vorbereitung und Anfangszeit der 'Asante Mission' in Abetifi, Kwawu." M. A. thesis, University of Basel.

Hofmeyr, Isabel. 1994. *"We Spend Our Years as a Tale That Is Told": Oral Historical Narrative in a South African Chiefdom.* Portsmouth, N.H.: Heinemann.

Hoppe, Kirk. 1993. "Whose Life Is It, Anyway? Issues of Representation in Life Narrative Texts of African Women." *International Journal of African Historical Studies* 26, no. 3: 623–36.

Keegan, Tim. 1988. *Facing the Storm: Portraits of Black Lives in Rural South Africa.* London: Zed.

Kendall, Limakatso K. 1996. Afterword to *Singing Away the Hunger: Stories of a Life in Lesotho*, by Mpho 'M'atsepo Nthunya, 164–71. Pietermaritzburg: University of Natal Press.

Killingray, David. 1982. "Military and Labour Recruitment in the Gold Coast during the Second World War." *Journal of African History* 23, no. 1: 83–95.

Mbilinyi, Marjorie. 1989. "'I'd Have Been a Man': Politics and the Labor Process in Producing Personal Narratives." In *Interpreting Women's Lives: Feminist Theory and Personal Narratives*, ed. Personal Narratives Group, 204–27. Bloomington: Indiana University Press.

McCaskie, T. C. 1995. *State and Society in Pre-colonial Asante.* Cambridge: Cambridge University Press.

Miescher, Stephan F. 1997a. "Becoming a Man in Kwawu: Gender, Law, Personhood, and the Construction of Masculinities in Colonial Ghana, 1875–1957." Ph.D. dissertation, Northwestern University.

———. 1997b. "Of Documents and Litigants: Disputes on Inheritance in Abetifi—a Town of Colonial Ghana." *Journal of Legal Pluralism* 39: 81–119.

———. Forthcoming. "The Making of Presbyterian Teachers: Masculinities and Programs of Education in Colonial Ghana." In *Men and Masculinities in Modern Africa*, ed. Lisa A. Lindsay and Stephan F. Miescher. Portsmouth, N.H.: Heinemann.

Mirza, Sarah, and Margaret Strobel. 1989. *Three Swahili Women: Life Histories from Mombasa, Kenya.* Bloomington: Indiana University Press.

Peacock, James L., and Dorothy C. Holland. 1993. "The Narrated Self: Life Stories in Process." *Ethos* 21, no. 4: 367–83.

Personal Narratives Group, ed. 1989. *Interpreting Women's Lives: Feminist Theory and Personal Narratives.* Bloomington: Indiana University Press.

Prell, Riv-Ellen. 1989. "The Double Frame of Life History in the Work of Barbara Myerhoff." In *Interpreting Women's Lives: Feminist Theory and Personal Narratives*, ed. Personal Narratives Group, 241–58. Bloomington: Indiana University Press.

Prodolliet, Simone. 1987. *Wider die Schamlosigkeit und das Elend der heidnischen Weiber. Der Export des europäischen Frauenideals in die Kolonien durch die Basler Frauenmission.* Zurich: Limmat Verlag.

Radin, Paul, ed. 1926. *Crashing Thunder: The Autobiography of an American Indian.* New York: Appleton.

Rathbone, Richard. 1993. *Murder and Politics in Colonial Ghana.* New Haven: Yale University Press.

Reindorf, Carl Christian. 1895. *History of the Gold Coast and Asante.* Basel: Missionsbuchhandlung.

Schlatter, Wilhelm. 1916. *Geschichte der Basel Mission, 1815–1915.* 3 vols. Basel: Missionsbuchhandlung.

Shostak, Marjorie. 1981. *Nisa: The Life and Words of a !Kung Woman.* Cambridge, Mass.: Harvard University Press.

Simensen, Jarle. 1975. "Commoners, Chiefs, and Colonial Government: British Policy and Local Politics in Akim Abuakwa, Ghana, under Colonial Rule." Ph.D. dissertation, University of Trondheim, Norway.

Smith, M. F. 1954. *Baba of Karo: A Woman of the Muslim Hausa.* London: Faber and Faber.

Smith, Noel. 1966. *The Presbyterian Church of Ghana, 1835–1960.* Accra: Ghana University Press.

Southall, Roger J. 1978. "Farmers, Traders, and Brokers in the Gold Coast Cocoa Economy." *Canadian Journal of African Studies* 12, no. 2: 185–211.

Tashjian, Victoria. 1995. "It's Mine and It's Ours Are Not the Same Thing: A History of Marriage in Rural Asante, 1900–1957." Ph.D. dissertation, Northwestern University.

Tonkin, Elizabeth. 1992. *Narrating Our Pasts: The Social Construction of Oral History.* Cambridge: Cambridge University Press.

van Onselen, Charles. 1990. "Race and Class in the South African Countryside: Cultural Osmosis and Social Relations in the Sharecropping Economy of the South-Western Transvaal, 1900–1950." *American Historical Review* 95, no. 1: 99–123.

———. 1993. "Peasants Speak: The Reconstruction of Rural Life from Oral Testimony: Critical Notes on the Methodology Employed in the Study of a Black South African Sharecropper." *Journal of Peasant Studies* 20, no. 3: 494–514.

———. 1996. *The Seed Is Mine: The Life of Kas Maine, a South African Sharecropper, 1894–1985.* New York: Hill and Wang.

Vaughan, Megan. 1991. *Curing Their Ills: Colonial Power and African Illness.* Stanford: Stanford University Press.

White, Luise. 1994. "Between Gluckman and Foucault: Historicizing Rumor and Gossip." *Social Dynamics* 20, no. 1: 75–92.

———. 1995. "'They Could Make Their Victims Dull': Genders and Genres, Fantasies and Cures in Colonial Southern Uganda." *American Historical Review* 100, no. 5: 1379–1402.

Witschi, Hermann. 1965. *Geschichte der Basler Mission.* Vol. 4, 1914–1919 (after a manuscript by W. Schlatter). Basel: Basileia.

———. 1970. *Geschichte der Basler Mission.* Vol. 5, 1920–1940. Basel: Basileia.

Wright, Marcia. 1993. *Strategies of Slaves and Women: Life-Stories from East/Central Africa.* New York: L. Barber.

Yankah, Kwesi. 1995. *Speaking for the Chief: Ɔkyeame and the Politics of Akan Royal Oratory.* Bloomington: Indiana University Press.

8

Lives, Histories, and Sites of Recollection

Tamara Giles-Vernick

When I first began to conduct historical research in Africa, I assumed that the interview and life history would constitute the centerpiece of my field methods.[1] I had formulated a research project that would identify how "migrants"[2] in the rain forests of the Sangha basin (Central African Republic) understood the history of environmental interventions. The study would explore how these environmental histories shaped "migrants'" interactions with a World Wildlife Fund conservation project in the region. Conducting interviews with elderly and middle-aged individuals about their lives seemed to be an appropriate method. I intended to organize these interviews around chronologies of individuals' lives, to gain insight into how they had subjectively experienced these environmental interventions over the course of the twentieth century. In framing interviews around individuals' lives, I presumed that our exchanges would yield much richer, more specific evidence about their past experiences than a series of questions about previous environmental interventions would. And thus, the interviews I conducted would accumulate as "life histories," revealing how "informants" conceived of their lives as they intersected with, responded to, and contributed to the massive changes sweeping the Sangha river basin from the early twentieth century to the present. These life histories would add up to a body of evidence from which I could construct a history of migrants' changing relations with and perceptions of a constantly changing landscape.

In this essay, however, I argue that conducting interviews to accumulate "life histories" in order to illuminate changing social, environmental, and economic relations rests on a plethora of misleading assumptions about "lives," "history," and the relationship between the two. In problematizing "life" and "history," I demonstrate how a particular African people remember their lives and pasts, as well as what field researchers writing about the past can gain from understanding those processes of recollection. I examine the specific ways that Mpiemu speakers in the Sangha basin of the Central African Republic recognize and organize their recollections of their developing selves and relationships with history. They recalled and expressed their developing lives (articulated as persons, or *bori*) and relationships to *doli*, or "history." They did so not only by recounting narratives of past events, but also through bodily and spatial practices, which differed substantially from narratives because they located and invoked, but did not explain or describe, past events.[3]

The essay thus compares how I and my Mpiemu teachers envisioned and expressed a particular self and its relations to the past. It first examines some of the assumptions about and problems of interviewing as a method for documenting a life and history that I experienced when first conducting research in the Sangha basin. I then take apart a conversation that I participated in with two Mpiemu men, as a means of exploring the different ways that we articulated our selves in relation to history. Through this comparison, I show that Mpiemu expressed various spatial and bodily definitions of the "person" and articulated multiple relationships with what they defined as history.

Excavating Mpiemu practices that articulate the self and its relationship with the past not only suggests different methodologies for conducting field research about the past. More importantly, it points to different ways of interpreting and writing about historical evidence. The oral, but also spatial and bodily, evidence we collect is not simply fodder for conventional narrative histories (cf. Vansina 1985, 1994), but is the product of confrontations with "other searches for truth and reality" (Fabian 1996: 298). These other searches challenge conventional historical interpretation and writing. Elaborating how a past life might be embodied in a field, a tree, a document, a person's stomach, or a corner of an elderly woman's kitchen does not fit easily within conventions of historical writing. Some scholars, confronted with these places and things, might query, "Where is the 'life'? Where is the 'history' here?" My response to them would be that we need to explore carefully just what teachers and their interlocutors mean by "life" and "history" and how these notions are connected.

THE PROBLEM OF INTERVIEWS

Researchers of several disciplinary persuasions have long relied on interviews to accumulate "life histories."[4] They have justified the collection of "life histories" on different grounds and have debated extensively what interviews and life histories can illuminate about a "life" or "history."[5] For some social science researchers, the life history has excavated the activities, developing consciousness, and historical contributions of people silenced by conventional political or economic histories (Geiger 1986: 334–51; van Onselen 1993: 494–501; Bozzoli 1991; Davison 1989). Others have seen the "life stories" method as an interaction through which the self is created, or as a process in which "[t]he telling of life stories, whether to others or self alone, is treated as an important, shaping event in social and psychological processes, yet the life stories themselves are considered to be developed in, and the outcomes of, the course of these and other life events" (Peacock and Holland

1993: 371; see also Briggs 1986). In particular, they have explored how interviews reflect developing relationships between a teller and an interlocutor and between a teller and a broader social context, and how tellers represent different selves even within the same performance (Mintz 1989: 786–96; Landau 1996: 89–93; Tonkin 1992: 39, 47–49).

Yet the notion that extensive interviews might produce a "life history" and thus shed light on people's experiences of past change, of developing selves and relationships, or of a storytelling process relies on a problematic assumption. All of these approaches conceive of interviews and life histories "as" products of and reflections of a life and history. Johannes Fabian has recently criticized the argument implicit in using "as," because it was part of the "task . . . to collect data that represented realities whose significance (indeed, whose reality) was determined by the agendas of our discipline [anthropology]. The little word 'as' . . . was a constant marker of such an epistemological position: Movements, for instance, were studied as social change; ritual as drama; religion (but also ideology, art, and what have you) as a system of symbols" (Fabian 1996: 297).

In his analysis of Tshibumba Kanda Matulu's painted history of Zaire, Fabian recognized that he could "experience all these *representations* of reality as *realities* . . . as practices" which "[confronted] my own ethnographic practice (of representing realities) . . . on the same level" (Fabian 1996: 297). He concluded that anthropology should focus not on representations, but rather on "other searches for truth and reality and [ways] to negotiate knowledge through critical reasoning" (298).

Historians have something to learn here from Fabian. In our efforts to excavate people's past activities and their contributions to and experiences and interpretations of historical change, we have presumed that extensive interviews and recorded narrative responses can be reconfigured and interpreted "as" a life and "as" history. In fact, tellers of history engage in a whole range of practices to express their "lives" and "histories." Historians who use only interviews to gain insight into a "life" and "history" will miss the broader context of practices that invoke and recollect the past. Thus, to explore these two notions and their interrelationships, historians (and other social scientists) need to confront how tellers articulate their "lives" and their connections with "history" through broad-ranging practices that are not exclusively narrative.

This effort demands a careful examination of how people generate and understand the self, or the "person" and its relationships to culturally specific notions of history. Such an analysis, as Ivan Karp has observed more generally of the person in Africa, would "explain why people act the way they do, interpret their experiences and predict their actions and fates . . . encode ideas about physical and social growth and development, motivation and personality and the consequences of action, entail descriptions of the capacities and powers persons have to carry out their actions . . . and locate these powers and capacities in the image of the body" (Karp 1997: 392). Mpiemu ideas about the person shaped how they remembered their "lives." And these lives, because they were in part about a person's growth, change, and development, were bound up in Mpiemu notions of history.

Karp's analysis of personhood also reminds us that many African cultures locate a person's powers and capacities in the body (Karp 1997: 392). Indeed, Mpiemu were no exception, for they organized and recollected their developing selves and relationships with doli, experiences and interpretations of the past, through bodily, but also spatial, practices. These non-narrative practices had a complex relationship to narrative practices of organizing, recalling, and expressing their selves and relationships to history. While Mpiemu speakers often evoked place and bodily sites of remembrance as a shorthand reference to a specific narrative, they also invoked these sites to stand on their own and to articulate a developing self in Mpiemu "history." I call these forms of organizing and remembering the past "non-narrative" to stress that they are not narratives themselves, and can evoke the past without relying on an explanation for it. Interviews alone, then, are not always the most appropriate means of examining how a person might conceive of his or her self and its relationship with "history." In posing questions that require tellers to respond through narratives, interviewers will not gain insight into other ways in which people might identify or organize their memories or imagine, articulate, and recall their developing selves.

During my field research among Mpiemu people in the Sangha basin, I did not initially realize that interviews foreclosed all sorts of practices that generated Mpiemu persons and history. I began by asking a series of questions to trace people's lives from their beginnings to the present, focusing particularly on their own and their parents' past uses and conceptions of farming lands, gardens, fishing waters, and hunting grounds. I fully expected that these interviews would yield insights into Mpiemu people's lives. I had previously used this method among Central African friends living elsewhere in the country and had been pleased and flattered by the shared confidences that such encounters brought. My exchanges with Mpiemu speakers, however, reflected more about my own definitions of a "life" and "history" than they did about those of my Mpiemu-speaking friends and teachers. Moreover, very few provided useful glimpses into how Mpiemu people perceived their changing relationships with the Sangha basin environment. I continually encountered indifference, antipathy, fear, suspicion, and expectations that I would fulfill a historical role as *patronne*. White *patrons* had resided in the village, Lindjombo, from 1926 until 1980, where they hired Africans to cultivate extensive coffee plantations, collect wild rubber in the forests, and hunt elephants and other game (Giles-Vernick 1999: 179–84). In exchange for this access to forest resources, white patrons would provide people with jobs and with access to such goods as clothing, whisky, and cooking pots. These relationships powerfully influenced how and with whom I interacted, for Sangha basin residents initially perceived me as yet another white patron who had come to extract yet another commodity—knowledge—from them.[6]

In one early interview, I had asked one woman, Elisabeth, to tell me about her life, but she was more interested in discussing her present circumstances than her past life. Her words, I later realized, were a request for me to fulfill the role of patronne and to provide her with material support.

E: There are words (stories) [of my past]. I think of them a lot. Oh, aging is bad.
TGV: Why is that?
E: Aging is bad . . . [she then interrupts to remark upon a child who is leaving the family compound]. Tamara, when I was younger . . . when I married my husband in Berberati, he was a truck driver. My husband traveled to Berberati and to Douala. He would drive to Douala. His name was Mamadou. His mother married, [and his parents] gave birth to him—where? In Senegal. He was Senegalese. Tamara, I now live as I am, you see me. I am living in this way. You see the clothing on my body? Who will wash it for me? Ay, I have returned to this village, but I am now so old. I have no more words [to tell you]. Mmm.
TGV: You just told me before that you were very beautiful when you were young.
E: My husband, Mamadou, his mother gave birth to him in Dakar. Kolowusa. He took me to Berberati. But my words are finished.
TGV: So this was before you worked for the whites?
E: [When I married] I hadn't worked for the whites yet. I worked for the whites after I gave birth to one child. When I came to my village, I slept with men and gave birth to one child, but he died. Then I went to marry a man in Ngbaka [east, where people of Ngbaka ethnicity live]. After that I returned and I worked [for the whites].
TGV: Why?
E: I returned because he married another woman, and that woman superseded me with medicine.
TGV: She poisoned you?
E: Mmm, no. She married by using the medicine. She used medicine so that my husband saw me in a poor light.

The interview did not continue much longer than that. Clearly, this woman was not interested in discussing her past. Although I persisted in asking questions, she repeated twice that she had no more to tell me. Instead, she mentioned the significant past events (though not in any chronological order, as I had wanted) that brought her to her lamentable current state, in which, she complained, she was poorly clothed and bereft of an attentive, caring husband or child to look after her in her old age. That past and present would be transformed, she suggested, if only I would step into the role of a white patron to provide her with material support.[7] Thus in retrospect, while the exchange reflected much about the past, at the time I chafed to extricate myself from these confining expectations, and to learn more about people's historical relations with their changing environments. Without that historical context, I could not begin to understand the vitriolic remarks so often voiced about the World Wildlife Fund project's conservation interventions. Many complained that "project" restrictions on hunting grounds and methods privileged the welfare of gorillas and elephants over the well-being of human beings.[8] And thus, they argued, as one man did in a meeting, the "project" condemned them to constant "hunger," with only cassava leaves—a poor substitute for meat—to sustain them.[9]

Sangha basin residents' refusal to say much about their lives and changing relationships with the environment resulted, too, from fear and suspicion. First, they feared that I was a spy for the World Wildlife Fund. Noting that many of the expatriate personnel were white American women, and that many WWF employees possessed, as I did, Japanese-made mountain bikes, some men clearly were convinced that I was a spy for the conservation project. I would, they believed, collect information on the locations of their snare traps and unregistered guns, so that antipoaching guards could arrest them. My arrival in the reserve also coincided with a period of national and regional political upheaval, and thus people feared that I would report their words to political authorities, who would imprison them. In such a context of fear and suspicion, I wondered, why on earth should these people *want* to talk to me? And why should I try to convince them to do so, if they believed that talking would endanger them?

I eventually stopped interviewing and resorted to an old activity that I had undertaken when I was a Peace Corps volunteer: I went to work in the fields. Farmers always enjoyed discussing their fields. By working with these farmers in their fields, I hoped I might glean some understanding about how their farming practices had changed over time, and thus might gain some insight into their perceptions of their changing environmental relationships.[10]

In retrospect, my time with people in their fields and forests illuminated far more than a history of agricultural practices within changing regional and global political economies. It also opened up a magnificent range of possibilities for thinking about how Mpiemu tellers articulated their "selves" and relationships with doli. African tellers of history did not just speak more easily as we worked together. Rather, they expressed a myriad of non-narrative practices remembering and expressing their own and others' lives. A woman in her field held up a yam vine and began to speak of her grandmother and the food she cooked. In the forest, one man pointed to a wide gash in a tree whose bark provided trapping medicines; this gouged tree reminded him of the dead hunter Ntuwo, who had used that very tree as a source of medicines to capture game for the coffee plantation workers. Still another woman swept one corner of her kitchen with great tenderness and care; only later did I learn that she had buried her infant son there. And countless times, men and women extracted small, plastic-wrapped packages of baptism cards, work identifications, and tax stubs that they had meticulously woven into the raffia roofs of their houses; they presented these documents to me as tangible expressions of their own or their parents' lives. As I began to write about these lives, I realized that I could not assume that Mpiemu speakers would generate and articulate their lives and histories in the chronological, narrative forms that I had been trained to elicit.

These acts of remembering in places helped to problematize the "life history" and "interview" in ways that I had not anticipated. First, these acts revealed that people do not always articulate "lives" in the context of question-and-answer sessions. These moments in fields, forests, and houses eloquently illustrated the multitude of non-narrative possibilities in remembering, condensing, and even creating a "life." They also demonstrated that the relationship between a "life" and "history" is not one that we can assume; rather, we must pay careful attention to the ways in which people define it.

Second, such acts raised questions about the multiple and contingent contexts in which such exchanges took place between me and my teachers. On the one hand, as some researchers have pointed out, what my teachers demonstrated to me had nothing to do with me, but rather with their efforts to articulate something about past lives and their places in history (Willis 1996: 319–22). Simultaneously, however, these exchanges reflected the intersection of multiple contexts and epistemologies, in which our notions of our selves and pasts mutually influenced one another.[11] Just as the display of documents, fields, or scarred trees can shed light on the ways in which tellers think about themselves, about lives, and about the past, these acts were also a response to my notions of myself and past social relations. My very presence in the fields, as I have noted, resulted in part from previous work I had done in the Central African Republic. And, similarly, many of the questions that I posed to these people stemmed in part from a long-standing fascination with mobile people, one that developed from my intellectual training as well as from my own past as a highly spatially mobile person.

NARRATING LIFE, NARRATING HISTORY

In 1993, I had what turned out to be a crucial exchange with two Mpiemu men in the forest outside of a small town along the Sangha river. This conversation illustrates how an exclusive focus on narrative expressions of the past can limit our understanding of how people generate lives and histories. But it also shows how non-narrative forms can expand our understanding of lives and histories. I had been conversing with these men about how Mpiemu migrants in the 1930s and 1940s had established their rights to exploit fields and forest streams in the town of Lindjombo. I asked the older man, "Patrice, when you are dead, what traces will you leave behind?" Mpiemu migrants had moved south in search of salaried employment on large, European-owned coffee plantations in Lindjombo. In introducing this question, I was seeking to understand how Mpiemu people imagined their places in history, and hoping to gain insight into the resources with and processes by which they remembered their individual and collective pasts.

"This isn't my home [*dadam*]," Patrice replied. "I am going to return home. If I don't die soon, I intend to return to Zankandi, my home village." The younger man, Anaclet, thinking that Patrice had not understood, repeated my question. Patrice hesitated, and then turned to him and remarked, "The place that your father once cultivated a manioc field. It's my place, my place. It is the place that my child had an accident." Just as Patrice was finishing his response, Anaclet interrupted, "People are what you possess during your life. The Mpiemu often say *leave a person [behind] [ligo mori]*. When you have done that, you have done a great thing. If you die and you don't give birth to children, your enemies will sleep in your house, and they'll eat your things. But if you give birth to a child, you are a person. Something of you is left [behind]." Patrice nodded vigorously and began to list all of the children and grandchildren who had been named Mpeng, after him.

I will explore the significance of Anaclet's and Patrice's responses shortly. But first, I want to pose a comparison, by exploring some questions of my own: what was I doing in the middle of the African equatorial forest with these two men? and why did I ask Patrice how he hoped people would remember him after his death? I want to show that my responses to these questions reflect one way of presenting a "life" and "history," but that it is not the only way of doing so.

I found myself in the middle of the equatorial forest for a whole host of personal, methodological, and intellectual reasons that continually shape the historical work that I do. It makes sense to begin with my past personal experiences. Although I find it difficult to identify a single moment in my own life when I could say, "My interest in living and working in equatorial Africa began there," for the sake of brevity, I will choose my late-1980s stint in the Peace Corps as a starting point. I had thought that Peace Corps work would introduce me to the challenges of pursuing development work in Africa. And in 1987, I received an assignment to work on a post-harvest food systems project in the Central African Republic.

When I read the assignment, I was delighted. A real development project! No small-scale projects to dig pit latrines or build mud stoves for me. I was going to rub elbows with government ministers and civil servants and professional development experts from Volunteers in Technical Assistance (VITA), Africare, and the World Bank. I assumed that I already knew how to work with these people, for they couldn't be much different from the political figures and policy analysts for whom I had provided consulting services in Washington, D.C.

The actual experience, however, was not one that I had anticipated, nor one that I relished. In fact, I found it infantilizing, both for me and for the agricultural extension workers whom I was supposed to supervise and teach. Our ostensible purpose was to promote grain-storage and labor-saving technologies advocated in a million-dollar study that the U.S. Agency for International Development had commissioned.[12] In the twisted logic that only development organizations could sustain, the study found that post-harvest food losses were not substantial in the northwestern Central African Republic, but nevertheless concluded that "Phase II"—the dissemination of grain- and labor-saving technologies—should proceed.[13] And thus, the post-harvest food systems project undertook a massive effort to teach farmers to set mousetraps in their homes, to fix aluminum rat guards on the legs of granaries, to encourage grain storage in clay pots, and to advocate the use of corn shellers and peanut mills. And we promoted these technologies through a variety of what were deemed to be "creative extension techniques": catchy songs about rat predations to the tunes of church hymns (imagine singing the words "Rats are bad, rats are bad, rats are animals that will fuck up everything, rats will give us sickness" to the tune of "Onward Christian Soldiers"); impromptu dramatic performances about a family attacked by rats; rat-guard installation demonstrations, in which we would nail up rat guards on the village chief's granary, even though he was only interested in these technologies because they were symbols of modernity, conferred by an expatriate-run project with access to expensive vehicles, free food, and money.

Even as it became clear that the Central Africans had little interest in adopting these grain-saving technologies, and that they would not have sought out the labor-saving devices if the project had not promoted them, project administrators threw themselves (and the rest of us) into a frenzy to document the project's "accomplishments" in order to justify their efforts to USAID: they measured the numbers of rat guards installed, of meetings and attendees, of training workshops and of people trained to use the technologies, of peanut mills purchased and corn shellers distributed.[14] And this massive data collection proceeded despite our awareness that the data were meaningless; they indicated nothing about whether or how people used the technologies, or how such technologies affected actual food availability or the relationships between men and women or elders and juniors.[15]

In short, I was entirely disillusioned by my experience with the project, and desperately sought ways of extricating myself from it. I wanted to move as far away as possible from the constraints of the project, to work in a village with women and gardens. And so I managed to escape after bandit attacks in the region where I was working forced the Peace Corps to evacuate me. I settled in a small village far away from any development projects, determined that I could work more effectively with African farmers than could a multi-million-dollar project promoting technologies to people who didn't want them. In the end, I was as ineffectual, and probably just as damaging, as the project. I set up six gardening cooperatives with women's groups and cultivated a demonstration plot intercropping maize and peanuts in different patterns than did the farmers with whom I lived. All six of the cooperatives failed, in part because I refused to work with men. As a staunch and uncritical convert to the Peace Corps's "Women in Development" fad,[16] I neglected to understand how women farmers were part of broader networks of kin and marriage alliances, which also had claims to their labor. In the end, I only helped to exacerbate tensions with Central African men over their access to their wives' labor, and the demonstration plot produced no more maize or peanuts than anyone else's.

As much of a travesty as my development experiences had been, I learned a great deal from spending time with farmers. They not only taught me about farming in the grassy savannas of the Central African Republic; they also conveyed the crucial importance of understanding how people live, work, create social relationships, and perceive their environments and histories before promoting "development," however it is defined. Following my Peace Corps years, then, I undertook graduate study in African history. History, I thought, would help me to begin to understand the ways in which Africans perceive their pasts and act upon them in the present, to create their own identities, to forge social relations, and to exploit their environments.

These interests took me again to the Central African Republic in 1991 and 1993, but others shaped my focus on migrants and the relationships they posit between their identities and histories. I had moved frequently as a child, and continued to do so as an adult. And so when people ask me where I am from, I say the first thing that comes to mind: California, where I spent my teenage and college years. But that response isn't entirely accurate. Before California, I had lived in Connecticut, Massachusetts, and North Carolina, and I have subsequently resided in London, Washington, D.C., the Central African Republic, and Baltimore, and now can boast two residences, in Charlottesville, Virginia, and New York City. In truth, I cannot identify one single location as "home."[17] And I wonder, why is it so important for people to understand where I am "from"? What does that indicate to them? Why have I chosen California as a locus of my place-based identity?

In equatorial Africa, where Africans have been especially mobile for the past two centuries, it is easy to see how my past experiences predisposed me to seek out mobile people and to search for their understanding of mobility, origins, identity, and history. And this is why I found myself with Patrice and Anaclet, discussing a kind of departure (death) in terms of how people would remember the departed.

Finally, an intellectual journey had also shaped my interaction in the forest with Patrice and Anaclet. My training had propelled me to search for "local" historical production, which, I assumed, everyone—or at least elderly and middle-aged Central Africans—practiced. And yet, during my field research in the southwestern Central African Republic, I encountered numerous Mpiemu-speaking people who claimed to know nothing about history. Several migrant workers and their descendants in the village of Lindjombo (including Anaclet and Patrice), in fact, referred to themselves as "a dead people." As a "dead people," they conceived of themselves as disconnected from "the things (and places) of history" (*bi san bi doli*) and from networks of powerful people, who would provide access to paying jobs and consumer goods. They remembered their past movements and resettlements not to connect themselves with historical identities, as some Mpiemu elsewhere do, but to conceive of themselves as cut off from both the past and the future. In this context, then, remembering past movement permits some Mpiemu to locate themselves outside of the time and place of history.

This stance toward the past challenged fundamental assumptions that historians, particularly those of Africa, hold so dearly: that all people have a history and cherish it, and that they can talk about it. But in the Sangha basin, I encountered people who claimed that they did not know history, and in fact were outside of it. Their claims, however, echoed in disturbing ways conservationists' conventional wisdom that "migrants," unlike "indigenous peoples," have no real history and know nothing about the environments to which they have moved and which they now exploit (Giles-Vernick 1999: 186). My intellectual training shaped how I grappled with these contradictory claims about mobile peoples and history: I sought to explore why this death had taken place, as well as how Mpiemu people practiced the "things of history" even as they professed not to. And thus as I sat in the forest with Patrice and Anaclet, I wanted to understand how two people who conceived of themselves as disconnected from history might become part of that history after their deaths.

Hence my reasons for participating in that exchange in the forest were methodological, personal, and intellectual. It is illuminating to examine how I have conveyed this explanation, for as I will show, my method differs substantially from the non-narrative ways of articulating life and history. I began by posing a historical question: how did I come to sit in the forest and converse with two migrants about death and remembering? I read that question as a inquiry about the past events which propelled me to construct a particular "self," as a historian who seeks to understand Africans' conceptions of their histories. And I answered the question by recounting narratives: about my first experiences of working in Africa, about past and present peregrinations that have shaped my questions about origins and mobility, and about my intellectual training as a historian. Of course, I don't always evoke my past in narrative, chronological form, and I do not intend to suggest that there is some sort of implicit difference between how I and African tellers express our selves and pasts. Nonetheless, in this context, I consciously chose to write interlocking narratives to explain my past choices and experiences that led me to a crucial exchange with the Mpiemu men, Patrice and Anaclet.

The construction of these narratives was a selective process in two ways. In the first place, I weeded out all sorts of uncomfortable and "extraneous" events that happened before and during those years to my personal and professional "selves." And secondly, these narratives reflect a selective process because I am only conveying to readers a developing "self" as interconnected narratives about my past. These interconnected narratives could be read as a form of ethnographic confession, in which the narrator owns up to his or her myopia when beginning field research, but achieves competence and insight after being grossly humiliated by informants. But I would argue that my accumulated past personal and professional experiences rendered me more open to asking questions about mobile peoples and their origins.

PLACING "LIVES," PLACING "HISTORIES"

Patrice's and Anaclet's responses to my questions, however, were underpinned by different ways of organizing their recollections and thus articulating their selves and histories. While we all shared knowledge of a narrative about Patrice's field and daughter, both men invoked other ways of articulating, imagining, and remembering persons, lives, and histories. For Mpiemu speakers, reproducing *mori* (person) is a central concern in their history and historiography. But "mori" does not translate easily into English, and in their responses, Patrice and Anaclet raised at least three different definitions of the term: a cyclical process which binds together multiple "lives," accumulated experience over a lifetime, and body and place memories. Nor did "history"—what Mpiemu call doli—correspond to a single English term, but rather had many meanings, including "long ago," "the recent past," and "unchanging knowledge and practices from the distant past" (Giles-Vernick forthcoming). The frequently invoked Mpiemu proverb *Ligo mori* ("leave a person behind") crystallized the multiple meanings of mori and interwove them with historical concerns, for Mpiemu invoked the proverb every time I asked about the traces they would leave of themselves after death.

In response to my question about the traces he would leave of himself after he died, Patrice first spoke of the field in which his child had had an accident. This field, which constituted the accumulation of many of Patrice's activities and memories, had a tragic history. Patrice had frequently recounted to me the story of his daughter's death in this field. Significantly, the first time was after I had stopped trying to interview him with a tape recorder, and instead went with him into the forest to search for medicinal plants. On our return to Lindjombo, we passed through the field, which had a large fallen tree in the middle of it. Patrice sat on the tree and began to speak of how his daughter had been crushed to death by the tree following a mild rainstorm. He contended that this death was not accidental. A woman living in Lindjombo had taken a dislike for him and caused the daughter to die. According to many Lindjombo inhabitants, Patrice possessed an active *alembo*, a "vital substance" that people contain in their bellies, and he had transmitted this active substance to his daughter.[18] An active alembo exists as a separate being, driving its host to commit acts on its part, but at the same time remains an integral part of its human carrier. Whether active or inactive, alembo is a historical substance, for it has been transmitted from generation to generation, shaping the lives and deaths of people who carry it. It is, in effect, one of many factors that influence a person's agency, which "includes not only one's effects on the world but also the extent to which one controls others' actions and effects as well" (Kratz 2000: 137). An active alembo serves, too, as a site of recollection, a marker that denominates members of a lineage (connected by kin in the past, present, and future) who are "different."[19] The woman who killed Patrice's daughter also possessed an active alembo, and perhaps she killed the girl to keep Patrice and his family from reproducing this vital substance and thus from "leaving a person behind."

In the field where his daughter died, Patrice claimed that for decades he had been continually reminded of his inability to leave his daughter behind him. He contended that he occasionally witnessed a gorilla exhibiting peculiar behavior at the very place that she died. The gorilla would sit at the field's edge and gaze at Patrice, and it displayed none of the aggressive behavior of gorillas when they encounter human beings. He believed that the gorilla was neither a "person" nor an "animal," but some manifestation of his dead daughter. This manifestation prevented him from abandoning that field, and he would continue to cultivate it as long as he was able.

Patrice's and Anaclet's responses to my question expressed multiple notions of the person and linked them to diverse definitions of doli. For Anaclet, the proverb *Ligo mori* evoked the cyclical process of creating a person. It succinctly summed up the importance of reproducing descendants and rights to one's house and belongings. It reminded Patrice of the futurity of his ties with subsequent generations of his lineage; he had left many children and grandchildren behind, thus reproducing himself and previous generations both biologically and socially. Those children and grandchildren would remember Patrice through his field and his home place, thus transforming him from a "person" into doli, or the recent or distant past.

Patrice's recounting of his past experiences in the field also alluded to this significance of the person as a cyclical process. But his stories rendered that process more complex, suggesting that leaving a person behind was neither inevitable nor always successful. Rather, each cycle had its own peculiar past, tied up with the "lives" that individuals or lineages had experienced. Hence Patrice invoked a second significance of the person: that of knowledge, or accumulated past experiences. In recounting to Anaclet and me his past experiences of migrating, acquiring use rights to farming lands, and suffering personal tragedy, Patrice was a person in this sense.

Finally, Patrice evoked a third definition of the person as place and body memory. When I asked him about the traces he would leave behind after his death, he mentioned the field where his daughter died as "my place." This place existed because of these past events and his labor, and thus was a means by which Patrice recognized and organized his recollections of his daughter's death and her subsequent reappearances as a gorilla. After he died, the field would not only serve as a mnemonic for future generations, but would become interchangeable with memories of Patrice himself (Küchler and Melion 1991: 7; Guyer and Belinga 1995: 113). This definition of the person as a place memory shaded into that of the person as accumulated experiences, for Patrice's continued cultivation of the field occurred because of his accumulated experiences there.

Relatedly, Patrice also invoked the notion of the person as a body memory, a site of recollection by which he phrased his memories of his daughter. By returning to the field and continuing to work there, as well as encountering the gorilla, Patrice could commemorate his daughter's life and death. But her memory was ambiguous, for his daughter had died without leaving a person behind, and thus her transformation into *bi san bi doli*, or "the things of history," manifested itself as a highly ambiguous forest mammal, the gorilla. In general, Mpiemu found gorillas compelling, shrewd, and menacing. These animals posed great sexual dangers to children and women—particularly menstruating women—in the forest. Patrice's daughter's transformation into a gorilla after death was a mnemonic of the incompleteness of her short life.

How did this exchange problematize and reconfigure the significances of "lives" and "life histories"? Different ways of expressing connections between a "life" and "history" underpinned this exchange. I recounted various interconnected narratives about past experiences that articulated different selves as they had developed over time and propelled me into the forest with Patrice and Anaclet. In a way, my narratives mirrored those of Elisabeth, who had spoken of past events to illuminate her present condition.

But Patrice and Anaclet used narrative and non-narrative practices to articulate connections between a person, his or her life, and history. Certainly, Patrice alluded to a narrative that he had recounted many times. Neither Anaclet nor I could have understood the significance of the field, the fallen tree, and the alembo that was not successfully passed on to another generation without knowing the narrative of his daughter's death. But he also referred to other ways of apprehending and organizing his memories, in particular the place and body sites of recollection that I have already discussed. Working a field year after year, sitting on a tree, referring indirectly to a bodily site, witnessing a gorilla—all of these bodily and spatial practices helped Patrice to remember his daughter's life in non-narrative ways. More-over, these were places and bodily sites that Patrice would "leave behind" after he died, and thus these sites, too, could be understood as evoking, and even embodying and spatializing, his "life."

These narrative and non-narrative practices linked "life" and "history." Recall that "doli" translates variously as the distant past, unchanging knowl-edge, and practices and beliefs discovered by unnamed people of the distant past. It also refers to experience accumulated by elders during past events in past and present places. This very broad term therefore encompasses a wide variety of knowledge, people, events, and places of the past. It is funda-mentally implicated in Mpiemu definitions of the person in multiple ways.

First, as Patrice and Anaclet observed, the person is a cyclical process, part of a larger process in which persons are created and ultimately trans-formed into a recent past, and later (through the processes of forgetting, eliding, and omitting) a distant one (doli). This creation of the person does not proceed as a series of chronologically arranged events, as social scientists might presume in their collection of life histories; rather, it is a cycle re-peated over and over, eventually homogenizing particular cycles into a sedi-ment of distant past.

Second, Patrice maintained that the person is accumulated knowledge based on past experience. This definition of a person accounts for the partic-ular events and people in the past that have shaped an individual's life. This definition, too, is historical, incorporating events, people, and places in the past.

And finally, Patrice and Anaclet claimed that the person is body and place memory. These sites of remembrance enable Mpiemu speakers to organize and recall their memories of past persons, events, and knowledge. Fields, trees, houses, plastic-wrapped packages of identification cards, and even alembo carry in themselves all of those past persons, events, and knowledge. Thus, even as Patrice, Anaclet, and other Mpiemu migrants professed not to know history and to be disconnected from it, they were simultaneously en-gaged in the process of producing persons and history through narrative and non-narrative practices.

How can we reconcile Mpiemu historical production with migrants' and their descendants' claims that they were "dead," disconnected from "the things of history"? Perhaps these divergent propositions do not necessarily require reconciliation. Mpiemu migrants and their descendants living in Lin-djombo were clearly engaged in practices of making people, and thus of pro-ducing history. Yet their efforts to gain access to historical places and to par-ticipate in historical practices in the forest were stymied by conservationist interventions. They consequently believed that efforts to "leave a person be-hind" and to connect themselves with "the things of history" and broader networks of economic and political power (also an important dynamic in twentieth-century Sangha basin history) were ineffectual. Their claims to be "dead" protested interventions by the Central African Republic and the World Wildlife Fund: the creation and patrolling of a national park rendered parts of the forest off-limits to Mpiemu and other hunters and gatherers. Hence, while Mpiemu continued to engage in practices of creating people and producing history, they believed that their efforts were overwhelmed by conservation interventions, and thus were in vain.

This essay has sought to interrogate some of the assumptions underpinning interviews as a method for capturing life histories. Interviews can elicit rich insights about a person's developing self and history, but field researchers can also overwhelm those insights with preconceived, limited notions of "persons" and "histories." Direct questions about past experiences and the narrative responses that they elicit, I have argued, do not necessarily produce a "life" or a "history" as many people (including researchers themselves) evoke, recall, and enact them.

Finding out how people create, express, and remember their developing selves and relationships to the past entails, in Fabian's words, confronting "other searches for truth and reality." Historical field researchers need to explore more than the words that people use. Paying careful attention to the sites of organizing and recollecting pasts can also help to excavate the myriad of ways that human beings define, produce, and weave together persons, lives, and histories.

NOTES

This essay is based upon field research in 1993 and archival research in the summers of 1994, 1996, and 1997. The research was assisted by a grant from the Joint Committee on African Studies of the Social Science Research Council and the American Council of Learned Societies with funds provided by the Rockefeller Foundation. A Fulbright Doctoral Dissertation Research Grant also funded the study. The University of Virginia provided funding for research in 1996 and 1997. I thank all of these organizations for their generous support. I am especially grateful to participants at the "Words and Voices" conference for their stimulating and challenging insights into the processes of remembering and of producing history.

1. For different perspectives on the process and challenges of conducting historical research in the "field," see Adenaike and Vansina 1996.

2. I use the term "migrant" with some reticence. As I show elsewhere, "migrant" has been historically used in the Sangha basin not as a neutral descriptive term, but as a category constructed against "indigenous" and used to facilitate statebuilding and access to and control over forest resources (Giles-Vernick 1999).

3. Following Raphael Samuel's work (1994: 17), I take history to be "an activity rather than a profession," to which a variety of practitioners can contribute. My work has addressed how Mpiemu speakers engage in this activity and the various kinds of historical knowledge they produce. In addition, I distinguish narrative from non-narrative practices within history on the basis of Elizabeth Tonkin's definition (1992: 62), which holds that a narrative explains, describes, and locates past events.

4. Both Corinne Kratz's and Stephan Miescher's insights into the interviewing

process and its relationships to "life histories" have significantly influenced my understanding of these problems. See their contributions to this volume.

5. There is even some debate about what to call accumulated interviews with a person. Some historians, anthropologists, and other social scientists use the term "life history" to denote "an extensive record of a person's life told to and recorded by another, who then edits and writes the life as though it were an autobiography" (Geiger 1986: 336, quoting Langness). Peacock and Holland, however, prefer "life story" ("the story of someone's life") to "life history," since they argue that the latter implies something about historical truth (1993: 368).

6. In fact, this extraction of knowledge was nothing new. Although no social scientists had worked in this corner of the Central African Republic before I arrived, explorers in the late nineteenth and early twentieth centuries, colonial administrators, expatriate plantation owners and traders, and, more recently, an American interested in BaAka (pygmy) music had relied on African knowledge to realize their own disparate goals, and had remunerated Africans for providing that knowledge (Giles-Vernick 1996; Hardin, Rupp, and Eves 1999: 18–20).

7. Elsewhere in the forested zone of the Central African Republic, Michelle Kisliuk has observed of ethnomusicologists, "[O]ur ancestors and our roles both diverge from and unite with those of anthropologists, missionaries, tourists, journalists, and artists, among others." I would agree that the situation is somewhat similar in the Sangha river basin, but that the influences of colonial and commercial agents have been even more pervasive in shaping how residents perceive historians and other field researchers (Kisliuk 1997: 32, 1998).

8. It is crucial to note here that many residents conflated the activities of the World Wildlife Fund project with those of certain agencies in the Central African Republic. In fact, the state set laws governing where, how, and what people could hunt. But it did so under pressure exerted by the WWF and the World Bank. Moreover, the presence of the WWF project in the upper and middle Sangha basin helped to ensure that these laws were enforced.

9. Clearly, "hunger" did not literally mean that people suffered from a dearth of food because of project and state interventions. Rather, "hunger" referred to a realization that unhindered movement, hunting, gathering, and diamond mining in some parts of the forest were now illegal, and that residents were powerless to alter state laws prohibiting these activities.

10. Tim Ingold's work on people-environment relations was and continues to be important in shaping my understanding of environmental history. Ingold has argued (1992: 51) that people and environments constitute one another over time, and that history is embedded in this "mutualism." The environment, he contends, encompasses past human activities, just as people embody their past environmental relations.

11. See Peacock and Holland 1993: 375; Mintz 1989; Hoppe 1993. For similar concerns, though focusing on relations between an ethnomusicologist, BaAka musicians, and the development of the self in analysis of musical performance, see Kisliuk 1997.

12. This "post-harvest food systems" project appears to have occurred as a result of multi- and bilateral aid organizations' obsession with food availability as a preventative measure against famine. The notion that hunger and famine resulted from inadequate food supplies had particular currency in the aftermath of the Sahelian famine from 1968 to 1974, although, as analysts have shown, food availability had less to do with the famine than did the long-term historical interventions of colonial administrators and development experts (Watts 1983; Franke and Chasin 1980).

13. James Ferguson has assessed multi- and bilateral aid organizations' discourse of development, in which they define "underdevelopment" in such a way that it justifies their interventions (Ferguson 1990: 31–37).

14. They undertook these efforts even as many grumbled under their breath that farmers needed to change their mentalities in order to realize that these grain- and labor-saving technologies would massively improve their lives. This notion of a holistic transformation of farmers' economic, cultural, and social relations echoes Escobar's observations of development rhetoric and practice in Colombia (Escobar 1988: 428–30, 438).

15. The effects of development interventions on gender and generational relations have been effectively explored in several works (Carney and Watts 1990; Schroeder 1997).

16. "Women in Development" (WID) programs promoted the notion that conventional development efforts neglected women's concerns and their contributions to local and regional economies and societies. They thus advocated working with women to spearhead "development."

17. Referring to different circumstances, Richard Shain (1996: 112) has insightfully noted that "home becomes an elusive state of mind where the local and the foreign intersect." His observations, however, have some relevance to my own questions about origins.

18. Patrice always denied having an active alembo, contending that his mother had given it to his child. He acknowledged that his father, too, possessed an active alembo.

19. Patrice's father was named Menkiya, an abbreviation of "Menki ya ya ri sangi," which translates as "my blood is different from yours."

BIBLIOGRAPHY

Adenaike, Carolyn Keyes, and Jan Vansina. 1996. *In Pursuit of History: Fieldwork in Africa*. Portsmouth, N.H.: Heinemann.

Bozzoli, Belinda, with the assistance of Mmantho Nkotsoe. 1991. *Women of Phokeng: Consciousness, Life Strategy, and Migrancy in South Africa*. Portsmouth, N.H.: Heinemann.

Briggs, Charles. 1986. *Learning How to Ask: A Sociolinguistic Appraisal of the Interview in Social Science Research*. Cambridge: Cambridge University Press.

Carney, Judith, and Michael Watts. 1990. "Manufacturing Dissent: Work, Gender, and the Politics of Meaning in Peasant Society." *Africa* 60, no. 2: 207–41.

Davison, Jean, with the women of Mutira. 1989. *Voices from Mutira: Lives of Rural Gikuyu Women*. Boulder: L. Rienner.

Escobar, Arturo. 1988. "Power and Visibility: Development and the Invention and Management of the Third World." *Cultural Anthropology* 3, no. 4: 428–43.

Fabian, Johannes. 1996. *Remembering the Present: Painting and Popular History in Zaire*. Berkeley: University of California Press.

Ferguson, James. 1990. *The Anti-Politics Machine: "Development," Depoliticization, and Bureaucratic Power in Lesotho*. Cambridge: Cambridge University Press.

Franke, Richard W., and Barbara H. Chasin. 1980. *Seeds of Famine: Ecological Destruction and the Development Dilemma in the West African Sahel*. Montclair, N.J.: Allanheld, Osmun.

Geiger, Susan. 1986. "Women's Life Histories: Method and Content." *Signs* 11, no. 2: 334–51.

Giles-Vernick, Tamara. 1996. "A Dead People? Migrants, Land, and History in the Rainforests of the Central African Republic." Ph.D. dissertation, Johns Hopkins University.

———. 1999. "'We Wander Like Birds': Migrants, Indigeneity, and the Fabrication of Frontiers in the Sangha River Basin of Equatorial Africa." *Environmental History* 4, no. 2: 168–97.

———. Forthcoming. "Doli: Translating an African Environmental History of Loss in the Sangha River Basin of Equatorial Africa." *Journal of African History.*

Guyer, Jane, and S. M. Eno Belinga. 1995. "Wealth in People as Wealth in Knowledge: Accumulation and Composition in Equatorial Africa." *Journal of African History* 36, no. 1: 91–120.

Hardin, Rebecca, Stephanie Rupp, and Heather E. Eves. 1998. Introduction to *Resource Use in the Trinational Sangha River Region of Equatorial Africa: Histories, Knowledge Forms, and Institutions,* ed. H. Eves, R. Hardin and S. Rupp, 8–28. Bulletin Series, Yale School of Forestry and Environmental Studies, no. 102. New Haven: Yale University Press.

Hoppe, Kirk. 1993. "Whose Life Is It, Anyway? Issues of Representation in Life Narrative Texts of African Women." *International Journal of African Historical Studies* 26, no. 3: 623–36.

Ingold, Tim. 1992. "Culture and the Perception of the Environment." In *Bush Base: Forest Farm: Culture, Environment, and Development,* ed. Elisabeth Croll and David Parkin, 39–56. London and New York: Routledge.

Karp, Ivan. 1997. "Notions of Person." In *Encyclopedia of Africa South of the Sahara,* vol. 3, ed. John Middleton, 392–96. New York: Simon and Schuster/Macmillan.

Kisliuk, Michelle. 1997. "(Un)Doing Fieldwork: Sharing Songs, Sharing Lives." In *Shadows in the Field: New Perspectives for Fieldwork in Ethnomusicology,* ed. Gregory F. Barz and Timothy J. Cooley, 23–44. New York: Oxford University Press.

———. 1998. *Seize the Dance! BaAka Musical Life and the Ethnography of Performance.* New York: Oxford University Press.

Kratz, Corinne A. 2000. "Forging Unions and Negotiating Ambivalence: Personhood and Complex Agency in Okiek Marriage Arrangement." In *African Philosophy as Cultural Inquiry,* ed. Ivan Karp and D. A. Masolo, 136–71. Bloomington: Indiana University Press.

Küchler, Susanne, and Walter Melion, eds. 1991. *Images of Memory: On Remembering and Representation.* Washington, D.C.: Smithsonian Institution Press.

Landau, Paul Stuart. 1996. "Falsehood, Truth, and Thinking Between: Histories of Affiliation and Ethnogenesis." In *In Pursuit of History: Fieldwork in Africa,* ed. Carolyn Keyes Adenaike and Jan Vansina, 75–93. Portsmouth, N.H.: Heinemann.

Mintz, Sidney. 1989. "The Sensation of Moving, While Standing Still." *American Ethnologist* 16, no. 4: 786–96.

Peacock, James L., and Dorothy C. Holland. 1993. "The Narrated Self: Life Stories in Process." *Ethos* 21, no. 4: 367–83.

Samuel, Raphael. 1994. *Theatres of Memory.* Vol. 1, *Past and Present in Contemporary Culture.* London and New York: Verso.

Schroeder, Richard A. 1997. "Re-claiming Land in The Gambia: Gendered Property Rights and Environmental Intervention." *Annals of the Association of American Geographers* 87, no. 3: 487–508.

Shain, Richard A. 1996. "A Double Exile: Extended African Residences and the Paradoxes of Homecoming." In *In Pursuit of History: Fieldwork in Africa,* ed. Carolyn Keyes Adenaike and Jan Vansina, 104–12. Portsmouth, N.H.: Heinemann.

Tonkin, Elizabeth. 1992. *Narrating Our Pasts: The Social Construction of Oral History.* Cambridge: Cambridge University Press.

van Onselen, Charles. 1993. "Peasants Speak: The Reconstruction of a Rural Life from Oral Testimony: Critical Notes on the Methodology Employed in the Study of a Black South African Sharecropper." *Journal of Peasant Studies* 20, no. 3: 494–514.

Vansina, Jan. 1985. *Oral Tradition as History.* Madison: University of Wisconsin Press.

———. 1994. *Living with Africa.* Madison: University of Wisconsin Press.

Watts, Michael. 1983. *Silent Violence: Food, Famine, and Peasantry in Northern Nigeria.* Berkeley: University of California Press.

Willis, Justin. 1996. "Two Lives of Mpamizo: Useful Dissonance in Oral History." *History in Africa* 23: 319–32.

9

Senegalese Women in Politics

A Portrait of Two Female Leaders, Arame Diène and Thioumbé Samb, 1945–1996

Babacar Fall

Presenting a portrait of a political leader is not common among Senegalese historians. The most well-known examples of such portraits are of renowned leaders or high-ranking officials in the hierarchy of political parties or the state. This paper goes against this tendency. It outlines and analyzes the career paths of two women who have variously marked Senegalese political evolution: Arame Diène and Thioumbé Samb.

The primary sources used for the article are interviews conducted with these two women. The women's testimony is part and parcel of the documentation collected by the oral history workshop at the Université Cheikh Anta Diop. The interviews took place in 1994, 1995, and 1996.

The interviewers chose to conduct the interviews as open discussions. Preliminary meetings were held to define the interviews' objectives and expected results. These first meetings allowed trust to build between the informants and the research team.

The principal difficulty was the transcription in French of the testimony obtained in the national language, Wolof. The narrators, illiterate, were unable to validate the transcribed testimony. Nevertheless, an accurate transcription was assured by repeatedly listening to the interview tapes.

Through their testimony, two adversaries in Senegalese political life, Arame Diène and Thioumbé Samb, have told their stories and their views of the principal events that marked their way. To understand the scope of this testimony, which was analyzed as a primary source, it is essential to understand the context of Senegalese political life. Such an understanding gives a singular sense of these women, whose paths are mapped out and compared by examining their political itineraries.

THE CONTEXT OF SENEGALESE POLITICAL LIFE

There are strong traditions in Senegalese political life, although they are limited to the four municipalities that benefited from French citizenship:

Dakar, Gorée, Rufisque, and Saint-Louis. Since 1848, Senegal has elected a representative to the French parliament. Until 1914, only whites and mulattos were elected. In 1914, a black, Blaise Diagne, acceded to the position of deputy for the first time. Upon Diagne's death in 1934, Galandou Diouf succeeded him to the parliament and dominated political life until 1941. Following the Second World War, the electorate grew with the Law of Lamine Guèye of May 7, 1946, which gave French citizenship to all nationals of overseas territories. Political life was expanding.

Political leaders all came from among the educated elites. Lamine Guèye was known as an attorney. Léopold Sédar Senghor was a professor of grammar. Cheikh Anta Diop and Abdoulaye Ly combined their political activities with their professions as historians. Caroline Diop, the first woman elected as a deputy to the Senegalese National Assembly, was an elementary school teacher who had earned her degree at the École Normale for girls in Rufisque. Such education confers status and gives access to leadership positions. During the first half of the twentieth century, advanced schooling for boys was encouraged (Coquery-Vidrovitch 1994: 239), but only assimilated or "cultivated" girls were enrolled in school. Because of the limited number of women who had attended school, the political elite was mostly masculine.

Nevertheless, women were present on the political scene. Sought after by educated political leaders because of their electoral weight and their abilities in mobilizing other social groups, they were nonetheless victims of prejudice. In addition, they were often given a weak role in decision-making. They ensured the liveliness of political meetings: they were the ones who sat on the sidelines and "applauded," according to Arame Diène. With their colorful clothing, they gave such functions an air of festivity.

The dominant image of the woman participating in political life is that of the socialite woman providing some folklore. But after 1945, women acquired the right to vote and now constitute a significant electoral weight because of their effective participation in elections. But even if they in large part ensure victory, they are no less confined to the symbolic representation. Caroline Diop is one example.

A renowned teacher and great orator having a significant electoral influence, she has been engaged in political life since 1945. Nevertheless, she was only elected and invested as the first female deputy in 1963. That is to say, women's electoral and political weight is not reflected in access to high-profile positions. This largely explains the weak presence of women in Senegalese historiography. Also, it is difficult to describe the role of women in the Senegalese political arena if the historian uses classic, official sources. That is nevertheless the challenge addressed by this essay. In addition, it attempts to reconstitute the paths of two women who are atypical militants, in that they did not receive an elite education in a French assimilationist school. Arame Diène and Thioumbé Samb are products of the popular tradition. Not having attended school, they gradually thrust themselves onto the political chessboard to become leading figures of female militancy. They have taken paths that are similar but divergent, and, above all, marked by different luck.

Common Traits

With their strong personalities and great abilities for social mobilization, both women come from the same milieu: the Lebou ethnic group, constituting the native population of Dakar. In addition, they are both self-made women. While the political leaders come predominantly from the elite intelligentsia formed in the French schools, these two women are the product of a "popular" culture. They did not attend the French schools. They are among those categorized as illiterate and traditionally destined to remain at home. The social status of women, which tended to marginalize them and keep them from the public sphere, hampered the emergence of female political leaders (Fall 1989).

Nevertheless, both played a significant role in the women's movement of their respective parties: Arame Diène is affectionately called the "mother" of the Socialist Party,[1] while Thioumbé Samb was vice president of the women's movement of the Senegalese Democratic Union (UDS)[2] and a founding member of the Union of Senegalese Women.

Arame Diène and Thioumbé Samb entered the political world in 1945 and 1946, respectively. They influenced opposition political groups until 1983.

Arame Diène declares with pride that she got into politics in 1945/46, following a family tradition. Her parents were among the notable Lebous. "We were with Goux Alfred, who is a *toubab* [white]. We fought to support Goux, the mayor of Dakar. The choice was dictated by loyalty to Galandou Diouf, allied to Goux Alfred and, above all, a friend of my father. After his death, only Goux was left. It was he whom we knew in Dakar. When Lamine Guèye ran against him, I stayed with Goux, following the family tradition. Of course, Lamine Guèye had a large following. He was very politically aware. He was a son of Senegal, a native of Saint-Louis. Yet he lived in France and there was no link between him and my Lebou family. God wanted Lamine Guèye and his party, Le Bloc Noir, to win the 1948 elections."

When Senghor became active in politics at Guèye's side, Arame Diène's family stayed with Alfred Goux. But with the rupture between Guèye and Senghor in 1948, Senghor created the Senegalese Democratic Bloc (BDS) and found support among the Lebou community in Dakar.

Arame Diène states, "Senghor joined us on our position and decided to come with us. The old Lebous, all notables, were still there: my grandfather Alieu Codou Diène; Ousmane Diop Coumba Pathé, who is the father of Mamadou Diop, the current mayor of Dakar; El Hadj Falla Paye, the father of Alioune Badara Paye, who was director of the Dakar Fair; El Hadj Ibrahima Diop, at the time the Grand Serigne of Dakar; El Hadj Assane Ndoye; and Mbaye Diagne Dégaye." The elders met, talked with Senghor, and promised to support him against Lamine Guèye. The political agreement sealed between Senghor and the Lebou community largely determined the selection of Abbas Guèye, a leading figure of the syndicalist movement, as a candidate for Deputy of Senegal.

Abbas Guèye was a native Lebou and held the prominent position of general secretary of commercial syndicats. At the primary elections of 21 October 1945, Lamine Guèye's French Section of the Socialist International (SFIS) and Senghor's BDS shared the two seats. But in the 17 June 1951 elections the BDS took both seats. Abbas Guèye was elected. On the evidence of a pact linking the members of the Lebou community to Senghor's BDS, the Lebou were satisfied with the final electoral agreement (Ly 1992: 11).

Thioumbé Samb also became involved in politics in support of Abbas Guèye. She explains, "Since Abbas Guèye is Lebou, the Lebou community came together to support his candidacy for the position of deputy. My husband, who was a member of the Senegalese Democratic Union (UDS/RDA), had given me permission to join the BDS youth group. After the victory of the BDS, I stopped my primary activity and in 1947 joined my husband in the Senegalese Democratic Union."

Arame Diène points out that "at that time politics was different than today. Yes! At that time if someone wanted to be represented in the elections they were the ones who financed the campaign . . . [but] with Senghor, it was the commitment and the money of the partisans that allowed his election. . . . [T]he men and women both contributed."

Arame Diène was affected by the loss of political ethics among the militants who are presently fighting each other for honors in the Socialist Party. She remembers that yesterday's militants showed greater commitment and motivation than those of today. Currently, political involvement is equated with material, financial gain. Political allegiance to a party, especially the one in power, is bought. Arame Diène criticizes this search for gain as "political nomadism," and consoles herself by remembering the pure sentiments that gave the militants of her generation the determination to fight for a cause. The same bitterness grips Thioumbé Samb when she says, "Today it's a game: see how much money can be siphoned off, have a good time."

In their intellectual profiles, Arame Diène and Thioumbé Samb are the opposite of the "cultivated" elite who earned their degrees in French schools. They did not attend school, but take pride in having been among the first militants, in the heroic phase of their party's formation. Arame Diène is proud to remember that during that time it was "us, the ignorant nobodies, who cheered and applauded, who fought, were insulted, and all that comes with it until our party was on its feet!"

Thioumbé Samb explains the reasons for her lack of schooling: the Lebous, especially, did not like to enroll girls in school. School was seen as a waste. It was thought to corrupt one's soul with cunning and trickery. It was the place where one could "learn how to win without being right," according to the Grande Royale, one of the key characters in Cheikh Hamidou Kane's book *The Ambiguous Adventure* (1961: 165).

But faced with the schooling imposed by the whites, the first children sent to learn were captives, followed by the sons of the leaders, and then other children. Girls, however, considered those who held to tradition, the soul, and the culture, had to be preserved. They were not to have any contact with the French school.

Apart from these resemblances, these two women had very dissimilar paths through life.

Two Diverse Fortunes

Thioumbé Samb was shaped by the UDS/RDA, the radical nationalist party which was created in Senegal after the constitutive Congress of the African Democratic Assembly, held 18 October 1946. This party counted on the training of its militants to enable them to cope with the ostracism and repression imposed by colonial power. Thioumbé Samb observes that the strength of the UDS, which was directed by Abdoulaye Guèye Cabri and Ba Thierno, lay in its militants' education and training. According to her, "the other political groups were preparing their militants for fights, insults, and praise, while the UDS/RDA was emphasizing the education of women."

> [W]e had high school students as our teachers; they taught us after 6:00, after they had finished their classes. We who lived in the Guele Tapée neighborhood, we were assigned Racine Ndiaye, who taught us how to take care of certain formalities, notably how to sign the bottom of a document . . . because we formed delegations to go ask around the governor's delegation for authorization to hold political meetings . . . and we were only given authorization to meet in movie theaters. We talked to the owners of the theaters, who let us use their theaters from 3:00 to 6:00. We did that to educate the militant [women] so that they would realize that they could take the reins of the country, which had become independent.

In 1957 the principal parts of the BDS and the UDS/RDA merged to create the Senegalese People's Bloc (BPS), which in 1958 became the Senegalese Progressive Union (UPS). This political group, since 1986 called the Socialist Party, had managed to dominate the Senegalese political chessboard since 1947.

But at the time the BPS was created, parts of the UDS/RDA rejected the pro–colonial reform line of the new party and prepared to put on its feet a political group that was heir to the anticolonial traditions. Thioumbé Samb was strongly involved with this group, which was directed by Majhmout Diop, a pharmacist who was a native of Saint-Louis. The project ended in Thies on 15 September 1957 with the creation of the African Party for Independence (PAI), the Marxist nationalist party. Between 1957 and 1983 Thioumbé Samb distinguished herself as the foremost leader of the PAI.

But in 1983, Thioumbé Samb rejoined the Socialist Party with hopes of participating in the construction of the country under the leadership of President Abdou Diouf. This change of allegiance in one way marks the end of a political career. It was a failure, because what appeared to be a political revival turned out to be more of a retreat from the political scene. This is a historical irony for one who had fought as a militant for so long, first for the Senegalese Democratic Union (UDS) section of the African Democratic Assembly (RDA), then for the African Party for Independence (PAI). All these political organizations represented the nationalist wing in the fight against the colonial system.

Arame Diène, a militant first in pro-colonial, then in neocolonial, reform, took part in the Senegalese Democratic Bloc, which became the Senegalese Progressive Union and then in 1976 the Socialist Party. She had a more fortunate destiny than her rival Samb. In 1983, her political career reached its summit with her election as deputy to the National Assembly. She took her revenge on the intellectuals who had joined the party only in their own interest. In analyzing her rise, Diène describes her great political insight. In fact, she characterizes her nomination for deputy as marking an epochal change in national political values.

In 1981, Prime Minister Abdou Diouf had succeeded Léopold Sédar Senghor as president. He set out to gain a new mandate, and the elections of 1983 offered Arame Diène a great opportunity. She recounts her interview with Diouf regarding the Socialist Party's choices for parliamentary candidates:

> I went to see him as the regional official for Dakar because they could not ignore me and accept some other woman, since it was I who had won the region. I told him, "Mister President, I came to see you because I heard that you were going to appoint eight women to the list of deputies and I'm the official of the region. When Senghor was here, our movement had the strength to elect me, but I wanted to be deputy; he would have rejected this request, because he only believed in those who'd been educated, but I know that you are aware of the realities of the situation and I'm part of the 'Lebou reality.'" He responded, "If the regional union presents you as a candidate, then I'll put you on my list."
>
> So my union nominated me with no problem. They nominated my substitute, Ramatoulaye Seck, as well. God blessed us; we were both elected. An-

other woman, Aida Mbaye, was the official of the regional union of Tamba-counda—she was a native of Saint-Louis and she was not schooled either. She was nominated by her regional union and then elected to the National Assembly.

For Arame Diène, a new head of the Senegalese state led to a change in the criteria for promotion. As long as Senghor was president, she had resigned herself to being deprived of the honors of a position as deputy. She expresses it this way: "If Senghor were still there, I'd never be deputy. Senghor only believes in those who were educated. Abdou Diouf also believes in diploma-holders, but he knows the realities. He combined the two."

Arame Diène interprets this change in the criteria for advancement as progress. She indicates that by the 1988 elections, "we were two women and two men, there were four of us, so it seemed that things had evolved. . . . Already in 1983, Aida Mbaye and I were two 'ignorant women,' not educated, within the National Assembly, but we were not insignificant." She knows she has come a long way. According to her, her election is also the reward for her patience and her sense of political opportunity. She expresses her satisfaction using philosophy as well as humor to evaluate her political development. "Politics is not a sprint, but a marathon. If you are in a hurry, you'll go nowhere; it's step by step, progressing slowly. Look at everything I went through before becoming deputy in 1983."

This determination animates her while she measures the difficulties facing her participation in the game of the parliamentary institution. She tells of the incident that allowed her to become known as a full-fledged member: "When I had been elected deputy for the first time, during a parliamentary session I was seated next to a male deputy, and when I asked for the floor, he answered in a mocking tone, 'If you want the floor we won't give it to you, because here we speak French.' I responded, 'Oh really! So today the National Assembly is going to break up [laughs], because if I have to be in an Assembly where I cannot express myself, I'm leaving.' I raised my hand and the president of the National Assembly said to me, 'Okay, Arame, I'll register your name. You'll speak Wolof because we can't elect someone whom we don't allow to speak, can we?' [laughs] I was the first to speak Wolof at the National Assembly."

During parliamentary sessions, Arame strictly limited her participation: "I don't speak when the sessions are about defense, finances, . . . but as soon as it's about farmers, health, women, and children I speak in Wolof; but what I say is clear and comprehensible to everybody—we all understand Wolof." With this attitude, Arame Diène refuses to play the role of benchwarmer. On the contrary, she is proud of her position as deputy and is determined to justify it.

Pride and disappointment are evident in the intersecting paths of these two female leaders of Senegalese political life.

CROSS-EXAMINATION OF TWO LIFE NARRATIVES

The reconstruction of these two women's paths opens up the field of historical discourse to oral sources. Giving their voices back to these two women who did not attend French schools enabled them to tell their own stories. They remembered events and rediscovered the logic and sense of their political commitment within the framework of the facts. Listening to their voices also gives us a sense of their ability to interpret the events in which they played determining roles.

The two people discussed here are among the "forgotten" of Senegalese historiography for two reasons. First, our collective memory is generally male. Second, they are not political stars or heroes. They are ordinary citizens who, by chance, were invited to recount their lives. Once past initial surprise that researchers were interested in their careers, they realized that their political activities had become visible, and participated in the rewriting of their stories. Consequently, they are very self-confident and describe their preoccupations, the state of their souls, even their evaluations of history. The resulting testimony is not a eulogy, but rather a reconstructed memory of another period of time: a past visited with an undisguised nostalgia.

Arame Diène is satisfied to have remained loyal to a political tradition and to see the result of her efforts. Her involvement having been rewarded after thirty-seven years of service, she repeats that politics is a long-distance race. She is conscious of remaining among the people and also shares her honors and disappointments with her extended family. Changing political circumstances have validated her journey. Her understanding of changing power structures allowed her to make her way to the National Assembly, which for a long time had been reserved for the French-schooled political elite. Consequently, she is no longer part of the anonymous mass of militants who toil in support of other political leaders. She is now an active player and intends to assume a central role in the community. She takes pride in the prestige she enjoys in the Socialist Party and among the general public.

Arame Diène, content with her success, contrasts greatly with Thioumbé Samb, who is a disappointed leader, bitter and retreating from the political scene. Samb, who was among the first activists in the fight for independence, now feels frustrated and marginalized. She was not one of what she calls "the beneficiaries of independence." Her quasi-solitary life in Fann Hock, the old PAI seat, contrasts with the opulence of Arame Diène's family home, located in the popular quarter of Medina in Dakar.

Thioumbé Samb does not try to hide her bitterness. The PAI militant, who was arrested and imprisoned in Saint-Louis in 1960 during the municipal elections, sees herself as a martyr. "We who fought for independence are forgotten today," she declares. Her disappointment is even stronger because she was a victim of humiliation and repression under Senghor's regime and, with the PAI, went underground between 1960 and 1976. Following the PAI's legalization, she was active in politics from 1976 to 1983, always on the side of Majhmout Diop.

In 1983, the final step for Thioumbé Samb was her decision to rejoin the Socialist Party, which she had fought for thirty-six years. After two months of what seemed a warm welcome, she came up against the hostility of her new allies, who still viewed her as a rival. Between the two leaders, past animosity was replaced with the fear that the newcomer would crystallize old resentments among the women in the Socialist Party in Dakar. Thioumbé Samb was uncomfortable in her new position. She realized too late that her disappointment was the price of her costly decision to renounce her past connection to the opposition. Her political naïveté turned into instability. She lost big in the game of political alliances.

Arame Diène is proud to declare herself a long-distance runner who has won. Thioumbé Samb only finds consolation by retreating to the memory of a certain past when, in 1957, the PAI awarded her the gold medal of the Women's Union of Senegal. She shows visitors her photo collection as supplementary testimony to the prestigious role she had in Senegalese political life.

One cannot be insensitive to the disappointment, even the drama, that she feels in the face of the almost total indifference of her milieu. Sharing Thioumbé Samb's disappointment, a female member of the research team leaves her with this comment: "'History is unfair." But shouldn't we also acknowledge that history is ironic as well?

NOTES

This essay was translated by Laura Gardner, with the help of Eric Prieto, Ph.D.

1. The Socialist Party in Senegal is the heir of the Senegalese Democratic Bloc, created by Léopold Sédar Senghor in 1948 after breaking with Lamine Guèye's French Section of the Socialist International (SFIS), and of the Senegalese Progressive Union, founded in 1958. The Socialist Party has governed Senegal since independence.

2. The Senegalese Democratic Union (UDS) is the Senegalese section of the African Democratic Assembly (RDA), founded in 1946 by Houphouët Boigny. This nationalist party, which had sections in different territories of French West Africa and French Equatorial Africa, had weak support in Senegal, where political life was dominated by the SFIS and then the Democratic Bloc.

BIBLIOGRAPHY

Awa, Kane. 1995. "Femmes et politique: des récits de vie et/ou de pratiques de quelques militantes sénégalaises." M.A. thesis, Université Cheikh Anta Diop.

Coquery-Vidrovitch, Catherine. 1994. *Les Africaines: histoire des femmes d'Afrique noire du XIXème au XXème siècle.* Paris: Editions Desjonquères.

Fall, Rokhqyq Gningue. 1989. "Femmes et pouvoirs politiques en Afrique—L'exemple du Sénégal." In *Cultures en crise: quelles alternatives pour les femmes africaines?*, 63–65. Special issue of *Fippu—Journal de Yewwu Yewwi, pour la libération des femmes.*

Jewsiewicki, Bogumil. 1987. "Le Récit de vie entre la mémoire collective et l'historiographie." In *Récits de vie et mémoires vers une anthropologie historique du souvenir*, ed. Fabrice Montal and Bogumil Jewsiewicki, 213–46. Paris: L'Harmattan.

Kane, Cheikh Hamidou. 1961. *L'aventure ambiguë*. Paris: R. Julliard.

Ly, Abdoulaye. 1992. *Les Regroupements politiques au Sénégal, 1965–1970*. Dakar: Codesria.

PART III

African Imaginations

10

Nana Ampadu, the Sung-Tale Metaphor, and Protest Discourse in Contemporary Ghana

Kwesi Yankah

> Every subordinate group creates, out of its ordeal, a hidden transcript that
> represents a critique of power spoken behind the back of the dominant. . . .
> Domination generates a hegemonic public conduct and a backstage discourse
> consisting of what cannot be spoken in the face of power.
>
> *(Scott 1990: xii)*

This essay seeks to articulate the resilience and efficacy of the folk tale as a hidden political text and examine the thematic and literary undercurrents that have made it a rallying force for protest within Ghana's contemporary political history. It is largely informed by the voice of a master narrator whose songs, spanning a quarter of a century, have virtually become a political charter, defining power relationships, lampooning political aberration, and advocating the restoration of ideal political values.

Noted for their skills in indirection, the Akan of Ghana would rather "speak to the wind" than directly speak to the Supreme Being. The construction of protest discourse under the surveillance of state and political authority could become a hazardous enterprise in power-laden situations. Prudence would require the deployment of revocable cultural representations in the construction of political dissent. Political critique under these conditions is handed over to the singer of tales, a culturally revered voice of the dominated, who creatively manipulates cultural symbols to convey themes celebrating the resilience of the deprived and exposing the gluttony of the dominant.

Not all tradition-based constructions of critical discourse succeed in withdrawing into comparative safety. In Africa, a few such clandestine texts have been met with executive censorship and other forms of sanction. In Malawi, Mkandawire, a forty-two-year-old musician drawing inspiration from the oral traditions of Tumbuka, became a victim of Kamuzu Banda in 1988 when he sang the tale of a bird that could not be stopped from singing about an incident involving a mysterious death and subsequent cover-up attempts. The government banned the song from the radio, concluding that Mkandawire was singing about atrocities allegedly committed by the Banda regime (Chamley 1994). At the time of this writing (1995), Kamuzu Banda, former president of Malawi, was being tried for the very murders of which the visionary bird sang.[1]

DISCOURSE IN POLITICAL CONTEXT

Discourse interaction in times of crisis has been expounded in various disciplines (sociology, politics, sociolinguistics, discourse analysis) and subsumed under related rubrics such as "conflict," "protest," or "problem" encounters. In face-to-face encounters, it is expressed in situations where identities are threatened, interactions are disrupted, and convictions are not in harmony or diametrically opposed (Stokes and Hewitt 1976: 842). Under such conditions, participants may interact voluntarily by various maneuvers or bargain a resolution to the problem and restore harmony (Okolo 1995; Gumperz 1982; Yankah 1985). In other situations, the encounter may further degenerate into straight verbal abuse or physical violence unmitigated by negotiation or any attempt at conflict resolution.

A significant aspect of everyday conversation in Africa is its close interaction with other verbal economies. Here, interpersonal discourse is not restricted to ordinary talk. Conversation is a megagenre that embraces related modes of interaction such as song and tale. Depending on the social context, song and other genres may constitute interactive or dialogic discourses in their own right,[2] or they may be evoked within the matrix of ordinary talk to heighten emotion or argument.

In conflict-oriented song, those involved in the interaction may take positions and lyrically register protest or disagreement or may lampoon or verbally assault one another, such as in the Ewe songs of abuse, in which the rules of the game require opposing groups to be present as part of the performance (Anyidoho 1983: 237).

In Africa, the face affront associated with such conflict-oriented songdialogues is sometimes reduced by concomitant activities, such as pounding, that provide supportive contexts and rhythms and also distract attention from the domestic crises being focused on (Mvula 1985). In effect, the latter fora provide socially approved mechanisms of indirection whereby conflict is successfully managed without recourse to open hostilities.

Protest against political authority in many cultures of Africa often finds expression in disguised discourses that are structured to preserve social relations and pose minimum threat to one's "face integrity" (Brown and Levinson 1978; Goffman 1967). This concept of minimum threat partly recognizes the power of the spoken word in preliterate societies and its immense capacity to threaten the face integrity of individuals. Owing to the high stakes inherent in the execution of speech, cultures have adopted various means to overcome or minimize the hazards of oral interaction. These strategies are especially useful in situations where protest discourse is targeted at the centers of power. Here, the cultural reverence often accorded to elders and political authorities considerably restrains the flow of open, critical discourse. But avoidance of direct protest may also be due to the repressive and vindictive tendencies of those in power when they feel exposed by open criticism. Indirection then becomes essential and is expressed in verbal disguises, such as circumlocution and the use of metaphors, proverbs, folk tales, and other modes of cultural representation.

Since Ghana's independence, constitutional governance has been constantly suspended and freedom of expression stifled by various oppressive governments. Newspapers have been shut down, journalists have been arbitrarily detained and tortured, and dissident politicians have been jailed and sometimes maimed. Under such conditions of fear and tension, journalists have resorted to allegories, proverbial discourse, and song or folk tale metaphors that are either politically motivated or adopted by audiences as clandestine discourse. Of the various modes of folk wisdom, the sung-tale metaphor adopted by Nana Kwame Ampadu, a pioneer in the use of politicized folk tales, has been the most important medium for articulating political critique in contemporary Ghana.

TALE AS RHETORIC

Being a discrete genre, the tale has a life of its own, with a fully developed plot, characterization, and norms of performance (Finnegan 1970; Bauman 1977: 11). Yet in certain cultural domains tales, like proverbs, are also rhetorical if they are tools for persuasion, and they can be spontaneously evoked in conventional talk to demonstrate a lesson, teach a moral, or reinforce an argument. The basis of the close link between the proverb (brief, dense) and the tale (longer, more explicit) is that despite their varying structural features, the proverb and folk tale are the most accessible genres in which moral lessons are embedded.

It is not surprising that in certain cultures, the two are given the same label (Finnegan 1970: 419–23; Yankah 1989: 88). In cultures where different labels are used, such as among the Akan of Ghana, the tale (*anansesem*) is called a proverb (*ebe*) when it is triggered in normal discourse outside its conventional "fireside" milieu. Here it is the logical and metaphorical link between the tale and discourse that appeals to the user.

The rhetorical function of the tale as metaphor also means that its major objective of upholding social values and exposing social flaws can be fully exploited for the purposes of satire, innuendo, or verbal assault. A further advantage is the greater leverage for character development and dramatization provided by the tale, which also facilitates its effective use for humor, parody, and satire.

Remarkably, the tale has been effectively used to protest, satirize, and transmit "hidden transcripts" in volatile political contexts in Africa's past. Here the aesthetic function of the folk tale is exploited by the teller, who weaves plot and characterization to reflect society's values while at the same time ridiculing social excesses and foibles within the political hierarchy. In societies where tales begin with a disclaimer that denies the factuality of the narration and foregrounds its purely artistic and aesthetic intent—"The tale is not to be believed," according to the Akan—it is only natural that a skillful narrator will exploit the situation to lampoon real-life characters, as long as no real names are mentioned.

Because the folk tale lends itself to dramatization, it is even more suitable for the purpose. The musical interludes and recesses it provides within the African context often offer opportunities for vivid satirization of real-life incidents. Here the performer and audience, during the interval, may collaborate to celebrate the story's moral by competitively impersonating favorite characters in the story amid music, dance, and general merriment.

CONTINUITIES IN THE DIASPORA

Clearly, there is a close interaction between the song and the tale in Africa, since song is an integral part of African folk tales, and tales may also be sung. This mutual interaction between tale and song applies also to the African diaspora in general. In the words of Zora Neale Hurston, referring to Jamaica,

> Now and then [the narrator] sang a little. A short squirt of song and then another song would come. . . . It fitted together beautifully because Anansi stories are partly sung anyway. So rhythmic and musical is the Jamaican dialect that the tale drifts naturally from words to chant, and from chant to song unconsciously. (1938: 260)

In situations of political censure where there is fear of reprisals, satirical song and tale provide a "backstage" conduit for self-expression and articulation of dissidence in Africa and the black diaspora. This has extended from traditional society, through the period of slavery and colonialism, to the era of the modern nation-state.

R. S. Rattray, early in this century, alluded to the use of folk tales by Akan slaves to ridicule oppressive masters (1930: x). The use of the tale to lampoon and caricature authority figures is made easier by the persistence of the wily, smallish trickster—call it "political spider" (Salkey 1969), hare, or tortoise— who in the tales manages to weave his way through a treacherous world of powerful and greedy animals out to devour him. This opposition between wit and force often provides fitting parallels in slave-master relationships and enables victims to satirize excesses of authority and to overcome adversaries vicariously. In the words of Sherlock,

Through the story the story-teller could often take his revenge on those who offended him. Some one in the village, or even the chief, could be ridiculed, and his failings exposed. The story-teller had a measure of freedom, and through the story he could raise a laugh against the greed or hypocrisy or jealousy or deceit of someone more powerful than himself. (1957: 12)[3]

The artistic strategy of modeling dramatic characters after folk tricksters has also been extensively used by playwrights.[4] In this way guile, cleverness, and resilience may be safely celebrated, whether in tales or stage dramas, without courting the hostility of dominant forces.[5]

Apart from satirical tales, songs of ridicule and lampoon are very widespread within Africa (Finnegan 1970) and have also been extensively used in slave cultures to "sing the master" or "put down ole massa."[6] Together with the proverb and the tale, the song constitutes a very effective mode of cultural discourse that helps to reinforce hatred of the powerful and celebrate the resilience of the underdog. In certain situations, such as festivals, sung protest is infused with a shock element, consisting in the open abuse of authority. Here, the normal rules of social intercourse are suspended and protest is ritually celebrated under the supervision of a demobilized state authority.

High Life and Political Satire

Oral satire in contemporary Ghana goes beyond pristine traditional discourse. Its power is enhanced by its "mediatization" on radio, as well as its incorporation within the matrix of popular high life music, which is a syncretic art combining Western instrumentation and indigenous rhythms and lyrics (Collins 1976). Introduced into the country in the nineteenth century and developed during the First and Second World Wars, the social and geographical base of high life music has broadened from its historical association with the coastal elite to encompass most of the urban and rural areas of Ghana (and other West African countries). It is also enjoyed by both higher and lower classes. The wide reach of high life music, particularly its grass-roots appeal, naturally makes it an important medium for political mobilization and propaganda. Indeed, the panegyrics of high life guitar bands helped to shape the political agenda of President Kwame Nkrumah around the time of Ghana's independence; some of the groups even traveled with him outside the country.

Over the years, however, musicians have generally avoided open critical comment on political processes for fear of censure. Significantly, though, several songs have been conventionally construed by the public as cryptic statements on the political process.[7]

In several cultures of Ghana, oblique criticism is an accepted part of the aesthetics of indigenous communication. Imaginative discourse in general tends to be susceptible to political interpretation, since a public starved for critical self-expression normally looks for appropriate public icons in which to anchor their repressed emotions.

But it is perhaps the electronic media, particularly radio, which have most substantially enhanced the power of political satire and its availability for public scrutiny. Even so, what constitutes political meaning in respect of sung discourse remains somewhat problematic, in that verbal artists would rather not openly admit political motivation in their discourse and often lament the subversive readings applied to them. Yet the public, in ascribing political meaning to such polysemous discourses, has been guided by a cultural aesthetic wherein the artful concealment of intentions by an artist is considered a hallmark of sophistication. The aesthetic maturity of a good artist is therefore taken for granted. The general preference for cryptic rhetoric as indicative of artistic sophistication is fostered by the relative absence of channels for open and spontaneous articulation of political opinion or opposition. Under such circumstances, refuge may be sought under suggestive symbols whose meanings (innocuous or otherwise) may be reinforced, transformed, or extended to suit a political purpose. When such protest symbolism in the public sphere coincides with a particularly suitable turn of political events, its efficacy as a weapon for insubordinate discourse (and as a shield) is further enhanced.

This is of course not to deny credit to the artist for consciously presenting a disguised text, but rather to note the delicate balance the artist must negotiate between private and public identities. As a guardian of community social values, the traditional artist is concerned with timeless ideals, and his "catch-words" and refrains become handy weapons for political activism when those ideals are subverted by those in power. Sometimes, catchwords and slogans may be reinforced by visual representations in textile designs that facilitate their adoption as cryptic discourse for conveying innuendo.

AKUTIA

The phenomenon of innuendo or indirect critique finds expression in what the Akan call *akutia*, a strategic verbal assault in which speakers in face-to-face confrontations avoid eye contact with their targets and make insinuations without mentioning names. Instances of innuendo, couched in songs and tales such as those discussed in this essay, are generally classified as akutia. *Akutia wo ne wura* (Akutia has a known target), the Akan say, implying not only that akutia is goal-oriented but also that its target, if well schooled in the genre, is often aware of the subtext. Yet like all cultural indirection, such as *sanza* among the Azande (Evans-Pritchard 1956, 1963), or *signifying* in African-American tradition, akutia speakers always have a potential line of retreat should their motives be challenged (Mitchell-Kernan 1972).

In certain domains, akutia overlaps stylistically with ebe (proverb) in that it is also a mode of indirection that can be replicated or recreated in other contexts. Yet akutia has a characteristic trait that lends itself readily for deployment in class- and power-laden contexts. It finds its best fulfillment in situations of power differentials—situations of conflict involving individuals of uneven sociopolitical status or class. Here it is deployed by the underdog as an offensive weapon and protective shield. Akutia in the hands of the powerful (to be used against the deprived) would be a redundant device, since the dominant class has nothing to lose by adopting direct strategies of confrontation, including open abuse and physical aggression.

In the proverb or sung-tale, akutia then finds a fitting social niche in which the powerless can use these forms to create sociopolitical awareness and celebrate an exclusive social identity. Yet it is probably the recursive potential of this mode of akutia that is more significant. In the form of a tale, the popular appeal of akutia lies in its dynamism, its responsiveness to emergent social forces, which compels its principles to be reinforced, adapted, or reconstituted to meet new historical challenges. This way, one who is socially deprived is not doubly handicapped through verbal deprivation; a performer can adopt and adapt "ready-made" therapies in novel situations of stress. Even while celebrating a group identity, the protest voice constantly resonates and affords the listener vicarious participation in the political process. The efficacy of akutia, however, rests on the performer's skills and integrity as an artist.

NANA KWAME AMPADU

The legitimization of the folk tale as part of the contemporary political process is largely based on the sung-tales of Nana Kwame Ampadu that came to public attention in 1967, a year after Nkrumah's overthrow. His African Brothers Band had been formed in 1963. Born on 31 March 1945, Nana Kwame Ampadu has attained preeminence as the single most important folk commentator in Ghana's contemporary history. He was indeed crowned *odwontofoohene* (singer-in-chief) in a nationwide competition in 1973.

Eloquent, prolific, and erudite in Akan oral traditions, Ampadu appeals to the rural folk with very philosophical lyrics and social commentary spiced with proverbs, witticisms, and idioms. He is certainly the most prolific high life artist, having composed and recorded more than five hundred songs in his career. His sung-tales span a variety of social and cultural themes, ranging from marriage, interpersonal harmony, and lineage disputes to love of country. Ampadu's songs are so commonly known that his sung-tale titles have often been adopted by traders as names of textile designs, shoes, and other materials, to facilitate marketing.

Born in Adiemmra in the Afram Plains of the eastern region of Ghana, Ampadu spontaneously broke into traditional song early in his life. His verbal wit and eloquence with proverbs and philosophical quips astounded his household. In primary school, storytelling was his favorite pastime, and he would monopolize the floor for extended periods during proverb competitions and storytelling, regular features in the school curriculum. He had learned stories in his immediate neighborhood and would often sit for hours on end listening to folk tales told by elders. But it was probably his father's knowledge and practice of oral traditions as a professional that helped to sharpen Ampadu's verbal wit. His father was a lineage head and a subchief whose daily duties of adjudication required a deep acquaintance with customary lore, lineage history, oral traditions, and forensic skills. Ampadu recalls that even as an eight-year-old he sat at his father's feet during judicial deliberations.

Ampadu's musical career started early in the sixties during Nkrumah's regime, but it was not until Nkrumah's overthrow that he came out with his first commercial recording. The political significance of Ampadu's folk tales came to public notice in 1967, when he released his single hit, "Ebi Te Yie" (Some are favorably positioned). Over nearly three decades, from Nkrumah's overthrow to the regime of J. J. Rawlings, Nana Ampadu's folk tales have become the most powerful metaphors for popular comment on contemporary Ghanaian politics.

Yet it is useful to consider how Ampadu's poetic agenda was partly shaped by the social and political context in which he launched his career, as well as the turbulence and uncertainties of Ghana's political history. His dominant imagery of brute force, intimidation, and oppression, represented by carnivorous beasts, is often countered by the wily maneuvers of small, oppressed creatures. However, it takes a closer look at the dynamics of Ampadu's tales to discern his message (whether benign or seditious). His maiden song releases coincided with a changing political order whose immediate past had been characterized by internal repression, political persecution, and inhibitions on free speech. In 1966 the *Legon Observer,* a fortnightly journal founded a few months after Nkrumah's overthrow, painted a vivid picture of the political context at the time and advocated an agenda for the oppressed:

We were held captive to a political tyranny which the Ghana army and police coup of 24th February 1966 has now rendered ridiculous and impertinent in retrospect, but which while it lasted made a pathetic spectacle of this country. We looked so bad at the height of the CPP ritual dance that a foreign news magazine described Ghana as a country inhabited by Kwame Nkrumah and seven million cowards. . . .

Among the people most culpable for these conditions were those of us, who for good reasons or bad, could speak out and damn the consequences, but did not. We only stood and waited, though believing quite sincerely that we were in that way also serving. We have learnt by bitter experience that that was not so, and many of us are resolved never again to be caught trying to save the future by sacrificing the present; never again to remain quiet if our liberties are being invaded and curtailed, hoping that somebody else would perform any risky national obligations for us.

ARTICULATION OF SOCIAL INJUSTICE

Ampadu's song "Ebi Te Yie" (Some are favorably positioned), released during the military regime of the National Liberation Council, highlights social injustice and the suppression of free speech in an imaginary animal world. Below is a summary of the tale:

> There was once a meeting of all animals to discuss the concerns of the animal world. All the animals were present, including Leopard and the orphan Antelope. It so happened that Leopard took a seat directly behind orphan Antelope and started mistreating him. He clawed Antelope's tail to the ground, making it impossible for him to actively participate in the discussion. No sooner would orphan Antelope begin to speak than Leopard would silence him, with the warning that the meeting was not meant for skinny creatures. The mistreatment went on until orphan Antelope could bear it no longer. He plucked up courage and made a loud plea to the presiding chairman. "Petition on the floor, point of order," he said. "Mr. Chairman, secretary, elders here assembled. I move for an immediate adjournment of the meeting, because some of us are not favorably positioned. Some are favorably positioned, others are not." As soon as the meeting saw through the words of orphan Antelope, there was an immediate adjournment.[8]

This tale depicts a world of social injustices under a veneer of peace and political order. Here, the democratic search for consensus within the decision-making process is quietly subverted by the tyrannical impulses of bullies, whose very legitimacy would be threatened by a dispensation of equal rights, democracy, and free speech. It is a world of class distinctions, where might and brute force prevail, the opinion of the deprived is censured, and representative forums are mere tokens. The fragile antelope, already anguished by orphanhood, is brutally suppressed in his attempt to represent the views of the needy. Besides the flushes of suppression and victimization, the tale is also a metacommunicative illustration of indirection as a safe channel of protest by the politically endangered. Antelope, under constant physical harassment, manages to muster enough courage to cleverly convey his agony without mentioning his tormentor. He avoids open confrontation by seeking the intervention of the fairminded majority through a protest judiciously constructed with an impersonal pronoun. This strategy is meant to transform a subjective concern into a shared experience. Note also the double entendre in Antelope's lexical depiction of his plight. The verb Ampadu uses, *te yie,* has the advantage of lexical ambiguity. Whereas it literally conveys an unfavorable seating position, it also depicts a world of social deprivation brought about by deviants and bullies who have been enriched (te yie) by ill-gotten wealth.

Since the antelope's community appears to be bound by the same cultural rules of indirection, they immediately decode his cryptic tale of agony and adjourn, to the relief of all assembled. The leopard's caution and muscle-flexing were clear signals that the antelope's sorry plight would perhaps have been tremendous comic relief based on code-switching at the climax, where Antelope's plea is dramatically presented in English, with all the jargon of formal parliamentary discourse.

The drama in this tale is indeed a microcosm of a modern nation-state encumbered with tyranny, oppression, and social inequity. Coming as the song did during a military dictatorship, where there was widespread social injustice and acquisition of ill-gotten wealth in Ghana, its adoption as a mode of political protest by the deprived was natural. Not only was the refrain sung as a form of lampoon; a new textile design instantly named "Ebi Te Yie" became an overnight commercial success. It is no wonder that the song disappeared from the government-controlled airwaves soon after it was released. It reappeared after the military regime granted power to civilians. Nearly thirty years after its coinage, the phrase "ebi te yie," with all its political connotations, is still widely used in the Akan popular lexicon.

Social Responsibility

Two years after the military government of the NLC handed over power to the democratically elected government headed by Dr. K. A. Busia in 1969, the transition from military muscle-flexing to a democratic order was marked by another popular tale composed by Kwame Ampadu, entitled "Article 204 (The Laws of Mmoadoma Kingdom)." The tale goes as follows:

> Animals in the kingdom passed a law, under Article 204 of their constitution, protecting weaker animals from being victimized by the powerful ones. As a result of this law, all carnivorous animals turned vegetarian. The timid not only started rejoicing, they also took advantage and started teasing the wild animals. One day, as Leopard relaxed under a tree with his mouth wide open, Bat took advantage and flew in and out of Leopard's mouth a couple of times. When Bat entered for the third time, Leopard shut his mouth. Witnessing all that was happening, Antelope reported the incident, and all animals met to deliberate on the matter. The meeting started with a roll call; whereas every-

body else responded to their names, Bat did not respond. When Leopard was charged with the responsibility for Bat's disappearance, he denied guilt until he was betrayed by surgery on his entrails. But Leopard defended himself, saying he was fast asleep and was not aware he had swallowed Bat. Leopard's lawyer also argued that Article 204 of the animals' constitution banning meat consumption was no license for the weak to turn the mouths of wild creatures into playgrounds.

This tale, recorded in 1971, is an apparent adjunct to the previous one and signals an improved political order in which animals basically conform to the rule of law in a world of peace. Yet it is the deprived, now enjoying a new lease on freedom, who indulge in acts of provocation and thereby threaten social stability. This story, coinciding with the return of democratic rule in Ghana, lent itself to easy political interpretation at the time. It cautions against the exercise of freedom without responsibility and overtly incorporates elements from the national constitutional agenda. Including in the tale juries, lawyers, and laws based on articles in the constitution (Article 204) signals a political transition to a democratic order, an era governed by the rule of law. Leopard, this time on the side of the law, resorts to victimization not on impulse, but only upon provocation and only after his patience has been stretched to the limit.

Although victimized by Leopard, Bat has only himself to blame for his unnecessary acts of provocation. Significantly, the role of Antelope is transformed from victim in the previous story to witness; the new dispensation of freedom and equal rights emboldens him to openly initiate judicial action without recourse to verbal indirection.

LIMITS OF POWER

In a new political era in Ghana, where the military had been withdrawn to the barracks, it took such traditional rhetoric to caution the civilian government, and Ghanaians in general, against actions that could provide an excuse for the return of the military. Less than a year after the release of this song, the military bounced back. The National Redemption Council took over power in a coup d'état in 1972 and made Lieutenant Colonel (later General) Acheampong head of state. In 1977, Nana Ampadu composed a tale whose release the following year coincided with Acheampong's overthrow in a military palace coup. It was titled "Obiara Wo Dee Etumi No" (Every power is subject to a superior force). The song consisted of a series of short tales including the following:

Cock embarked on a journey to look for a wife. On his way, he met Fox, who offered to accompany him. Suspicious that Fox would attack him on the way, Cock answered that Dog was among the party and that he was hiding behind a tree. Scared, Fox then said, "Well, if Dog is going with you, I will stay back; you seem to be in good company." . . .

A talkative woman provoked a driver's assistant, who gave her a sound beating at the bus station. The woman reported the case to her husband, who bared his chest and, in a flight of fury, went to the station to fight. "Give way, give way, I will beat up my wife's assailant," he boasted. When the driver's assistant emerged, he happened to be a giant of sorts. Setting eyes on the giant, the "brave" husband recoiled, thanking the giant for trouncing his loquacious wife.

These stories portray a series of potentially explosive situations defused by a tactical, even if humorous and humiliating, retreat of inferior forces. Following the principle that no man is invincible, those who are aware of the limits of their strength arrange a timely withdrawal to avoid humiliation. The cock, a virile force in his own right, is suspicious of his traditional predator's unusual offer of companionship on a perilous journey. But Fox himself tactically recoils at the announced proximity of a superior predator, Dog. The peace that results from this cloak-and-dagger dialogue can only be said to be tenuous, for social chaos might take over if the weaker animals relax their vigilance.

In the second tale, a major confrontation between two self-assured parties is once again averted by a tactical retreat of the weaker one, but this time only after a woman has been victimized. The husband here acknowledges the relative inferiority of his own strength and thereby avoids public humiliation. But the woman is doubly agonized, not just by physical assault, but by her husband's cowardice in the face of a superior force.

Whereas the stories portray the limitations of self-proclaimed prowess, they also deride the absurd pretexts to which boastful cowards resort when faced with imminent danger. Arising as these tales did within Ghana's current political context, in which a military leader had been toppled by another soldier, after a series of botched takeover attempts, they appeared to be proverbial capsule versions of contemporary events. Predictably, they were adopted by General Acheampong's opponents as *akutia* (attack by innuendo) against the fallen head of state.

NEGLIGENCE AND IRRESPONSIBILITY

Since J. J. Rawlings's appearance on the political scene in 1979, his political agenda has been critiqued by at least three sung-tales of Nana Kwame Ampadu. In all cases, though, the master storyteller attributes the outcome to subversive public readings by Rawlings's opponents, since he openly declared his support for Rawlings. Indeed, the witty singer of tales helped to campaign by song and deed for Rawlings's NDC party prior to the democratic elections in 1992 that gave constitutional legitimacy to its political agenda.

In 1982 Rawlings had made a tactical plea to musicians to use their art to mobilize support for his revolution and join in the crusade against greed, corruption, and commercial malpractices. In response, Nana Ampadu released what he considered a promotional song but which he claims was subverted and used for political critique. Its title foreshadowed danger, "Asem Beba Da Bi" (There will be trouble someday). The tale goes as follows:

> Tortoise noticed that a raffia palm tree had sprouted at the bank of the river and suggested that all animals should join hands to uproot it, since it might pose a danger in the future. Nobody paid heed to Tortoise. Fish shrugged him off, saying that fishes live in water and have nothing to do with vegetation at the river's bank. Bird declined, with the excuse that birds fly in the sky; Antelope did not cooperate either. Disappointed, Tortoise maintained an embarrassed silence. Later, the raffia palm grew wild and was cut by Man, who constructed a fish trap and left it in the river and also made a bird trap out of it. Bird and Fish were both caught in the traps. A hunting trap made of the wild raffia also entangled Antelope. Tortoise was thereby vindicated, since he had warned of imminent danger.

This tale (reminiscent of the Anglo-Saxon proverb "A stitch in time saves nine") demonstrates how a small problem can get out of hand because of negligence. The Akan would normally advise against *mma mfofo nnane kwaee* (allowing shrubs to become a forest).

The call by Tortoise for an immediate solution could not have been based on selfish interest, since his own crusty exterior insulates him against any prickly plant, and the tortoise is by nature not liable to violent captivity. The Akan say, *Ekaa akyekyedee ne nwa nko ara a nka otuo nntu wo kwaee mu* (If tortoise and snail were the only creatures, there would be no gunshots in the forest). The various creatures that are eventually endangered by their own sloth and negligence display a lack of foresight and maturity, ignoring that a mature raffia palm could be put to uses that may endanger their own lives. As it turns out, the short-sighted animals had wrongly made Tortoise the object of suspicion, forgetting that man's destructive propensities in his desperate search for survival may endanger their own lives.

This tale, on the one hand, advocates preventive action against social evils—quick redress of problems. Within Ghana's political circumstances, it would then equate Tortoise with Rawlings (as the singer said he intended) and his wise counsel with Rawlings's vision of a problematic future if social evils were not immediately arrested. In this case, the victimized animals would represent a cross section of Ghanaians who might ignore the leader's counsel only to regret it later.

On the other hand, the tale was interpreted by opponents of Rawlings's regime as signaling his negligence toward the country's problems and predicting imminent political instability. In this interpretation, metaphorical equivalents are reversed: the wise tortoise is equated with opponents of the regime, advocating the immediate removal of the head of state (the raffia palm tree) who might otherwise pose a bigger problem to Ghanaians. In addition to being evoked in situations of tension and confrontation, the song's title, "Asem Beba Da Bi" (There will be trouble someday), is occasionally inscribed on placards of activists and opposition groups demonstrating against the Rawlings government.

POLITICAL RESPONSIBILITY

It was not until 1991 that political meaning was widely attributed to another song-tale by Nana Ampadu. If his song composed in the eighties called for the deployment of swift remedies, its sequel in the early nineties, according to folk interpretation, saw the key to sociopolitical order in exemplary behavior on the part of political functionaries. The agent of the admonition this time was the most renowned trickster in Ghana—Kweku Ananse, the spider:

> When all animals met for elections to executive positions, Pataku the wolf lobbied to be *tankese,* the chief sanitary inspector. Having a hidden agenda, Wolf said he would be responsible for all burials at the cemetery. After each burial, he would then secretly visit the cemetery, exhume the body, and eat it. Kwaku Ananse had seen it all but kept quiet. Soon, Ananse lost his mother and vowed never to allow Wolf to have his own way with the corpse. After the burial, Ananse secretly dug an underground tunnel to his mother's grave and spent the night in the tunnel. As Wolf visited the grave and started digging to exhume the body, the downward thrust of his digging implement made the sound *kukrukukru.* Whenever Ananse heard that noise, he would reply with a metallic jingle: *kikekike.* Hearing this, Wolf concluded it was a ghost and went home in frustration. The next day when he tried *kukrukukru* again, it produced the echo *kikekike.* Wolf reported the matter to the elders, arguing that rituals performed by Ananse on the death of his mother were incomplete and must be done again. It was at this point that Ananse intervened and said there was no need for another round of rituals, adding, proverbially, that "When *kukrukukru* ceases, *kikekike* will also cease."

The story here draws attention to the inherent challenges of leadership, advocating exemplary behavior in positions of responsibility and pointing out the ripple effect of irresponsible behavior in the high echelons of society. Whereas the previous story highlights the adverse effects of negligence, this one focuses on the causes. Significantly, the social disorder depicted by the tale is not a function of political tyranny, but the by-product of a democratic order, where governance devolves on popular will and personal liberties are not in jeopardy. As exemplified by Wolf, greed often supersedes public interest in the performance of public duties; but one can also blame the relaxation of public vigilance on the cultural symbols of gluttony in the animal world. In appointing Wolf to that position, was the animal world not guided by its typical habits?

Wolf's eventual exposure and public betrayal constitute the ultimate social sanction, but note the wily mechanism the trickster uses to ensnare Wolf. Ananse avoids open apprehension of the culprit as well as responsibility for initiating judicial action. He is not the plaintiff. It is Wolf, the culprit, who is trapped into the role of plaintiff and ends up as defendant. His move to make Ananse answerable for the spooky graveyard experience redounds on him.

Note also here the significance of the semantic contrast between the two ideophonic expressions, partly based on contrast in vowel quality: the wolf's sound symbolism, *kùkrúkùkrú*, denoting a heavy, immense impact of power; and Ananse's metallic jingle, *k\kék\ké*, depicting lightweight marginality. The two ideophones, though contrasting in meaning, share the alliterative plosive sound *k* and have similar tone patterns. This tonal parallelism helps to heighten the cause-effect correlation and foregrounds the underlying irony. But one cannot miss the semantic effect of the sound symbolism: the heavy impact of the culprit's tool triggering an echo and cautioning that "there is no smoke without fire."

Significantly, Ananse's echo is not an attempt to replicate Wolf's gluttony: it is only a playful deterrent. As it turns out, the ploy betrays the coward in the predator who, for fear of a vindictive phantom, beats a quick retreat.

Ananse's detached public comment that betrayed Wolf is also reminiscent of the cryptic protest by the orphan Antelope under the intimidating gaze of Leopard. In Ananse's example, though, the proverbial punch line can only be quietly decoded between the speaker and "he whom the cap fits," even though the ironic truth is bound to be public knowledge.

Once again, we witness here the timely deployment of akutia innuendo within the confines of the tale itself, recalling another case in Akan traditional lore where the scavenging wolf is proverbially betrayed by a vigilant vulture who, quietly perched on a tree, sees it all. The proverbial refrain of the above tale, "When *kukrukukru* ceases, *kikekike* will also cease," is often used as a political innuendo protesting irresponsible behavior in high places.

However, as the singer himself lamented to me, the original meaning of his song has been subverted for political gains by opponents of the Rawlings government. In his words,

> The folk tale was given to me by a friend in the late eighties, and I recorded it mainly because of the rampant grave looting in the country at the time. It was meant to advise against the criminal looting of graves, but its message is

so important that I wish it would be played every morning on radio to help eradicate social vices in general, and promote honesty in life. I did not have any political meaning in mind; it is the public's own inscription.

But has the singer of tales himself ever made a conscious effort to compose political songs? Yes, he says, even though the meanings of some may have been "subverted." To underscore Ampadu's point, note that he has publicly endorsed President Jerry Rawlings since 1982. In more recent times, the famous singer has appeared on public platforms, rallying rural support for Rawlings in his campaign for constitutional presidency. He explained, "I admire Rawlings very much and would be the last to sing a tale to hurt him. I have admired him since the beginning of the revolution. He is a simple man who likes the rural folk and I like him for that." Prior to the 1992 elections, Nana Ampadu composed and recorded a promotional song for Rawlings's National Democratic Congress. "I did it from the bottom of my heart, and it became an overnight hit," he added.

In 1992 Ampadu released a sung-tale meant to advise and frustrate opponents of Rawlings who were scheming to disqualify him in court as a presidential candidate on the basis of his half-Scottish parentage. Nana Ampadu intervened with a cautionary tale warning that laws deliberately made to create problems for opponents eventually become a burden for all. This was the song "Oda Mo Do Yi Oda Wo Do" (A burden on me is a burden on you):

> There lived a king who was very just and very popular among his people. Soon the king's wife fell seriously ill, and it looked as though she wouldn't survive. Enemies of the king then took advantage and conspired against him. The kingmakers quickly made a law that husbands would henceforth accompany their dying wives to the grave. The king did not protest; he agreed and signed it into law. Very soon his wife died, and the king was bound to comply with the law. Before departing, however, he shook hands with all the elders, accompanying each handshake with the words "Oda mo do yi oda wo do" (A burden on me is a burden on you). Puzzled by the words, the elders went into consultation and decided to withdraw the law, since some of their own wives were very prone to illness.

Despite the tale's apparent meaning, its philosophical refain, "Oda mo do yi oda wo do," is now generally sung as a political innuendo, insinuating that government policies perceived to hurt only a segment of the population would eventually be a burden on all, including the policy makers and their party members.

Thus whereas Nana Apadu's political stance has been openly declared to be pro-government, his philosophical ideals appear intact. He may preach the ideals of the president, rally support for his policies, and publicly seek his reelection; but Ampadu remains a philosopher, a visionary with an abiding faith in cultural truths that stand the test of time.

As a sage, he knows the power of folk wisdom, the multiple voices encoded in its messages, its vast potential for bringing deviants into line with social ideals, and its tremendous appeal to the masses. With this knowledge, he has managed somehow to maintain separate private and public identities.

For nearly thirty years, Nana Ampadu's folk wisdom has provided a cultural prism through which the masses interpret and comment on political behavior. His vast resources of tales, proverbs, folk songs, and historical narratives collectively constitute a cultural megaphone by which the powerless exercise "free speech" even under political surveillance. His sung-tales continue to enjoy tremendous airplay; none has recently been censured for political reasons, nor has he himself been reprimanded, despite allegations to the contrary.[9]

Yet Ampadu's animal world is dynamic and has not been static over the years. Actors have been changed, some renewed with vigor; roles have been shifted, realigned, shaped by the dynamics of the political landscape—from the intimidating glances of ferocious tyrants and bullies, through their domestication, to the haunted premises of a graveyard where the political spider betrays the nocturnal exploits of social deviants. In all cases, however, truth and social ideals have triumphed through the timely replication of time-honored conventions.

As Ampadu told me in a final word, "The hunter's hammock is not the monopoly of the antelope, it's for the smaller species too." The above proverb is itself a philosophical capsule of the intrinsic mechanisms undergirding the potency of the sung-tale metaphor as a form of popular cultural production: the hunter's hammock, like popular culture itself, subsists on fluidity, multiple uses, and applications. Its power revolves partly on its rustic appeal, but also on a flexible scope of application that defies time and space and facilitates constant reproduction to meet new challenges. Like the oral poetry of Sotho migrant workers, the sung-tale metaphor has helped to define new realities, formulate new images (Coplan 1986), and articulate class-based contradictions that threaten social stability.

Thus akutia, as cultural production, does not emerge in a social vacuum; it is attuned to addressing the complexities of social experience, even as it constitutes a rallying point for the celebration of sociopolitical identities and the articulation of the vox populi. The sung-tale metaphor sustains and empowers the silent majority, who see this medium of popular culture as the only weapon by which to articulate their political consciousness and seek to gain empowerment.

NOTES

"Nana Ampadu, the Sung-Tale Metaphor, and Protest Discourse in Contemporary Ghana" by Kwesi Yankah, from *Language, Rhythm, and Sound: Black Popular Cultures into the Twenty-First Century*, Joseph K. Adjaye and Adrianne R. Andrews, eds. ©1997 by the University of Pittsburgh Press. Reprinted by permission of the University of Pittsburgh Press.

1. See also Nkanga 1994.
2. See Anyidoho 1983; Mvula 1985; Omoniyi 1995.
3. See also Bascom 1969: 473.
4. See Imbuga 1995.
5. See also Purchas-Tulloch 1976: 242.
6. See Herskovits 1969; Piersen 1977; Blassingame 1979; Abrahams 1992.
7. See van der Geest and Asante-Darko 1982; Yankah 1985.
8. This and all other songs in this essay are translated from the original Akan by the author.
9. See van der Geest and Asante-Darko 1982.

BIBLIOGRAPHY

Abrahams, Roger D. 1992. *Singing the Master: The Emergence of African American Culture in the Plantation South.* New York: Pantheon.

Anyidoho, Kofi. 1983. "Oral Poetics and Traditions of Verbal Art in Africa." Ph.D. dissertation, University of Texas, Austin.

Bascom, William. 1969. *The Yoruba of Southwestern Nigeria.* New York: Holt, Rinehart and Winston.

Bauman, Richard. 1977. *Verbal Art as Performance.* Rowley, Mass.: Newbury House.

Blassingame, John W. 1979. *The Slave Community: Plantation Life in the Antebellum South.* Rev. ed. New York: Oxford University Press.

Brown, Penelope, and Stephen Levinson. 1978. "Universals in Language Usage: Politeness Phenomena." In *Questions and Politeness: Strategies in Social Interaction,* ed. Esther Goody, 56–289. Cambridge: Cambridge University Press.

Chamley, Santorri. 1994. "How Banda Ruined Malawi Music." *New African,* 27 November.

Collins, E. J. 1976. "Ghanaian Highlife." *African Arts* 10, no. 1: 62–69.

Coplan, David. 1986. "Performance, Self-Definition, and Social Experience in the Oral Poetry of Sotho Migrant Mineworkers." *African Studies Review* 29: 29–40.

Evans-Pritchard, E. E. 1956. "Sanza, a Characteristic Feature of the Zande Language and Thought." *Bulletin of the School of Oriental and African Studies* 20 (June): 165–79.

———. 1963. "Meaning in Zande Proverbs." *Man* 63: 4–7.

Finnegan, Ruth. 1970. *Oral Literature in Africa.* Oxford: Clarendon.

Goffman, Erving. 1967. *Interaction Ritual: Essays on Face-to-Face Behavior.* Chicago: Aldine.

Gumperz, John J. 1982. *Discourse Strategies.* Cambridge: Cambridge University Press.

Herskovits, Melville. 1969. *The New World Negro.* New York: Minerva Press.

Hurston, Zora Neale. 1938. *Tell My Horse.* New York: Lippincott.

Imbuga, Francis D. 1995. "Folkloric Transpositions and Tricksterism in African Drama: The Case of John Ruganda's Drama." Paper presented at the conference on Scholarly Authority and Intellectual Production in African Studies, Northwestern University.

Legon Observer. 1966. University of Ghana, July.

Mitchell-Kernan, Claudia. 1972. "Signifying and Marking: Two Afro-American Speech Acts." In *Directions in Sociolinguistics: The Ethnography of Communication,* ed. John J. Gumperz and Dell Hymes, 161–79. Oxford: Blackwell.

Mvula, Enoch. 1985. "Tumbuka Pounding Songs in the Management of Familial Conflicts." In *Cross Rhythms,* vol. 2, ed. Daniel Avorgbedor and Kwesi Yankah, 93–113. Bloomington: Trickster.

Nkanga, Mbala. 1994. "The Hidden Text in the Rhetoric of Social and Political Criticism in Central African Performing Arts." Paper delivered at the African Humanities Institute, Northwestern University.

Okolo, Bertram A. 1995. "Opening-Up Closings: Negotiating Settlements in Problematic Discourse Encounters." In *Discursive Strategies in Africa,* ed. Kwesi Yankah. Special issue of *Text: An Interdisciplinary Journal for the Study of Discourse* 15, no. 2: 191–208.

Omoniyi, Tope. 1995. "Song-Lashing as a Communicative Strategy in Yoruba Interpersonal Conflicts." In *Discursive Strategies in Africa,* ed. Kwesi Yankah. Special issue of *Text: An Interdisciplinary Journal for the Study of Discourse* 15, no. 2: 299–315.

Piersen, William D. 1977. "Puttin' down Ole Massa: African Satire in the New World." In *African Folklore in the New World,* ed. Daniel J. Crowley, 20–34. Austin: University of Texas Press.

Purchas-Tulloch, Jean A. 1976. "Jamaica Anansi: A Survival of the African Oral Tradition." Ph.D. dissertation, Howard University.

Rattray, R. S. 1930. *Akan-Ashanti Folk-Tales.* Oxford: Clarendon.

Salkey, Andrew. 1969. "Political Spider." In *Political Spider: An Anthology of Stories from Black Orpheus,* ed. Ulli Beier, 21–30. London: Heinemann.

Scott, James C. 1990. *Domination and the Arts of Resistance: Hidden Transcripts.* New Haven: Yale University Press.

Sherlock, Philip M. 1957. Introduction to *Anancy Stories and Dialect Verse,* ed. Louise Bennett, 11–14. Kingston: Pioneer.

Stokes, Randal, and John P. Hewitt. 1976. "Aligning Actions." *American Sociological Review* 41, no. 5: 838–49.

van der Geest, Sjaak, and N. K. Asante-Darko. 1982. "The Political Meaning of Highlife Songs in Ghana." *African Studies Review* 25: 27–35.

Yankah, Kwesi. 1985. "The Making and Breaking of Kwame Nkrumah: The Role of Oral Poetry." *Journal of African Studies* 12: 86–92.

———. 1989. *The Proverb in the Context of Akan Rhetoric: A Theory of Proverb Praxis.* New York: Peter Lang.

11

Voice, Authority, and Memory

THE KISWAHILI RECORDINGS OF SITI BINTI SAADI

Laura Fair

This chapter examines the music and career of Siti binti Saadi,[1] a famous *taarab* musician who performed in Zanzibar during the 1920s and 1930s. Taarab is a form of coastal east African music whose lyrics consist of Swahili poems. Relying on four distinctive types of evidence—her recorded music, written documentation produced in East Africa, interviews with men and women who heard her perform, and records of company executives—I compare perspectives on the source of the power and authority attributed to her voice as well as on the meaning of her music. Siti binti Saadi was the first East African to have her voice captured and reproduced on 78-rpm gramophone disks. The production of these records enhanced her status and imbued her voice with a sense of authority that it otherwise might never have attained. Written histories of taarab, particularly those authored in the 1950s and 1960s, often memorialize her as literally "giving voice to the voiceless," allowing the voice of East Africa to be heard internationally. In written accounts of Siti's music and career, her success as a published author is often credited with granting her the authority to speak. In oral accounts, however, Siti's songs are said to have power because they represent a composite of local voices and past historical events. Elderly men and women used these songs, whether recorded or not, to confer authority on themselves as interpreters of the words and as agents in the making of the history on which the songs were based.

According to oral sources, one can listen to Siti's recordings yet never hear what she is remembered for having said. Siti and her band recorded over 250 songs with various companies between 1928 and 1930 (Graebner 1989; Vernon 1995).[2] While this voice, captured and marketed across East Africa, sold extremely well, it did not represent "the truth" as recalled by elderly Zanzibaris. As with all texts, be they oral, written, or recorded, how the text was received and interpreted by an audience was just as important as the production of the text itself. Without comment from the artists *and audience* during the course of performance regarding the "deeper" meaning buried within the prose, or the social and political context from which the songs emerged, the lyrics, many contend, were meaningless (Fatma 1991; Mwajuma 1992; Muhamed 1991; Mwalim Idd 1991b; Nasra 1991; Mohamed 1992; Said 1992; Amina 1992). Far from seeing themselves as voiceless, these men and women often considered themselves coauthors of Siti's work. Siti's work relied on indirection, a form of speech in which the hearer's role is critical to creating meaning and defining how the texts as spoken are understood (Brenneis 1986). Without the context, analysis, and debate that the audience provided, a recorded voice was only so many words.

Perhaps not surprisingly, the songs preserved in recordings differ from those preserved in memory. The former, on their own, hint at only part of the story, while the latter often serve as a metaphor to which larger historical events and processes are attached. In interviews, Siti's songs were rarely recollected without commentary. Frequently a few lines from a song were accompanied by a much longer discussion of the class, gender, and political struggles in which Siti and her contemporaries were enmeshed in colonial Zanzibar.

SITI AS ICON

The early decades of the twentieth century were a period of large-scale social, economic, and political change. In 1895, some three-fourths of Zanzibar's population were either slaves or recently manumitted slaves, most of whom labored on clove plantations owned by the islands' Omani aristocracy (*Report of the Commission* 1923: 38; Christie 1876: 415–19; Sheriff 1987). In 1897, an abolition decree was passed in Zanzibar, and over the course of the next several decades former slaves gradually abandoned their status as social dependents and began demanding recognition of their place as independent members of island society (Cooper 1997; Fair 2001).

Siti's own biography parallels many of the larger transformations that occurred during this period. Siti binti Saadi was born in the countryside just outside of the town of Zanzibar, in the 1880s. Her given name, Mtumwa, translates literally as "slave" or "servant" and reflects the subordinate status into which she was born. In 1911, fourteen years after abolition, Mtumwa binti Saadi moved to the town of Zanzibar in search of better economic opportunities, greater personal autonomy, and a place to make a new start in life (Shaaban 1991: 8–11). Siti moved into an area of town known as Ng'ambo (literally "the other side"), the former residential quarter of urban slaves, which was separated by a tidal creek from Stone Town, where the elaborate stone homes of the Arab, Asian, and European ruling classes were located. Between 1890 and 1930, the size of Ng'ambo more than doubled, as tens of thousands of men and women like Siti abandoned the rural plantations and moved to town. However, as Mtumwa binti Saadi and others soon discovered, although the city certainly offered limited opportunities for enhanced autonomy, systems of class, ethnic, and gender oppression continued to structure their lives in fundamental ways.

During World War I, Siti's fame as a performer began to spread throughout Ng'ambo. Her popularity was rooted in her use of song to depict the joys and sorrows of daily life in Ng'ambo, as well as her willingness to use her performance to critique acts of injustice to which her friends and neighbors were subjected (Mwalim Idd 1991a; Fatma 1991; Hilal 1995; Mohamed 1992; Nasra 1991; Said 1992). Siti and the other members of her band lived, practiced, and performed in Ng'ambo, and the rumors and debates within the community frequently found their way into song (Fatma 1991; Nasra 1991; Amina 1992; Mohamed 1992; Said 1992). Poverty, the smug superiority of the Arab ruling class, and the injustices of British colonial courts filled the daily lives of Ng'ambo inhabitants as well as the songs of Siti's band.

While Siti is widely praised by her contemporaries for never forgetting where she came from (Hilal 1995; Fatma 1991; Mwajuma 1992), published accounts of her life frequently depict her as transcending her poor background—an icon representing the fulfilled dreams of an entire generation. The daughter of slaves from the countryside, Mtumwa became widely known in the 1920s by the title of "Siti" (Arabic "lady").[3] During this period her popularity spread beyond Ng'ambo, as she frequently performed religious and secular tunes at the weddings and celebrations of coastal East Africa's leading families. As one author wrote, "No occasion was deemed successful, be it a wedding or the celebration of a birth, amongst Zanzibar's elite, without Siti's performance" (Sheikh-Hashim 1988: 3). While her position at these events may have been interpreted by the elite as that of the singing slave girl, in the written folklore she is eulogized for hobnobbing with the most important members of coastal society. The financial rewards she earned for these performances were well beyond the dreams of most Ng'ambo residents. She received gifts of gold jewelry, silks, and embroidered cloth; the payment she received for one performance for these wealthy clients earned her more money than a typical urban laborer earned in a year (Shaaban 1991: 55–59; Nasra 1990; Sheikh-Hashim 1988: 3; Suleiman 1969; Whitely 1966: 4–5). At a time when many Ng'ambo residents were only welcomed in Stone Town as domestic laborers, Siti was invited into the inner rooms of the Sultan's palaces, where she dined and talked with the ruling family and their guests (Mgana 1991: 47–48; Shaaban 1991: 55–56; Jahadhmy 1966: 69, 98). Siti's presence amongst the elite and her growing wealth epitomized the transformative potential of the era. Her power as a cultural hero was enhanced when she was chosen, in 1928, as the first artist from East Africa to produce a gramophone recording (Suleiman 1969: 87; Mgana 1991: 47; Shaaban 1991: 45–48; Whitely 1966: 96).

THE POLITICS OF RECORDING THE AFRICAN VOICE

Through the late 1920s, the only commercial recordings available in East Africa were in the languages of India, Europe, and the Middle East. The Gramophone Company, the Asian and African arm of His Master's Voice (HMV), left the development of the East African trade to its Bombay branch. Local Asian traders were appointed to act as agents as well as sellers and promoters of gramophones and gramophone discs. In 1928, HMV's agent in Zanzibar, Abdulkarim Hakim Khan, persuaded the company to take a gamble on the production of records in Kiswahili, and he arranged for Siti and the other members of the band, Budda Swedi, Maalim Shaaban, and Mbaruk Talsam, to travel to Bombay to record. International recording companies were slowly awakening to the potential buying power of black audiences, and in the next few years records directed at previously ignored audiences were marketed across the globe.

The twenty-eight records (containing fifty-six songs) that were released from Siti's first session sold over twenty-three thousand copies by 1931 (EMI 1931: 4). Overwhelmed by its initial success, especially considering the fact that a paltry sixty-four rupees (approximately a hundred shillings) had been spent to advertise and promote these first recordings, HMV invited Siti and her band back to Bombay for another session in March 1929. On this second trip the band recorded another ninety-eight songs, which sold 40,666 copies over the next two years (EMI 1931: 5). The skyrocketing sales, as well as profits, being realized by HMV in East Africa prompted other recording companies to follow its lead and venture into previously unrecorded territory. By 1930, HMV, Odeon, Columbia, and Pathe were all recording in East Africa (Graebner 1989: 3; Vernon 1995: 26). Although HMV's sales dropped considerably in 1931, as a result of increasing competition and the Depression, by mid-1931 it had sold over seventy-two thousand records in East Africa, the vast majority of which were recordings of Siti binti Saadi, as well as a few other taarab performers.

From a marketing point of view, the decision to produce music recorded in Kiswahili appears to have been a wise one, since Kiswahili is and was the most widely spoken language in East Africa. As Werner Graebner (1989: 5) has argued, however, the practices of company executives were also influenced to a large extent by the ideas of colonial administrators and missionaries in East Africa, who promoted Kiswahili taarab because it was considered to be a more "developed" and "civilized" form of music than what they imagined African music to be. After the merger of HMV, Odeon, Pathe, and Columbia in 1931, the new company, EMI, sent a representative to East Africa to investigate the current state and future prospects of gramophone promotion. In his report, the agent proposed a continued emphasis on Kiswahili recording, arguing that Kiswahili possessed power as a lingua franca as well as prestige as a "vehicle of Arab ideas and civilization" (EMI 1931: 6). The EMI agent even went so far as to suggest that Kiswahili would ultimately replace the numerous other East African languages as the "natives" became "civilized" and adopted it as a symbol of their advancement.

Echoing European ideas of the day, which attributed the development of Kiswahili as well as of the Swahili people to the civilizing influence of Arabia, he saw Swahili music (in Kiswahili) as a refinement "on the original crude Native Music" through the influence of Arabic music. He concluded that this Arabic influence brought not only civilization to coastal East Africans, but creativity as well; Swahili music had definite commercial potential for the recording industry because Swahili culture, unlike that of other East African peoples, changed and developed over time. What the agent neglected to recognize, however, was that the Kiswahili-speaking peoples had many musics. The taarab genre, which dominated recording until after World War II, was only one of many musical possibilities.[4] Despite this, EMI and its predecessors accorded taarab singular authority as *the* Swahili voice.

EMI's conclusions regarding the quality and commercial promise of other languages and musics were not as positive as those for Swahili taarab. Though colonial and missionary informants from Mozambique to Uganda assured the agent that local musical genres were commercially viable, they warned of "native" music's "unhealthy," "immoral," and "crude" associations. The EMI agent took the company's responsibility to "uplift" and "civilize" seriously, and he suggested that any future development of the recording industry in East Africa must endeavor to educate the native as well as cater to his commercial and musical appetites. From a business standpoint, he also noted that "primitive African tribes," which he assumed to be culturally and musically stagnant, would "naturally" have a fairly limited repertoire of songs to record. While some peoples, like the Buganda, might be civilized enough to continually create new tunes, he did not favor investing company resources in recording the music of small, uncivilized, and static peoples (Graebner 1989: 5–7; EMI 1931: 7–12). It was really only after World War II that EMI began to experiment with recording a variety of East African music in languages such as Bunyore, Luo, Gikuyu, Luganda, and Nandi (Vernon 1995: 27; Graebner 1989: 8–16).

THE AUTHORITY OF VOICE

Only after reading the 1931 EMI report did I fully appreciate Siti's contemporaries' understanding of the politics of language in colonial East Africa, as well as of their own positionality within those battles. Numerous sources, both oral and written, stress the symbolic importance these Kiswahili recordings had in enhancing the self-esteem of Kiswahili speakers. Prior to Siti's 1928 recordings, the only gramophone records available in East Africa were in the languages of the economic and political overlords of the colonies. By recording in Kiswahili, Siti managed to elevate the status of Kiswahili, and thus of Kiswahili speakers, to that of one amongst equals (Sheikh-Hashim 1988: 4; Suleiman 1969: 87–88; Mwalim Idd 1991b; Fatma 1991; Said 1992; Nasra 1991). One man who spent a great deal of time in Siti's home as a youth suggested that these recordings symbolized "[t]he importance of Swahili as *one of the most advanced* African languages" (Suleiman 1969: 87). He and many other Zanzibaris interpreted the production of Siti's recordings as evidence of European and Asian recognition of their status as civilized beings—no small feat in the colonial world of the 1930s.

While sources both oral and written praise Siti binti Saadi's music, there are interesting differences in emphasis between the two. Written sources universally highlight the significance of her recordings, often defining the moment when she went to Bombay to record with HMV as the apex of her career (Suleiman 1969: 87; Shaaban 1991: 45–48; Sheikh-Hashim 1988: 4; Mgana 1991: 47; Whitely 1966: 6). Shaaban Robert, the famous Swahili poet, referred to her songs as "the pride of East Africa" and to her recordings as "a great light in the darkness," left to posterity (1991: 16). Aware of the ephemeral nature of the spoken word, these authors identify the act of recording with the ability to preserve. Imbued with the sense of the authority of authorship that often accompanies literacy, they also attributed a power to Siti as a creator that oral sources did not.

Many of these authors also applauded the ability of Siti's records to promote Zanzibari cultural imperialism. The commercial sale of Siti's voice helped to spread the dialect of Kiswahili spoken in Zanzibar, then also being promoted as "standard" by the British, across East Africa. These recordings were heralded by some as contributing "to the growth of the Swahili language [in a way that] can never be matched" (Sheikh-Hashim 1988: 4). Others claimed that the production of these recordings attuned fellow East Africans to the internationally recognized importance of Zanzibari culture. Shaaban Robert's 1956 biography proclaimed Siti's importance, and by extension that of Zanzibar:

> Her voice began to rumble like a drum in the air; praises of her spread like fire across a dry grassland. People of every age-group, men and women, in the villages and in towns, inside huts and stone homes, from the islands throughout the coast, everywhere in East Africa; they were taken by an overwhelming desire to talk about her.[5] (Shaaban 1991: 15)

Other authors echoed Shaaban's sentiments: "Once this voice was heard coming from a gramophone everyone started singing the songs, children, elders, women and men, everyone was singing. . . . Even beni bands started to copy taarab songs" (Whiteley 1966: 6). Whiteley implies that the commercial production of Siti's music transformed taarab into a musical lingua franca which other peoples quickly sought to adopt. However, Gramophone Company sales records indicate that such perceptions of upcountry enthusiasm for Zanzibari culture, language, and music were somewhat exaggerated (EMI 1931: 2, 7). The bulk of these recordings were purchased by people living along the coast. Kiswahili speakers, outside and even within Zanzibar, resisted company attempts to define *the* Swahili music. Taarab was fine as one form of music, but other musical genres continued to be performed and widely appreciated.

Yet commercial production of taarab did often exaggerate local perceptions of Zanzibar's position on the cutting edge of the regional social scene. Siti's captured voice symbolized Zanzibar's role as a force of modernization, argued Suleiman, spreading new technology, as well as taarab music, from Tanganyika to Uganda, Kenya, the Belgian Congo, Comoro, Somalia, and southern Arabia. He pointed to this as "a fine example of Swahili leadership" and even went so far as to praise Siti's records for returning Zanzibar to its former glory, giving new meaning to the old saying "When the pipes play in Zanzibar, they dance on the lakes" (Suleiman 1969: 88).

Elderly men and women whom I interviewed also referred to Siti's music with a great deal of pride. However, their emphasis was on the power of live performances rather than of commercially produced renditions. This emphasis may reflect sour grapes, as few of the people I interviewed lived in a household capable of affording a gramophone, let alone the monthly releases of new records, whose average cost was more than half the monthly salary of an unskilled urban laborer.[6] Of course, even those who could not afford to own the recordings had ample opportunity to hear them at the homes of friends and neighbors, or while sitting on the baraza of a favorite coffee shop. Having a gramophone and playing the new releases for others was a sign of status and modernity, and households with the financial means used the regular release of new records to amass social capital. What enhanced the status of even those without a gramophone was the fact that "one of their own" (i.e., poor, black, and Kiswahili-speaking) had been recorded, rather than one of the bands from Stone Town that sang in Arabic, the language of the island's aristocracy (Salum 1992; Fatma 1991; Said 1992; Nasra 1991; Mwalim Idd 1991b).

While written sources highlight Siti's significance in the arena of international cultural politics, oral sources focus almost exclusively on her role as an agent in local struggles. Similarly, while the former identify her as "giving voice to the voiceless," the later praise her for echoing what they were already saying. The memories of Siti that brought the most excitement to the faces of the elderly men and women whom I interviewed were of the lively debates that took place in Siti's home during practices and performances, and the impromptu way she could transform their talk into a song (Fatma 1991; Amina 1992; Said 1992; Muhamed 1991; Mwalim Idd 1991a; Mohamed 1992; Nasra 1991). Siti's home became one of the central gathering places in Ng'ambo in the 1920s and 1930s, where she joked, exchanged gossip, analyzed local politics, and absorbed new material for her songs.[7] The band's practices were open events. Siti and the other members of the band composed the poetry which formed the songs' lyrics, but they did this with feedback from the members of the community who were in attendance. Creation was not an individual act, according to oral sources, but a public and collective one. The power of her music was in the context of its creation—a process in which everyone took part—and not in the act of recording, where Siti was given sole credit as author (Mohamed 1992; Fatma 1991; Amina 1992; Said 1992; Muhamed 1991; Mwalim Idd 1991a; Nasra 1991, 1992).

RECORDED VS. REMEMBERED SONGS

Siti and her band recorded well over 250 songs on various labels (Graebner 1989: 3; Vernon 1995: 26).[8] Obviously, not all of these songs were memorable, nor were all of her most memorable songs recorded. An analysis of one hundred of these song texts reveals that some 60 percent of the band's music centered on issues of love, 2 percent on religion, and another 20 percent on a range of topics dealing with social and cultural life. The material for which Siti is most widely remembered—her trenchant criticisms of local class, gender, and colonial politics—made up less than a quarter of her published repertoire.[9] Company records that could provide greater insight into exactly what was recorded, how the material was selected, and whether or not it was subject to censorship by company or colonial officials are unavailable.[10] The available evidence does not permit me to state conclusively how representative these hundred songs are of the band's recorded or live music. What is abundantly clear, however, is that the songs which have stuck in people's minds over the last half-century are those that echoed either important personal experiences or events of major significance to the Ng'ambo community at large.

Sites of struggle between the urban poor and the forces of colonial power were numerous, yet two particularly explosive points of contestation were the courts and the jails. From the 1920s through the 1950s, crowds of angry residents brought court proceedings to a boisterous end or liberated neighbors from jail on numerous occasions. According to Ng'ambo residents, colonial "justice" was blind to the interests of the unpropertied (Zanzibar National Archives, AB 28/12; Said 1992; Adija Salum 1992; Adija Haji Simai 1992). Only by banding together and intervening on behalf of those wrongfully convicted could the poor protect their interests. Although verbal appeals to the state for fairness frequently fell on deaf ears, community debates over the meaning of justice found expression not only in jailbreaks, but in the songs of Siti's band as well. Many of these songs are still widely remembered, and their performance often serves to crystallize memories of the violent struggles which pitted the African poor against Asian and Arab property owners, as well as the colonial administration.

One such song, "Wala Hapana Hasara" (There is no loss), commemorated the conviction of Mselem bin Mohamed el-Khalasi, a wealthy and powerful Arab who was employed as a local colonial official. Mselem was renowned for using his position to deceive and exploit the poor. He was also despised for his work as a government informant during a particularly tumultuous period in the late 1920s, when Ng'ambo residents organized a ground rent strike which propelled them into numerous clashes with the state. For years Mselem had stolen the property of Zanzibar's poor and illiterate and never been punished by his British superiors. When he was later convicted for embezzling money from government accounts in order to finance his daughter's lavish wedding, many in Ng'ambo took his conviction as a vindication by God for the wrongs that he had committed against them. Mselem was sentenced to hard labor in the town's rock quarry, and Siti performed this song in honor of his fall. It is said that the song became so popular that a *kanga* (a cloth worn by coastal women) was even printed titled "Mselem's Rock," bearing a picture of Mselem carrying a rock on his head (Nasra 1992; Whiteley 1966: 101).

There Is No Loss

There is no pedigree, I am the child of so and so
A word like a sudden blow which burns in the chest
The name is yours, my man, and the rock is on your head.
    And the rock is on your head. . . .

You men should stop your oppression and stealing from the poor
Especially from those who are said to be the stupidest of the stupid
Forever their pen is ink upon the thumb[11]
    Is ink upon the thumb. . . .

It isn't right to pinch, to embezzle from the government
Their books are all open with each and every signature
Something from years ago can always be investigated.
    Can always be investigated. . . .

You people should not be deceived, this is mine, I should take it
A memento should be created so it doesn't leave their hearts
You clerks should be satisfied with what you are entitled to.
    With what you are entitled to. . . .

As one elderly woman suggested, this case evoked appreciation for the wit of the Lord's justice, which entrapped Mselem with the very forces that he had used to undermine the poor for years: affectation, literacy, theft, and the colonial courts (Adija Salum 1992).

Mselem's sentencing to hard labor represented a rare instance in which local and colonial notions of justice happened to coincide. More typically, argued one man, "the rich man, whose parents could buy him out, got off, while the poor man went to jail" (Said 1992). An analysis of court records from these decades indicates that women were particularly liable to lose their cases. In cases of rape and domestic abuse women were frequently told by European court officials that their own immoral behavior was the ultimate cause of their problems (Zanzibar National Archives, HC 3/, HC 4/, HC 8/). The commentary of Ng'ambo residents on the outcome of such cases was reflected in many of Siti's songs (Fair 2001). One such song, which is widely remembered and still occasionally performed by the women's taarab group Sahib el-Arry, is titled "Kijiti." It documents the rape and murder of a woman from Dar es Salaam who came to Zanzibar to visit friends in Ng'ambo. She was invited by neighbors for a night "out on the town," where she met her death at the hands of one of the men in the group, who was named Kijiti. The guilty man escaped from the police and ran to the mainland, while two women who had helped to organize the outing, as well as provide the alcohol for the occasion, were found guilty of the woman's death (some oral sources claim they were sentenced to hang) after testifying against Kijiti in court. This song suggests that not only were Ng'ambo residents aghast at the court's ruling, but they had their own ideas of the justice that might ultimately befall Kijiti.

Kijiti

Look you all, look at what Kijiti has done
To take a guest and play the game of chase with her
He went with her to the bush and brought her back as a corpse.

We left home, we did not ask for permission
Our alcohol in the bag, we took it with us
The dance is in Chukwani, death in Sharifmsa.

Kijiti said to me, "Come on girl, let's go!"
Oh, if only I had known I would have refused, I wouldn't have gone
Kijiti, you are killing me for a single shot of booze.

The judge was mad in his chair where he sat
And said, "You bloody fools!" to the witnesses of Kijiti
We put you in jail, Sumaili and K the daughter of Subeiti.

These things are amazing every time we look at them
Kijiti killed someone and in her stomach was a baby
Kijiti crossed the river, the witnesses have drowned.

Kijiti, I warn you, don't go to Dar es Salaam
You will meet an old man and he has worn a razor just for you
People are swearing about you, may God give you elephantiasis.

Songs about the colonial courts are not the only items in Siti's repertoire that are widely recalled, but I would suggest that they stand out in people's memories precisely because the courts were such an important battleground during the heyday of Siti's career. As the Ng'ambo ground-rent strike gained increasing momentum between 1925 and 1928, the courts were repeatedly called upon to enforce eviction notices on Ng'ambo tenants. In the space of one year, over five hundred eviction notices were served by two of Ng'ambo's more notorious landlords (examples are in Zanzibar National Archives AB 36/13, 36/22; AE 8/10). By March of 1928, as Siti and her band departed for their first recording engagement in Bombay, the ground-rent strike had become nearly universal. At demonstrations attended by hundreds of residents, angry crowds affirmed their commitment to protecting each other from the talons of "justice." They kept good on their promises. On at least five separate occasions in 1928, crowds of several hundred men and women freed friends and neighbors from the grip of the police, the courts, and even the jail (examples are in Zanzibar National Archives, AB 28/12). After more than a year of marches, demonstrations, and attacks on its institutions of "justice," the state finally ended up conceding to the crowds. Ground rents were reduced by an average of 50 percent and a moratorium was imposed on court actions by landlords against tenants in arrears (Zanzibar National Archives, AB 36/13, AB 36/22, AB 36/23, AE 8/19). Although songs about the colonial justice system make up less than 10 percent of the songs whose lyrics have been published, they figure very prominently in the memories of men and women who lived through this era.

Oral sources suggest that Siti binti Saadi was an important historical figure not because her voice was recorded and marketed from Zanzibar to Kinshasa, but rather because her songs reflected the lives, the ideas, and the struggles of their times. Despite the written claims of Zanzibari authors regarding the popularity of Siti's gramophone recordings across East Africa, Gramophone Company records indicate that her sales were mainly confined to the coast. Graebner (1989: 5) has suggested that one possible explanation for this is the nuanced and elusive nature of the lyrics of her songs. An additional answer can also be found in the fact that listeners in Lumbumbashi or Nairobi were most likely unaware of the local events and people who gave these songs their significance. Without context in which to evaluate the lyrics, the music lost much of its power to speak.

DONKEYS, RUPEES, AND METAPHOR

On 7 February 1936, Zanzibar was rocked by another series of violent events, which one elderly man referred to "as the war between the Omani Arabs [Wamanga] and the Europeans" (Mohammed 1992). By the end of this brief war, fought at the central market and lasting less than one day, the assistant district commissioner and the assistant inspector of police had been beheaded by sword-wielding Arabs and four Wamanga had been shot dead by colonial police (Said 1992; Annual Report of the Zanzibar Colony, 1936; Zanzibar National Archives, BA 106/15). Memories of these events, while basically "true," are in some instances more metaphorical than actual. Reflections on the place of Siti's music in the struggle also reveal the way in which her songs have sometimes served as hooks on which events have been hung in the closets of memory.

In January 1936, the East African shilling officially replaced the British Indian rupee and the Seyyidieh copper pice as the currency of Zanzibar. At the beginning of the following month, the produce inspectors at the port also began imposing much more stringent standards of quality on the copra being produced in Zanzibar and shipped overseas. According to one man, the war began when an Arab who was returning from the copra sheds stopped at the water trough near the market to give his donkey some water. While waiting, he made a necklace by stringing the new coins (which had holes in the center) together with some cord. He then adorned his donkey with his creation. A "big" European saw how the man had defaced the "Queen's" currency and ordered him to remove the necklace from the donkey. Before anyone knew what happened, the European had been hit with a sword (Mohammed 1992).

A second man, who was unlucky enough to be one of the policemen called to the market that day, recalled that the violence erupted when the district commissioner went to the water trough near the market and began forcing people in the vicinity to exchange their old rupees for the new shillings. He recalled that no one wanted the new currency, because of confusion over what it was worth (Said 1992). This confusion was exacerbated by the fact that the official exchange rate was calculated at ten cents (one-tenth of a shilling) to five pice, yet ten cents were being exchanged for only four pice. People were no longer sure what anything was worth, but they were certain that they were being cheated every time they went to the market (Zanzibar National Archives, BA 106/15). When the district commissioner tried to force the Arabs gathered at the market to exchange their rupees and pice for shillings, they resisted. When he became increasingly adamant, they pulled out their swords and slaughtered him, "just like a chicken" (Said 1992).

The official report of the Commission of Enquiry makes mention of the changeover in currency, but concludes that the riots were primarily caused by the Wamanga's inability to sell their inferior copra, as well as their "wild, ungoverned and turbulent nature." In the days before the outbreak of "the war," over a hundred Wamanga had had their copra rejected by the inspectors. To make matters worse, their bags of sub-grade copra were also confiscated, allegedly to keep them from returning again with the same goods. Over fifteen hundred bags of copra were confiscated, leading many of these men to conclude that this was a further attempt by the government to "rip them off" and get their copra without paying for it (BA 106/15). While these men owned land, most of them lived fairly marginal economic lives. Their bags of sub-grade copra may have been deemed worthless by the agricultural authorities, but they represented months of hard work to them. They had brought their produce to town, not by car or lorry, but by walking five, ten, or fifteen miles while leading a donkey cart. The official report suggests that the violence began at the inspection sheds and only gradually spread out to the central market, not because markets and money were at the core of the dispute, but because the water trough served as a gathering place for "idle" Wamanga "lazing" in town before their trip back home. If only the Wamanga were more industrious and put more time into drying their copra, they could have easily met the new standards, it concludes.

However, ultimately, this war really was about money. New produce standards and confusing exchange rates combined to ensure decreasing earnings for rural producers. It is thus not surprising that the memories of these two men focused more on the coins—whether adorning donkeys or forcibly exchanged—and the marketplace, where these dynamics of unequal exchange were most apparent, than on soggy, sub-grade copra. After relating how events unfolded at the market, leading up to the slaughter of the police inspector, Said Mohamed continued,

> At that time there was an artist, a musician, named Siti binti Saadi . . . who sang taarab. She was acclaimed throughout Zanzibar for her wonderful songs. She had a song, "Goodbye rupee, goodbye rupee, you are being sent away. These new coins have no value, they are pieces of tin stamped from metal cooking pots." The colonial government hated this song; the government was furious at being disrespected in this way. "Goodbye rupee, goodbye rupee, you are being sent away. These new coins have no value, they are pieces of tin stamped from metal cooking pots." The government detested this song! So they gave an order, if the police heard this song coming from inside your house they should break down your door, smash your gramophone, bring you to court, and sentence you to a two-thousand-shilling fine. But the song continued to be played.

I had gone to Said's house to interview him neither about copra riots nor about Siti binti Saadi. I left charged by his fascinating stories and amazed at the ability of this man, well into his eighties, to recall names, dates, and wage rates with an accuracy that neither I nor any other informants could come close to. Nonetheless, I was also highly skeptical of his version of the copra riots. Could the district commissioner and the inspector of police really have been beheaded at the market? The next day I ordered the 1936 Annual Report at the archives and discovered that the assistant district commissioner and the assistant inspector of police had in fact been murdered in the course of a riot by Manga Arabs.[12]

I was also reluctant to accept at face value the image of police breaking into people's homes and smashing their gramophones. I knew that the Zanzibari police at this time were neither that bold nor that committed. And could a song, as amusing as it was, really have been that important? It was only while writing this paper that I came to believe that this part of Said Mohamed's story was more fiction than fact. These events took place in 1936, six years after the last documented recording of Siti's music. There is a slim chance that she may have recorded with Columbia in Zanzibar in 1937 or 1938, and that this song may have been amongst those recorded, but this does not seem very likely. If there was no record, then there would be no reason for breaking down people's doors, smashing their gramophone players, and hauling them off to jail.

It appears as though Said's memory of "Kwa Heri Rupia" (Goodbye rupee) conflates the role of Siti's music as a vehicle for reflecting the events of the time and the effect of the recordings themselves in preserving her songs. In Said's memory, and I would suggest in the memories of many others, Siti's music and her records become a metaphor for the times. The song itself doesn't invoke the violence that accompanied the new standards for copra or the change in currency, but that violence is projected onto the song through Said's memory of police recklessly smashing the gramophone players that were playing her tune. The raised copra standards were also as difficult to meet, from the perspective of rural producers, as the exorbitant fines imposed on those playing the tune in Said's recollection of events. The record, whether it existed or not, embodies all that the song implied. At the same time, however, the focus on the recorded version of the song decenters Siti as both a subject and an object in this violence. Said's memory focuses instead on widespread involvement of hundreds of people, who continued to play the record even though the song was "banned," in the riots. The police were not beating up Siti, but they were attempting to silence those who played "Kwa Heri Rupia."

Comparing Said's memories of events at the market in February 1936 with those of Mohammed Ali, more commonly known as Mzee Jahare, drew me to consider other aspects of their accounts as metaphor, as well. Following orders from their European superior, the Zanzibari police opened fire on the men at the market, killing four and seriously wounding three others, resulting in one of the largest uses of deadly force by police in the history of twentieth-century colonial Zanzibar. According to Jahare Mohammed, Zanzibari men who were members of the police force were later so afraid and ashamed to walk the streets that they borrowed *buibui* (veils worn by coastal East African women, which cover them from head to ankle) from female friends and relatives near the market so that they could safely make their way back home. For a period after the riots, local policemen left their homes to report for duty only under the cover of buibui, and once assigned they quickly went off to hide until their shift was over (Mohammed 1992). There are several accounts of earlier moments in Zanzibar's history when men used the cover of buibui to escape from danger, so, while I found this anecdote

both amusing and somewhat odd, I did not completely dismiss it as "untrue."
I don't really "know" if policemen covered themselves with buibui and I
never had the chance to put the question directly to Said. However, my interview with Said suggests that Jahere's larger point, for which the buibui becomes a literal cover, is, in at least some instances, quite accurate. Although
Said made no mention of either he or his fellow officers wearing veils, in the
course of a rather long and embellished discussion of events that day at the
market he completely avoided any reference to his own involvement either
in the shootings or the violence which followed. Whether he donned a buibui
or not, this was apparently something he preferred to keep under cover.

   This examination of the recorded music of Siti binti Saadi, as well as of
the memories of her songs and her career, suggests that the "capture" and
production of her music did in fact grant her an authority, at least in the
minds of some, that she might otherwise never have attained. I hope I have
illustrated, however, that the ultimate source of this authority, as well as its
meaning, was highly contested. Texts—even if erroneously produced and
marketed internationally as the authentic "civilized" voice—have value as
sources to be argued with and against. Local agents continue to use Siti's
songs as metaphors, as tools with which they recall and construct their own
versions of Zanzibar's pasts. Elderly men and women who lived through
these times frequently draw on Siti's songs as mnemonics of memory, triggers that allow them to see and hear the struggles and debates of the times.
While aspects of what is revealed about the past might seem rather far-
fetched at first glance, these strange and grandiose stories can perhaps provide rare insights into discourses of power, discourses that might otherwise
be left entirely out of recorded history.

NOTES

   An earlier version of this essay appeared as "Music, Memory, and Meaning: The
Kiswahili Recordings of Siti bint Saad," *Swahili Forum* 5 (1998). It is published here
with permission.
   1. Readers unfamiliar with Swahili may find the use and citation of names difficult
to follow. Swahili names do not easily translate into first and last names, or family
names, the way Western names do. Thus Amina Aboud has the given name "Amina"
followed by her father's name, "Aboud," although her siblings may not all use Aboud
as their second name. Given names, however, are not always the names individuals
use throughout their lives, and the line between a given name and a nickname is
indistinct. "Siti binti Saadi" means, literally, "lady, daughter of Saadi." This was the
name she used as an adult instead of her given name, Mtumwa binti Saadi, which
means "slave (or servant), daughter of Saadi." She was called Siti by almost everyone,
however; not because she was famous, but because she was known by her first name,
as were most people on the East African coast. I have tried to use both Swahili and
Western practices of citation when each is appropriate, so that, for example, the author and poet Shaaban Robert is referred to as Shaaban in parenthetical citations,

just as Amina Aboud is cited as Amina. However, because the Library of Congress catalogues authors by their second name, Shaaban Robert is listed under "Robert" in the bibliography.

2. The band recorded 250 songs with the Gramophone Company over the course of three successive annual sessions. According to an EMI report, Odeon and Columbia also recorded the band in 1930, though it appears that they recorded many of the same songs, with variations (EMI 1931: 16). This report is identified by Graebner as having been written by H. Evans, a representative of EMI, which was formed in 1931. I am extremely grateful to Werner Graebner for his generosity in sharing his research findings (Graebner 1989) and directing me to obscure and difficult-to-find company records. I am also thankful to Janet Topp Fargion for providing me with a copy of EMI's 1931 "Review of the Present Vernacular Record Trade." See also Vernon 1995.

3. Many sources argue that she was given this title by a member of the island's landed gentry impressed by her knowledge of religious music and her pronunciation of Arabic (Sheikh-Hashim 1988; Hilal 1991; Mwalim Idd 1991a). Khatib (1992: 15) contests this account, arguing that it was in fact her fans who changed her name, because she was no longer a slave but a lady, the equivalent of the female members of the aristocracy. Mgana (1991: 35) adds a further twist, arguing that the word "siti" simply refers to any female singer. Certainly in the post-independence period this has become the case.

4. Graebner 1989 includes an extensive analysis of East African recorded music by language and genre from 1928 to 1963.

5. This and all other translations from Kiswahili are my own. In some cases I have strayed from the literal translation in order to more accurately convey a meaning as it might be understood in English.

6. Records in East Africa were priced at one shilling, nine and a half pence (1/9½) each, although Suleiman says that prices in Zanzibar ranged from 4/50 to 7/50, depending on popularity and public demand. Rather than release all of the records at once, the companies released ten or so each month, thereby sustaining sales over the course of the year. At this time the average monthly wage for unskilled laborers working in town was thirty shillings. See EMI 1931: 4–5; Vernon 1995: 26; Suleiman 1969: 88; Zanzibar Colony Blue Books 1930–32.

7. The historical importance of her music as a venue for communicating the issues and concerns of the Ng'ambo community was memorialized, in 1988, by the Tanzania Media Women's Association (TAMWA), which chose to name the nation's first feminist popular journal *Sauti ya Siti* (The voice of Siti), in commemoration of her work as a journalist in an oral genre. What is perhaps more significant is the fact that the journal's founders, who were barely learning to walk when Siti died in 1950, were introduced to the importance of her songs through the memories and unrecorded voices of their elders. See Alloo 1988: 1; Sheikh-Hashim 1988; Nasra 1991, 1992.

8. The lyrics of one hundred of these songs were published by Whiteley in 1966. I have managed to collect the music and lyrics of another thirty-five from sources in Zanzibar.

9. This analysis is based on the one hundred song texts published by Whiteley. Categorizing these songs was in some instances an entirely subjective call on my part. In addition, a large portion of the songs which I placed in the "love" category actually provide a very pointed critique of gender and sexual relationships.

10. Available records give no hint whatsoever regarding these matters as they relate to the band's recordings. EMI records from the 1930s, as mentioned above, do make numerous references to the importance of carefully selecting "vernacular" material for recording, and ensuring that it is not of an immoral nature. Both Graebner and Vernon suggest that censorship, particularly in Kenya and Uganda, was a prominent

concern by the 1940s and especially after the declaration of the Mau Mau emergency. EMI apparently had employees in Nairobi whose job it was to translate lyrics, assess their suitability, and make recommendations regarding publication. By the 1950s, Graebner argues, this task became so difficult that company and radio executives in Kenya decided to simply ignore local music and promote Swahili music from the Congo instead. Graebner also hints that censorship of "offensive" music may have been in place from at least 1931, since Columbia's session in Dar es Salaam that year, which was intended to capture the most popular local music, included not a single recording of *beni,* a musical form which we know was extremely popular. See Graebner 1989: 9–16; Vernon 1995: 27.

11. A reference to the practice of requiring the illiterate to place their thumbprint on written documents to indicate their acceptance of the contract. This practice was detested by many in Ng'ambo, because written documents were often quite different from what they had verbally agreed to. See Zanzibar National Archives, AB 14/67, AB 14/68.

12. Those killed were Assistant District Commissioner I. H. D. Rolleston and Assistant Inspector Camur-un-deen of the Zanzibar Police (PRO CO 618/66/3: Erection of Headstones for Officers Killed in 1936 Riots; Margaret Irving Papers, Rhodes House, Oxford Mss. Afr. S. 816).

BIBLIOGRAPHY

Interviews by the Author

Adija Salum, 23 March 1992.
Adija Haji Simai, 3 February 1992.
Amina Aboud, 13 January 1992.
Fatma binti Baraka (Bibi Kidude), 30 September 1991.
Hilal Amour Seif, 15 July 1995.
Mohamed Salum, 26 June 1992.
Mohammed Ali (Mzee Jahare), 9 June 1992.
Muhamed Seif Khatib, 24 February 1991.
Mwajuma Ali, 26 April 1992.
Mwalim Idd Farahan, 24 September 1991a and 23 December 1991b.
Nasra Mohamed Hilal, 28 August 1991 and 14 July 1992.
Said Mohamed, 25 March 1992.
Salum Baraka Said, 13 July 1992.

Records in the Zanzibar National Archives

AB 14/67: Moneylenders Decree, 1927–55.
AB 14/68: Native Mortgages to Moneylenders, 1930–31.
AB 28/12: Demonstration by Native Hut Owners against Payment of Ground Rent on January 11, 1929.
AB 36/13: Ground Rent Restriction Decree.
AB 36/22: Ground Rents.
AB 36/23: Procedure Regarding Compensation Paid to Hut Owners in Ngambo in Relation to Ground Rent Due Them.
AE 8/10: Land at Mlandege Claimed by Gulamhussein Remtulla Hemani.
AE 8/19: Claim over Land at Kisimamajongo by M. H. Taria Topan.

BA 106/15: Report of the Commission of Enquiry Concerning the Riot in Zanzibar on the Seventh of February, 1936.

HC 3/ High Court Civil Cases.

HC 4/ High Court Criminal Cases.

HC 8/ The Sultan's Court.

Published and Unpublished Manuscripts

Alloo, Fatma. 1988. "Umuhimu wa Kuwa na Gazeti la Wanawake Nchini" (The importance of a magazine for the women of the country). *Sauti ya Siti* 1, no. 1: 1.

Brenneis, Donald. 1986. "Shared Territory: Audience, Indirection, and Meaning." *Text* 6, no. 3: 9–47.

Christie, James. 1876. *Cholera Epidemics in East Africa, from 1821 till 1872.* London: Macmillan.

Cooper, Frederick. 1997. *From Slaves to Squatters: Plantation Labor and Agriculture in Zanzibar and Coastal Kenya, 1890–1925.* 1980. Reprint, Portsmouth, N.H.: Heinemann.

EMI. 1931. "Review of Present Vernacular Record Trade." Unpublished manuscript in the possession of Janet Topp, London.

Fair, Laura. 2001. *Pastimes and Politics: Culture, Community, and Identity in Post-abolition Urban Zanzibar, 1890–1945.* Athens: Ohio University Press.

Graebner, Werner. 1989. "The First Thirty-Five Years of Commercial Recording in East Africa, 1928–1963." Paper delivered at the Institute of African Studies, University of Nairobi.

Khatib, Muhammed Seif. 1992. *Taarab Zanzibar.* Dar es Salaam, Tanzania: Tanzania Publishing House.

Mgana, Issa. 1991. *Jukwaa la Taarab Zanzibar.* Helsinki: Mediafrica.

Nasra, Mohamed Hilal. 1990. *Siti binti Saad.* Video documentary. Produced by the Tanzania Media Women's Association (TAMWA), Dar es Salaam, Tanzania.

Report of the Commission on Agriculture. 1923. Zanzibar: Government Printing Office.

Robert, Shaaban. 1991. *Wasifu wa Siti binti Saad.* 1956. Reprint, Dar es Salaam, Tanzania: Mkuki na Nyota.

Shaaban, Robert. 1991. *See* Robert, Shaaban.

Sheikh-Hashim, Leila. 1988. "Siti's Magnetic Voice." *Sauti ya Siti* 1, no. 1: 3–4.

Sheriff, Abdul. 1987. *Slaves, Spices, and Ivory in Zanzibar: Integration of an East African Commercial Empire into the World Economy, 1770–1873.* London: James Currey.

Suleiman, A. A. 1969. "The Swahili Singing Star Siti binti Saad." *Swahili* 39, no. 1: 87–90.

Vernon, Paul. 1995. "Feast of East." *Folk Roots* (July), 26–27, 29.

Whiteley, W. H., ed. 1966. *Waimbaji wa Juzi.* Dar es Salaam, Tanzania: Chuo cha Uchunguzi wa Lugha ya Kiswahili.

Zanzibar Colony. 1937. Annual report, 1936. Zanzibar: Government Printer.

———. 1930–32. Blue books. Zanzibar: Government Printer.

12

In a Nation of White Cars . . . One White Car, or "A White Car," Becomes a Truth

David William Cohen

On 17 February 1990, the *Daily Nation* (Nairobi) reported on the search for the missing Kenyan Minister of Foreign Affairs Robert Ouko and the subsequent discovery of his mutilated body. *Nation* reporter Catherine Gichero related various leads:

> Unconfirmed reports said that a car of an unknown make, but white in colour, was seen at the end of the driveway leading to the [Oukos'] farmhouse early on Tuesday morning, apparently at the same time that Dr Ouko went missing. No one could confirm the report but police sources said they were investigating the information.

More specifically, in the same article, the *Daily Nation* reported that it had

> learned that a woman, who was at the house when Dr Ouko disappeared, found the front door of the main house open when she woke up on Tuesday morning.
> The woman, believed to be the housekeeper, was identified as Selina. She was, however, told not to talk to the Press by family members, who said: "She has been interviewed and questioned so many times that there is nothing she can tell you." (3)

Within a few days, the Kenyan news media had connected these two narrative segments, thenceforward attributing the sighting of a white car in the driveway to the Oukos' housekeeper at the Koru farm, Selina Ndalo Were.

The Weekly Review (Nairobi), in its 23 February 1990 edition, provided a more detailed account, based on an interview with Selina (referred to as "Aoko" in the story) by a *Weekly Review* team. The interview was conducted in "the large well-furnished sitting-room" of the Oukos' Koru farmhouse.

> She [Selina Ndalo Were] recounts that, at around 3 o'clock on Tuesday morning, she was woken up by the sound of a door banging shut, coming from the direction of the late minister's bedroom. She got up a little later, preparing to make a cup of tea for Ouko as usual, in case he intended to leave at that early hour. After a while, hearing no further sounds from the direction of his

bedroom, she says she decided to go out to check on whether *Japuonj* [Ouko] had already left the house. It was then, she says, that she saw a white car turning and driving away on the main road—which on a clear night, may well be visible from the front of the house, as far as *The Weekly Review* staff could tell. An even better view of the road can be gathered from the entertainment hut which is built in front of the main house, closer to the road (10–11).

Following the announcement of the discovery of Robert Ouko's body, Selina Ndalo Were's observation of a white car acquired the status of the last known sighting of the living Robert Ouko, Kenya's Minister of Foreign Affairs and International Cooperation. The question of when, and to whom, Selina Ndalo Were first disclosed her observation has itself become a matter of debate . . . but what Selina Ndalo Were saw, what she said she saw, and what others heard and claimed she said that she saw came to constitute an important—perhaps *the*—centerpiece of months and years of debates, investigations, and deliberations involving the still unsolved questions of how Robert Ouko died, at whose hand, at what place, and for what reason.

The material considered here is largely drawn from the proceedings of the Judicial Commission of Inquiry into the Disappearance and Death of John Robert Ouko in Kenya in 1990 and 1991. The material opens views not only of the procedures and protocols of evaluation and critique of the commission itself—as an "authoring institution"—but also of a range of interrogative and discursive sessions (referenced in the commission proceedings) in which "voice" is variously authorized or authenticated, critiqued, examined, and evaluated. The specific focus of this reading is a purported "eyewitness account" of one individual . . . but more particularly how this specific eyewitness account achieved standing and centrality in a long and complex murder investigation.

This reading is then, essentially, an inquiry as to how, within a complex of interrogative settings, an observation, or alleged observation—transformed into a statement through oral testimony—acquired and maintained standing, influence, and the status of "truth."[1] It is also about the power of incomplete and unfinished accounts, the power of intermediate and indeterminate knowledge, and the power not so much of "a truth" or "the truth" but of, rather, *a claim to truth.*

❀ ❀ ❀

Selina Ndalo Were's report of "a white car" between midnight and dawn on the thirteenth of February, 1990, is but one data point along a trajectory of events, situations, conditions, and observations, subject to the several Ouko investigations. This trajectory stretches back into the early 1980s and, as far as the Judicial Commission of Inquiry was concerned, reaches forward into the time of the commission's own work. In respect to the expertise and experience that Selina Ndalo Were herself brought before the commission, her testimony regarding "a white car" attended to but one item among many observations extending back to the weeks before Robert Ouko's disappearance and forward to the time of her appearance before the commission. But her observation of a white car gained an immense life of its own.

As noted above, on the very day Ouko's body was found, Ouko family members pointed out that Selina "has been interviewed and questioned so many times that there is nothing she can tell you." They could hardly have imagined that, over the next thirty-six months, Selina Ndalo Were would give numerous statements to various investigating agencies—the Kenya Special Branch, the Kenya Police, the New Scotland Yard investigation led by Detective Superintendent John Troon, and the Judicial Commission of Inquiry (where she testified for eight days, beginning her testimony on 13 February 1991 and concluding on 23 February). Nor could they anticipate that her statements would draw attention for another three years, during the unsuccessful prosecution of Jonah Anguka (Anguka 1998) for the murder of Robert Ouko. Nor could they have imagined that references to, and appropriations of, her observations would carry significance within the testimonies of dozens of other "witnesses."[2] Nor could they have foreseen that her observations, as presented in testimony, would become talismanic . . . that the worth and truth of the testimony of others would be evaluated in regard to its conformity with the testimony of Selina Ndalo Were.

Familiarly referred to as "Selina," Selina Ndalo Were acquired celebrity status in the press. During the thirteen months of the Judicial Commission of Inquiry, and the many subsequent months of the murder trial, headlines frequently announced her presence at the core of the inquiries, whether she was on the witness stand or not. On 8 November 1990 the *Daily Nation*, referring to "Day 14" of the proceedings, captured one witness's extensive testimony with the headline "Selina saw a white car moving—Otieno." This was the first of many headline references to "Selina" in the *Daily Nation*. On certain days the reports of Selina Ndalo Were's testimony were front-page news in the *Daily Nation*, paralleling and at times eclipsing reports of the Gulf War: for example, on 16 February 1991, the paper began the coverage of the previous day's proceedings at the top of page one, under the headline "Selina: I heard banging doors, then saw white car." Below this story, the *Nation* had its day's story on the Gulf War, under the headline "Saddam offers to quit Kuwait but . . ."

✲ ✲ ✲

When Selina Ndalo Were first disclosed what she observed that night,[3] and during her early reiterations of her first statements, she probably did not comprehend the extraordinary singularity of her knowledge, the powerful and perhaps dangerous uniqueness of her observational position, and the remarkable centrality that her eyewitness account, however brief her observation, would attain in the elaboration of investigations, inquiries, and narratives regarding Robert Ouko's "disappearance" on the night of 12–13 February and his death.

The presence and the force of Selina's words—of her observations as rendered into words by herself and by others speaking for her and about her—are constituted in a field of tensions between, on the one hand, the very singularity of her account and of her observational position and, on the other, the contingent embeddedness of her experience amidst the broader folds of Kenyan life and Kenyan society in the last decades of the twentieth century: between the voice that stands alone and the voice that makes sense and has credibility only within its broader resonances. Indeed, the evaluations of Selina Ndalo Were's observation of "a white car" or "the white car"—the standing of her account among various interested audiences—searched for substantiation in the credibility and groundedness of Selina's own accounts of her everyday farm and household routines amidst the complicated schedules of the Oukos' public and private lives, and in the interplay of her accounts with those of other Ouko employees and of Ouko family members and friends who interacted with her at the farm and via the telephone. As other Ouko employees, friends, and family members testified about the activities of various parties both before and after Robert Ouko's disappearance on 12–13 February, Selina Ndalo Were's account became the reference point by which their testimony was evaluated.[4]

More subtly, the evaluations of Selina's observations, of her interests, and of her credibility are grounded in less fully explicated, even less speakable, understandings in Kenya of the relations of work, household, and family appropriate to an "enterprise" as complex and multistranded as the Oukos' public and private realms, which comprised residences, property, offices, businesses, bank accounts, cars, trucks, tractors, cattle, poultry, sugar cane, school fees, investments, accountants, family responsibilities, civic interests, political organizations and political supporters, farm, business, and government employees, personal secretaries and personal assistants, colleagues, friends, advisors, and patrons in Kenya and abroad. More than a decade ago, E. S. Atieno Odhiambo and I brought attention (1989: 53–56) to "a new Luo habitus," a way of living in the sugar belt in western Kenya in which civil servants and professionals put sugar on their land by telephone while traveling to their farms at the weekends to establish a third life: neither in Nairobi and its suburbs nor in the birth "home" in the old Luo homelands, but rather in these new freehold spaces, which have been termed "the Kenyatta Bequest." The Oukos' Koru farm was and is a perfect example. In *Siaya*, we noted that

> what the proprietors usually find is that the telephone brings them news that planting, cutting, transport and the work force on their lands are badly disarranged. Many have come to see the absentee farm as unlikely to succeed, but the farm remains for most an avocation, and in some senses is being trans-

ferred slowly from fully productive land, to a reserve for precious capital, to new status, and to a new locus for living. (1989: 55)

This was where Robert Ouko spent his last living hours, and the Oukos' exemplary farm at Koru was only two or three kilometers from the site where his body was found. So, of the thousands of pages of testimony and reportage from the investigations into the death of Robert Ouko, a great part revolves around the spatial dimensions of the last hours of Robert Ouko's life, the activities of members of his immediate and extended family, of his friends and visitors, and of the thirteen or fourteen employees at his farm in Koru in the heart of this sugar belt. Selina Ndalo Were was one of the Oukos' key employees at the Koru farm, frequently on the phone to Nairobi receiving instructions from Mr. and Mrs. Ouko regarding the management of their household.

○ ○ ○

In "a nation of white cars," Selina Ndalo Were's observation of one white car gripped the attention of multiple publics, and it was especially arresting to the chief of the New Scotland Yard investigative team in Kenya. On 28 September 1990, soon after Superintendent Troon had personally handed the New Scotland Yard team's final report to Kenya's Attorney General, the *Weekly Review* commented,

> The white car which was seen at Ouko's Koru home late the night the late minister disappeared is another mystery. On several occasions during the 110-day investigation, Troon publicly appealed to the driver and the occupants of the car to contact his team at their base at the Sunset Hotel in Kisumu, but it is not certain if anybody ever did. At one point, late in the investigations, Troon lamented that it was regrettable that despite his numerous appeals, neither the driver nor the occupants of the car had contacted him. The car may form an important chapter in the Troon report, given that he seemed to have been preoccupied with it for quite some time. (8–9)

More than a year later, during examination before the Judicial Commission of Inquiry, now-former Superintendent John Troon put the issue in his own words. In responding to a question from commission member Justice Aki-lano Akiwumi concerning whether the car that Selina reported she saw might have been there innocently, Troon offered,

> My lords, my experience has always been on these matters that if the appropriate appeal goes in the Press requesting assistance in a murder case, usually there is a positive response. In this particular case, I would have expected that if that vehicle and its occupants were innocently there at the Minister's farm that morning with nothing to hide, the occupants of the car would have come forward and declared their interests. (*Daily Nation,* 12 November 1991, 16)

This is not the only moment in his testimony and under examination when Troon attempted to unveil or articulate his methodology for establishing confidence in a particular observation or assertion. However, this is certainly the most interesting of Troon's methodological discursions, for in establishing the basis of his confidence that "the white car" was not innocently on the Oukos' drive on the night of 13 February, Troon erased any contingency or conditionality in Selina's observation.

The next day, under questioning from commission counsel Bernard Chunga, Troon not only restated his "method" but underlined his conviction that the car which Selina reported she observed was directly involved in the disappearance of the minister.

> *Chunga:* It was (Selina) Ndalo's evidence that she did not see the vehicle stop; she did not see anybody get into or out of the car; she did not see the Minister around the compound at the moment and she did not see the occupants of that vehicle at all, were you aware of these factors?
> *Troon:* Yes, I understand. At the point where the vehicle disappeared from her view, according to later experiments, is the junction where the vehicle turned down to Got Alila Hill. She would not have known that because she could not see it. The other matter is that the vehicle corresponds with her evidence of hearing a noise like a door being slammed and, some few minutes later, seeing the vehicle proceeding up the path, which, in my view, the obviously logical explanation is that the Minister left his farm at that moment of time and was either voluntarily or involuntarily placed in the car. I am convinced that he left the farm in that vehicle that morning. . . .
> *Chunga:* Now that I have put the four factors of Selina's evidence to you, would they affect your opinion that the vehicle transported the Minister?
> *Troon:* No, because I am convinced that the Minister left in that vehicle. There is no other logical explanation as to why the vehicle was there. As I mentioned yesterday, if it was innocently there, the persons responsible would have come forward as a result of my appeal through the media. (*Daily Nation,* 13 November 1991, 14)

Selina's observation was not only a piece of Troon's evidence; it had, by November 1991, reconstituted itself as the means through which Troon could discover the intentions of an unknown number of unseen individuals in a vehicle of unknown make, year, and registration.

In his official report, his additional testimony, and his examination before the Judicial Commission of Inquiry, we can not only observe Troon's methods in his own words, but understand the implicit logical apparatus—or some of the problematics of logic—in his approach to evidence, in his interpretative practice. Selina's report of a sound like a door being slammed was, at some points in his testimony and examination, an integral part of Troon's hearing of, and support for, Selina's account of "a white car" on the drive. But Troon and other members of his team, as reported in *The Standard*

(8 November 1991, 14–15), undertook an experiment on the farm on the night of 22 February 1990, in which they asked Selina to remain in or near her room and indicate with her raised arm whether a specific sound—and they tried a number of different sounds—resembled the one that she claimed to have heard on the night of 12–13 February. The Scotland Yard team reported that the sound that she identified most closely was not a door slamming but rather a gunshot. So, while associating Selina's idea that she heard a door slamming with the observation of a car a few moments later, Troon knew that she had herself, in a blind experiment, identified the sound of a gunshot, not a door slamming, as the sound she heard.

From the present "privileged observational position" accorded by time and distance, we can also observe what might be reckoned a "progression" from "a white car" to "the white car": the transcendence of difference between the Kenya press's references in February 1990 to Selina's observation of "a white car" and the mid-November 1991 references to "the white car" and "that vehicle" in the testimony of the head of the New Scotland Yard team.

Ultimately, it became clear that Selina Ndalo Were's observation of "a white car" on the Ouko drive on 12–13 February 1990 was singular; no other claim of sighting "a white car" or "the white car" gathered or maintained any credibility or authority across the several years of investigation of Ouko's disappearance and death. Indeed, in a quixotic way, the authority and credibility of Selina's account managed to sustain itself against, and through its sustained opposition to, an essentially corroborative account by Administrative Policeman Agalo Obonyo, who initially claimed to have observed "the white car" or "a white car" from a different position on the Oukos' farm. At different times and in different fora, Obonyo asserted that he saw "a white car" or "the white car"; acknowledged that he did not see "a white car"; admitted to lying about seeing the car, or a car; claimed to have only *said* that he saw a white car but not that he actually saw it; denied saying that he saw the white car; argued that he was "only following Selina's story"; and claimed that Selina told him to say that he had seen a white car.[5]

∘ ∘ ∘

One may project onto or into the records within and surrounding the five investigations of Ouko's disappearance and death an almost palpable tension between an assurance that one is close to understanding what happened and a need for still more foundation (evidence, testimony, coherent accounts) as to what actually happened. Whether one is considering the judicial process or the wider terrains in which the judicial process is seated and surveilled, a critical distinction is realized between a readiness to fill in, or construct, *a* narrative and the challenge of constituting *the* narrative. Selina's singular report of "a white car" on the drive became the central fixture in the forensic narrative of Ouko's disappearance. The car was as necessary to the constitution of the narrative of Ouko's disappearance and murder as this narrative was in the dispatch of a "suicide theory," a theory which sustained itself for a number of officials across more than eighteen months of investigations and commission hearings, and which rested on an observation parallel to "the white car": that on his last night on earth Robert Ouko had asked for someone to bring him his "gumboots" (Wellingtons), which were found near the smoldering body on 16 February. The white car and the gumboots were, in the narrativization of Ouko's disappearance, incompatible props. The car is the necessary implement of the murder account. Ouko had to be removed from his home as a prelude to his murder. The "distance" between a living Ouko at home on the evening of 12 February and a murdered Ouko's corpse at Got Alila—two to three kilometers away—could only be traversed by a car. There having been no other car in or near the Ouko farm on his last night on earth, the car must have come from elsewhere, from outside, as a piece of the murder account. But the "distance" between a living Ouko at home on the evening of the twelfth and a suicidal Ouko at Got Alila could only be traversed by gumboots. The "white car" represented a range of possibility stretching from a voluntary to an involuntary departure from the Ouko farm. The "gumboots" implied only a single possibility: Ouko putting them on and walking off from his farm in a voluntary and solitary manner appropriate to an interpretation of suicide.

Critically important across the investigations and inquiries into Ouko's disappearance and death was the question of whether his death was a suicide. A suicide scenario was slightly hinted at by government sources on the day the body was found. A number of those centrally involved in the investigations, including significant witnesses in the Scotland Yard proceedings and before the Commission of Inquiry, maintained the suicide theory—the "gumboots" or "Wellingtons" scenario—long after it had been abandoned by the Scotland Yard team, and even after it was strongly ridiculed in the Commission of Inquiry. The interpretative split between the "murder school" and the "suicide school" was an impasse across which the believers in murder could only imagine advocates of the suicide theory as part of an elaborate conspiracy to murder Ouko and cover up the crime. Yet witnesses before the Judicial Commission of Inquiry continued to offer evidence giving support to the "suicide school" long after this association with conspiracy had been established.

Senior Superintendent Emmanuel Mwachiti and District Commissioner Godfrey Mate were witting or unwitting exemplars of the "suicide school." According to them, they stood with Selina at the grass-thatched hut. From that spot, they claimed, it was quite improbable that Selina could have seen a white car at night. At the same time, these doubters of Selina's observations gave considerable attention to the alternative account of Ouko's last moments, the gumboot story. In a significant sense, to follow this argument through its various stages, the report of the gumboots was inherently part of the constitutive force of Selina's account of "a white car" on the Oukos' drive, for the one gave force to the other. To seek an interpretation of murder, one would "see" Selina's white car; to seek an interpretation of suicide, one would see no white car from the grass-thatched house, but one would see the gumboots, and Ouko's request to have the gumboots available, as a preface to his taking his own life.

A car on the drive, of any color, made no sense to those who would narrate Ouko's demise as a suicide. But a car on the drive was highly visible to those who sought to situate Robert Ouko's death as a core issue in the campaign for multiparty democracy. The "white car" in 1991 stood for Kenya's particular political embarrassments: corruption, government-provoked violence against its opposition, fixed elections, and a lack of transparency. The democracy campaign would claim a significant, if not also hideously paradoxical, victory as the Commission of Inquiry's proceedings were brought to a sudden end by President Moi, and the ruling party almost simultaneously voted to change the constitution to permit other parties into the organized political field of Kenya. Selina's claim to have seen "a white car" not only overwhelmed corroborative claims (most especially Administrative Policeman Agalo Obonyo's) but also overwhelmed assertions regarding Ouko and the gumboots and stood against the Kenyan government's attempts to mask its role in Ouko's death and the subsequent cover-up of the crime. Curiously, and without explication by any party to the investigations, Selina's account stands at the center of the contest between these two narratives, and seems to gain at least part of its standing through the force or effect of this contest. Selina Ndalo Were's ability to convince diverse audiences that she saw a white car on an unlit drive and yet could not see its occupants created an extraordinary yet delimited space for the public and forensic imaginations of Robert Ouko's end, and for the public instantiation—through months and months of testimony and examination of witnesses—of the significantly present and sometimes spoken, yet never inscribed and hardly ever interrogated, worlds of farms, ministries, investments, families, and friendships in the late twentieth century.

◦ ◦ ◦

Considering the records of Selina's reports regarding her observation of "a white car" or "the white car," it might look as if she were telling it to everyone she encountered over more than thirty-six months. Or, to say this differently, it might seem as though everyone who encountered Selina during more than thirty-six months following Ouko's disappearance from his Koru residence heard her speak of "a white car" or "the white car": in person, on the phone, in the Oukos' bedroom, at the grass-thatched hut, before the press, at police stations, at the Sunset Hotel in Kisumu, before the Commission of Inquiry, and at the Anguka trial.

But the record of the Judicial Commission of Inquiry actually indicates that Selina was selective in whom she told. For the commission, Selina's evident ambivalence about telling on 13 and 14 February 1990—when the search for the disappeared Ouko had begun—was from the beginning of the inquiry an opening to doubt the credibility of her account. Why did she not tell Administrative Policeman Agalo Obonyo, when she saw him early on the morning of the thirteenth, that she had seen and heard something strange during the previous night? Why didn't she speak to Obonyo about the issue of the minister's whereabouts, when Ouko was not in his bedroom awaiting his morning tea as she had expected? After all, Obonyo was the instantiation of the official security system on the Minister's farm. Why did she avoid the question with other farmworkers, even telling some that she was going to prepare tea for the minister when she purportedly knew (or by her own words was convinced) that Ouko was not there to ask her for it? Why did she not tell the secretary from the Ministry of Foreign Affairs, who called Koru early on the thirteenth inquiring about the minister's travel plans to Nairobi? Why did she not tell the group who came visiting in the afternoon with former Kisumu mayor George Owino, bringing Robert Ouko an array of food to congratulate him on having been spared injury in a road accident a few days before? Equally, what did it mean that she was later uncertain whether she had told certain individuals or not?

For the commissioners and counsel in the Judicial Commission of Inquiry, Selina's supposed oversights, her evident reluctance to speak, her uncertain recollections, raised questions about her veracity and reliability. Implicitly and explicitly, and regardless of Superintendent Troon's convictions, all this tested confidence that there had been a white car on the drive at the farm, long before Kenya's publics had access to Troon's report and heard and read his commission testimony. Selina was closely questioned on these issues, as were those to whom she had had the opportunity to relate her account and those who claimed to have crossed paths with her—in person or by phone—in the two days following Ouko's disappearance. Piece by piece, Selina struggled to explain each circumstance—whether she told, whether she withheld, whether she forgot which she had done—and she did so by unveiling a set of operative procedures relating to authority, protocol, and deference in her life and on the farm that were substantially different from those held by the commissioners and counsel themselves at the outset. To affirm her own credibility and her observation of "a white car," Selina not only had to tell the story again and again but also had to establish the priority of her own regime of protocol over that of the commission. Consequently, these texts—relating to "a white car" or "the white car" and to the surrounding frameworks of this alleged sighting—expose the formal and informal rules by which the thirteen or fourteen employees worked in the Oukos' absence. Likewise any knowledge of, or supposition regarding, the nature of the Oukos' farm—and others like it—itself became a commentary on Selina's credibility, and on the verisimilitude of Selina's account of the procedures and protocols of everyday work, management, and sociability on the farm. The commission's expectations and protocols clearly differed from Selina's in regard to what one would, normatively, say to whom about what. In this sense, the texts arising in the examination of Selina Ndalo Were are very much about *talk*, the ways in which individuals, workers, employees speak of themselves, their work, their employers, their lives, and their peers. The status of Selina's account rested on prevalent, and not necessarily homogeneous, notions of how people talk to each other. And it would rest on Selina's power to establish her notions of how people talk to one another, and to establish her credibility against all other views.

The repetition, or near repetition, of Selina's observation, and of reports of it by others—what Selina saw, what Selina said, what others said Selina saw, what others said Selina said she saw, and what others said others said Selina said and saw—was an important element in the constitution of Selina's observation of "a white car" as "a truth." Over time, the "Selina discourse" crowded out alternative discourses and sustained itself across both larger and narrower distinctions in the accounting of what Selina saw and said she saw. The dramaturgical quality of several sites and moments in which Selina—as well as others—was heard to speak regarding her observation of "a white car" helped enable it to do so. The reconstruction of these sites and moments, not once but several times over three or four years, reconvened the contingent elements of Selina's voice and Selina's observation. All of these sites and moments involved several persons, each of whom was capable of producing partial accounts of what was seen or heard, producing intricate topographies of coherence and incoherence at the center of which was, invariably, Selina's voice and Selina's observation. For example:

• Apollo Ageng'o, manager of the Oukos' Shoe Den Shop in Kisumu, helped Administrative Police Corporal Gordon Okoth Ondu place a call to the Koru farm on 13 February, with Okoth speaking to Selina about the minister's whereabouts while Ageng'o listened to the conversation from Okoth's end of the line.

• Mrs. Christabel Ouko, wife (and then widow) of Robert Ouko, placed a call to the Koru farm on the thirteenth, around 2:00 P.M., and spoke with Selina regarding her husband's whereabouts. She also spoke to Amos Agalo, son of Administrative Policeman Agalo Obonyo, possibly as Selina listened; Amos Agalo may have been listening to her speak with Selina.

• On the fourteenth of February, Constable George Otieno Ndege, a police bodyguard attached to Minister Robert Ouko, called the Koru home from Nairobi and spoke with Selina. He asked her to bring Philip Rodi, the Koru gateman, farm manager Samson Odoyo, and Obonyo to the phone, and each spoke to Otieno while the others were nearby and possibly within earshot.

• At around five o'clock on the morning of 15 February 1990, Mrs. Ouko arrived at the Koru home from Nairobi in the minister's government-owned Mercedes, driven by Joseph Yogo and accompanied by Otieno (the body-guard) and James Mathew Onyango K'Oyoo, a friend of the family. Selina greeted them, and other workers at the farm were rounded up, brought to the main house, and questioned. Selina was heard and overheard by differ-ent parties in different spaces, including near where the car was being un-loaded, in Mrs. Ouko's bedroom, and near and within the grass-thatched house from which she claimed to have seen "a white car." Different arrays of some ten individuals were in different listening configurations in respect to Selina's speaking and answering questions during an hour or so of conver-sation and inquiry, with the different parties later asserting what they heard Selina say and who was listening or within earshot when they heard her speak.

• As reported in his testimony before the Judicial Commission of Inquiry, James Mathew Onyango K'Oyoo heard Selina's account of a white car on that morning of 15 February. According to the *Daily Nation*, K'Oyoo, Ouko's "chief campaigner," related that he, Mrs. Ouko, and Otieno left Mrs. Ouko's Loresho home at 1:00 A.M. and reached Koru at 5:00 A.M. When they ar-rived they

> interviewed workers at the home, including the house-keeper, Selina Were Ndalo, gateman Philip Rodi, an askari and another man.
> [Commission counsel Bernard] *Chunga*: What did Mrs. Ouko ask Selina if you can remember?
> *Oyoo*: She asked Selina when *japuonj* (Ouko) left and by what means. Selina replied she heard the outer door bang then she thought *japuonj* had woken up and she went to check if he was already up so that she could make him coffee or tea.
> *Chunga*: Continue.
> *Oyoo*: Then when she went out she saw *japuonj* enter a white car which was parked outside the gate and the car was leaving. So she rushed to a small house the Minister had built for resting or entertaining his political strategists (laughter), then she saw the car leave. That is what I heard her tell Mrs Ouko and I posed a question to her [Selina]. I told her: "At your age and it was about 3 am, how did you manage to see the car and the colour?" She gave me a reply which convinced me she saw a car when she was in the grass-thatched house.
> He [Oyoo] said he went to where Selina claimed to have seen the car from. "She insisted and she looked sincere—she is an ordinary woman! (laughter). You can see sincerity in her!" (*Daily Nation*, 23 July 1991, 15).

• On 22 February 1990, Detective Superintendent Troon made his first visit to the Koru farm, in the company of some Kenya police officers and others. He interviewed Selina in the presence of Kenyan police officer Christopher

Timbwa and Nakuru District Commissioner Jonah Anguka (also a neighbor of the Oukos' at Koru), who assisted with the translation during Troon's questioning of Selina. According to Troon, an "altercation" broke out between Timbwa and Anguka "in relation to the quality of the interpretation." It was settled by each being given an opportunity to translate what Selina was saying. It was in the midst of this dispute that Troon first heard from Selina—or, better, he was told by Anguka what Selina said—about "a white car" or "the white car."[6]

Speaking about and speaking for Selina were major "trades" for an array of participants in and observers of the Ouko case. But at the heart of all this speaking about and speaking for—and present in spite of all the formal methodologies and informal appropriations through which her words, postures, gestures, and observations were pressed to produce fuller insight—was the notion of Selina's authentic voice, and her authentic presence, as a woman and as a worker, within the Ouko household and in Kenya. This production of Selina's authenticity reflects a broader, global rendering of the African woman and of the African woman's voice as wholly authentic, as standing firm and powerful against any and all interventions and mediations. The interactions of the construction of Selina's voice and presence within the Ouko saga and the broader programs to recognize or attribute authenticity to the African woman's "voice"—and to the notions of "voice" itself—invite further attention, and only more so after some three or four decades of development and reproduction of scientific methodologies to manage the complexities and problematics of African oral discourse. Luise White has observed,

In African history, the search for African voices with which to write has been an academic obsession for almost thirty years. While the formal study of oral tradition was to provide a concrete methodology with which historians might study a precolonial past filled with mythical heroes and landscapes, colonial historians were not supposed to have such images to interpret. Oral histories were by definition about things that were within a living memory; facts could be checked by interviewing a number of informants. The emphasis was on how to verify, not how to interpret. Even a long overdue feminist critique of oral history addressed the politics of the collection of oral materials, not their interpretation. As ethnography and anthropological objects have been decentered in the last decade, academic attentions have subtly shifted to the individual; methodological debates in oral history have concentrated, like those in literature, on establishing the authority and authenticity of the voice of the colonized. Life histories have come to be considered more authentic than simple interviews; letting African voices speak for themselves has not only become a methodology, it has become a minor publishing enterprise. (1997: 438)

There was of course a palpable tension, and an important distinction, between how Selina's testimony was received by the official parties who heard it—and particularly by the Judicial Commission of Inquiry—and how, just four years before, Wambui Otieno's testimony was heard in the High Court of Kenya, in the extraordinary civil proceedings over the disposition of her husband S. M. Otieno's remains. It was not lost on Kenyans that one of the commission members, Justice Richard Kwach, who nurtured Selina's authenticity in February 1991 and throughout the commission's proceedings, had in 1987, as counsel to S. M. Otieno's clan—Wambui Otieno's adversaries—disparaged any authority she would claim as a "modern woman," widow, or Kenyan (Cohen and Odhiambo 1992; Stamp 1991).

◦ ◦ ◦

For Detective Superintendent Troon and for others, Selina's account constituted a truth. But how did Selina's story work? As well as anyone, Isabel Hofmeyr (1994: 175) has framed the essential problem:

> Any literary discussion of oral history is forced to shuttle between four major co-ordinates: the event/s referred to by the informants; the present-day context in which those narrations occur; the conventions and forms which enable narration; and an intervening period during which both the conditions and craft of telling, as well as the meaning and form of the story itself, have undergone considerable changes.[7]

Of course, in respect to the "work" of Selina's story, the "intervening period" was only three or four years. Selina's story stood by itself, without corroboration. To a certain extent, as suggested above, it worked because it resisted the efforts of others, and of other potentially more problematic stories, to corroborate it. There is little doubt that simple *repetition* had an impact on the authority of Selina's account, as it was offered, repeated, reiterated, and recited time after time. Listeners and readers certainly found support for Selina's story in their observations of Selina's character, and of the character of her work and devotion within the Ouko household.

◦ ◦ ◦

Early in my examination of the Ouko materials, the question "Who killed Ouko?" was persistently forced forward, as if this were the only question of value, the only concrete ground from which to act as a historian or historical anthropologist upon the public record of the Ouko inquiries. This essay resists that ground, seeking to understand the workings and powers of knowledge within the Ouko inquiries. Within these official inquiries, the central question of whether there was or was not a vehicle, possibly white, on the Oukos' drive around 3:00 A.M. on the night of 12–13 February 1990 remanifested itself as a question of who was in the car and with what intent. Further, for many, like Troon, the question of intent was eminently satisfied and speculation focused upon the identities and interests of the occupants of "the white car." The question of whether there was "a white car" on the drive would still be open today were it not for the complex interplay of Selina's account with those who heard it and reheard it.

But none of this made Selina's account more true. The story operated as "a truth" rather than as "the truth" upon broader fields of contest over the larger story. As "a truth" the story had momentous impact on other takings within the inquiries, and through its usages, through its mediative workings, Selina's account drew to itself additional authority, or authenticity. Some members of the Ouko farm workforce and some police told stories that did not cohere with Selina's account, and their testimony, their accounts, their observations, indeed their forensic skills, were disparaged, attacked. They themselves were subjected to personal ridicule and were humiliated. Some were threatened with, and some actually faced, charges of perjury. The "truth" of Selina's account shone a powerful light on those who would attempt to conceal details of the murder and to distort the investigations, and it drew renewed attention to the corruption and terror that were hallmarks of the Moi state in Kenya. This is a power of "a truth," a power that still allows contention, opposition, revision, and dissension, and this is the force of stories that might be as much "wrong" as they are "a truth." They still bear the vitality and problematics of interstitial knowledge and unfinished accounts, of a "place-holder" for truth . . . the potentially unlimited force of "a truth" against "the truth," of what is held to be "authentic" against "what is true."

NOTES

A number of individuals have generously provided comment and advice during the development of this essay (some in ways they may not want to acknowledge), beginning with Keith Breckenridge, Catherine Burns, and Gretchen Elsner-Sommer, and including Karin Barber, Tim Burke, Ben Cohen, Carolyn Hamilton, Gunther Lottes, Hans Medick, Stephan Miescher, Jeff Paige, Stephen Pierce, Martin Schaffner, Gay Seidman, Keith Shear, Lynn Thomas, Katherine Verdery, Maris Vinovskis, Kerry Ward, and Luise White. I have appreciated the extraordinary opportunity to read and discuss many of these materials and issues with E. S. Atieno Odhiambo. I am grateful to the Bellagio Conference and Research Center and the Max-Planck Institut fuer Geschichte in Goettingen, Germany, as well as to the Dean of the College of Literature, Science, and the Arts of the University of Michigan for affording me time to work on these materials and to write, part of this opportunity being devoted to the present project. The staff of the International Institute, especially Christy Yenkel, did so much to provide me with time and space for work on this project.

1. Steven Shapin (1995) valuably complicates the constitution of truth within historical practice through an analysis of the role or work of trust in the shaping of bodies of knowledge. Similarly, Kwasi Wiredu (1996: chapter 8) introduces the notion of "agreement" into a discussion of the sense of truth for or within Akan society.

2. See Cohen and Atieno Odhiambo (forthcoming) for an inventory of thirty-three reports of Selina Ndalo Were's observation of "a white car" within the record

of the Judicial Commission of Inquiry. Neither the proceedings nor a final report of the Commission were ever published; rather a public record of the Commission's takings was constituted day-by-day in the reports of the *Daily Nation* and *The Standard.*

3. The reports in the *Daily Nation* and the *Weekly Review* of Selina Ndalo Were's observation of "a white car" followed disclosures she made more privately to Robert Ouko's wife, Christabel Ouko, to police, and to others. Selina's statements were in Dholuo; according to many witnesses before the Commission of Inquiry, she could not speak or understand English. Translating her was itself a major field of endeavor and controversy. The Commission of Inquiry employed a series of translators, and would draft one when another failed. That one commissioner and various counsel were themselves Luo speakers complicated the work of the translators, as the commissioner and counsel often intervened during the proceedings, correcting or checking on the translation of terms and statements. Questions were also often raised about the linguistic facility of various witnesses, and some were asked to accept an interpreter. Officially, the proceedings were conducted in English. The newspapers covering the proceedings generally reported the English translations of questions, answers, and testimony, but occasionally the reports include Dholuo text. One highly regarded translator, Charles Pacho, died during the proceedings and the commissioners took time to note his passing.

4. Within the public record of the Judicial Commission of Inquiry, there are a number of expositions by various witnesses, from a farmworker to Detective Superintendent Troon, of what one might term "theories of Selina," groundings for assessments of Selina's credibility and veracity that verge on theoretical statements. These expositions or statements were typically voiced, it seems, as ways of explaining discrepancies between Selina's account or behavior and that of others, and between what witnesses, commissioners, and counsel (and also Selina) seemed to consider normative in a particular situation and what actually happened or was said to have happened. These expositions and statements make up, in a certain sense, a holographic portrait of Selina.

5. At the conclusion of his testimony before the Judicial Commission of Inquiry, the commission ordered Agalo Obonyo arrested and prosecuted for perjury.

6. For more examples and detail of such sites and moments of speech, see Cohen and Odhiambo (forthcoming).

7. I would only add one further element, a fifth coordinate: the listening/hearing/reading work of audiences in respect to the oral accounts. See also Elizabeth Tonkin (1992, especially chapter 2).

BIBLIOGRAPHY

Anguka, Jonah. 1998. *Absolute Power: The Ouko Murder Mystery.* London: Pen Press.
Cohen, David William, and E. S. Atieno Odhiambo. 1989. *Siaya: The Historical Anthropology of an African Landscape.* London: James Currey.
————. 1992. *Burying SM: The Politics of Knowledge and the Sociology of Power in Africa.* Portsmouth, N.H.: Heinemann.
————. Forthcoming. *The Risks of Knowledge.*
Daily Nation (Nairobi).
Hofmeyr, Isabel. 1994. *"We Spend Our Years as a Tale That Is Told": Oral Historical Narrative in a South African Chiefdom.* Portsmouth, N.H.: Heinemann.
Shapin, Steven. 1995. *A Social History of Truth: Civility and Science in Seventeenth-Century England.* Chicago: University of Chicago Press.

Stamp, Patricia. 1991. "Burying Otieno: The Politics of Gender and Ethnicity in Kenya." *Signs* 16, no. 4: 808–45.

The Standard (Nairobi).

Tonkin, Elizabeth. 1992. *Narrating Our Pasts: The Social Construction of Oral History.* Cambridge: Cambridge University Press.

The Weekly Review (Nairobi).

White, Luise. 1997. "Cars Out of Place: Vampires, Technology, and Labor in East and Central Africa." In *Tensions of Empire: Colonial Cultures in a Bourgeois World,* ed. Frederick Cooper and Ann Laura Stoler, 436–60. Berkeley: University of California Press. First published in *Representations* 43 (1993): 27–50.

Wiredu, Kwasi. 1996. *Cultural Universal and Particulars: An African Perspective.* Bloomington: Indiana University Press.

13

True Stories

Narrative, Event, History, and Blood in the Lake Victoria Basin

Luise White

This essay is about reliability, accuracy, and what is true and what is false and when and where those distinctions might be best deployed. I am not concerned with how Africans understand these concepts but with how historians understand them. This is an article about reading texts and interpreting oral data; it is about evidence.

Leading Questions

This essay is based on two sets of interviews that were conducted four years apart in western Kenya and Uganda with different research assistants. I write about them together because they form a regional cohort: most informants were male, former migrant laborers and artisans, and born between about 1900 and 1940, although a few Kenyan men were proud of their identity cards showing birth dates in 1884 and 1892. Many of the Kenyan men had worked in Uganda at one time or another; none of the Ugandan men had left the country to work, and several were the sons of wealthy farmers who had employed Luo migrants. These interviews were designed to be about commonplace colonial rumors (prevalent in both Uganda and Kenya) according to which some agency of the state captured Africans and took their blood. I use these interviews as if they were a set; that is because I am interested not in what happened in Uganda or Kenya but in something that never happened. I do not believe this bloodsucking ever happened, and while I think much richer research could be conducted by someone who did believe these stories, the strategy I have taught my research assistants (I speak neither Luo nor Luganda) has been to treat these stories as though they were both true and false in an interview. Thus informants have been asked about their experiences with these vampires—a term I will use in conjunction with the local terms, *bazimamoto*, *wazimamoto*, *kachinja*, and sometimes *kachi-*

nja-chinja, throughout this essay—and about whether these vampires were real or not, and what they think these stories mean. This has involved more direct questioning than many oral historians allow, but I have been asking direct and leading questions for years, and have usually found that informants respond by arguing with me, or at least by implying that I was inattentive. I have argued that being reprimanded by an informant is more than an ethnographic experience: it reveals what information informants care about enough to argue about and defend (White 1990b: 20–28). Indeed, the title of this essay comes from a man in Uganda who became exasperated with having to explain why some people believed vampire stories and others did not: "they existed as stories."[1] Vampire stories were a widespread oral genre and were told and retold as true stories; whether or not they described an actual event or events is another issue entirely.

Elizabeth Tonkin has argued that oral genres do not have an either/or status; people go in and out of genre as often as they need to, to get their point across. Genres have no special performative or historical status, although a speaker might not want to be interrupted while in genre. In interviews people tend to be cued or prompted into genre, either because the answer is one that the speaker has already thought about in a generic form or because a question occasions a response with specific narrative conventions. Genres can be true or false; a well-rehearsed narrative is no more suspect or historically inaccurate than a blurted-out comment (Tonkin 1992: 50–55). But the idea of people speaking in genres problematizes many recent concerns about the politics of interviewing and the evaluation of testimony so obtained (Law 1984: 195–99, Rosaldo 1986; Geiger 1986, 1990; Patai 1987; Mbilinyi 1989; van Onselen 1993; Hoppe 1993; Gengenbach 1994).

My goal in this essay is not to defend any methods I might have used but to look at the range of oral accounts generated by my and my research assistants' questions. Much of the material in this essay comes from oral statements about these vampires, but I will also look at men's and women's accounts of their wartime experiences, because they too trouble the boundary between true and false, between a real event and an imagined occurrence. But this boundary may be a false issue for historians. "What really happened" is hardly set in stone; new information changes the past far more often than we like to admit: the very term "revision" glosses the processes by which data once thought to be true has been declared false.

I want to resuscitate some older debates about oral traditions—were they true, were they Braudelian (Clarence-Smith 1977; Vansina 1978b), were they different from memory and from myth (Beidelman 1970)—because these debates addressed questions of evidence in some very imaginative and important ways. Most of these debates were as petty as they were short-lived, but many also addressed issues that concern me here: how do historians access what shaped the past, and how can they use oral sources to discern these causes? Such a question—categorically different from that of what really happened—may link oral histories and the study of oral tradition in re-warding ways. These two areas of orality have been maintained as separate areas of research for decades, despite David William Cohen's (1977, 1980) protests, for reasons that are as strident as they are unexamined: oral tradi-tions are unlike personal reminiscences because experts say they are (Van-sina 1980, 1985: 18–19; Miller 1980: 9–12). One result of this segregation has been an implicit construction of oral history and oral tradition as oppo-sites: oral traditions had to be interpreted with the greatest care and caution, but subalterns were buried under so many garbled texts that only by speak-ing for themselves could they be understood (Spivak 1988; but see White 1995b, 2000). But as Carolyn Hamilton (1987) has pointed out, oral history and oral traditions have a great deal in common: people draw on the forms in which the past has been presented to them to represent their own experi-ences and ideas. Oral history and personal narrative may require as much methodological interrogation as oral traditions do, as well as close attention to the political purposes for which Africans have been encouraged to "speak for themselves."

Debates about oral tradition and oral history have not taken place in a vacuum, of course. Scholarship on Africa has taken some flak, not only in the world of dwindling academic resources, but in the world of cultural politics and African politics. The subject of ethnographic enquiry has been prob-lematized in recent years (Fabian, 1983; Rosaldo 1986) and historians have cast their topics wider than the boundaries of beleaguered African nation-states (Feierman 1990, 1995). Academic attention has, in a variety of disci-plines, shifted subtly to the individual. For those doing oral history, method-ological debates have concentrated, not on interpreting words, but on estab-lishing the authority of the speaker—words were true because of what the speaker had experienced. Whereas scholars once talked about oral history or personal reminiscences, they now had a methodology, the life history. It was said to be more authentic than simple interviews, and only Tonkin protested that "life" is not a universal category that all informants and interviewers share (Tonkin 1992: 49, 56). Nevertheless, letting African voices speak for themselves has not only become a methodology, it has become a significant publishing enterprise (Smith 1981; Shostak 1981; Davison 1989; Strobel and Mirza 1989; Bozzoli 1991; Geiger 1997). But concerns about the validity and authenticity of African voices, and about who they speak for, are concerns about how African experiences can be represented to a larger world. Sixty years ago the Russell Commission, investigating the causes of the 1935 Cop-perbelt disturbances, apologized to its readers for the amount of irrelevant testimony published in *The Evidence*, but it found that "in the case of native witnesses, it saved time to allow witnesses to proceed with their evidence without attempting to abbreviate it" (Government of Northern Rhodesia 1935, 2). More recently, Gyan Prakash (1990: 402) has located concerns about speech and representation in the very academic processes by which colonial history has been what he calls "third worlded"—made into an object of study in the first world and given new and powerful meanings by subordinated groups there.

Writing a history of Africa from oral sources that seeks to make sense within Africa as much as it seeks to "explain" Africa to the wider world requires vigorous methodological work. Rather than make pronouncements about what historians should do, let me ask another question: what do people say about the past, and why do they say it the way they do? People have many ways of talking about the past, of course—one of which is to talk about the present—but the question posed above may be a way to access all the different modes of speech, of recollection, of fantasy and ideology that might appear in an interview—or indeed, in any oral form (Barber 1989, 1991; Hofmeyr 1994). If historians ask what an account describes, can we begin to use that description in our historical reconstruction? And if we do, what kind of history do we get?

HEARSAY, HISTORY, AND EVIDENCE

Almost all the men and women interviewed in western Kenya and Uganda said that the men of the colonial and early postcolonial fire brigade—generally called by some version of the Swahili term *wazimamoto*, the men who extinguish the fire or heat, or sometimes by the intensive *kachinja-chinja*, slaughterer—captured Africans and took their blood. These ideas were not unique to men in Kampala and Siaya District. Stories about bloodsucking firemen, or game rangers in Zambia, or mine managers in Zaire, were commonplace. How Africans were captured and what was done with them during and after their captivity had distinctive and well-known regional variations. "[T]he nature of the stories was not much different from place to place," said the wife of one of the first Africans to drive a locomotive for the Kenya and Uganda Railways; "the stories I heard were different from place to place," said her husband.[2] In Uganda many people thought the Yellow Fever Department captured people (using fire brigade vehicles), and a few others thought the Welfare Department took their blood; in Siaya District people actively debated whether the wazimamoto acted alone or with (or in fact were) the police. Within a region people debated how blood was taken and who were the most likely victims—women, old people, drunkards. These variations were regional rather than individual and idiosyncratic, but they were neither true nor false: no one doubted a wazimamoto story because the abductors were said to be police, or Yellow Fever Department workers. Indeed, no one doubted these stories because they seemed unlikely. If people doubted these stories at all, it was because they had never met anyone who was abducted. But these versions taken together, in the daily exchange of conversation and news, formed a debate, a continual reevaluation and reexamination of the story's key elements. Talk about wazima-moto, with versions in which wazimamoto were the police or in which the victims were all female, did not make wazimamoto stories false, or even suspicious. Instead, a fluid cluster of persons, organizations, and events established a wazimamoto story; the absence of one organization and the presence of another did not make a story sound unlikely, it made it sound true (Vansina 1978a: 29–74; Hofmeyr 1994: 78–101). Hofmeyr (1994: 94–100) has observed that in much historical storytelling facts were contested as they were told. They didn't have to be passively accepted to be true; rather, they were true because they were part of an established narrative. The interaction between narrator and audience foregrounds the meaning of the stories (Seitel 1980: 30–31); it may be that only leading questions reproduce such interactions. The "popular consensus" that troubled Paul Irwin (1981; see also Wright 1982) when he discovered that Liptako genealogies had erased a French-appointed village headman of slave origin did the same. As David Newbury (1991) has argued for the Lake Kivu region, consensus is achieved by ideology, not history; people agree on facts they like: slaves should not be village headmen. But genealogies are historical tools only to historians; they are true—or believed—by the people who keep them, however negotiated and fictive that keeping is, because they allow names and relationships to be juggled and arranged (Blount 1975; but see Vansina 1974). I have argued elsewhere that these differences of details are what make a wazimamoto story powerful and credible locally—pits in many parts of Kenya, chloroform in Kampala, or butterfly nets in northeastern Zambia explain local concerns and meanings as nothing else would (1990a, 1993, 1995a, 1995b; see also Musambachime 1988). These differences not only proved that the story wasn't just a rumor, they proved that it had happened to someone nearby.

Telling wazimamoto stories with fluid details was one thing; not telling the story, or only telling part of the story, was another. The men in these interviews do not form an undifferentiated mass of storytellers. Indeed, not all of them believed these stories: some thought they were false, another thought Africans misunderstood medical research.[3] But there were men who considered wazimamoto stories true and who were said not to be able to talk about them. Some occupations were especially suspect: "policemen are always careful about what they leave out. Retired policemen cannot tell you exactly what they were doing when they worked."[4] Anyango Mahondo, who claimed to have done the work of capturing people, said, "Because of the nature of my work I could not tell anyone, even my wife . . . even my brothers I could not tell."[5] Men and women did not seem to tell different stories—although I did not do the research that would have actively foregrounded such differences—but they heard different stories. Several men said they told their wives these stories, but a few said they did not: "my wives were adults and they could get the stories from other sources," said a man who warned his children about wazimamoto.[6] But such gendered tellings, and their place in household interactions, did not make the stories any less credible.

What made wazimamoto stories true, and powerful, was that they were rumors, they were hearsay, they were part of the news and small talk of the day. Because news and small talk were held to be true, wazimamoto stories were true. "I told my children so they could know what was happening . . . I told my wife and friends during normal conversation."[7] It was policemen's and others' refusal to participate in small talk that made their omissions suspicious. Most people argued that the bloodsucking firemen were real because of how they were talked about; speech was not just the expression of something that happened, it was the proof. A man who barely escaped capture by the Nairobi fire brigade in 1923 said he told many people the story because "I am lucky enough to have escaped and therefore must talk freely about it to people," although he admitted that his wives often called him a liar.[8] Eyewitness evidence was important too, but it was not crucial to an understanding of truth and talk: "people were not crazy just to start talking about something that was not already there."[9] Some people described how experience changed the way they evaluated narrative. The present does not shape oral history in the simplistic ways its critics have imagined; rather, a specific present valorizes specific accounts of the past (Beach 1983; Ewald 1985; Malkki 1995: 51–152). Something that seemed false in 1955 seemed all too true in 1975. "During the colonial period I could not believe there were some people who could abduct people. I would ask myself, how could someone go missing? Could somebody disappear like a goat? But when I learned of my brother-in-law . . . taken by the Amin regime . . . then I understood. But for some of us, who did not know anybody captured by the bazimamoto, it was impossible to understand it."[10]

It was widely believed that talk was rigorously grounded in fact. Its opposite was the "loose talk" that some said characterized Swahili people.[11] Children were brought up not to gossip or speculate idly.[12] Experience shaped narrative. Some people used the present to explain how talk about bloodsucking firemen was always grounded in experience. "If I am stealing bananas and they talk about me, they say I always steal bananas. But can they talk about somebody they don't know, and say that he is stealing? . . . Now I have seen this recording machine. If I had not seen it, I wouldn't be able to talk about it, but because I have seen it, now I can talk about it."[13] Because people spoke from experience, there was in eastern Africa a widespread belief that hearsay was absolutely trustworthy; truth was in everyday talk. The issue was not how well argued something was (Veyne 1988: 79–93), but how readily and commonly it was spoken about. "It was a true story because it was known by many people and many people talked about it. Therefore it was a true story and it is wrong to say that it is not because they would not talk about it if it were not true."[14] The following exchange between interviewer and informant makes this point forcefully, and suggests that questions of interviewing techniques may be overwhelmed by local standards of evidence, of talk rather than fact:

> *q:* Some people have told us that wazimamoto kept their victims in pits. Did you ever hear this?
> *a:* No, I never heard anything like that.
> *q:* Some people have said that wazimamoto used prostitutes to help them get victims. Did you hear that also?
> *a:* Yes, I heard that wazimamoto used prostitutes for such purposes.
> *q:* That means these stories were true?
> *a:* Of course they were. Who told you they weren't?
> *q:* Nobody told me, it was just my personal feeling that these stories were false.
> *a:* These stories were very much true. Those stories started in Nairobi when racial segregation was there. Whites never shared anything with other races and whites were also eating in their own hotels like Muthiaga.[15]

This kind of account, in which hearsay slides into historical geography, is not atypical of the wazimamoto stories of men in Siaya District. Urban landmarks—the hospital at Tanga, the disguised pits of the Kampala police station, hotels and thoroughfares of Nairobi—were not spatial ways of "proving" the reality of wazimamoto; that proof was accomplished with storytelling. While some of these urban details established the authority of the speakers—each a world-wise migrant—I think these informants would say the details were essential to these stories: wazimamoto worked in towns at precise places; stories about them would describe these places. Nevertheless, it is unlikely that former migrants see this as an either-or question: talk of urban landmarks could both establish their knowledge of these cities and situate historical knowledge in these places (Giles-Vernick 1996; Hofmeyr 1994: 161–67; Wachs 1988).

The account above raises other questions, however. Which parts of the story are true, and how do partial truths shape historians' use of the account? The answers may lie not in making more rules for oral historians and what they take to be true, but in problematizing what a true story is, and when and where it becomes true. In an early, important critique of the use of oral tradition, T. O. Beidelman (1970) complained that historians tended to make culture static, to make traditions into historical facts; finding out what really happened obscured how traditions were used to "hold social 'truths' independent of historical facts" (78). But the line between different kinds of truth is as flexible as any genealogy; historical facts emerge from social truths just as social truths develop from readings of historical facts. Hearsay is fact when people believe it. It is impossible to say that wazimamoto stories, told and retold in East African cities, are independent of historical, or social, or sociological fact. In 1947 rioters at the Mombasa fire station demanded the release of a woman; in October 1958 Nusula Bua was arrested at the Kampala fire station for offering to sell a man for fifteen hundred shillings. He told the fireman he spoke to that he had "about 100 people to sell." Bua was sentenced to three years' imprisonment, because it was his first offence and because "[p]eople must know that the Fire Brigade is not buying people, but is intended to extinguish fires in burning buildings and vehicles" (Huxley 1948: 23n; White 2000: 34).

EXPERIENCE, MEMORY, AND THE POLITICS OF INTERVIEWING

Even when repeating hearsay, speaking without personal experience, informants insisted that there was much they did not know about wazimamoto. "How could I know what they did with the blood?" said a near-victim, while another thought it was sold to America but "I don't know what Americans were doing with African blood."[16] A man in Uganda did not know why, or when, bazimamoto stopped capturing people, but "[s]omeone who worked for the bazimamoto, he can tell you why they stopped."[17]

This combination of social facts and empiricism means, quite simply, that informants cannot be dismissed as "inaccurate" or "unreliable"; portions of interviews cannot be labeled "flights of fancy" when they simply repeat well-known truths. The idea that a story might be true while its details are unknown to its tellers is at odds with most of the methodologies that interrogate the reliability of testimony or of an informant. Stories are neither true nor false in the sense that they do not have to be proven beyond their being talked about; but as they are told they contain different empirical elements that carry different valorizations: stories are told with truths, commentaries, and statements of ignorance. These do not make wazimamoto stories seem unlikely; each is a true story and no one would make a compositional effort to change it to make it credible. Anyango Mahondo, for example, explained that the police were actually the bloodsuckers; it was "ordinary people" who could not distinguish between police and firemen. In Kampala,

> When a man joined the police he had to undergo the initial training of blood-sucking. . . . When one qualified there, he was absorbed into the police force as a constable. . . . At night we did the job of manhunting. . . . from the station we used to leave in a group of four with one white man in charge. . . . Once in town we would hide the vehicle somewhere that no one could see it. We would leave the vehicle and walk around in pairs. When we saw a person, we would catch him and take him to the vehicle. . . . Whites are a really bad race. . . . They used to keep victims in big pits. . . . blood would be sucked from those people until they were considered useless. . . . Inside the pits lights were on whether it was day or night. The victims were fed really good food to make them produce more blood. . . . The job of the police recruit was

to get victims and nothing else. Occasionally we could go down into the pits and if we are lucky we can see the bloodsucking but nothing else.[18]

This is presumably the account Mahondo could not tell his wife. I have already noted how this particular chunk of narrative describes on-the-job experience, supervision, promotion, and the place of race and rank therein (White 1993). Now I want to examine this account as testimony, as a narrative told with different kinds of truths, experiences, and frank admissions of ignorance. I am not interested in why he told this story, but how. In this account, Mahondo has made hearsay into a narrative of personal experience: the vehicles, the nighttime abductions, the pits, the feeding of victims were all commonplace in the region's wazimamoto stories. Mahondo has taken these elements and made a story structured neatly by the sequence of events and his own role as a participant and then a bystander. This account was structured around the idea of experience; Mahondo spoke about the world he was relieved to have left behind (Kratz 1991; Miller 1980). There is a difference between this structuring and that idealized by Joseph Miller in his discussion of how oral traditions develop. The victorious leader of a hypothetical battle might well revise an account to make central his role in defeating the enemy, but there would be definite limits on what he could say: other people told their own versions and they could not be convinced by a single account; traditions emerged from versions of events that coexisted for generations (Miller 1980; Hofmeyr 1994). But Mahondo does not seem to be talking simply to enhance his dubious prestige;[19] instead he seems to be establishing truth about wazimamoto—the role of the police, the evils of white people—by telling the story as personal experience. It may be that this was a wazimamoto story that he could not have told locally without inviting argument; the problem with interviewing is the way interviews domesticate contested facts and contested fictions. What may be important here is the way that Mahondo informs his own storytelling. The process of making a personal narrative was constrained by hearsay: if Mahondo was doing what we could call lying, why didn't he make up a story about what happened in the pits?

It is possible that only by conforming to hearsay could Mahondo have been thought credible. Had he stated what actually went on in the secret pits under the Kampala police station, or what whites did with the blood, he might have revealed himself to be a fraud, rather than a man with insider knowledge. Richard Bauman has warned scholars who expect straightforward answers to their questions that we are often performed to, and that we need to understand "the forces of performance" before we unpack the answers to our questions (Bauman 1993). Performance is not the work of specific practitioners in specific places (Vansina 1985: 34–41); it is part of conversation and answering questions. Mahondo's eyewitness account was told the way hearsay wazimamoto stories were told. How the story was performed, and the elements with which it was performed, made it credible. Where it stood on some imaginary line between hearsay and experience had nothing to do with how accurate it was.

People who described narrow escapes from the wazimamoto spoke with both hearsay and memory, as well. A woman who claimed to have escaped from wazimamoto told a story in which she explained her near capture by hearsay. Mwajuma Alexander was going to her farm late one moonlit night in 1959, after an evening's drinking with her husband and co-wife. At the farm of a neighbor she saw a group of men around a parked vehicle with no lights; one man was white. A man threw her to the ground and demanded she open the main gate of the boma. She managed to run away but heard one of the men say in Luo that she was too heavy too run far; she hid in bushes and heard them searching for her. "When they were still looking for me the first cock crowed and one of them said, 'oh oh oh the time is over.'" The following day her husband heard that the wazimamoto had caught a woman in the area; for him and his other wife, this confirmed that Mwajuma had been saved from certain death.[20] Although Mwajuma told her story as one of good fortune, with some key images from wazimamoto stories, the proof that she had escaped certain death was the logic of hearsay: if someone told someone who told someone who told her husband that wazimamoto were in the area that night, then they were.

Zebede Oyoyo had been captured by Nairobi's fire brigade in the early 1920s. All his neighbors knew his story, which is how I came to be sent to him early on during my stay in Yimbo. My research assistant and I interviewed him twice. The first interview was a barely disguised boast of his strength—"my fists were like sledgehammers"; "nobody could come near me"; "when I saw the chance, I dashed out of the room. . . . I out-paced them." "Those kachinjas really chased me and when I had completely beaten them one of them told me, 'Eh, eh you! You were really very lucky. You will stay in this world and really multiply.'"[21] The second, ten days later, provided a much more detailed and subtle account.

> I was caught near River Road. It was near the police station. I had gone for a short call in one of those town toilets. The time was before noon. . . . When I finished urinating someone came from nowhere and grabbed my shirt collar. He started asking me funny questions like "what are you doing here?" I told him I was urinating in a public toilet. On hearing that the man started beating me. He slapped me several times and pulled me toward a certain room. On reaching that room I realized that something was wrong. It was then that I started to become wild and since I was still young . . . that man could not hold me. . . . I fought with the man until I got the chance to open the door. I shot out at terrific speed. . . . When they realized they could not catch me, one of them told me, "you, you are really lucky. You will really give birth to many

children and will only die of old age. You were lucky and pray to god for that luck."[22]

I am not the first to notice that people often revise the answers they gave in a first interview when they are interviewed for a second time. I am not the first to find this unremarkable, as well. Historians routinely mediate between different accounts of the same event; why should this mediation be method-ologically any different when the different accounts are provided by one per-son? It is only when "the voice" is granted authority that this is a problem. It is only when a voice becomes a single, spoken rendition of experience that contradictions become extraordinary rather than ordinary. To argue that an informant is mistaken because he or she says different things at different times, or even to argue that one account is wrong, makes linear demands on speech and self. But lives and experiences are not such simple and straight-forward things that they lend themselves to easy representation; people do not give testimony that fits neatly into chronological or cosmological ac-counts. Instead they talk about different things in personal terms; they talk both about what happened to them and what they did about it, but they also use themselves as a medium by which to talk about other things. They are not inventing themselves on a moment-to-moment basis; they are talking.

A voice, however produced, that does not change its mind or its words is a voice that serves historians, not its own complicated interests. And what constitutes the authority of the voice? That historians use what it says? What then makes oral evidence reliable? That it can be verified just like docu-ments, or that it is taken as a kind of evidence produced in circumstances unlike the ones in which people write diaries, reports, and memos? Is oral evidence the truth spoken during an interview, or the social facts and hearsay with which people talk and that give us insight into local knowledge beyond one man's or woman's experience? If Mwajuma Alexander or Zebede Oyoyo or even Anyango Mahondo are not telling "the truth" but misrepresenting and misconstruing events that did happen, turning them into vampire sto-ries, are they wrong, are they lying, or are they using widely held conventions to explain experience? Are they telling a story with well-known truths rather than with personal experience? But if they had not based their accounts on some personal experience, why did they use that particular invention; why did they bring vampires into daily life at all?

Zebede Oyoyo may not have been what North Americans would call hen-pecked, but his wives seemed wary of his bravado. Once after visiting his compound my research assistant overheard his senior wife asking him why he spoke English to her and not to me. I would argue that the first version of his near-abduction was the one he wanted his wives to appreciate: it was the story of his strength and his fame. It may not have been a story Oyoyo told with any success anywhere else; we may have heard it precisely because it was received so badly at home. The first interview may have been Oyoyo's chance to get his story, with its bravado, taken seriously. He tried to make clear that if this story was not appreciated at home it was because it was a men's story: "none of my wives could realize the seriousness of these stories but a man like you [he turned to my research assistant, a man] can realize the value and seriousness of any story."[23] The story he told us ten days later is what I like to think was the result of his reflection: having thought about the incident, he may have recalled more, and he was able to tell me this version when we returned to interview him again. While this interpretation "explains" the second interview, it's one that puts me at the center, just as Oyoyo's first story puts him at the center. In a provocative article Justin Willis (1996) notes that informants may change key parts of their lives in different interviews not because of anything the interviewer says or does, but because of other people in the room: the audience for whom lives are negotiated and re-presented (as opposed to represented) may not even include the inter-viewer. Such an insight problematizes concerns about the politics of inter-viewing—the interview and his or her questionnaire may have little to do with what's being said or why. Leading questions may neither hinder nor promote good data or a reliable interview; they may be irrelevant.

But what about informants who stick to the same story? Does it mean the story is true, or something historians should worry about? Charles van Onselen (1993) reports that Kas Maine told of how in his first rough seasons as an independent farmer a local trader praised his honesty in paying his debts. Five years later, Maine repeated the story, almost word for word, to a different researcher. Do such repetitions speak to issues of memory and cognition, van Onselen asks, or were they performed, shaped perhaps by the religious teachings Maine favored at that time? If this event had been pulled from a diary, would the interpretation have been as troublesome? I suggest that such repetitions occur when stories were stories long before a re-searcher showed up and recorded them for the first time; that this story was told over and over, as Maine both showed himself to be honorable and re-buked the younger men he found irresponsible.

But van Onselen's quandary—expressed in terms of how memory is stored and retrieved and what cues it—and the two tales of Zebede Oyoyo raise another question: what is remembered and what is constructed during the process of interviewing? Such a question, however, may make unreason-able demands on oral evidence, since, as Stephan Miescher (1997) points out, there is no single version of a person's own life; personal narratives change because they are a dialogue between the speaker and the audiences he or she imagines.[24] There is a difference—and not a static one—between the person and the narrator (Tonkin 1992: 49). In the case of Oyoyo, I would argue that the first story was the one he wanted his wives to believe; it may well have been the story all his neighbors had heard over and over again. Tonkin has noted that genres evolve through successful storytelling (1992:

97), but I want to suggest that in some interview situations researchers' questions cue unsuccessful oral genres, those that have not met with local belief or appreciation. When Bibi Titi Mohammed told Susan Geiger (1996) that she taught Julius Nyerere to speak Swahili in their early nationalist days, for example, she may not have been exaggerating her role in the education of the first Tanganyikan to study abroad and her correction of the book-learned Swahili he knew. Understanding Bibi Titi's words may not have required contextualizing the kind of Swahili spoken in Tanganyika in the 1950s. Bibi Titi's assertion may have been one of many that showed Nyerere to be out of touch, a sentiment she had stated elsewhere many times. Boasts and exaggerations and lies may well be constructed for audiences other than the interviewer: the historian's task may be not to contextualize these statements but to sort out who the intended audience was—Oyoyo's imagined household or Bibi Titi's comrades all too eager to find more reasons to condemn Nyerere. My point is not that historians should not try to contextualize exaggerated statements, but that historians should also use such statements to glimpse an audience not present, the audience for whom such statements are appropriate. Oyoyo's first story may have been what he imagined obedient wives would listen to politely. Perhaps historians should ask not "is it true?" but "who does the speaker think would believe that statement?"

But does all the above mean that I can call Oyoyo's second story a memory? And if it was a memory, why is it more real or reliable or accurate than the memory he had of his strength as a youth? Is it a more reliable memory because I in fact rely on it? Is memory really a shorthand by which oral historians classify the information they want to write on and dismiss the rest? Memory, Ian Hacking has suggested, is the perfect science of crisis: memory can legitimate a version of moral dilemma in a way little else can. Labeling one version of the past memory reinscribes other versions with less authority. Memory does far more than legitimate a specific voice; it legitimates words and specific narratives (Hacking 1995: 126). So if I label Oyoyo's second account his memory, how can I defend my use of that term? Can I show it to be an accurate memory? Oyoyo's account gave a good description of where this toilet was, a detail that is difficult to verify. The archives are useless on this point; not only were most Nairobi housing records destroyed in a 1936 fire, but official writings on the amenities provided for Africans were imaginative and often praised buildings years before they were erected (White 1990b). Whenever that urinal was built, however, it never had an additional room to which victims or anyone else could be taken. Even without verification from the archives, this imaginary urinal is a far more interesting one than officials would ever have constructed. This town toilet is an anachronism, but it is also the site of Oyoyo's story (Miller 1980: 15). It is perhaps all the more interesting because it exists in Oyoyo's depiction of the contradictions of the world of wage labor, a world furnished with details of shirts, recalled time of day, pride in proper toilet habits, and buildings whose extent and nature are unknown and dangerous. Oyoyo's second account describes his being accosted and says little about the activities of wazimamoto; can it be interpreted as Oyoyo's imagined sense of violation, the intrusion into private space of assaulting a man after a pee? This is not to say that Oyoyo's second account was really about something else; vampires were not so unimportant to Oyoyo that he spoke about them without thought. Rather, in this instance, Oyoyo's wazimamoto story described the ways that the experience of urban wage labor trespassed on his most intimate needs.

But Oyoyo's second story seems to have been one that was circulating throughout East Africa in the early 1920s. In 1923 a "Believer" (Adiyisadiki 1923) wrote to the Tanganyikan Swahili-language newspaper *Mambo Leo,* saying that he was now convinced that "mumiani are cruel and merciless and kill people to get their blood." He had seen this himself in Nairobi. Near the new mosque in River Road there was a long narrow building and a "government toilet but no permission was given for people to use these toilets. Inside the long narrow house, people stay, wear black clothes and are called Zima Moto, but the thing that is astonishing is that somebody isn't in this group and they go inside this building, they never come out again." A Luo man who worked there would not allow his brother to come near the building, not even to greet him. Did Oyoyo bring this story home and craft it to depict his own strength, his own talents, and his own memories?

The question may not be whether this account is a memory, or even an accurate memory, but how historians can tell what is someone's memory and what is not. After all, if Oyoyo was telling a 1920s story as his own, it was certainly a memory of sorts; the fact that it had been a story in the early 1920s hardly matters. But he was telling it for other reasons: because I wanted wazimamoto stories, and because this account so wonderfully described his youthful strength and his belief—apparently shared by many East Africans in the 1920s—that there was no space or activity that the colonial state could not invade. Without getting too far afield, and without oversimplifying too much literature, much recent work suggests that memories actually reside somewhere in a person and can be generated, cued, retrieved, or recovered by careful and probing questions (Vansina 1980; van Onselen 1993; Hacking 1995). Such ideas make minds and what happens within them too close to computers for my comfort—everything is stored and can be accessed by the right commands. I want to suggest, based on this research, that the distinctions between memory, experience, well-known fact, and fantasy might be clear to our informants, even though these genres do not occupy special parts of performed or personal histories and may not be presented in an interview as one or the other. Halbwachs argues that memories do not reside in individual consciousness, but are the products of daily interaction—they are cued, recalled, and negotiated because of the other people in the many collectivities a person participates in. A recollection of a visit to a farm with a brother is not fixed; sometimes it is the brother and what he said that is recalled, another time it might be the landscape (Halbwachs 1992: 38–39, 62). As this part of the essay has argued, memories, experiences, and social facts are how people talk, not what they talk about, and the material presented in an interview—whatever the questions and whatever the politics of interviewing—is told with truths of various sorts, but may not be the truth. People speak with truth, memory, and social facts; that is how they talk about experience, the past and the present and their place in both of those times.

But what are oral historians to do with stories that are patently untrue, stories of such a dubious nature that even I began this essay noting my disbelief? To doubt these stories—systematically, scientifically, or any other way—would be to dismiss them; to hypothesize that they were actually misunderstandings, that they were really about something else, would do the same (see Vansina 1974; Henige 1994; but compare Santino 1988; Scott 1991; Stoler 1992). How then do I write the history of things that never happened? Is the methodology the same as for the history of states and battles? Are the tools for studying representation the same for studying misrepresentation? What do I do with the precise geographies and chronologies of wazimamoto stories? Was Zebede Oyoyo wrong because he imagined a urinal years before colonial officials did? When some women in Nairobi told me that wazimamoto stopped in 1939 and others said abductions continued to 1942 (White 1990b, 1993, 1995b, 2000), did I need to establish who was right? I want to answer by arguing two linked issues. The first is that the distinction between true and false may not be necessary, or, more correctly, may not be useful to all texts. Second, I want to suggest that a form of truth may be the appreciation of evidence in contemporary terms—evidence that contemporaries hear as reasonable and reliable may be taken as locally true. In other words, if we treat all versions of false stories as if they were true, we get a glimpse into the world our informants described to us.

The boundary between the fictive and the true may not be so important that historians are well served by policing it. In Uganda I wrote a number of questions for my research assistants to ask. One question asked about *embalasassa*, the speckled lizard that was said to be poisonous and was said to be sent by President Obote to kill the Baganda people in the late 1960s. It was neither poisonous nor any more common in the 1960s than it had been in previous decades, as Makerere University science professors announced on the radio and stated in print (Banage, Byarugaba, and Goodman 1972). But it was something I was curious about when I did research in Uganda, and in one of those moments of true disengagement, I wrote the question, what is the difference between bazimamoto and embalasassa? Anyone who knows anything about a Bantu language—myself included—would know the answer was contained in the question: humans and reptiles are different living things and belong to different noun classes. "There is a big difference between them; bazimamoto are people and embalasassa is a lizard,"[25] many people said, but others went beyond my question to talk about the history of the constructs without the slightest hesitation: "bazimamoto finished by the time of embalasassa; that was during independence."[26] Where people expressed confusion, it was not about the differences between species, but about the differences between the policies of the late colonial era and those of the first decade of independence: while most people said that embalasassa came during Obote's first regime, a few said it was "sent" by Governor Cohen or by Amin in his first years in power.[27] My point is not about the truth of embalasassa or even the inadvertent good sense of my questionnaire, but rather that the labeling of one thing as "true" and the other as "fictive" or "metaphorical"—all the usual polite academic terms for false—may eclipse all the intricate ways that people use social truths to talk about the past. Moreover, chronological contradictions may foreground the fuzziness of certain ideas and policies, and that fuzziness may be more accurate than any exact historical reconstruction—the very area where oral history has suffered the most sustained and reasonable attacks (Henige 1974; but see Vansina 1985: 175–85). Whether embalasassa was real was hardly the issue; there was a real, harmless lizard and there was a real time when people in and around Kampala feared it. They feared it in part because of beliefs about lizards, but mainly people were frightened by their beliefs about their government and the lengths to which it would go to harm them. The confusions and the misunderstandings show what's important; knowledge about the actual lizard would not.

BUT WHO WON WORLD WAR II?

So far, I've implied that one way to privilege informants' words is to stop privileging the interviewer. The idea that the interviewer, her questions, her technique, her ethnographic knowledge, and her hidden and unhidden agendas shape the content of oral interviews may be wrong: people may speak about what they want, rather than what scholars want, and besides, such an idea makes the scholar the center of the world from which oral material comes. I now want to take these suggestions one step further and insinuate that there is no gaze of oral historians, that there is no point of observation so strong and controlling that it determines what we see or, in this case, hear: our subjects talk back as documents never do. I want to suggest instead that there is a cogent moment in which we glimpse a small fraction of the world our informants saw, as they saw it. I argue that these glimpsed fragments are the tools with which we reconstruct the past. This is not another demand that historians listen to African voices; on the contrary, it is a request that historians work hard to understand all the things a voice says (Barber 1991; White 2000).

Oral history has rested on an uneasy premise: that people should have history and should be able to tell it to us, historians (Schrager 1983; Geiger

1990; White 1990b). If the study of oral tradition rested on a firm idea that some people were experts and others were not (Vansina 1985: 36–58; Alagoa 1994), the study of oral history was rooted in more popular ground—that people were experts on their own experiences, and should be able to speak for themselves directly into our studies. When people did not know, or declined to say, or had forgotten, this was noteworthy. If they suggested other directions of enquiry, that was a footnote at best (see Klein 1989: 217). The problem here is not oral sources, but historians' belief in what they should be. It is almost as if oral historiography, developed to solve the problem of how to study the history of nonliterate societies, was never allowed to fail; when there was no material, historians could study the silences and omissions. Voices were there for our use.

This section is an attempt to make modest claims for oral history; I want to show the world we can glimpse through the fissures and contradictions of oral testimonies. I will discuss oral histories about World War II, three interviews done over a decade that give an unconventional but unmetaphorical and unimaginative account of the Italian campaign in East Africa. Zaina Kachui, a woman my research assistant and I interviewed in 1976 in Nairobi, gave this particular history:

> [T]hose people who built with *mabati* [corrugated iron], the government painted mabati over with black paint so that the people coming with airplanes could not see the house, so they couldn't know where to drop the bombs. You couldn't even leave your house at night to go to the toilet. After four o'clock the government refused to allow charcoal to burn and you couldn't even wear white in your dress. . . . Nairobi is not that far from Garissa and they were shooting and fighting with tanks there, that was how Italians fought in Garissa, and Garissa is right near Kitui, you know, so there was a real danger that the Italians were coming here, to Nairobi. The Italians said, "there is good tea, you'll drink it in Nairobi, the cup you'll wash in Kampala." That's what they wanted to do. The government of Kenya sent big boats full of men to take over from the Italians in Somalia. Golgos [the Gold Coast Regiment of the West African Frontier Force], South African people, those are the ones who went in the boat, the English sent them, they took over Somali towns, but all of them died fighting there. The English knew how to come in front of people and take them over. Then we heard the airplanes. Then the Italians left, they had no other way to fight, we heard very nice, very long *kingora* [sirens] and the police opened our doors and people ran out and started to laugh and clap, saying Italians down, English up.[28]

In one sense, this account is factually true—it is an extremely local history of World War II in East Africa, in which blackouts and curfews are made to make a military sense that they did not "really" have. In another sense, this account is false—it argues an Italian threat that never existed except in the talk of Italian prisoners of war in Kenya and it telescopes the sequence of curfews, invasions, battles, and airplanes overhead (the RAF base was two miles from Kachui's house) as if they were events of the distant past. But usually when Kachui telescoped events, she was profound: "Mau Mau was bad, because it was African people killing African people. . . . the white people could have won, you know, look at the way they defeated the Italians, but they didn't want to do that. The white men agreed among themselves to leave this place."

Kachui was one of my most reliable informants—which means I relied on her testimony a lot. She was an astute observer and in my time in Nairobi I frequently sought her out to discuss aspects of township life in the 1930s and '40s. My sense, based on my experiences with her, is that the account above was not a generic performance on her part. It had all the hallmarks of a good spontaneous response to an interview question: it was not something she had been asked before nor did it seem to be something she had thought about and ordered as a coherent narrative.

But is there a problem here? No one really tries to find out the military success of the Italians from Nairobi residents alone. A false section of an interview is also not a problem; the words of a reliable informant might be reliable but have no particular authority. False sections of testimony do not make the informant unreliable but may make her reveal more (Tonkin 1992: 114–15). Kachui seems to have taken the words of Italian prisoners of war— of whom thirty thousand ended up in wartime Kenya—far more seriously than she took the words of Kenyan nationalists: her own standards for evaluating eyewitness accounts, and assessing the credibility of eyewitnesses, shaped the account above.

But Kachui was not the only Kenyan to have been concerned with the threat of Italian invasion. A veteran of the King's African Rifles recalled the campaign in Somaliland, from which he took very different insights about European power:

> [O]ur battalion went to British Somaliland. People were fighting in Gondar. We stayed there and our main job was to board Kenya-bound ships with Italian men who were prisoners of war. We used to separate men from women. Women were put on Roma-bound ships. Eh! it was then I learned that *wazungu* are very clever people. Some Italian men would come dressed in complete women's dresses and shoes and try and cheat their way into the Roma-bound ships, but they were always discovered by the British.[29]

Another man's recollection troubles the boundary between true and false, between memory and imagination. He was a labor recruiter for a sisal plantation near the coast; his white boss sent him home to Siaya to recruit workers. After World War II began, he was taking some men to the plantation when he was stopped by white soldiers. The commander of the white soldiers told me, "Supervisor Oundo, you are not taking these men to work in the sisal plantation, they are going to work for us. I am going to recruit them in our army. You also must come with us." I obeyed him and followed. In the army my labor recruits were given the job of building a wire fence along the ocean shore from somewhere near Mombasa on the Tanzanian [south] side to almost Malindi. The aim of this fence was to prevent the Italians from entering Kenya's soil. Surely this fence is still there?[30]

It would of course be possible to argue that this man and his recruits did construct a fence, but that it was one of many installations to keep Italians, or soldiers, in, not out, and that he was extrapolating the length of this structure from his own vision of the war. In the absence of detailed histories of construction during World War II this would be a good guess. But what's important about all these accounts is not what they say about World War II, but what they say about oral history. Here are two or possibly three examples that provide a glimpse into an early wartime experience in which an Italian invasion seemed dangerously imminent. Whether this experience was the result of Africans "misunderstanding" or "misrepresenting" what Europeans said and did or whether it was an accurate summary of the commands of overzealous British officers is impossible to say and perhaps not all that worth finding out. What are worth noting are the modest gains and insight that this kind of oral material gives scholars, a vision of momentary and intense concerns at the start of the war, a vision of administrative power and the mobilization of African labor and daily life that has lasted for decades. It is these glimpses, these windows into worlds of colonial control and containment, of imagined invasions and wartime strengths, worlds where Europeans prove their smarts not by military might but by cross-dressing—it is these insights that oral history provides as no other source does. The historiography that has argued for authentic voices, speaking for themselves, and the historiography that has warned about the inherent weaknesses of oral history may both be making greater demands on source material than source material can bear. In the case of Kachui her "experience" during World War II in Nairobi informed her analysis of decolonization in Kenya. If her experience was false or imagined it was by no means insignificant, and it is a rich and vivid account when read for what it describes; but it is an account historians cannot use if they seek to label it true or false.

NOTES

1. Gregory Sseluwagi, Lubya, Uganda, 28 August 1990. All interviews in Uganda were conducted either by myself and Remigius Kigongo or by myself, Fred Bukulu,

and Godfrey Kigozi. For this essay I haven't bothered to distinguish which interviews were done with which research assistants.

2. Achola Ofwete, Uchonga Village, Siaya District, Kenya, 11 August 1986; Ofwete Muriar, Uchonga Village, Siaya District, Kenya, 11 August 1986. All the interviews in Siaya were done by myself and Odhiambo Opiyo.

3. George Ggingo, Kasubi, Uganda, 15 August 1990.

4. Timothy Omondo, Goma Village, Yimbo, Siaya District, Kenya, 22 August 1986.

5. Anyango Mahondo, Sigoma Village, Siaya District, Kenya, 15 August 1986.

6. Peter Hayombe, Uhunyi, Siaya District, Kenya, 20 August 1986.

7. Cosmas Oundo, Uchonga Village, Siaya District, Kenya, 20 August, 1986.

8. Zebede Oyoyo, Yimbo, Siaya District, Kenya, 13 August 1986.

9. Nichodamus Okumu-Ogutu, Uhuyi, Siaya District, Kenya, 20 August 1986.

10. Gregory Sseluwagi.

11. Anthony Odhiambo, Uranga, Siaya District, Kenya, 11 August 1986. According to a few old men, the undiscipline of the Swahili protected them from the vampires, who could not risk capturing people in Mombasa "because people were very wild." Zebede Oyoyo, 13 August 1986.

12. Domtita Achola, Uchonga Ukudi, Alego, Siaya District, Kenya, 11 August 1986.

13. Julia Nakibuuka Nalongo, Lubya, Uganda, 21 August 1990.

14. Samuel Mubiru, Lubya, Uganda, 28 August 1990.

15. Nyakida Omolo, Kabura, Siaya District, Kenya, 19 August 1986.

16. Zebede Oyoyo, 13 August 1986; Nyakida Omolo.

17. Sapiriya Kasule, Kisenyi, Uganda, 28 August 1990.

18. Anyango Mahondo, Sigoma, Siaya District, Kenya, 15 August 1986.

19. This seemed to have been accomplished by the number of people in the area he had threatened to have arrested at one time or another (author's fieldnotes, 15 August 1986).

20. Alexander Opaka, Mwajuma Alexander, Helena Ogada, Ndegro Uranga Village, Siaya District, Kenya, 11 August 1986.

21. Zebede Oyoyo, 13 August 1986.

22. Zebede Oyoyo, Yimbo, Kenya, 23 August 1986.

23. Zebede Oyoyo, 13 August 1986.

24. There is no single way a person is remembered (Miescher 1997). People in Uganda named Dr. Duke—presumably Lyndal Duke of the Tsetse Research Service, who retired in 1934—as the man in Entebbe who collected the blood, and they also spoke of him with great humor as the founder of what became the Entebbe Zoo; he was remembered as both. See Joseph Nsubuga, Kisasi, Uganda, 22 August 1990; Samuel Mubiru; Gregory Sseluwagi; Julia Nakibuuka Nalongo. The living are often constrained by the experiences they recall about the deceased (see Cohen and Odhiambo 1992).

25. Bibiana Nalwanga, Bwaise, Uganda, 24 August 1990; see also Joseph Nsubuga, Kisasi, Uganda, 22 August 1990; Samuel Mubiru, Lubya, Uganda, 28 August 1990.

26. Daniel Sekiraata, Katwe, Uganda, 22 August 1990.

27. Gregory Sseluwagi; Samuel Mubiru; Joseph Nsubuga; Ahmed Kizir, Katwe, Uganda, 20 August 1990; Sapirya Kasule, Kisenyi, Uganda, 28 August 1990.

28. Zaina Kachui, Pumwani, Nairobi, interview with myself and Margaret Makuna, 14 June 1976.

29. Alexander Opaka, Ndegro Uranga Village, Siaya District, Kenya, 11 August 1986.

30. Cosmas Oundo, Uchonga Village, Alego, Siaya District, Kenya, 20 August 1986. In answer to his question my assistant answered, "No, I think they might have removed it after the end of the war."

BIBLIOGRAPHY

Adiyisadiki [Believer]. 1923. Letter to the editor. *Mambo Leo* (November): 13–14.

Alagoa, E. J. 1994. "An African Philosophy of History in the Oral Tradition." In *Paths toward the Past: African Historical Essays in Honor of Jan Vansina*, ed. Robert Harms et al., 15–25. Atlanta: Crossroads.

Banage, W. B., W. N. Byarugaba, and J. D. Goodman. 1972. "The 'Embalasassa' (*Riopa fernandi*): A Story of Real and Mythical Zoology." *The Uganda Journal* 36: 67–72.

Barber, Karin. 1989. "Interpreting Oriki as History and Literature." In *Discourse and Its Disguises: The Interpretation of African Oral Texts*, ed. Karin Barber and P. F. de Moraes Farias, 13–34. Birmingham: Centre of West African Studies, University of Birmingham.

———. 1991. *I Could Speak until Tomorrow: Oriki, Women, and the Past in a Yoruba Town*. Washington, D.C.: Smithsonian Institution Press for the International African Institute.

Bauman, Richard. 1993. "Disclaimers of Performance." In *Responsibility and Evidence in Oral Discourse*, ed. Jane H. Hill and Judith T. Irvine, 182–96. Cambridge: Cambridge University Press.

Beach, David N. 1983. "The Rozvi in Search of Their Past." *History in Africa* 10: 13–33.

Beidelman, Thomas O. 1970. "Myth, Legend, and Oral History: A Kaguru Traditional Text." *Anthropos* 5–6: 74–97.

Blount, Ben G. 1975. "Agreeing to Agree on Genealogy: A Luo Sociology of Knowledge." In *Sociocultural Dimensions of Language Use*, ed. Mary Sanchez and Ben G. Blount, 117–35. New York: Academic.

Bozzoli, Belinda, with the assistance of Mmantho Nkotsoe. 1991. *Women of Phokeng: Consciousness, Life Strategy, and Migrancy in South Africa, 1900–1983*. Portsmouth, N.H.: Heinemann.

Clarence-Smith, W. G. 1977. "For Braudel: A Note on the 'Ecole des *Annales*' and the Historiography of Africa." *History in Africa* 4: 275–81.

Cohen, David William. 1977. *Womunafu's Bunafu: A Study of Authority in a Nineteenth-Century African Community*. Princeton: Princeton University Press.

———. 1980. "Reconstructing a Conflict in Bunafu: Seeking Evidence outside the Narrative Tradition." In *The African Past Speaks: Essays in Oral Tradition and History*, ed. Joseph C. Miller, 201–20. Folkstone: Dawson.

———. 1989. "The Undefining of Oral Tradition." *Ethnohistory* 36, no. 1: 9–18.

Cohen, David William, and E. S. Atieno Odhiambo. 1992. *Burying SM: The Politics of Knowledge and the Sociology of Power in Africa*. Portsmouth, N.H.: Heinemann.

Davison, Jean, with the women of Mutira. 1989. *Voices from Mutira: Lives of Rural Gikuyu Women*. Boulder: Westview.

Ewald, Janet. 1985. "History and Speculation: History and Founding Stories in the Kingdom of Taqali, 1780–1935." *International Journal of African Historical Studies* 18, no. 2: 265–87.

Fabian, Johannes. 1983. *Time and the Other: How Anthropology Makes Its Object*. New York: Columbia University Press.

Feierman, Steven. 1990. *Peasant Intellectuals: Anthropology and History in Tanzania*. Madison: University of Wisconsin Press.

————. 1995. "Africa in History: The End of Universal Narratives." In *After Colonialism: Imperial Histories and Postcolonial Displacements*, ed. Gyan Prakash, 40–65. Princeton: Princeton University Press.

Geiger, Susan. 1986. "Women's Life Histories: Method and Content." *Signs* 11, no. 2: 334–51.

————. 1990. "What's So Feminist about Women's Oral History?" *Journal of Women's History* 2, no. 1: 169–80.

————. 1996. "Tanganyikan Nationalism as 'Women's Work': Life Histories, Collective Biography, and Changing Historiography." *Journal of African History* 37: 465–80.

————. 1997. *TANU Women: Gender and Culture in the Making of Tanganyikan Nationalism*. Portsmouth, N.H.: Heinemann.

Gengenbach, Heidi. 1994. " Truth-Telling and the Life Narrative of African Women: A Reply to Kirk Hoppe." *International Journal of African Historical Studies* 27, no. 3: 619–27.

Giles-Vernick, Tamara. 1996. "Na lege ti guriri (On the Road of History): Mapping out the Past and Present in M'Bres Region, Central African Republic." *Ethnohistory* 43, no. 2: 245–75.

Government of Northern Rhodesia [Russell Commission]. 1935. "Report of the Commission Appointed to Enquire into the Disturbances on the Copperbelt of Northern Rhodesia." Lusaka: Government Printer.

Hacking, Ian. 1995. *Rewriting the Soul: Multiple Personality and the Sciences of Memory*. Princeton: Princeton University Press.

Halbwachs, Maurice. 1992. *On Collective Memory*. Chicago: University of Chicago Press.

Hamilton, C. A. 1987. "Ideology and Oral Traditions: Listening to the Voices 'from Below.'" *History in Africa* 14: 57–86.

Henige, David P. 1974. *The Chronology of Oral Tradition: Quest for a Chimera*. Oxford: Clarendon.

————. 1994. "Gambit Decline: Pervasive Doubt about Systematic Doubt." In *Paths toward the Past: African Historical Essays in Honor of Jan Vansina*, ed. Robert Harms et al., 77–95. Atlanta: Crossroads.

Hofmeyr, Isabel. 1994. *"We Spend Our Years as a Tale Is Told": Oral Historical Narrative in a South African Chiefdom*. Portsmouth, N.H.: Heinemann.

Hoppe, Kirk. 1993. "Whose Life Is It, Anyway? Issues of Representation in Life Narrative Texts of African Women." *International Journal of African Historical Studies* 26, no. 3: 623–36.

Huxley, Elspeth. 1948. *The Sorcerer's Apprentice: A Journey through East Africa*. London: Chatto and Windus.

Irwin, Paul. 1981. *Liptako Speaks: History from Oral Tradition in Africa*. Princeton: Princeton University Press.

Klein, Martin A. 1989. "Studying the History of Those Who Would Rather Forget: Oral History and the Experience of Slavery." *History in Africa* 16, 209–17.

Kratz, Corinne A. 1991. "Amusement and Absolution: Transforming Narratives during Confession of Social Debts." *American Anthropologist* 93, no. 4: 826–51.

Law, Robin. 1984. "How Truly Traditional Is Our Traditional History? The Case of

Samuel Johnson and the Recording of Yoruba Oral History." *History in Africa* 11: 172–99.

Malkki, Liisa H. 1995. *Purity and Exile: Violence, Memory, and National Cosmology among Hutu Refugees in Tanzania*. Chicago: University of Chicago Press.

Mbilinyi, Marjorie. 1989. "'I'd Have Been a Man': Politics and the Labor Process in Producing Personal Narratives." In *Interpreting Women's Lives: Feminist Theory and Personal Narratives*, ed. Personal Narratives Group, 204–207. Bloomington: Indiana University Press.

Miescher, Stephan F. 1997. "Becoming a Man in Kwawu: Gender, Law, Personhood, and the Construction of Masculinities in Colonial Ghana, 1875–1957." Ph.D. dissertation, Northwestern University.

Miller, Joseph C. 1980. "Listening for the African Past." Introduction to *The African Past Speaks: Essays on Oral Tradition and History*, ed. Joseph C. Miller, 4–51. Folkstone: Dawson.

Musambachime, Mwelwa C. 1988. "The Impact of Rumor: The Case of Banyama (Vampire-Men) Scares in Northern Rhodesia, 1930–1964." *International Journal of African Historical Studies* 21, no. 2: 201–15.

Newbury, David. 1991. *Kings and Clans: Ijwi Island and the Lake Kivu Region*. Madison: University of Wisconsin Press.

Patai, Daphne. 1987. "Ethical Problems of Personal Narratives, or, Who Should Eat the Last Piece of Cake?" *International Journal of Oral History* 8, no. 1: 5–27.

Prakash, Gyan. 1990. "Writing Post-Orientalist Histories of the Third World: Perspectives from Indian Historiography." *Comparative Studies in Society and History* 32, no. 2: 383–408.

Rosaldo, Renato. 1986. "From the Door of His Tent: The Fieldworker and the Inquisitor." In *Writing Culture: The Politics and Poetics of Ethnography*, ed. James Clifford and George Marcus, 77–97. Berkeley and Los Angeles: University of California Press.

Santino, Jack. 1988. "Occupational Ghostlore: Social Context and the Expression of Belief." *Journal of American Folklore* 101: 44, 207–18.

Schrager, Samuel. 1983. "What Is Social about Oral History?" *International Journal of Oral History* 4, no. 2: 78–98.

Scott, Joan W. 1991. "The Evidence of Experience." *Critical Inquiry* 17, 773–97.

Seitel, Peter. 1980. *See So That We May See: Performance and Interpretation of Traditional Tales from Tanzania*. Bloomington: Indiana University Press.

Shostak, Marjorie. 1981. *Nisa: The Life and Words of a !Kung Woman*. New York: Vantage.

Smith, Mary. 1981. *Baba of Karo: A Woman of the Muslim Hausa*. 1954. Reprint, New Haven: Yale University Press.

Spivak, Gayatri Chakrovarty. 1988. "Can the Subaltern Speak?" In *Marxism and the Interpretation of Culture*, ed. Cary Nelson and Lawrence Grossberg, 217–313. Urbana: University of Illinois Press.

Stoler, Ann Laura. 1992. "'In Cold Blood': Hierarchies of Credibility and the Politics of Colonial Narratives." *Representation* 37: 151–89.

Strobel, Margaret, and Sara Mirza. 1989. *Three Swahili Women: Life Histories from Mombasa, Kenya*. Bloomington: Indiana University Press. A Swahili edition was published in 1991: *Wanawake watatu wa Kiswahili: hadithi za maisha kutoka Mombasa, Kenya*. Bloomington: Indiana University Press.

Tonkin, Elizabeth. 1992. *Narrating Our Pasts: The Social Construction of Oral History*. Cambridge: Cambridge University Press.

van Onselen, Charles. 1993. "Peasants Speak: The Reconstruction of Rural Life from Oral Testimony: Critical Notes on the Methodology Employed in the Study of a Black South African Sharecropper." *Journal of Peasant Studies* 20, no. 3: 495–514.

Vansina, Jan. 1974. "The Power of Systematic Doubt in Historical Enquiry." *History in Africa* 1: 109–27.

———. 1978a. *The Children of Woot: A History of the Kuba Peoples*. Madison: University of Wisconsin Press.

———. 1978b. "For Oral Tradition (But Not against Braudel)." *History in Africa* 5: 351–56.

———. 1980. "Memory and Oral Tradition." In *The African Past Speaks: Essays on Oral Tradition and History,* ed. Joseph C. Miller, 262–79. Folkstone: Dawson.

———. 1985. *Oral Tradition as History*. Madison: University of Wisconsin Press.

Veyne, Paul. 1988. *Did the Greeks Believe in Their Myths? An Essay in Constitutive Imagination*. Trans. Paula Wissing. Chicago: University of Chicago Press.

Wachs, Elinor. 1988. *Crime Victim Stories: New York City's Urban Folklore*. Bloomington: Indiana University Press.

White, Luise. 1990a. "Bodily Fluids and Usufruct: Controlling Property in Nairobi, 1919–39." *Canadian Journal of African Studies* 24, no. 3: 418–38.

———. 1990b. *The Comforts of Home: Prostitution in Colonial Nairobi*. Chicago: University of Chicago Press.

———. 1993. "Cars out of Place: Vampires, Technology, and Labor in East and Central Africa." *Representations* 43: 27–50.

———. 1995a. "'They Could Make Their Victims Dull': Genders and Genres, Fantasies and Cures in Colonial Southern Uganda." *American Historical Review* 100, no. 5: 1379–1402.

———. 1995b. "Tsetse Visions: Narratives of Blood and Bugs in Colonial Northern Rhodesia, 1931–39." *Journal of African History* 36: 219–45.

———. 2000. *Speaking with Vampires: Rumor and History in Colonial Africa*. Berkeley and Los Angeles: University of California Press.

Willis, Justin. 1996. "The Two Lives of Mpamizo: Understanding Dissonance in Oral History." *History in Africa* 23: 319–32.

Wright, Donald R. 1982. "Can a Blind Man Really Know an Elephant? Lessons on the Limitations of Oral Tradition from Paul Irwin's *Liptako Speaks*." *History in Africa* 9: 303–22.

Participants in the "Words and Voices" Conference

*February 24–28, 1997, Bellagio Study and
Conference Center, Bellagio, Italy*

E. J. Alagoa
Boubacar Barry
David Beach
David William Cohen
Paulla Ebron
Laura Fair
Babacar Fall
Tamara Giles-Vernick
Carolyn Hamilton
Isabel Hofmeyr
Abdullahi Ali Ibrahim
Corinne Kratz
Gregory Maddox
Stephan F. Miescher
Mwelwa Musambachine
David Newbury
Bethwell A. Ogot
Richard M. Shain
Elizabeth Tonkin
Megan Vaughan
Luise White
Kwesi Yankah

Participants in the "Words and Voices" Follow-up Conference

*March 20–23, 1997, International Institute,
University of Michigan, Ann Arbor*

E. J. Alagoa
David Beach
Bryan Callahan
David William Cohen
Catherine M. Cole
Mamadou Diawara
Babacar Fall
Anjan Ghosh
Janet Hart
Angelique Haugerud
Clare Ignatowski
Windsor Leroke
Julie Livingston
Elizabeth MacGonagle
Michael Mahoney
Patrick Malloy
Gregory Mann
Patrick U. Mbajekwe
Stephan F. Miescher
Susan O'Brien
Agnes Odinga
Bethwell A. Ogot
Tejumola Olaniyan
Derek Peterson
Peter Seitel
Jan Shetler
Lynn M. Thomas
Luise White
Kwesi Yankah

Contributors

E. J. Alagoa was, until his retirement in 1998, Professor of History at the University of Port Harcourt, Nigeria. He is the author of *The Small Brave City-State: A History of Nembe-Brass in the Niger Delta* (1964), *People of the Fish and Eagle: A History of Okpoama in the Eastern Niger Delta* (1996), and a number of articles on oral tradition and the history of Nigeria. He edited the 1990 volume *Oral Tradition and Oral History in Africa and the Diaspora: Theory and Practice.*

David William Cohen is the author (with E. S. Atieno Odhiambo) of a forthcoming study of the multiple investigations into the disappearance and death of Kenya's foreign minister, Robert Ouko. He is the author of *The Historical Tradition of Busoga, Mukama, and Kintu* (1972), *Womunafu's Bunafu: A Study of Authority in a Nineteenth-Century African Community* (1977), *Towards a Reconstructed Past: Historical Texts from Busoga, Uganda* (1977), and *Siaya: The Historical Anthropology of an African Landscape* (with E. S. Atieno Odhiambo, 1989), all based on research in Uganda and Kenya. He is also the author (also with Atieno Odhiambo) of *Burying SM: The Politics of Knowledge and the Sociology of Power in Africa* (1992), as well as *The Combing of History* (1994). Cohen is Professor of History and Anthropology at the University of Michigan, having formerly served on the faculties of Northwestern University and The Johns Hopkins University.

Laura Fair is Associate Professor of African History at the University of Oregon. She is the author of *Pastimes and Politics: Culture, Community, and Identity in Post-abolition Urban Zanzibar, 1890–1945* (2001), as well as articles on leisure and urban popular culture.

Babacar Fall is a member of the Department of History and Geography, École Normale Supérieure, Université Cheikh Anta Diop, in Dakar. He has held appointments as a Visiting Fellow at the University of Michigan. He has been involved in an oral history project on the lives of trade unionists in Senegal from the 1940s through the 1960s.

Tamara Giles-Vernick is Assistant Professor of History at Baruch College of the City University of New York. She has conducted research on equatorial African conceptions of environment and history and has published in *Ethnohistory, Environmental History,* the *Journal of African History* and the *International Journal of African Historical Studies.* Her book, titled *Cutting* *the Vines of the Past: Environmental Histories of Loss in the Central African Republic, 1894–1994,* will be published in 2002. Her next research project will focus on the historical production of knowledge about malaria.

Isabel Hofmeyr is Professor of African Literature at the University of the Witwatersrand in Johannesburg, South Africa. She has published extensively in the field of southern African literature and culture. Her book on oral historical narrative, *"We Spend Our Years as a Tale that Is Told": Oral Historical Narrative in a South African Chiefdom* (1994), was shortlisted for the Herskovits Award in 1995. She is currently working on a book on John Bunyan in Africa.

Abdullahi A. Ibrahim is Associate Professor of History, University of Missouri-Columbia. Educated at the University of Khartoum, he received his Ph.D. from Indiana University. He is the author of *Assaulting with Words: Popular Discourse and the Bridle of Shari'ah* (1994) and a number of articles on legal culture, politics, and popular culture in the Sudan. He is a founder of the Sudan Studies Association and has been a Visiting Fellow of the Institute for Advanced Study and Research in the African Humanities (Evanston, Ill.).

Corinne A. Kratz is the author of *Affecting Performance: Meaning, Movement, and Experience in Okiek Women's Initiation* (1994) and *"The Ones That Are Wanted": Communication and the Politics of Representation in a Photographic Exhibition* (2001). She is currently Associate Professor of African Studies and Anthropology at Emory University.

Stephan F. Miescher is Assistant Professor at the University of California, Santa Barbara. He is the coeditor (with Lisa Lindsay) of the forthcoming volume *Men and Masculinities in Modern Africa* and is preparing a monograph on the construction of masculinities in twentieth-century Ghana.

Bethwell A. Ogot is Director of Graduate Studies at Maseno University College, Kenya. Educated at Alliance High School, Kenya, Makerere University College, St. Andrews University, and the School of Oriental and African Studies, London, Ogot received his Ph.D. from the University of London in 1967. He served as Professor and Head of the History Department of the University of Nairobi from 1967 to 1977 and Director of the International Louis Leakey Memorial Institute for African Prehistory (Nairobi) from 1977 to 1980. Founder of the East African Publishing House and the Historical Association of Kenya, Ogot was a lead figure in the development of the UNESCO General History of Africa. He has authored and edited more than twenty books on the history of East Africa, including *History of* the *Southern Luo* (1967) and *The Jii-Speaking Peoples of Eastern Africa* (1996).

Megan Vaughan is Professor of Commonwealth Studies, University of Oxford, and Fellow of Nuffield College. She taught at the University of Malawi for a number of years. She is the author of *The Story of an African Famine: Gender and Famine in Twentieth-Century Malawi* (1987), *Curing Their Ills: Colonial Power and African Illness* (1991), and (with Henrietta Moore) *Cutting Down Trees: Gender, Nutrition, and Agricultural Change in Northern Zambia* (1994). She is completing a book on creolization in eighteenth-century Mauritius and conducting further research on precolonial identities in Malawi.

Luise White is Professor of History at the University of Florida. Her first book, *The Comforts of Home: Prostitution in Colonial Nairobi* (1990) won the African Studies Association's Herskovits Prize in 1991. Her second book, *Speaking with Vampires: Rumor and History in Colonial Africa* (2000) is a comparative study of Kenya, Uganda, and Zambia.

Kwesi Yankah is a member of the Department of Linguistics, University of Ghana, Legon. With long-standing interests in royal and political oratory, folklore, and popular culture, he is the author of *The Proverb in the Context of Akan Rhetoric: A Theory of Proverb Praxis* (1989), *Speaking for the Chief: Okyeame and the Politics of Akan Royal Oratory* (1995), and a large number of articles in the field of African linguistics.

Index